Against the
Multicultural Agenda

Against the Multicultural Agenda

A Critical Thinking Alternative

Yehudi O. Webster

Westport, Connecticut
London

Library of Congress Cataloging-in-Publication Data

Webster, Yehudi O.
    Against the multicultural agenda : a critical thinking alternative
/ Yehudi O. Webster.
        p.   cm.
    Includes bibliographical references and index.
    ISBN 0–275–95876–0 (alk. paper).—ISBN 0–275–95877–9 (pbk. :
alk. paper)
        1. Multicultural education—United States.   2. Multiculturalism—
United States.   3. Critical thinking—Study and teaching—United
States.   4. Knowledge, Theory of.   5. Pluralism (Social sciences)—
United States.   I. Title.
LC1099.3.W43   1997
370.117′0973—DC21   96–37690

British Library Cataloguing in Publication Data is available.

Library of Congress Catalog Card Number: 96–37690
ISBN: 0–275–95876–0
        0–275–95877–9 (pbk.)

First published in 1997

Praeger Publishers, 88 Post Road West, Westport, CT 06881
An imprint of Greenwood Publishing Group, Inc.

Printed in the United States of America

The paper used in this book complies with the
Permanent Paper Standard issued by the National
Information Standards Organization (Z39.48–1984).

10 9 8 7 6 5 4 3 2 1

To those educators who teach for critical thinking and who believe as H. G. Wells did that history is more and more a race between education and catastrophe.

Contents

Acknowledgments   ix

Introduction   1

1. Multicultural Education: Development, Variants, and   13
   Controversies

2. Multiculturalism: Egalitarian Social Reconstruction through   69
   Education Reform

3. Multiculturalism: An Assessment of Its Analytical Foundations   101

4. Education Reform, Multiculturalism, and Critical Thinking   169

Bibliography   201

Index   225

Acknowledgments

Of course, the persons named here should not be held in any way responsible for this book's limitations. Many thanks to Erich Martel who, several years ago, ignited my interest in multicultural education and provided "tons" of reading material as well as innumerable insights on the subject. Aldo Garbellini, Anita Ghazarian, and Haykaz Hambarassomian supported my efforts as friends should, as did my sister, Pauline (Motee). I would like to thank also Edward Damer, Bill Dorman, Russ Lindgren, Richard Paul, and Mark Weinstein for many years of annual discussions of philosophy, critical thinking, culture, and human relations at International Conferences on Critical Thinking at Sonoma State University. I am grateful to Victor Quevedo, computing consultant, for his efforts to make me "camera-ready." My gratitude extends also to the library staff at California State University, Los Angeles, and Alfred Gonsalves and the rest of the library staff at Occidental College, who were unfailingly cooperative and good-humored about my "deadlines."

Introduction

Various state and local legislatures, school boards, and colleges are recommending and establishing some form of multicultural education. A significant number of teachers also support curriculum reform that would imbue students with tolerance and respect for cultural differences and include various perspectives that represent the racial and ethnic diversity in schools and society. Students would be taught that cultural differences are enriching and in no way suggestive of inferiority. Stereotyping and prejudice could be diminished, if the relative value of all cultures and perspectives were to be stressed. Through multicultural education, then, students can be encouraged to respect differences and genuinely celebrate America's cultural diversity. With the inclusion of "minority" cultures and experiences in the curriculum, the self-esteem of students of color enhanced, and their academic performances improved. However, this movement for culturally pluralistic educational processes, equity, and equality has attracted a fair share of criticisms. Indeed, mutual political accusations deform discussions of inequality of educational opportunities and "the diversity revolution" in U.S. society. Both media reports and the literature on multicultural education indicate that its implementation has been met with staunch objections. Moreover, general discussions are ensnared in charges of Eurocentrism and insensitivity to excluded voices, on the one hand, and political correctness on the other.

The discussions also reveal that there are competing schools of thought within multicultural education's advocacy. Some conceive it as a means of raising self-esteem and remedying educational failure among "students of color." Others restrict its goal to an appreciation of cultural diversity, while "pluralists" see its objective as the preservation of "the common culture," including America's European intellectual heritage. A perusal of the growing literature indicates that the list of objectives lengthens—celebrate cultural differences, enhance global-human awareness, equalize educational opportunities, and eradicate prejudice, intolerance, and stereotypical behavior. The expected outcomes of multicultural education are as diverse as its portrayal of cultures in U.S. society. Moreover, over the last decade, a new genre of multicultural education has emerged. Its advocates present multicultural education not so much as an academic discipline as social reconstructionist programs or eradicating "white racism" and achieving equality among groups. Closely aligned to this genre are education reform proposals for empowering students to eliminate the oppression of women, people of color, homosexuals, and the poor, and establish "cultural democracy." This development also contains various perspectives, strategies, and objectives, and its sponsors describe their arguments and recommendations as *multiculturalism*, not multicultural education.

The implementation of multicultural education and multiculturalism would have profound sociopolitical consequences. For, considering the vast number of possible groups in U.S. society, an inclusion of gender, racial, and ethnic *experiences* and *perspectives* in the curriculum would amount to a restructuring of not only the organization of public education but also socially necessary identities. Thus discussions of the multicultural agenda raise challenging questions, such as: How can America's racial-cultural diversity be celebrated and enriched without promoting segregation and separatism, or destroying the unifying purpose of educational experiences? Is cultural pluralism a valid basis for curriculum development, given the amorphousness and disputes surrounding the culture concept? Within the finite space in the curriculum, which group's experiences should be included and by representatives of which ethnic group should the selection be made? What other justification is there for such an inclusion, apart from the thesis that every group should know its historical experiences and culture? Since each group in U.S. society can conceive a historical injustice at the hands of another group, would stories of group victimization not become central to the history and social studies curriculum? What are the behavioral implication of such a development? Would a curriculum designed within an accentuation of group differences not lead to a marginalization of empathy for others? But in the eruption of "culture wars," a most pertinent question emerges: Can participants in intellectual exchanges make dismissive references to each other's racial and ethnic attributes and politics, without multiplying accusations of political correctness /incorrectness? These questions renew centuries of debate over the relationships among group classification, culture, and educational policies; they also introduce complex concepts from sociology, history, anthropology, and philosophy. In this discursive vortex, the crucial issue becomes whether disputes over education reform can be resolved without a consensus among protagonists on standards of argument evaluation. It is here that concepts and principles from critical thinking may have some relevance.

A guiding principle of this work is that critical thinking is an essential condition of both dispute resolution and intellectual progress. In aspiring to a critical thinking analysis, the arguments avoid denunciation, rejection, and repudiation of multicultural education proposals. Rather, these proposals are assessed within certain ground rules of discourse that focus on the classifications, premises, implications, purposes, and policy consequences of multicultural education proposals. *No allusion is made to the "race," "ethnicity," "gender," "class," or "politics" of advocates or critics of multicultural education and multiculturalism.* Comments are directed at the reasoning processes that surface in arguments, the coherence of definitions of key terms, and the analytical depth of observations. This work, then, adheres to a standard of fair-mindedness and principles of refutation developed by critical thinking theorists. Arguments for multicultural education and multiculturalism are presented in a manner that their advocates should find agreeable, for neither their writings, nor those of their opponents, are politically or morally evaluated and dismissed, or approved. Thus this work goes beyond a rejection of multicultural education and multiculturalism. Nevertheless, it demonstrates significant inadequacies in their social scientific and philosophical foundations, such as their use of certain anthropologists' conceptions of separate races and single cultures and their affiliations with realist and postmodernist currents in philosophy. Finally, it introduces education reform proposals grounded in critical thinking principles.

Chapter 1 presents the development of multicultural education, its genesis in the debate over the place of cultures in schools, its various definitions, and the disputes among its proponents and opponents. Multicultural education may be defined as education reform proposals whose purposes are: to make students appreciative of diversity, respectful of all cultures, cognizant of the perspectives and historical contributions of women and persons of color to American and world civilization, and free of the racist, sexist, and homophobic prejudices that are condoned in traditional textbooks. Its rationale is embodied in the following observations:

(a)   changing migration and demographic patterns that dramatically increase the racial and ethnic diversity of the student and general population;

(b)   a rise of expressions of intolerance and hate crimes on campuses and in society as a whole;

(c)   ethnocentric biases in textbooks that prioritize European cultural values, or present these values as canons;

(d)   some teachers' inability to deal effectively with the learning styles and the culture-specific needs of "students of color";

(e)   inequality of educational opportunities and chronic patterns of educational underachievement among African-American students; and

(f)   a general, monocultural curriculum and school ethos that severely diminish the self-esteem of "students of color."

Sponsors of multicultural education argue that, because schools are powerful socializing agencies, they should serve the goal of promoting the cultural pluralism and diversity that are such obvious features of U.S. society. In order to achieve this goal, the various racial minority experiences and the multicultural nature of this society must be recognized and even-handedly dealt with in curriculum design and pedagogic practices. Students, teachers, and indeed all citizens must be divested of the notion that this is a white society of European cultural origin. Otherwise the racist, sexist, and class prejudices that permeate everyday utterances and attitudes will continue to flourish.

According to its proponents, multicultural education is most relevant to specific problems facing students of color—low self-esteem, under-representation in colleges, overrepresentation in dropout or pushout rates, comparatively low educational achievements and consequent economic deprivation, and the unpreparedness of some faculty to teach culturally diverse student populations. What schools need is a curriculum that includes the perspectives, or "voices," of the different. What they must cultivate in students is understanding of, and respect for, different cultural expressions and practices in both schools and society. This transformation of the schools' social system would contribute to better-informed students, prejudice-reduction in the larger society, and respect for diversity. While these appear to be worthwhile objectives, the construction and implementation of multicultural curricula in schools in New York City, Portland, and Oakland have led to volatile discussions of the relationships among education, the teaching of history and social sciences, the nature of the social fabric, and "racial" problems.

Chapter 1 presents: (a) the analytical roots of multicultural education in certain anthropologists' conceptions of races and cultures, (b) the related cultural pluralist tenets that gave rise to "melting pot" and "salad bowl" portrayals of U.S. society; (c) the principal approaches to multicultural education; (d) the dispute between "pluralists" and "Afrocentrists," and (e) the "values education" proposed by some critics of Afrocentrism. This chapter concludes with a summary of analytical weaknesses in the overall advocacy of multicultural education, its specific perspectives, and the values education alternative suggested by certain critics. For example, it would be generally agreed that sound reasoning is essential to intellectual progress, and according to its proponents, multicultural education is indeed a liberating educational project. Yet the entire advocacy is grounded in unclear and arbitrary racial and ethnic distinctions. Second, the discussions among the various schools of thought and between advocates and detractors are characterized by the use of political and cultural standards for argument evaluation. Disputants are described as "white," "black," "conservative," "Eurocentric," "racist," and so on. What is needed from advocates of multicultural education, *as a prelude to its implementation*, are clearly-defined standards for argument assessment and ground rules for intellectual exchanges.

Chapter 2 outlines multicultural education's evolution from: a call for cultural pluralism in schools, to demands for *equal* representation of "cultures of color," the development of antisexist and antiracist education reform proposals, solicitation for representation of the experiences and perspectives of the disempowered and oppressed, and exhortations to teachers, as "transformative intellectuals," to engage in practices that resist and challenge domination and oppression. This evolutionary trajectory reveals the transformation of multicultural education into multiculturalism, which extends egalitarian and social reconstructionist interpretations of cultural pluralism. Its objectives range from the eradication of all forms of racism, sexism, and oppression in schools to an egalitarian and democratic renewal of culture and society.

Chapter 2 also develops on the distinction between multicultural education and multiculturalism. This distinction facilitates an understanding of both the difficulties surrounding the implementation of multicultural education and the protracted nature of the disputes among its advocates. The idea of multicultural education is implicit in multiculturalism, but multicultural education is not synonymous with multiculturalism. What obscures their dissimilarities is their common emphasis on cultural differences, claims on cultural pluralism, and their interchangeable use by some of their advocates. Multicultural education and multiculturalism are overlapping elements of a cultural pluralist agenda. The former's proposals include the schools' nurturing of distinct cultures, incorporation of the voices of people of color and women, and consolidation of a common cultural heritage allegedly rooted in Western traditions. The latter addresses issues of educational equity, social inequality, democracy, and domination. Its major proponents go further than a call for pluralist inclusiveness, the cultivation of different identities, and appreciation of cultural diversity. They conceive schools as sites of political domination that, at the same time, present opportunities for resistance and emancipation, and argue that the schools' mission should be the eradication of domination and injustice as well as racist, sexist, ethnocentric, and other biases from educational experiences, culture, and society. This can be achieved through the transformation of school knowledge and the promotion of a critical pedagogy that empowers both teachers and students.

Overall, advocates of multiculturalism seek to transform educational policies in order to achieve equality of educational opportunity and redress power imbalances in knowledge-construction, schools, and society. However, their individual arguments and prescriptions are often divergent. Some explicitly champion the interests of "oppressed" groups, and regard differences as essential to cultural identities. The schools' cultivation of different identities is therefore to be maintained, even intensified. By contrast, advocates of "critical multiculturalism" and "resistance multiculturalism" oppose any "essentialization of differences"; they recommend a "critical pedagogy" that, while generating students' opposition to racism, Eurocentrism, ethnocentrism, sexism, and homophobia, also inculcates an awareness of the political and theoretical contexts of differences. Students must not only know their individual cultures, appreciate cultural differences, and perceive the links among culture, power, politics, and identities, they must also understand patterns of inequality and oppression, and be committed to social transformation.

Proponents of antiracist and antisexist multiculturalism describe the curriculum as politically, epistemologically, and culturally limited creations of "dead white males." Schools, they argue, represent patriarchal, Eurocentric outposts of cultural imperialism whose narratives are treated as canons, even as they disempower women and students of color. This observation represents the basic justification for the development of antiracist and antisexist curricula. A central feature of Chapter 2 is the clarification of the theoretical origins of antisexist and antiracist curriculum reforms, for an understanding of their philosophical and social scientific lineage can prevent their dismissal and condemnation as radical and liberal excesses of political correctness. Thus Chapter 2 outlines the conceptual structures of these reform proposals, tracing them to the theses on inequality, domination, and oppression prevailing in the radical feminist and cultural nationalist wings of gender and racial theories of social relations. While these proposals may be conceived as extensions of the conflict perspective in sociology, they also draw on the following intellectual developments: (1) Pan-Africanist and cultural nationalist perspectives on black liberation; (2) opposition to Arthur Jensen's revival of discussions of black-white differences in intelligence in the late 1960s; (3) the failure of school desegregation to generate equality of results; and (4) "progressivist" educational doctrines that propose an egalitarian restructuring of the social order through the schools' reorganization. Other developments in social sciences, however, suggest caution in basing education reform proposals on the concepts of power, equality, and oppression.

Dissertations on gender in feminist writings, race in physical anthropology, power in political science, and racism in sociology are rich and complex enough to warrant reservations about factual assertions on women's oppression, racism's pervasiveness, and its explanatory value. It follows that the description *black educational underachievement* cannot be taken for granted and explained as a consequence of a racist school system. The culture concept is also surrounded by complex and controversial analyses of its definitions, its significance for behavior, and its relationship to racial categorization. Lack of consideration for these developments weakens the multicultural agenda and reduces it to a mere activist opposition to racism and sexism. Nor do proponents of multicultural reforms offer any sustained analysis of the various other explanations of "minority" educational failure: lack of active parental involvement in children's education, the system of school funding, the absence of parental choice of school, inadequate welfare and health care policies, and economic deprivation in households. Indeed, if the racial classification of students were to be discarded, it would be perceived that it is not "students of color" who underachieve educationally, but all students who are trapped in schools not equipped to foster learning. Some students are successful, despite the absence of courses in racial and ethnic history in their school. Others fail to learn or graduate, even with the presence of such courses. Students are failed not because of the absence of women's, African-centered, and Hispanic-centered history in the curriculum. Rather, insofar as a wide variety of socioeconomic and philosophical-educational conditions affect students' performances, the multiculturalists' focus on gender, race, and culture would not stem the tide of school failure.

Chapter 3 examines key arguments in various multiculturalist schools of thought. It focuses especially on their debts to "classical" biology (anatomical classifications), sociology (power, conflict, and domination) anthropology (distinct races and single cultures), and postmodernist objections to metanarrative and discursive consensus. Critical multiculturalism presents a rich exposition of these themes; it combines theoretical contributions from Jean-François

Lyotard, Michel Foucault, Max Weber, Karl Marx, the Frankfurt School of Critical Theory, and Paulo Freire to develop liberationist pedagogical criticisms of certain educational theories, practices, and school organization. Its linking of knowledge, interests, and culture reflects its appropriation of a postmodernist contextualization of knowledge. In conceiving signs and significations as unstable and shifting, postmodernism deprecates fixed identities and authoritative, knowing subjects. Nevertheless, despite its expressed allegiance to the postmodernist deconstruction of metanarrative, critical multiculturalism conserves the canon of anatomical differences, which are deemed "real." In this context, critical multiculturalism is not faithful to Lyotard's antirealism. On the other hand, Lyotard's postmodernism does not constitute a radical rupturing of modernism. It retains the idea of a subject as a producer of knowledge. The subject's authority is merely challenged on the basis of the specificity of language games, the relative equality of all subjects, and the cultural peculiarities within any thinking or knowing subject. Thus postmodernism mirrors the classical philosophers' subject-object conception of knowledge. It simply localizes and individualizes an element of the subject-object epistemology—the subject's cultural and political presence—to deepen modernism's contextualization of knowledge. Postmodernism is, therefore, not a rupture with, but a continuation of modern philosophy's quest for a subject's theoretical or linguistic mirror of the real world.

In the writings of most classical philosophers, both the thinking subjects' attributes and the nature of objects in the real world are said to affect significantly the status of thought, while in the postmodernist version of the subject-object epistemology, the culture, politics, and power of thinking subjects necessarily localize knowledge as narratives. Because all narratives are subjectively, politically, and culturally contextual, no knowledge claim has universal validity, and no consensus on rules can be achieved. All "language games" and cultures are legitimate things-in-themselves and relatively equal. By further implication, no person's arguments can be refuted by another, only rejected, denounced, or repudiated. These features are expressed in multiculturalists' characterizations of arguments as politically necessary/unnecessary, reductionist, essentialist, morally desirable/undesirable, Eurocentric, racist, sexist, ethnocentric, and Western traditionalist, as well as their accusations of complicity in domination and declarations of partisanship for the oppressed. However, while these descriptions and confessions may stake someone's claim to superior moral-political virtues, they cannot serve as indices of the validity or invalidity of arguments. And if the conviction of truth is crucial to decision making, critical multiculturalism, in rendering all arguments and standards "unstable," destroys its own knowledge base for transformative action.

The multiculturalists' appropriation of aspects of postmodernism results in an opposition to the search for a consensus among disputants on standards for validating/invalidating arguments, and rational ground rules for intellectual exchanges. Indeed, they utilize a theory of knowledge that denies the possibility of such a consensus on grounds that all standards are politically and culturally determined. This amounts to saying: "I, as an autonomous subject and being of a distinct culture, can make even the most absurd and incoherent claims that no other subject may invalidate." Within this standard that is not a standard, multiculturalism's proposals proliferate. The standard of clarity is abjured so that multiculturalism's foundational categories such as reality, truth, experience, race, and culture remain unclarified. Arguments for its adoption by school administrators and teachers are taken into philosophical waters and abandoned for lack of attention to logical and epistemological relationships. The justifications for multiculturalism are moral and political and its critics are also morally and politically castigated as liberal, conservative, racist, sexist, Eurocentric, traditionalist, mainstream, and so forth. "Liberal" and "conservative" camps are thereby formed in stalemated discussions of the direction of education reform.

The stalemate is discernible in the acrimonious quality of the debate over multicultural education, and in the fact that its definitions, proposals, and objectives are diverse to the point of being motley: Multicultural education should move in a globalist direction. No, it should address cultural pluralism in U.S. society. No, its focus should be on racism, sexism, and ethnocentrism in education. No, it must be concerned with the legacies, values, and experiences that unify all Americans. No, it should displace the overarching Eurocentric ethos in education, culture, and society. No, it should unify human beings as such, by introducing the interactive and complex variations of human experiences and creations throughout the world. Admittedly, education reform cannot be expected to proceed without challenges and counterchallenges, but the cul-de-sac in the debate over multicultural education could have been avoided by paying greater attention to theories of knowledge, the relationship between "moral literacy" and logical reasoning, standards for argument assessment and ground rules for intellectual exchanges.

Chapter 4 is organized around three theses: (1) an education model, with roots in a specific theory of human nature, and characterized by a commodification and politicization of schooling, dominates educational organization; (2) an educability model, the philosophical-educational foundation of critical thinking reforms, contains remedies for education's crises; (3) the multicultural agenda and critical thinking are incompatible, and the latter provides reasonable alternatives to standard educational practices. This chapter demonstrates that discussions of multicultural education and multiculturalism encompass themes in: educational philosophy, various theories of knowledge, biological, and cultural classifications from anthropology and sociology, and different perspectives on schooling and social change.

Three sets of criticisms of schooling—corporatist, critical pedagogist, and critical thinking—bring to light an "education model" that designs schooling not for the maximum development of students' analytical, reasoning, and empathic abilities, but for accommodation to political and labor market exigencies. In its stipulation that students be prepared for the world of work, this model shows its derivation from a conception of human beings as materialistic, egotistic, and consuming bodies with untrustworthy reasoning. This Hobbesian conception of human nature virtually guarantees the choice of a form of economic organization whose purpose is the production of commodities through the buying and selling of labor power. The education model is eminently suited to such an economy. Indeed, its adoption by corporate and political leaders as well as educators is virtually global. It is expressed in the subordination of educational aims to the vicissitudes of the labor market and politically defined goals; it produces qualifications of education such as, citizenship education, defense education, values education, drug education, sex education, vocational education, multicultural education, education governors, and education presidents. Advocates of multicultural education reform, in seeking simply to imbue educational delivery with cultural and political additives, do not challenge the education model that yields students as commodity hustlers in labor and consumer markets. Such a challenge is eminently necessary, however, if the purpose of education reform is the consolidation of democracy, the equalization of educational opportunities, or the cultivation of a reasonable citizenry. Such outcomes require, above all, a decommodification of educational delivery, that is, the exemption of all phases of education from commercial processes. A multicultural curriculum will not stem the attrition rate among "students of color," if economic deprivation and family destabilization prevent them from concentrating on learning, or if teachers impose a learn-to-earn ethos on students to the extent that these students conceive schooling simply as a means toward monetary ends. Money can be made without much schooling.

Schools must return to the drawing board on instruction in reasoning. Social justice cannot be achieved through logically flawed arguments. Such arguments lack persuasive power, and their behavioral effects are unpredictable, or contrary to a purpose of human affirmation. Teachers cannot become empowered, if they disregard the need for reasoning within intellectual standards or conceive their role as preparing students to celebrate *their* group's culture. Such students will hardly be interested in knowledge of "other cultures;" they would become agents of social justice only in the sense of demanding their group's ascendancy, or equality, in occupations and consumption patterns. Thus the core feature of "bourgeois society"—the reduction of human endeavors to a pursuit of commodities—remains unchallenged in multiculturalism. How it has acquired a reputation as being on "the Left" is a mystery. However, what the popularity of the terms *Left* and *Right* reveals is educators' failure to prevent political denunciation from becoming a standard for evaluating arguments.

The education model may be contrasted with an *educability model* in which the humanities play a key role in the curriculum, and learning is not subordinated to labor market and political vicissitudes. Teachers would concentrate on cultivating analytical, reasoning, and empathic abilities, strive for *theoretical* inclusiveness in the curriculum, and attend to the intellectual potential of all students. Students ought not to be taught cultural differences b*ut how to reason about cultural differences and similarities*. These recommendations are at the center of the critical thinking advocacy. Admittedly, there is considerable dissension regarding the definition of critical thinking, adequate strategies of infusion, and the locus of its initiation—in colleges, corporations, kindergarten, media, or the family. What is most significant, however, is that these discussions, are characterized by an implicit and explicit commitment to rational ground rules, and intellectual standards such as conceptual clarity, plausible assumptions, coherent classifications, logical consistency, and analytical depth. By contrast, advocacies of the multicultural agenda are replete with mutual moral denunciations and accusations of political biases. This condition reveals a significant incompatibility between critical thinking and multicultural education /multiculturalism.

In the interest of clarity and consistency, advocates of critical thinking proposals must be self-reflexive, that is, sensitive to the implications of classificatory criteria, epistemological assumptions, and implicit and explicit purposes. This means that the proposals would have to be corrected or withdrawn, if their basic categories were shown to contravene logical rules, or if the implications of the arguments in which the proposals are couched are demonstrably contrary to their purposes. By contrast, the defense of multicultural education and multiculturalism focuses on the "cultures" and "interests" of specific populations. This lack of attention to standards for reasoning facilitates tolerance of a certain contradiction—cultivating gender, racial, and ethnic identities while at the same time protesting against the accompanying forms of discrimination. Multicultural education programs compound this contradiction by heightening awareness of identities that foster nepotism, or discrimination for one's group. People who are constantly being made aware of their gender, whiteness, blackness, and cultural differences should be expected to: worship their ancestors, make requests for their own histories, favor their own kind, become educationally "centric," and ignore human commonalties. Thus multicultural education requires stronger doses of multicultural education to combat its own effects; it evolves into demands for group centeredness and liberation, which are justified on the grounds that all education is politics. Thus educators empower political zealots in schools and abandon control of learning processes.

Chapter 4 proposes a curriculum for intellectual diversity that is inclusive of gender, racial, ethnic, class, and human *theories* of social relations in order to foster understanding of how differences are constructed. Through a critical thinking focus on the relationship among theories, identities, group formation, and behavior, students can be invited to appreciate the behavioral significance of theories and offered standards to evaluate them. Gender, racial, class, and human self-identifications are derived from corresponding theories that are disseminated by educational and socializing institutions. In critical thinking classrooms, students would be asked to become conscious users and evaluators of theories, not activists for egalitarianism or anti-egalitarianism. Such classrooms would cultivate that which is most human about the species—the capacity to reason and be reasonable. The curriculum would also be inclusive of a human perspective on social relations, which may be necessary for understanding the infinite *variations* on culture. If students are to pursue such an understanding, teachers would have to embrace a goal of educability and seek to nurture students' passion for knowing, as well as their analytical, reasoning, and empathic skills. Were educators to reach agreement on the ground rules for intellectual exchanges and the standards to be used in assessing arguments, the sought-after balance between attention to different voices and humanism/universalism in the curriculum would be relatively easy to discover.

1

Multicultural Education: Development, Variants, and Controversies

> Whoever attempts to classify material must first have in mind certain notions, ideas, or characteristics by means of which he will separate one object from another.
>
> —Otis Mason (1887) cited in George W. Stocking Jr. (ed.), *The Shaping of American Anthropology, 1883-1911: A Franz Boas Reader* (New York: Basic Books, 1974), p. 3.

Over the last two decades, schools have been subjected to a most intense scrutiny and found wanting.[1] By the late 1980s, much of the discussion of education reforms focused on education's relationships to culture, gender, racial and ethnic inequalities, and national economic competitiveness. Among the variety of prescriptions for problems of prejudice, intolerance, and educational underachievement, multicultural education proposals have been most intensely debated, and their implementation have received substantial attention and resources from policy makers. It is generally presented as the most viable means of maintaining America's pluralistic heritage and egalitarian ideals. As curriculum and pedagogic reforms, it constitutes a set of measures aimed at building the self-esteem of "students of color," creating respect for cultural differences, removing racist, sexist, and ethnocentric biases from textbooks, and ensuring excellence and equity in educational outcomes.[2]

Donna Gollnick and Philip Chinn present a catalogue of seemingly unobjectionable aims. They argue that, through multicultural education students will:

(1) learn basic academic skills;

(2) acquire a knowledge of the historical and social realities of U.S. society in order to understand racism, sexism, and poverty;

(3) overcome their fear of differences that leads to cultural misunderstandings and inter-cultural conflicts;

(4) function effectively in their own and other cultural situations;

(5) value cultural differences among people and view differences in an egalitarian mode rather than in an inferior-superior mode; and

(6) understand the multicultural nation and interdependent world in which they live.[3]

However, for some of its advocates, multicultural education must go beyond these goals. Its texts, programs, and courses should give expression to the "silenced voices," that is, the experiences and perspectives of women and "people of color" that are generally omitted from the curriculum. Thus Gollnick and Chinn's specifications of multicultural educational objectives would be challenged by some scholars, teachers, and community activists for failing to mention the transformative purposes of multicultural education reform—the eradication of educational inequities and inequalities as well as the empowerment of oppressed and excluded groups.

According to some of its definitions, multicultural educational processes include the introduction of textbooks, testing, and teaching methods that are inclusive of the cultural backgrounds of all students. In other stipulations, it is a set of school reforms that prioritize the experiences of "students of color" in an effort to improve their self-esteem, motivation, and academic performances. Still other conceptions of multicultural education envisage textbook, pedagogical, and personnel changes that are inclusive of women and people of color, students' experiences, cultures, and perspectives in order not only to raise self-esteem but to motivate students toward action to alter power imbalances and unjust social arrangements. These different objectives result in a striking programmatic diversity within the general concept of multicultural education. Francis J. Ryan, professor of education at La Salle University, writes:

The term "multicultural education" is a slogan. It means different things to different people, and it assumes different purposes in different contexts. For instance, in some minority communities, multicultural education programs usually attempt, like some progressive efforts during the 1930s, to foster pride and self-esteem among minority students. . . . In white communities, however, multicultural programs are generally designed not so much to instill ethnic pride in students (although this clearly often occurs) so much as to cultivate an appreciation of various cultural, racial, and ethnic traditions both in the United States and abroad.[4]

These divergent goals and recommendations are united, however, by a focus on cultural differences. On the other hand, culture is variously conceived so that some approaches to multicultural education introduce prescriptions for remedying educational, as well as psychological and sociopolitical problems. The overall result is not only different schools of thought on multicultural education but the necessity of drawing a distinction between multicultural education and multiculturalism. The latter is grounded in a purpose of justice for all silenced, marginalized, and oppressed groups through the transformation of the culture and power structures in educational institutions. The ramifications of this distinction are explored further in Chapter 2. Suffice it to note here that all multicultural educational proposals derive from a common culturalist agenda that places a significant emphasis on coexisting but also conflicting group cultures. The relatively recent addition of a theme of social reconstruction through multicultural education marks a deviation from multicultural education as equal cultural representation and celebration of cultural differences.

Roots of Multicultural Education

From the historian's standpoint, multicultural education constitutes a series of reform proposals for preserving the cultural heritage of individual groups. Its basic assumption is that society comprises a macroculture that is divided into microcultures, and its clarion call is cultural inclusiveness. Because groups are necessarily protective of their heritage, the demand for multicultural education cannot be just a twentieth-century phenomenon. Some historians trace its origins beyond the culture-ferment in the 1920's assimilationist-pluralist debates over the place of cultures in schools. In *The Great School Wars, New York City, 1805-1973: A History of the Public Schools as Battlefields of Social Change*, Diane Ravitch identifies protracted controversies over the place of cultures in schools as contests over the direction of social transformations. Like Ravitch, Nathan Glazer notes links between the renaissance of contemporary disputes over multicultural education and the school wars of the 1840s, and concludes that multicultural education represents "a new word for an old problem."[5] Both authors indicate that one reason for the abiding disputes over multicultural education is the recognition by all sides that how children are taught has consequences for their identities, intellectual development, and social mobility.

As a concept and an education reform strategy in the twentieth century, multicultural education echoes specific disciplinary legacies and political activism: (1) the early twentieth-century Boas Revolution in cultural anthropology, which presents culture, not biology, as the axis of social relations; (2) the assimilationist-cultural pluralist debate of the 1920s; (3) the struggle against racism and thrust toward racial equality in the 1960s; (4) 1970's "culturalist" criticisms of schooling; and (5) ethnic revivalism, also of the mid-1970s. The 1970s, in particular, witnessed the emergence of semiofficial proposals for a culturally pluralistic education—an embracing of all cultures and inclusion of different ethnic experiences in the curriculum. What has hardly been noticed throughout the protracted debate over cultural pluralism is that it implicitly legitimizes the concept of culture as a standard for evaluating proposals for curriculum construction. Hence its progeny, multicultural education, embodies not only the proposition that schools must reflect America's various cultures, but also the suggestion that knowledge be evaluated in terms of its cultural ramifications.

Multicultural education, then, should be expected to generate a smorgasbord of reactions, for it represents an overall ethnic theory of social relations that constructs ethnic groups through cultural demarcation, and places culture at the center of knowledge construction and assessment, as well as social action and social change.[6] The evolving popularity of this theory is discernible in cultural prescriptions for conflicts among employees, students, and communities as well as proposals for cultural literacy, multicultural literacy, diversity management, intercultural proficiency, and intercultural communication.

Initially, the construction of the concept of multicultural education drew on an ethnic theory of society that centralizes the culture concept. Early twentieth-century contributions to this theory are discernible in the writings of the Boas School of Cultural Anthropology, as well as philosopher Horace Kallen's. The concept of single cultures, with corresponding ethnic groups, figures eminently in the "culture wars" of the 1920s between those who preferred the "melting pot" (assimilationist) over the "salad bowl" (pluralist) metaphor to describe the ethnic dimensions and dynamics of American society.[7] Two crucial issues, having implications for immigration policies especially toward Central and Eastern Europe, were whether people of different cultures can integrate, and the necessity of their becoming Americanized. In the discussions, various conceptions of race, culture, cultural differences, and cultural determination took center stage as scholars and activists struggled to conceptualize the effects of, and educational policies needed to deal with, an influx and mixing of "different peoples." Their exchanges reveal the salient influence of certain anthropologists' notion of single cultures, and especially the contributions of the Boas School of Cultural Anthropology.

According to George W. Stocking Jr., Boas himself used the culture concept to refute what he regarded as an unwarranted notion of racial determinism in studies of the relationships among race, language, and culture. As Boas writes:

The claim is not tenable that mental qualities of races are biologically determined. Much less have we a right to speak of biologically determined superiority of one race over another. Every race contains so many genetically distinct strains, and the social behavior is so entirely dependent upon the life experience to which every individual is exposed, that individuals of the same type when exposed to different surroundings will react quite differently, while individuals of different types when exposed to the same environment may react the same way.[8]

Stocking argues that Boas' writings strongly influenced the development of American anthropology in the twentieth century, generating: "on the one hand a rejection of the traditional nineteenth-century linkage of race and culture in a single hierarchical evolutionary sequence, on the other the elaboration of the concept of culture as a relativistic, pluralistic, holistic, integrated, and historically conditioned framework for the study of the determination of human behavior."[9] Boas' influence may be said to be even more extensive. He pioneered the rejection of the naturalist, social Darwinist, or biological determinist association of racial attributes and intelligence, and his influence on contemporary discussions of "race relations" is described by Vernon J. Williams Jr.:

In fact, although harboring doubts about the eventual achievement of a biracial egalitarian society, Boas trained, corresponded, and was actively involved with blacks in reform movements based on the belief that African Americans should be assimilated. Thus, despite the confines of his period, Boas was a prisoner there to a lesser extent than most other white scholars: he defined the parameters of the current controversy concerning the saliency of "race," "culture," or "class" as the chief determinant of African Americans' life chances.[10]

What, however, of Boas' own intellectual debts? His arguments and "empirical" research do deny the validity of any hierarchical arranging of races, and certainly demonstrate that "race" does not determine behavior. However, they affirm an equation of race and culture—the idea that a race has its own culture. Underlying this idea is a view of culture not so much as human-species creations as individual or group possessions. This view of culture is strongly developed in the writings of Johann Herder, an eighteenth-century philosopher. In tracing the emergence of anthropology to late eighteenth-century intellectual developments, Boas comments on Herder's work as follows: "To this period belongs Herder's Ideen zur Geschicte der Menschheit, in which, perhaps for the first time, the fundamental thought of development of the culture of mankind as a whole is clearly expressed."[11] However, Herder is more concerned with identifying *cultures* than (human) culture. His notion of single cultures seeped into anthropological studies, perhaps because of its compatibility with the race concept. Through its adoption and popularization by the Boas School, Horace Kallen, and ethnic activists, the idea of single cultures was consolidated in social studies and social consciousness; it underlies the culture wars of the 1920s; the formation of the concept of multicultural education, and the ethnic revivalism of the 1970s.

According to the ethnic perspective, society comprises a plurality of cultures, or culturally defined groups. If education is a transmission of culture, the central question for legislators and educators is: what kinds of educational policies are needed to include the cultures of the different ethnic groups in American society? In *The Disuniting of America*, Arthur M. Schlesinger Jr. notes that this question touched off intense discussions of immigration and education in the 1920s. However, what should also be noted that these discussions were based on the assumption of single cultures. In keeping with Boas' emphasis on the pliability and equality of all cultures, "assimilationists" argued that urban immigrants— whether originating from the Deep South or Southern and Eastern Europe—can shed their cultural peculiarities and be assimilated into a general American culture. The contrasting argument, expressed in Horace Kallen's *Culture and Democracy in the United States* and *Cultural Pluralism and the American Idea*, is that these different cultures need not be amalgamated or dissolved.[12] Rather, each should be preserved and allowed free and full expression. Kallen's rejection of the melting pot is curiously Boasian. Boas proposed that behavior was culturally determined to counter any suggestion that different peoples could not become harmoniously integrated. Kallen took cultural determination a step further, that is, toward ethnic exclusivity and cultural inviolability.

Kallen coined the term *cultural pluralism* to describe his recommended policy toward the different cultures in American society. His writings emphasize the individual's indelible, inner ethnic self, America's cosmopolitan character, and necessary connections between culturally pluralistic educational institutions and the preservation of democratic values. These "progressivist" notions were linked to a conception of ethnic groups as culturally autonomous entities voluntarily fused within the American nation. None should be "assimilated," in the sense of being made to lose its heritage, or have it marginalized under the guise of creating a homogeneous American culture. As Baptise and Baptise write: "Multicultural education is education which values cultural pluralism . . . to endorse cultural pluralism is to endorse the principle that there is no one model American."[13] The influence of the cultural pluralist idea on the formulation of multicultural education in the 1970s is also manifest in the goals outlined by the Association for Supervision and Curriculum Development (ASCD) Multicultural Education Commission:

In educational terms, the recognition of cultural pluralism has been labeled "multicultural education." The essential goals of multicultural education embrace: (a) recognizing and prizing diversity; (b) developing greater understanding of other cultural patterns; (c) respecting individuals of all cultures; and (d) developing positive and productive interaction among people *and* among experiences of diverse cultural groups.[14]

The concept of multicultural education is undergirded by a thesis that American society constitutes a macroculture with many microcultures. This thesis raises questions that continue to trouble both advocates and detractors of multicultural education: What makes the macroculture "American," if it is a composition of many *different* microcultures? Or, is there a distinct American culture, and *then* other, microcultures? Which of the microcultures is most American? Perhaps the missing question is: Is the term *culture* being used equivalently in the thesis about macro and microcultures?

For advocates of multicultural education, insofar as the United States is said to be a democratic society with democratic educational institutions, each culture should be represented n the curriculum, and this would foreclose an image of the United States as white, Anglo-Saxon, and Protestant. The thesis of many, distinct cultures, as well as opposition to a one-culture America was clearly stated by the ASCD Multicultural Education Commission: "Multicultural education goes beyond an understanding and acceptance of different cultures. It recognizes the right of different cultures to exist, as separate and distinct entities, and acknowledges their contribution to the social entity. It evolves from fundamental understandings of the interaction of divergent cultures *within* the culture of the United States."[15] There is no single culture that may be said to represent America's cultures, and all students should experience an immersion into these different cultures, if they are to function effectively in the society. By implication, multicultural education is not only for "people of color." The writings of its advocates do contain constant references to racial and ethnic minority experiences of exclusion and victimization. However, their defense might be that these references appear race-specific only because of a traditional silencing of "cultures of color."

In 1972, the AACTE's (American Association of Colleges for Teacher Education) Commission on Multicultural Education outlined elements of a culturally pluralistic education:

Education for cultural pluralism includes four major thrusts: (1) the teaching of values which support cultural diversity and individual uniqueness; (2) the encouragement of the qualitative expansion of existing ethnic cultures and their incorporation into the mainstream of American socioeconomic and political life; (3) the support of explorations in alternative and emerging life styles; and (4) the encouragement of multiculturalism, multilingualism, and multi-dialectism.[16]

The aims of the early advocates of multicultural education were tolerance of intergroup differences and the preservation of cultural heritages, not the realization of equality of educational opportunities or the eradication of oppression. However, the Commission's recommendations hint at different interpretations of cultural pluralism and foreshadow conflicts over the teaching of "alternative life styles" and bilingual education. For example, critics of the "expansion of existing ethnic cultures," could argue that a curriculum sensitive to, or grounded in, many autonomous cultures would unleash forces threatening the cohesion of U.S. society. Rather than out of many one, *E pluribus Unum*, the cultivation of "microcultures" would lead to the dissolution of the macroculture. As the argument goes, the scramble among racial and ethnic groups for their place in the curriculum will result in a Balkanization of both the curriculum and U.S. society. The schools' emphasis on cultural differences may improve students' self-esteem but not necessarily their academic performance, and, once such differences become educationally institutionalized, they would hardly be manageable. These may be said to be the pluralists' criticisms and apprehensions; they echo those of the early assimilationists, and for this reason they are frequently described as "conservative" and "traditionalist."

The anti-assimilationists of the 1930s protested against the WASP cultural hegemony that was being maintained under the guise of preserving the common American culture, and insisted on the nonabsorption of ethnic cultures. Their arguments were echoed by the "black nationalists" of the 1960s who also insisted on the distinctiveness of black culture, and black cultural reorientation as a strategic prerequisite of black liberation. The promotion of black culture in schools—*as a solution to educational underachievement*—was fueled by perceptions of "scientific racism" in Arthur Jensen's thesis that genetic, racial inferiority is responsible for black educational underachievement. Fueled by the Coleman Report's (1966) emphasis on conditions in the home as the decisive variable in educational outcomes, headstart, compensatory, and cultural enrichment programs were implemented. Jensen's criticisms of these policies were presented in an a paper: "How Much Can We Boost IQ and Scholastic Achievement?" Published in the *Harvard Educational Review* in 1969, the article claimed that there is a correlation between intelligence, measured by IQ tests, and racial genes. In "empirical" substantiation, Jensen carried out a series of tests on black and white students and concluded that black intelligence was congenitally inferior to that of whites, and that this partly explains unequal educational achievements.[17] He argued further that, because a certain level of underachievement was due to the inferior genetic attributes of blacks, compensatory and enrichment programs are bound to be ineffective in closing the racial gap in educational achievements.

One of the criticisms of Jensen's "scientific racism" pointed to the salient influence of culture. As the argument goes, the compensatory programs did not go far enough to counter the influence of a white racist culture on the black psyche, and thereby boost black self-esteem and test scores. An analysis of the poor performance of black students on IQ tests must begin with a hard look at the white (racist) culture that provides the standards for these tests. This racist culture is a much more plausible explanation of underachievement than black genetic inferiority, for it shapes the curriculum and the entire organization of schools. Black students were being educated and tested in an alien European culture, a culture that dehumanizes them and destroys their incentives to achieve. Test results confirm what racial discrimination in the economic sphere and cultural racism in the schools perpetuate—low achievements. These are also key Afrocentric arguments; they bear a striking similarity to the cultural nationalist themes presented in Harold Cruse's, *The Crisis of the Negro Intellectual*.

The advocacy of multicultural education also strikes a note of quantitative historical redress; it is a proactive response to long-standing policies of educational deprivation. According to Francesco Cordasco, policies of rejection and forced cultural assimilation have traditionally characterized schooling in America:

Skeletally framed, American schools rejected black pupils, repudiated the cultural differences of the children of immigrants, and encapsulated within separate spheres other subcommunities (e.g., Mexicans and Indians) which threatened what the American schools envisioned as a homogeneous social order oriented to models which were white, Anglo-Saxon, Protestant and middle class. It sorted out the blacks, enforced the assimilation of different social enclaves, and generally ignored the educational needs of intransigent groups. In the process, the American school practiced both racial and ethnic discrimination against the children of the poor.[18]

Most commentators on education would agree that residues of this discrimination persist in the form of glaring and related inequalities in school districts' funding and patterns of educational achievement. By and large, students from "inner city" schools are outperformed by their suburban peers on all tests. Multicultural education proponents argue that in order to stem this hemorrhage of educational failure, the equal educational opportunity programs that were established during the 1960s must be supplemented with a curriculum that is relevant to the experiences of students of color.

Although contemporary justifications for multicultural education vary considerably, most advocates cite the failure of educational institutions to address recent demographic changes. As the argument goes, there is an imperative for quality academic programs that address the increasing presence of culturally diverse student populations. James A. Banks writes: "The color of the nation's student body is changing rapidly. Nearly half (about 45.5%) of the nation's school-age youths will be young people of color by 2020."[19] Banks, a principal architect of multicultural educational programs, argues that these changing racial proportions have significant implications for educational delivery, especially because these minorities are not positively presented in traditional texts, and have special needs deriving from linguistic and cultural differences from the majority. Moreover, the established curriculum is so Eurocentric and monocultural that most students are unaware of the racial and ethnic composition of American society, much less the contributions of persons of color to philosophy, literature, art, and the sciences. As Banks writes: "Feeling that their voices often have been silenced and their experiences minimized, women and people of color are struggling to be recognized in the curriculum and to have their important historical and cultural works canonized."[20]

Advocates of a multicultural curriculum and school environment argue that they would create an ethos of inclusiveness that is necessary for an appreciation of differences. Students and citizens would come to recognize that American society is richer for its cultural variety, that it need not be a "melting pot." Rather, it could be a "salad bowl" of infinite diversity. A "world of difference" is the world to be cultivated, and in embracing differences, students can come to treat others fairly. If differences are to be truly appreciated, a systemic multicultural reconstitution of education must be initiated. Textbooks must be carefully chosen. Many should be ejected from the curriculum, having been written from either blatantly racist, sexist, and Eurocentric perspectives that often subtly denigrate women, the handicapped, homosexuals, and people of color. To ask for the ejection of such textbooks is not an expression of censorship or an illiberal political correctness. On the contrary, such textbooks illustrate the worst kind of political correctness—exclusion based on color and gender classifications.

For multicultural education's sponsors the school is a society in microcosm that can function either to minimize or exacerbate racial and ethnic conflicts on its campuses and in the larger community. By this token, if the alleviation of such conflicts is desirable, educators should create a multicultural ethos in schools. Students should become acquainted with not only the histories of white male European thought and sciences, but also various ethnic perspectives. As Gerald Pine and Asa Hilliard III write: "An effective multicultural curriculum is achieved when we change the basic assumptions of the curriculum: enable students to view concepts, themes, issues and problems from several ethnic perspectives and infuse throughout the curriculum the frames of reference, history, culture, and perspectives of various ethnic groups."[21] Knowledge of various ethnic perspectives on American history and society should be part of the learning experience of every citizen. An infusion of such knowledge would lead to an increase in group empathy and a reduction of prejudice and discrimination. Its effectiveness would be discernible in attitudinal and intellectual transformations among students, and greater motivation and better performance from students of color. However, Hilliard professes a multicultural education that is pluralist in the sense of promoting curriculum diversity and setting the record straight on human history. In his view, the development of motivation and self-esteem of African-American students is not the major thrust of multicultural education.

Schools are major transmitters of both knowledge and cultural images, and their student populations are richly culturally diversified. Teachers need to take note of this diversity, and foster respect for differences by inculcating knowledge of the contributions of women and different racial and ethnic groups to history and social development. Because of a dominant monocultural school ethos, teachers are reinforcing stereotypes, ignoring the specific needs of students of color and thereby failing them. Too many teachers enter the classroom with old-school misconceptions about racial minorities, an unawareness of different learning styles, and a misunderstanding of the behavioral and linguistic codes used by black students, who are thus deemed "failures." Hence it is the teachers' biased perceptions and attitudes that are fatal to the realization of equal educational outcomes. This line of reasoning surfaces in Geneva Gay's advocacy of multicultural education, as she offers the following reasons for educational underachievement among "ethnic minority groups":

First, the sameness of educational resources for diverse individuals and groups does not constitute comparability of quality or opportunity. . . . Second, most graduates of typical teacher-education programs know little about the cultural traits, behaviors, values, and attitudes different ethnic minority groups bring to the classroom, and how they affect the ways these students act and react to instructional situations. . . . Third, like teacher training, most curriculum designs and instructional materials are Eurocentric. As such, they reflect middle-class, Anglo experiences, perspectives, and value priorities. They are likely to be more readily meaningful and to have a greater appeal to the life experiences and aspirations of Anglo students than to ethnic minorities.[22]

Not only is the number of students of color in U.S. schools rapidly increasing, but cultural and other socioeconomic differences between teachers and students are also widening. It follows that mere curriculum reform in K-12 and colleges would not be enough to improve educational outcomes. New faculty and staff development programs need to be devised to lessen "the sociocultural gap between students and teachers," a gap that has pernicious effects on learning processes. Multicultural education necessarily involves a revamping of teachers' attitudes.

Convinced that cultural predispositions of participants in educational institutions fundamentally affect learning processes, James Banks proposes attitudinal changes among teachers. He writes: "Because the teacher is the most important variable in the child's learning environment, classroom teachers must develop more positive attitudes toward ethnic minorities and their cultures and must develop higher academic expectations from ethnic youth."[23] Indeed, nothing short of the transformation of schools in the direction of equal representation of all cultures and the empowerment of students will do, and so teachers must reshape their attitudes, perspectives, and teaching styles. These arguments have implications for relations among teachers and for their livelihood. Who can become a teacher, and who is to teach whom? Should there be a fit between teach-ers' and students' cultures? Who should teach about different cultures, and should they be taught neutrally or evaluatively? These issues reveal that imple-mentation of multicultural education programs would affect curriculum con-struction, textbook selection, and faculty appointments, as cultural competence and correspondence become necessary components of teaching credentials.

"Multiculturalist" critics of educational practices generally insist that teach-ers who are not sensitive to their own cultural assumptions and to the different cultural practices, experiences, and expectations of "ethnically diverse students" *will* fail these students. Teachers bring culture-specific traits and behaviors to the classroom; they might even hold biased and stereotypical expectations that could significantly limit both their effectiveness and the performances of "students of color." Some advocates of multicultural education therefore recommend staff development programs and workshops, led by multicultural education consult-ants, as well as teacher preparation programs geared to increasing cultural com-petence and intercultural proficiency. However, this transformation could be voluntarily initiated, as indicated by Linda McCormick's "tips for helping" teachers:

1. As you identify the different ethnic groups in your classroom, become informed about their characteristics and learning styles.

2. Encourage and assist students in sharing their culture in the classroom; you can start the process by sharing your own cultural values and traditions.

3. Avoid textbooks and materials that present cultural stereotypes.

4. Learn as much as possible about minority students' home and community, in-terests, talents, skills, and potentials and develop an instructional program ac-cordingly.

5. Find out how the minority students in your class wish you to refer to their eth-nic group; for example, some Mexican-Americans prefer to be called Chicanos where as others may take offense at the term.

6. Include ethnic studies in the curriculum to help minority students gain a more positive self-image.

7. Make parents your partners in helping minority students.

8. Treat all students equally; do not fall into the trap of reverse racism.

9. Make sure assessment techniques used are appropriate and take into account cultural differences.

10. Avoid imitating speech patterns of minority students; rather than an aid in edu-cation, this may be viewed as mockery.[24]

These suggestions are presented as a means of realizing an "equitable treatment of culturally diverse students." Teachers are advised to adopt a series of self-examinations and self-corrective measures. They should not teach as if all, or even most, students are white, culturally mainstream, and middle class, and they should be attentive to the cultural biases in their own perceptions and expectations. In effect, the ramifications of cultural differences should become the organizational foundation of education.

Cultural Pluralism Plus Equality

The suggestion that educational practices and inputs reflect America's cultural diversity is not just about culture. It is also about attaining equality of educational opportunity and generating social mobility for women and people of color. However, some advocates of multicultural education are concerned only that the curriculum reflect America's cultural diversity; they would challenge a description of American education and society as unequal and oppressive for women and people of color. Both clusters of advocates claim an allegiance to cultural pluralism, but they offer contrasting answers to the following question: Does education for cultural pluralism necessarily involve a goal of equality? Baptise and Baptise answer in the affirmative: "Whatever the area of concern, underlying the definition of cultural pluralism is a philosophy that strongly recommends a particular set of beliefs, principles, and ideas that should govern the relationship of people of diverse cultures. The cornerstone principles of cultural pluralism are equality, mutual acceptance and understanding, and a sense of moral commitment."[25] Cultural pluralism necessarily involves a principle of equality; it means that all the cultures in schools are to be given equal play and their equal representation must be assured in the allocation of resources. But the standard predicament over equality emerges: the proof of equal opportunity is equal results, but equal results are not guaranteed by the presence of equal opportunity. Moreover, how can it be claimed that cultures are not equally represented in schools. Neither bicultural and transcultural students, nor textbooks depicting many diverse cultures are being banned from American schools, which cannot guarantee equal outcomes for students. These are some of the issues raised in the "conservative" opposition to multicultural education programs that promote cultural equality, antiracism, antisexism, and bilingualism.[26]

Explicit in the writings of Franz Boas is the notion that each race has a single culture, and that all cultures are relatively equal. Also explicit in the writings of Horace Kallen is an affirmation of notions of cultural distinctiveness and equivalence. Absent from their writings, however, is a justification for conceiving culture as distinct individual and group endowments, and comparing cultures within criteria of equivalence. Such comparisons are, indeed, part and parcel of anthropological research characterized more by a concern with measurement and comparison of cultures than conceptual specification of the culture concept and consistent usages of the chosen meaning. Nevertheless, it may be argued that inequality /equality is not a standard that can be applied to cultures, that cultures consist of qualitative, symbolic phenomena, unfolding in specific ecological and political-economic contexts. Thus cultures are neither equal, nor unequal. Nor should "cultural differences" be taken for granted. They are observed through the lens of a specific concept of culture. Nevertheless, how can cultural difference be observed without a simultaneous observation of cultural similarities? In emphasizing the transcultural nature of human experiences, Wolfgang Welsch urges advocates of "interculturality" and "multiculturality" to take a closer look at their usage of "the classical concept of single cultures" that certain anthropologists adopted from the writings of Johann Herder.[27] Subsequent usage of the concept of culture took a "volk" turn to serve purposes and processes of group construction and political mobilization.

The advocacy of multicultural education is deeply indebted to a Herderian tradition in anthropology that conceives single cultures in operation and interaction. However, as is shown in Chapter 3, universalistic conceptions of culture are also favored by the anthropologists Claude Levi-Strauss, Leslie White, Richard Tullar, and Joseph Campbell. And there is some justification for their more inclusive conception of culture. For the concept of single cultures lends itself to: (1) the discovery of an infinite number of cultures, (2) a merger with "race," or any social category, (3) cultural determinist explanations of behavior, and (4) conflicts over cultural space and resources that require government interventions. "Culture" comes to be all politics. Within the assumption of single cultures, the question generally asked is: What is to be done, educationally, with the enormous cultural diversity in American society? More radical questions, however, could be raised: Why does this diversity need official attention? What is the rationale for counting single races and cultures? What role does the Census Bureau play in constructing different racial and cultural identities? Once citizens are classified as belonging to different cultures, and their proportions in the population emphasized, how can their pursuit of equal cultural representation in education, the arts, and social life be avoided, or controlled. On the other hand, what should be considered as evidence of equal cultural representation in educational institutions? Should all "white-looking" and "brown-looking" students be categorized as members of different cultures? Is multicultural education cultural affirmative action? These are troubling questions, and they underlie much of the controversy over multicultural education, if not perceptions of racial and ethnic tensions. Noticeably, however, neither "liberals," nor "conservatives" direct critical attention to government's racializing practices that surely perpetuate this controversy and concomitant tensions. Yet the contradiction is stark. On the one hand, official policies cultivate images of inalienable racial and cultural differences, which constitutes a virtual Balkanization of identities. On the other hand, one of the consequences of this cultivation—demands for separate but equal cultural spaces in schools—is resisted, especially by "conservatives," for fear of Balkanization.

The issue of equal treatment of cultures and the races representing these cultures remains central to multicultural education. In its Afrocentric, antisexist, and antiracist versions, U.S. society is conceived as being dominated by a particular group—the white race, White Anglo-Saxon Protestants (WASPs), and white males. This domination is said to be manifest in the fact that nonmainstream cultures are marginalized in education and institutional life generally. The curriculum is organized around Western, monocultural canons that hinder learning for students of color. It reflects Eurocentric, racist, and sexist notions that must be uprooted, if education is to be faithful to its liberating and democratic goals. Thus Afrocentric, antisexist, and antiracist approaches to multicultural education take aim at the entire social system, seeking education reforms to equalize opportunities for those classified as "women" and "people of color." Proposed Afrocentric reforms are particularly interesting in the pungency of their criticisms of U.S. education.

Afrocentric Education Reform: Origins, Postulates, and Purposes

Criticisms of the monocultural focus of the curriculum, "Eurocentric hegemonism" in schools, and the damage done to the psyches of African American students form points of departure for Afrocentric education reforms.[28] According to this perspective, schools decenter and demotivate students of color. Their textbooks, courses, and pedagogical practices maintain a patterns of white hegemony. For the culture being transmitted by schools is based on traditions and images representing and favoring white students. Given the fact that the curriculum is based on Eurocentric assumptions, schools are not bastions of intellectual and cultural neutrality. On the contrary, in their omission of cultures of color, they practice "cultural racism," which according to Camille A. Clay, is "a belief in the superiority of the Eurocentric cultural heritage. Curricula that omit the contributions of minorities are culturally racist."[29] Such racism is discernible in textbooks' omissions of the contributions of persons of color to world civilization and American society. Geneva Gay makes the broader case:

Too often school curricula have omitted blacks, Puerto Ricans, American Indians, Cubans, Mexican Americans, and Asian Americans entirely, or depicted them in negative ways. Multicultural curricula can correct these distortions by explaining the contributions these minorities have made to American history and culture, and by presenting honest, comprehensive portrayals of their life experiences. This means including information about their status in American society in contemporary and historical perspective and their characteristic as functional cultural entities, as well as their contributions.[30]

This goal of equal representation of racial and ethnic groups remains a core feature of multicultural education proposals. Advocates of an Afrocentric curriculum take this feature in a particular direction; they construct a causal relationship among portrayals of black history, low self-esteem and educational underachievement. The remedy, they suggest, is the infusion of an Afrocentric perspective throughout the learning process.

A major impetus to the development of Afrocentric education reforms comes from not only cultural nationalist writings on the black experience in the 1960s, but also from a decade of "culturalist" criticisms of the organization and functioning of schools. As Cameron McCarthy and Michael Apple write: "American education took a decisively more culturalist approach to schooling in the mid-seventies, partly out of a dissatisfaction with structural economic explanations of schooling and society."[31] These critics claimed that schools fail students more through cultural omission than commission. Many teachers, they charged, ignore group-specific cognitive processes, the experiences students bring to the classroom, and the implications of the school's own cultural practices for different learning styles. The genes of the victims, that is, those forced to underachieve, are then blamed.

References to deficient black genes, evident in the work of Arthur Jensen and others, are part of a "naturalist" explanation of educational and socioeconomic differences, where nature is endowed with a purpose and held to be an unalterable determinant of group destinies.[32] In rejecting this explanation, certain scholars suggested a focus not on genes but on a racist white culture and corresponding educational inputs that have devastating effects on black self-esteem, motivation, and educational outcomes. Historian Stephan Thernstrom, while not an advocate of multicultural education, writes:

In any event, in virtually every area of the economy it appears that the main barriers to black achievement have been not internal but external, the result not of peculiarities in black culture but of peculiarities in white culture. For three quarters of a century following Emancipation there was a pervasive belief in Negro inferiority that fostered overt discrimination in many industries, and left blacks with little choice but to accept traditional "Negro jobs."[33]

These remarks capture a basic theme of the cultural nationalist approach to black liberation. Culture is to be the starting point of all educational and political organizational efforts to liberate black Americans. Crucial to this objective is the claim that American culture is racist, oppressive, and psychologically destructive of black Americans. This culture, a white culture, has penetrated and poisoned the black mind to such an extent that the strategy for black liberation must be grounded in African-centered cultural-educational inputs.

Cultural-educational proposals for black liberation can be found in "black nationalist" writings in the 1960s as well as in the works of late nineteenth-century Pan-Africanists and mid-twentieth-century "black cultural nationalists."[34] Afrocentric education reform represents the most recent reappearance of black cultural nationalism. One of its foremost advocates, Molefi Asante, presents Afrocentricity as "an ideology for liberation" that rivals Marxism, Islam, Christianity, Buddhism, or Judaism.[35] Afrocentricity means prioritizing the interests of African people in all endeavors. Nevertheless, for Asante, the infusion of Afrocentricity is not merely a matter of politicizing the curriculum or imposing an Afrocentric perspective on schools. Truth and accuracy in scholarship and pedagogy are also at stake. African-American students are being indoctrinated with false interpretations about the past, and especially about the influence of ancient Egyptian civilization on Greece. Afrocentrists argue that, were the accomplishments of classical Africa to be given a small amount of the prime time that is accorded Europe's, African-American students would fare much better in schools. More significantly, overall African-American attitudes to self and other African Americans would be positively different.

Central to Afrocentricity is the claim that dominant Eurocentric educational practices exclude other perspectives, ignore the cultural heritage of African-American students, and marginalize Africa's contributions to world and American history. It is these practices that chronically fail these students, who are not given a historically positive grounding of their identity. On the contrary, they are taught that theirs is a race of nonachievers. If African-American students are to achieve on equal terms with white students, the curriculum must be infused with Afrocentric values, standards, and concepts. At one level, African-American students must participate in courses that center their identity, culture, contemporary experiences, and historical memory. Molefi Asante writes: "*Afrocentricity* is a frame of reference wherein phenomena are viewed from the perspective of the African person. The Afrocentric approach seeks in every situation the appropriate centrality of the African person."[36] An Afrocentric curriculum, then, is specifically for African-American students. At another level, the Afrocentric perspective on history should be included in all educational institutions and be part of *both black and white educational experiences*. In the process of learning historical truths about black people, whites will come to recognize blacks as their historic equals and cease to question the intellectual abilities of modern African Americans. In effect, both blacks and whites will be intellectually and socially liberated by Afrocentric education reforms.

The Afrocentric perspective also represents a liberationist variant of a racial theory of history and social relations that was developed in nineteenth-century Europe. Like its founders, Afrocentrists identify *racial* problems in society. However, they claim to be champions of black interests, and seek to counter racism and Eurocentrism in schools with an infusion of specifically, "black" interpretations of the past and the present. These proposals take the idea of black liberation in a specific, psychohistorical direction by focusing on the relationships among courses on history, the self-esteem of students, and their academic performance. Black students underachieve because the curriculum demotivates and disempowers them. If they are to have an incentive to learn, they must be centered in the knowledge they assimilate. Therefore, specific information about Africa must be infused throughout their educational experiences. Molefi Asante writes: "We do not seek segments or modules in the classroom but rather the infusion of African-American studies in every segment and in every module. The difference is between 'incorporating the experiences' and infusing the curriculum with an entirely new life."[37] While "pluralists" seek a mere inclusion of experiences, Afrocentrists insist on the inclusion of an Afrocentric perspective on world history. How can there be objections to this recommendation, they ask, given the recognition that the knowledge being transmitted by the current curriculum is so obviously Eurocentric? And worse, this Eurocentrism is presented as the intellectual apex and representative of the human experience!

Afrocentrists claim that the ideas and images of European civilization are overrepresented in an educational system that is supposed to serve a variety of cultures. Thus courses on Western civilization should be radically transformed or discontinued and replaced with courses and texts that psychologically "center" black students. However, this centering is a means to an end—liberation—for the ultimate purpose of Afrocentricity is not just to celebrate black culture or ancient Egyptian civilization, but to liberate black people spiritually, culturally, and politically. The proposed philosophical, cultural, and educational reconstructions are meant, ultimately, to serve the political-economic emancipation of a people. African Americans still constitute a disproportionate share of the poor, the uneducated, the unemployed, and the incarcerated, despite the legal and political-economic solutions to racial problems that were initiated during the 1960s, such as civil rights and affirmative action programs. Some studies of economic trends suggest that African Americans faced an economic crisis of unprecedented proportions in the 1980s that has continued into the 1990s.[38] For Afrocentrists, this situation is the outcome of centuries of miseducation of black people, and the cardinal reason that black students underachieve educationally, which prevents black socioeconomic mobility, is that the cultural images they receive in schools depreciate their sense of self. A white-culture biased education destroys their self-esteem and motivation to learn. This leads to chronic patterns of maladjustment, isolation, and comparatively high dropout rates among black students. Official remedies have registered failure after failure, for they do not attend to the cultural and spiritual devastation being inflicted on black students by a racist and Eurocentric educational system. The alternative is Afrocentricity. Once the school environment becomes user-friendly for black students, the hemorrhage of black educational failure could be terminated. Once blacks are freed from the historical distortions that are imposed on them by a Eurocentric education, they will gain racial pride and self-esteem. Through this, they will proceed to liberate themselves from all other forms of white domination and oppression.

Afrocentrists continue the Pan-Africanist, Garveyite, and black nationalist pursuit of black cultural regeneration and liberation through a reconstruction of the past. Their quest for black liberation explicitly centralizes racial identities, as is manifest in Jon M. Spencer's depiction of the significance of racial categorization for the multicultural movement: "For us to transcend the notion of race—when the quest for racial equality is a central motivating factor in multiculturalism, is to undermine this historical movement. . . . We cannot expect the unprivileged and oppressed to discard their mythologies and mystifications regarding race and the essential blessings of their race until the privileged and powerful discard their particular mythologies and mystifications."[39] It is not for black people to abandon the "mythologies and mystifications" about race, first. Indeed, the black race even has certain "essential blessings." But surely, because the very act of discarding the idea of race would negate one's racial identity, neither "white people" nor "black people" can abandon racial classification without at the same time ceasing to be white people and black people. And they should be expected to resist appeals for an end to racial classification, given the relatively massive official and academic investments in such classification.

Spencer argues for a retention of racial classification as a means of instilling racial pride and liberating the oppressed and the powerless. His argument expresses one of the cardinal purposes of Afrocentrism—to transform, positively, the self-image and political perspective of African Americans through accurate depictions of Africa's history. In pursuit of the intellectual and spiritual emancipation of African-origin people, Afrocentrists expound the following theses:

1. The human species was originally black; it radiated from Africa to all other parts of the world, and it now comprises different but biologically equal racial groups.

2. Nonblack races emerged as a result of millions of years of adaptation to specific climatic conditions, and miscegenation. The white race, for example, is a mutant species of a black human prototype.

3. Modern blacks and whites are offshoots of primordial black and white races that are traceable to Africa and Europe, respectively.

4. Ancient Egyptians were black. Egyptian civilization was greater than Greece's, and Egyptian scholars' influence on Greek scholars was profound. Indeed, many Greek philosophers were schooled in Egypt, from which a vast number of intellectual treasures were stolen, and renamed Western, European, and white.

5. Egypt is the fountainhead of Western civilization, including its philosophical, scientific, and technological achievements. Egypt's achievements, in turn, are indebted to the Nubian civilization up the Nile.

6. For the last two centuries, racist and Eurocentric historians have systematically denied that ancient Egypt was a black civilization, the first human civilization.

However, it should be noted that the degree of endorsement of these tenets varies among those self-characterized as Afrocentrists. Thus Afrocentrism is far from a homogeneous school of thought. As Gerald Early writes:

Afrocentrism is not monolithic—there are actually many varieties of Afrocentrism. Some are demagogic and even fascist or racist in their assertions. Others are more nuanced, thoughtful, and probably worth our attention and engagement. Despite their own diversity, most Afrocentrists tend to hold three beliefs in common. They believe that society's dominant body of scholarship exhibits a decidedly "white" or "Eurocentric" bias in support of a "white" or "Eurocentric" political and social hegemony. They believe that the Western world has smothered divergent ideas that promote a distinctly African or nonwhite viewpoint. They believe that African peoples around the globe can come to a full self-determination and complete humanity only when they are permitted to overthrow "white" or Eurocentric premises and when they can fully realize and articulate themselves through self-creation.[40]

One of the explicit purposes of Afrocentric writings is the restoration of the black race to the eminence it enjoyed in the ancient world. This necessitates a call to intellectual arms, an appeal to "black scholars" for unity and struggle to rescue black history from distortions and the black race from centuries of oppression. Thus blackness should be a spiritually and politically unifying attribute. To facilitate this transformation of black consciousness, Africa must be conceived as the spiritual home of all Africans in Diaspora. Black scholars should be committed to the realization of their people's interests. Those who oppose the call for unity and cultural revolution are psychologically decentered and dislocated ideologues deluded by Eurocentric scholarship and trapped within white culture.

Afrocentric scholars take African-American educational experiences and interests as one of the points of departure for criticisms of American education; they insist on the elimination of racist and Eurocentric assumptions and texts from the curriculum as a necessary prelude to black educational progress. For example, Gerald Pine and Asa Hilliard III write:

Through the omission of information, America's schools have become monocultural environments. They dispense a curriculum centered on western civilization that encapsulates only narrowly the truth, reality and breadth of human experience. . . . Because the U.S. system of education is built so solidly on a monocultural, Euro-American world view, it tends to benefit white students, whose cultural patterns and styles are more attuned to this world view.[41]

Because educational institutions reflect the value system of the white race, it incapacitates non-European students, who fail because they are unable to identify with the material being presented, and because teachers generally ignore non-European cultures and experiences. Thus the schools' practices are damaging to the psyche and performance of students of color. The remedy, and it is relevant to the education of not only African Americans, is the infusion of an Afrocentric perspective in the curriculum. Such an infusion would be neither antiwhite nor anti-American. What would make it appear as such is that in U.S. society, white people are politically dominant and their culture is being presented as the mainstream American, if not world, culture.

A genuinely multicultural education would not accept the monoethnic and centrist distortions that pass as education in schools. In Asante's words:

Multiculturalism in education is a nonhierarchical approach that respects and celebrates a variety of cultural perspectives on world phenomena. The multicultural approach holds that although European culture is the majority culture in the United States, that is not sufficient reason for it to be imposed on diverse student populations as "universal." Multiculturalists assert that education, to have integrity, must begin with the proposition that all humans have contributed to world development and the flow of knowledge and information, and that most human achievements are the result of mutually interactive, international effort.[42]

Asante argues further that the "Eurocentric claim to universalism" not only flies in the face of cultural pluralism, but also miseducates students of color. Such students, then, are programmed to fail by an educational system geared to further the culture and interests of white people. This failure, however, could be remedied with educational inputs that promote the equality of all cultures. Indeed, it may be necessary to construct special curricula for students of color to impress on them that they come from a long line of "classical" cultures and civilizations in Africa, Asia, and Latin America.

In a multiracial and multicultural society, schools need grounded knowledge, that is, texts and instruction that touch base with the background, identity, and experiences of all students. Otherwise, schools lose their raison d'être as a place where African American students want to, or can, be educated. Asante writes:

African American children who have never heard the Spirituals; never heard the names of African ethnic groups; never read Paul Laurence Dunbar, Langston Hughes, and Phillis Wheatley nor the stories of High John de Conqueror, Anansi, and the Signifying Monkey are severely injured in the most fragile parts of their psyches. Lacking reinforcement in their own historical experiences, they become psychologically crippled, hobbling along in the margins of the European experiences of most of the curriculum.[43]

It is Asante's argument that African-American students perform poorly because of low self-esteem and poor motivation. Both are the result of negative, or the absence of positive, black historical images in the school environment. However, these students will be powerfully motivated to learn, as African students are in African schools, when they are presented with their own historical models, myths, and heroes. For this reason, the achievements of ancient, black civilizations and their contributions to modern civilization must be part of the curriculum. Indeed, it should be generally known that these achievements and contributions were pivotal to the development of Western philosophy, science, and civilization. This information should be at the center of the learning experience in this multiracial and multicultural society. Nevertheless, certain special circumstances must also be addressed. Black students have specific needs. They bring cognitive styles that are peculiar to black culture, a culture dismissed by the mainstream, Eurocentric culture. This long tradition of dismissal necessitates an introduction of the Afrocentric perspective on world history and civilization into all phases of education. The perspective must also be incorporated into teacher training and staff development programs, if schools are to become relevant to the black experience, and if black students are to be given a chance at equal educational outcomes.

There are reasons to believe that Asante's explanation of black educational underachievement is guilty of non-sequitur. First, if a racial fit is so essential to the assimilation of a message and the motivation to be, what explains Africans' and African Americans' embracing of Christianity's "white" Jesus? Second, as Diane Ravitch has observed, the explanation reduces complex matters of cognition, motivation to learn, and self-esteem to the one-dimensionality of historical racial images. The presence of positive, historical Greek images in the curriculum has not produced overachieving Greek-American students, and the absence of positive, historical Asian images does not appear to cause academic underachievement among Asian-American students.

Afrocentricity: A Continuation of "European" Racial Studies

Principal opposition to Afrocentrism emerged in the form of a series of criticisms from those scholars for whom American society is multiracial and multicultural but also unified by a common culture. They propose multicultural education reform as a means of strengthening the common culture, not to promote any particular culture. In defense, Afrocentrists argue, however, that "pluralists" fail to emphasize the fact that one race is culturally dominant in U.S. society, the white race, and that that, indeed, there is no common culture as such. Under the guise of promoting the so-called common culture, schools add a Eurocentric twist to knowledge, and are especially diligent in falsifying the role of Ancient Egypt in the evolution of Western civilization.

One of the purposes of the Afrocentric reading of ancient history is to redness the Eurocentric imbalance in the curriculum and demonstrate that the black race is, indeed, creative and that its accomplishments are central to the development of all civilizations. Knowledge of the role of black people in history is regarded as crucial to black psychological and political rehabilitation. But there is also a question of accuracy in studies of the past. Within the dominant Eurocentric studies a certain whitening and falsification of history has taken place. Its propagation through educational institutions destroys African Americans morally and spiritually. In order to remedy this devastation, blacks throughout the world must be told that African people are the first human beings—making Africa the cradle of civilization—and that their achievements are brilliantly expressed in ancient Egypt.[44]

Afrocentric arguments on race and history draw principally on the Egyptological studies of Cheikh Anta Diop, who in his magnum opus, *Civilization or Barbarism*, writes:

For us, the return to Egypt in all domains is the necessary condition for reconciling African civilization with history, in order to be able to construct a body of modern human sciences, in order to renovate African culture. Far from being a reveling in the past, a look toward the Egypt of antiquity is the best way to conceive and build our cultural future. In re-conceived and renewed African culture, Egypt will play the same role that Greco-Latin antiquity plays in Western culture.[45]

Diop's writings on ancient Egyptian history, like those of W.E.B. Du Bois and Marcus Garvey, are opposed to the white-favored interpretation of the past. But the past is still regarded as a process of racial contacts, confrontations, and cultural repression. This pursuit of the racial pedigree of ancient history continues the tradition of racial studies developed in certain ethnological and anthropological studies from the eighteenth century onward.

Arthur de Gobineau's remarks set the tone for much of nineteenth-century racial studies: "I was gradually penetrated by the conviction that the racial question overshadows all other problems of history, that it holds the key to them all, and that the inequality of the races from whose fusion a people is formed is enough to explain the whole course of its destiny."[46] Gobineau, often called "the father of racist ideology," presented his classification of types of people as follows: "Considering it by myself, I have been able to distinguish, on physiological grounds alone, three great and clearly marked types, the black, the yellow, and the white. However uncertain the aims of physiology may be, however meagre its resources, however defective its methods, it can proceed thus far with absolute certainty."[47] The author of *The Inequality of Human Races* links these races to specific historical conditions to demonstrate that natural differences in racial endowments result in unequal regional and continental progress.

Gobineau considered his analysis to be "a work of moral geology." His demonstration of the inferior nature of "black people" serves to elevate "white people" to the status of nature's chosen people, a biologically predestined role of civilizers. However, his correlation of racial attributes and civilizational progress makes light of logical reasoning. First, it fails to demonstrate that white achievements (sic) are a result of biological endowments. Indeed, Gobineau's assertions are eminently circular—white people are biologically superior because they alone created Western civilization and this civilization is superior to all others because it was created by white people. Second, the concept of inequality is nowhere clarified in Gobineau's work. This conceptual looseness allows him to speculate further that all whites are not biologically equal. Within his ladder of racial excellence he constructs a second ladder whose top rung is occupied by a superior white race—Aryans.[48] Thus there are races within a race, which implies that the original criteria of racial classification are not being maintained. By further implication, given the infinite number of human biological attributes, races and sub-races may come and go into perpetuity. All that would be required are investments in their creation from prospective Fuhrers, political representatives, and scientists.

Like Gobineau, Diop makes forays into a variety of disciplines to demonstrate that there are racial types that correspond to cultural and civilizational achievements. In Diop's writings, however, Gobineau's ladder is upturned. The black race occupies the top rung. Diop dismisses as "ideology," but does not refute, the denial by some physical anthropologists, molecular biologists, and geneticists that races exist.[49] He, too, constructs black, white, and yellow races, with the black race being the progenitor of all other races and "mixed breeds." Nevertheless, in his analysis of racial achievements, the terms *black people* and *white people* have no fixed conceptual status. His demarcation of races depends primarily on skin color and facial form. However, blood type, area of habitation, shape and size of skull and jawbone, and physical stature are also sporadically mentioned as racial distinctions. Thus Diop's racial inventory reproduces the same arbitrariness that characterizes earlier attempts at racial classification.

Racial classification lies at the core of Diop's studies of ancient Egypt. He affirms this by his comments on criticisms of the concept of race: "They tell us that molecular biology and genetics recognize the existence of populations alone, the concept of race being no longer meaningful. Yet whenever there is any question of the transmission of a hereditary taint, the concept of race in the most classic sense of the term comes into its own again."[50] Some of Diop's remarks rival those of Gobineau in their fixation on parts of the human anatomy and on race-mixing:

Race et intelligence raises the question of miscegenation: Is it a positive or negative factor in the course of historic evolution? History has already answered the question. All Semites (Arabs and Jews), as well as the quasi-totality of Latin Americans, are mixed breeds of Blacks and Whites. All prejudice aside, this interbreeding can still be detected in the eyes, lips, nails, and hair of most Jews. The Yellows, the Japanese in particular, are also crossbreeds, and their own specialists today are acknowledging this important fact.[51]

White and yellow races are said to be derived from the black race; these races are identified basically by skin color, in conjunction with blood type, stature, and shape of skull. In other words, Diop uses a conception of race developed by "white" scientists who, he claims, deny that the ancient Egyptians were black and distort Egypt's and world history. Were the ancient Egyptians black? This is a premature question. The prior question must be: How do human beings become a color? Skins, however, do take colorings, and reportedly the skin colors of ancient and modern Egyptians and Europeans vary through copper, dark brown, pink, tan, olive, etc. Logically, to maintain the skin color criterion of racial classification, these would all be "coppers," "dark browns," "pinks," "tans," and "olives." The fact that these races are never carved out for dissertations on history indicates that skin color is not a decisive criterion of racial demarcation.

Black and white races are arbitrary constructs designed to justify specific policies, missions, and patterns of resource allocation; they serve to foster a collective consciousness and political mobilization. These functions require that these races be defended to the death of classificatory accuracy. For example, Diop's comments on human species affiliations place a "black race" as the ancestor of even "Aryans." He writes: "All the other races derive from the Black race by a more or less direct filiation, and the other continents were populated from Africa at the *Homo erectus* and *Homo sapiens* stages, 150,000 years ago."[52] However, these assertions equate species evolution and regional diffusions with racial divisions and derivations. Arguably, pre-historic Africa contained many "races," some of whom migrated to other continents. Diop's sighting of one black race in Africa, however, is understandable. Racial demarcation by skin color is pivotal to the Afrocentric project. The resulting races are therefore presented without any consideration of: the difficulties in identifying a representative of such races, criticisms of the conservative ideological functions of race, and arguments claiming that it is humankind's most dangerous fallacy.[53] For Diop, ancient Egypt is to be the black race's metaphorical Greece because Greece belongs to the white race. Thus his depiction of ancient Egyptian civilization as the work of "Blacks" pursues Africa's cultural renovation in order to liberate contemporary "Blacks." His studies of the past, then, are instrumentalist; they mirror those of the "ill-intentioned Egyptologists" who chose and whitened Greece as the fountainhead of "the West," which was then used to instill white pride and justify a civilizing mission in the Americas, Asia, and Africa.

References to persons as black people and white people in not only Afrocentric writings indicate a peculiar refusal to confront the substantial criticisms of racial classification that have emerged over the last two decades. A most compelling criticism is that human beings cannot be said to belong to a race, for the term *race* merely denotes certain anatomical attributes, not the persons who possess them. For good reasons, the practice of racial classification is recognized by some anthropologists as logically indefensible. It produces "blacks" and "whites" as referents of persons, but these persons' attributes go far beyond the colors of their skin. The indefensible nature of the racial classification of human beings is marginally recognized in the transition from "blacks" to "African Americans," which is allegedly an ethnic or cultural identification. However, the underlying notion of an African culture serves to retain the category "blacks."

In the advocacy of multicultural education, "African American" and "blacks" are used interchangeably, indicating that African American is simply a cultural denomination of "blacks." But some 80 percent of so-called blacks can claim "white" ancestry, and all participate in a culture that is called "white." Why, then, are they "blacks?" Who indeed are people of color? as Naomi Zack writes:

The words "black" and "white" purport to categorize people racially on the basis of their skin color. There are some, but very few, Americans who have skin the actual color of objects that are accurately described as having black and white surfaces. As colors, black and white are anomalous: In quasi-scientific language, black is the perceptual experience of the absence of all colors from the visible spectrum, and white is the perceptual experience of the presence of all colors from the visible spectrum. (These optical facts make a joke out of the use of the sobriquet "of color" for all non-white people.)[54]

Neither persons, blood, family, behavior, nor socioeconomic conditions can be described literally as black or white. Indeed, given the wide range of considerations that affect behavior and policies, the socioeconomic conditions facing so-called people of color cannot be said to be caused by their anatomical attributes. However, *racialized* perceptions of persons do lead to decisions that exclude them, as "others," from access to resources. The question that should, therefore, be posed is: how do such perceptions come into being, and maintained? The indisputable answer would be that, government racial classifications and policies on race relations and racial problems, media commentaries on racial experiences, the propagation of racial studies in educational institutions, and corporate funding of research on racial problems play significant roles in the racialization of self-consciousness. Advocates of Afrocentricity supplement government and media practices of racialization, consolidating the racial classifications developed by "Eurocentric" and "racist" scientists—eighteenth- and nineteenth-century zoologists, biologists, anthropologists, and social philosophers.[55] Afrocentricity is part of a relatively long tradition of racial studies. Its textbooks are allowed to be used in schools because it they buttress modern politicians' project of maintaining electorally useful racial divisions. Nor can its march be halted, given the official cultivation of black and white identities and commitment to "education for diversity." Nor should it be concluded that Afrocentrists are unaware of the theoretical and functional underpinnings of racial classification.

Initially, racial classifications formed the basis of a "natural" explanation of behavior and historical developments. Races were carved out and presented as beings created by forces beyond human control—God and nature. Molefi Asante's remark amounts to a radical insight: "Classification schemes created *Negroid, Mongoloid and Caucasoid* races."[56] These races, then, are not "real," in the sense of being products of nature, for the "classification schemes" are analytical constructs designed by classifiers. However, Asante does not follow up on the antirealist implication of his observation; he does not notice that, in its pursuit of black liberation, Afrocentricity endorses the arbitrariness and contradictions within these racial classification schemes. This endorsement is compounded by Asante's placing of the responsibility for the propagation of the myth of race on the shoulders of "white social sciences." He writes: "Race can only lose its political potency by attacking the white social sciences that persist in creating myths to further enhance the idea of racial purity and superiority."[57] But surely an uncritical usage of "white social sciences" and "black people" is also part of racial myth construction. In opposition to this practice, should not all racial myth-making studies, including Afrocentricity, be "attacked?" Asante describes race as a myth, and at the same time claims membership of a racial group.

Further justification for the proposition that Afrocentricity is but an extension of a "race science" developed by biologists and anthropologists from the eighteenth century can be found in arguments from Clinton M. Jean's *Behind the Eurocentric Veils*. This observation is not an attempt to prove guilt by association. Rather, it is made in the context of the frequently voiced Afrocentric accusation that these scientists were "Eurocentric" and "racist." Afrocentrists then compound their mimicry of the Eurocentrists' and racists' construction of "races" by endorsing, but not clarifying, the terms *black people* and *white people*. The reliance on Eurocentric scientists and acceptance of their racial categories are presented simultaneously with a claim of Afrocentricity's basis in African philosophy, historiography, and African-American interests. Jean, for example, offers "a specifically Afrocentric alternative to liberal and Marxist arguments concerning Africa."[58] Just as class is the analytical heart of Marxism, and the individual central to classical liberalism, so "black people" are the kernel of Afrocentricity.

Afrocentricity writes the Negro, or the black race, into history as its moving finger. Its advocates present an archaeological Negro—the Grimaldi Race—as the ancestor of the modern Negro, and Cro-Magnon man as "the prototype of the white race." These races march through eons of time and glacial spaces. Jean notes that the racial characteristics of certain skeletons discovered in 1895 were identified by R. Vernau, for whom the Negroness of two of the four discovered skeletons was confirmed as follows:

The Grimaldi Race was identified as black. This identity is indicated by the characteristics of the skeletons. Among these may be mentioned: the disproportionate length of the leg in relation to the thigh, the forearm to the whole arm, and the lower limb to the upper limb—all proportions that "reproduce, but in greatly exaggerated degree, the characteristics presented by the modern Negro": the regular elliptical shape of the skull (seen from above) with flattened parietal bosses; broad nose depressed at the root; facial prognathism, four cusps on the upper molars and five on the lower, a dentition with "many primitive characteristics" resembling that of the Australian aborigines and seldom found among the "higher races", "the vertical direction of the haunch bones . . . the curve of the iliac crest . . . the reduced dimensions of the great sciatic notch." All of these indicated that "the pelvis of the old woman differs from the pelvis of the modern European female, and resembles, on the contrary, that of a Negress."[59]

In other words, Negroes have broad noses, high behinds, long lower extremities, a primitive dental structure, and a reduced pelvic curvature. The skin colors of the skeletons were not ascertainable, and thickness of lips was also impossible to confirm. However, breadth of nose is a perennial second, or third, line of racial demarcation, and, in the case of the female skeletons, comparative pelvic regions proved which is "a Negress." An explanation of how the skeletons came to be conceived as racial artifacts would consider the following possibility: a certain scientist took the categories "Negro" and "white" into caves with skeletal remains and then claimed a discovery of Negro and white skeletons, rather than mere skeletons.

Neither Jean nor Asante deviates from Diop's "authentic anthropology," which is a replay of "classical anthropology," and each of them criticizes the discipline of anthropology as Eurocentric, while at the same time propagating its basic racial categories—black people and white people.[60] Their launching of these races backward into the ancient world inspired Frank M. Snowden Jr. to write:

Though Afrocentrists may be competent in their own specialties, many of their statements about blacks in the ancient world demonstrate clearly that they have not approached the ancient evidence with the relevant scholarly apparatus. Many shortcomings have resulted: unfamiliarity with and a failure to use primary sources; a reliance on the undocumented opinions of fellow Afrocentrists (always the same few); a tendency to make general statements on the basis of a few lines from a single author or from a few texts without considering the total picture of blacks in antiquity; the use of language charged with political rhetoric; and a tendency to read a "white conspiracy" into scholarly interpretations of the ancient evidence. . . . Afrocentrists have assumed that the word "African" and color adjectives as used by ancient writers were always the equivalent of words such as "Negroes" and "blacks" in twentieth-century usage.[61]

The similarities between "blacks" in ancient Egypt and contemporary blacks are similarities found among human beings everywhere. The skeletal remains of millions of "black Americans" could have more in common with the Cro-Magnon rather than the Grimaldi race, whose identification as "black" represents a case of reading the past forward. Nonetheless, the idea of "blacks in antiquity," which is the title of one of Snowden's books, forges connections between ancient and contemporary "blacks"—the Afrocentrists' project. A commitment to greater clarity in basic classifications would lead to consideration of playwright Jean Genet's questions: "But what exactly is a black? First of all, what's his color?"[62]

In the early eighteenth century, Africans were characterized as a black race by the naturalist and "father of zoology," Carl Linnaeus. This race, Homo Afer, was said to have specific mental and cultural traits. In Molefi Asante's *Afrocentricity*, "African" is both a racial and a cultural classification that has behavioral connotations. For Asante, Africans are black people, members of a black race, and also part of an organic, black, cultural bloc. Hence those defined as "blacks" anywhere in the world can claim both African cultural roots and membership of this race. Because "black people" in the United States bear cultural traits that are traceable to Africa, as the anthropologist Melville Herskovits insisted, and as is strongly reinforced in Sterling Stuckey's *Slave Culture*, their claim to being African is indisputable.[63] "Black people," then, are historically, anatomically, and culturally affiliated to Africa. However, by the same method of tracing affiliations "black people" in the United States can also claim to be historically, anatomically, and culturally related to Europe and Asia. Because these continents contain multitudes of culture's variations—family forms, customs, religions, languages—and an anatomical variety that defies racial categorization, those classified as "black" in the United States come close to being most all-American, as Stanley Crouch argues, and "omni people."[64]

Attempts to forge psychohistorical linkages between African Americans and an African culture reproduce the "Eurocentric" homogenizing of African cultures, and ignore the implications of the concept of "African-American culture." Such a culture is necessarily a combination of "many cultures." In other words, to select African cultural traits to identify African Americans as *Africans* would be to ignore their European cultural traits. As George Levesque comments: "That blacks in America have never developed a hegemonic race culture is hardly surprising since the homogeneous African culture which Negroes are told they must reclaim as exclusively theirs is a figment of hysterical imagination."[65] These remarks reflect some of the difficulties involved in imputing a culture to a race. A member of a race, defined by skin color, can belong to another, differently constructed race that is defined, for example, by shape of skull. Members of different "white" and "black" races can belong to the same race defined according to shape of skull. Where would they stand culturally? What are the implications of the thesis that races have their own cultures, given that cultural characteristics are themselves used to construct races?

Afrocentricity continues a (Eurocentric?) tradition of racial classification, but it imbues this practice with a liberationist purpose that evokes sympathy from some of its critics. For example, Cornel West writes:

Afrocentrism, a contemporary species of black nationalism, is a gallant yet misguided attempt to define an African identity in a white society perceived to be hostile. It is gallant because it puts black doings and sufferings, not white anxieties and fears, at the center of discussion. It is misguided because—out of fear of cultural hybridization and through silence on the issue of class, retrograde views on black women, gay men, and lesbians, and a reluctance to link race to the common good—it reinforces the narrow discussions about race.[66]

Noticeably, however, the Afrocentrists' reinforcement of racial interpretations also permeates West's *Race Matters*. West writes: "All people with black skin and African phenotype are subject to white supremacist abuse."[67] But what is black skin, if not the most-favored but frail crutch of racial classifiers, and how dark/light must the skin be for a human being to be deemed black or white? There are numerous skin colors among those classified as Africans and African Americans. Some persons born and living on the African continent certainly look

alike. Others look most unlike one another. What, then, can an African phenotype be?

Given his recognition that racial classification is a questionable practice,
West understandably seeks to move beyond "race." He suggests: "To establish a
new framework, we need to begin with a frank acknowledgment of the basic
humanness and Americanness of each of us."[68] What should also be recognized
is that *the continued propagation of the classification, black people, or African
Americans, is not consistent with an acknowledgment of humanness.* In order to
escape from "the narrow discussions about race" and focus on the human experience it would be necessary to suggest: "Some human beings are identified by
their skin color and phenotype and subject to abuse and violence by other human
beings." West's description of Afrocentricity as "gallant" constitutes an act of
perhaps pardonable chivalry. If liberation requires clear, progressive, and inno-
vative thinking, Afrocentricity's "retrograde views on race" are in no way a contribution to liberation. If racial identification is logically flawed, and if suffering
is one of its effects, the Afrocentrists' vilification of "whites" prolongs the life of
an absurd practice of racial classification, legitimizes white self-consciousness,
and perpetuates the resulting nepotistic actions that cause "black suffering." On
its own terms, Afrocentricity is no friend of "black people."

Key arguments in Afrocentricity are based on the same race-culture equation
that underlies the classification of inhabitants of Africa as a Negro race and the
reduction of their anatomical variety to a single race—black people. The designation *African American* simply pursues the cultural roots of "black people" in
Africa. Such people and their counterparts, white people, are products of a certain analytical confusion—an equation of skin color and self-hood. No human
being is black, or white. But surely there are cultural differences. Are there not?
Perhaps, but among whom? Obviously not among different cultures. Among
different races? Yes. This is the answer given by the classical anthropologists
who refuse to consider the possibility that cultural differences, like racial differences, are in the eyes, that is, the classificatory criteria used by the beholder.
Molefi Asante observes that there are more than a thousand ethnicities in Africa,
but still suggests that all black people share *a* culture: "Culture can vary over
time, but in the case of the African culture, it will always be articulated in a
similar way."[69] This "unanimism" moved Kwame Anthony Appiah to suggest
that the Afrocentrists' homogenizing of Africa's multiplicity of cultures replicates a practice of Victorian anthropology. Indeed, outside of certain perspectives within natural and social sciences, there are no black people or white people, no African race, value system, culture, or worldview. Of course, racial terms
serve certain purposes. Afrocentric and other scholars and political activists use
them to present themselves as representatives of the groups these terms allegedly
depict and to dismiss each other's arguments.

In exchanges among theorists holding divergent perspectives on "the black
experience," the term *black* is not a mere referent of skin color. It is also used as
a standard for political evaluation, a denotation of group membership, an expression of loyalty to certain ideas, and as a form of self-identification. Each of these

usages, however, is disputed. Thus the selection of the persons or perspectives who should represent blacks generates holier-than-thou disputes over genuine blackness, as expressed in the terms *sell-out*, *Uncle Tom*, and *Oreo*. The problem is only exacerbated by any "representative" claiming: *my* conception of blacks accurately depicts blacks. In the melee over the real blacks, some authors resort to ad hominem denunciations of critics and refer to them as "hypocrites," "ignorant," and "enemies" of African Americans.[70] Such expressions cannot but generate more intense political cleavages. Black disunity is bound to increase in tandem with emphases on its necessity.

Afrocentricity centers racial classification, a practice pivotal to its criticisms of education and also discernible in the designation of certain ideas, or critics, as "white," and by this token unacceptable to "blacks." Thus "black" knowledge, gains legitimacy, and Afrocentricity can be claimed as the knowledge's representation. In this way, issues of analytical rigor, accuracy, and logical consistency are avoided. In order to bolster the status of Afrocentric knowledge, its advocates merely have to proclaim their representation of, and loyalty to "black people." Their knowledge is righteous by virtue of their condemnation of white knowledge and their expressed commitment to the interests of black people. Thus an author's race becomes epistemologically significant; it can be used as evidence for or against the author's arguments. This leads to arbitrary readings. W.E.B. Du Bois was reputedly one-quarter white. Or was it three-quarters black? Historian Basil Davidson's writings would be classified as "white," but not Booker T. Washington's, unless Washington's writings are deemed not black enough. Then they become "white." Whiteness and blackness may be stipulated according to blood-color and/or political criteria. A person may claim membership of both "black" and "white" races, be white of skin and "black," or have black skin and be "white." The Afrocentric claim on black knowledge, interests, and representation represents nothing but poor reasoning. What, then, is to be said of those school boards that have adopted Afrocentric curricula?

Drawing its principal classifications from "classical" biology and anthropology, Afrocentricity constitutes an extension of certain currents in nineteenth-century endeavors that failed to achieve their objective of demarcating races, quantifying their achievements, and correlating them with naturally determined attributes. Thus Afrocentricity's advocates cannot develop an adequate specification of Afrocentricity. Asante defines it as a centering of African interests in all social and political thought and activities.[71] He does not offer a definition of African interests, but admits that a common black skin color does not guarantee perceptions of congruent interests. This admission, however, is inconsistent with the Afrocentric expectation that black skin and resulting experiences coupled with an assimilation of the Afrocentric perspective would unify black people. Advocates of Afrocentricity must demonstrate that it represents African-American interests, and that these interests are indeed collectively identifiable and congruent. The crucial obstacle is that such interests are differently conceived by self-characterized African Americans, and even antagonistically constituted within various perspectives on "the black experience." "Black interests," and it is not clear what kind of interests Asante has in mind, do not appear to be identical or in harmony among "blacks" in the United States, South Africa, Rwanda, Nigeria, Liberia, Kenya, Jamaica, or Brazil. What intellectual standards should be used to assess arguments on the black experience? That is the question that should be pre-occupying advocates of Afrocentricity, racial equality, and "black liberation."

The Pluralist Approach to Multicultural Education

All versions of multicultural education promote the idea of cultural diversity. It is argued that if this diversity is to be harmoniously sustained, a multicultural awareness must be established in schools through the inclusion of various ethnic experiences and perspectives. This appeal for an institutional recognition of America's diversity can be found in the otherwise mutually antagonistic writings of multicultural education advocates such as Molefi Asante and James Banks, and of historians such as Diane Ravitch and Arthur M. Schlesinger Jr. Ravitch champions a "pluralist" conception of multicultural education, that is, one based on the recognition that: "the United States has a common culture that is multicultural.[72] For Ravitch, cultural pluralism is a basic feature of American society. Deviations from its principles are expressed in the marginalization of the historical experiences of women and persons of color in traditional history and social science textbooks. However, these deviations can be, and are being, corrected by a variety of "new social historians." Pluralists seek further revisions of history and social sciences textbooks to cultivate a deeper understanding of "the pluralistic nature of American culture" and strengthen the common culture, while at the same time stressing the European foundations of American society. Ravitch writes:

The pluralist approach to multiculturalism promotes a broader interpretation of the common American culture and seeks due recognition for the ways that the nation's many racial, ethnic, and cultural groups have transformed the national culture. The pluralists say, in effect, "American culture belongs to us, all of us; the U.S. is us, and we remake it in every generation."[73]

Pluralists recommend history and social science textbooks that reflect the multicultural and multiracial nature of American society without demonizing any group. As an example, Ravitch points to history and social sciences curricula in New York and California schools, arguing that, in 1987, extensive revisions of the former had created "one of the most advanced multicultural history-social studies curricula" in the United States. However, a task force appointed by then New York State Commissioner of Education Thomas Sobol characterized the curricula as biased and Eurocentric. Ravitch, in turn, deemed the task force report "consistently Europhobic."

Ravitch also presents *The California History-Social Science Framework* as an example of a sound multicultural education text.[74] The authors themselves suggest:

The framework incorporates a multicultural perspective throughout the history-social science curriculum. It calls on teachers to recognize that the history of a community, state, region, nation, and world must reflect the experiences of men and women and of different racial, religious, and ethnic groups. California has always been a state of many different cultural groups, just as the United States has always been a nation of many different cultural groups. The experiences of all these groups are to be integrated at every grade level in the history-social science curriculum.[75]

As if in testimony to the intrinsically contestable nature of multicultural education reform, the *Framework* was strongly criticized by some teachers and activists, and even rejected by the Oakland School Board.[76] Some critics claimed that it distorts the cultures of various racial and ethnic groups and promotes racist stereotypes. Diane Ravitch and Arthur Schlesinger Jr. counter that their critics represent a "particularistic" approach to multicultural education that is inimical to America's cohesion. These criticisms and countercriticisms have not lead to a resolution of disagreements, for the standards for argument assessment within the multicultural agenda are themselves open to "cultural" rejections.

Another source of contention concerns the relationship between the inclusion of ethnic experiences and infusing ethnic perspectives. Any curricular inclusion of the *experiences* of racial and ethnic groups could generate a further request for an inclusion of their perspectives on their experiences also, and that these perspectives be presented by members of the given group. It is but a short step to the suggestion that these experiences be *favorably* presented and that the presentation be "transformative," that is, critical of the "mainstream perspective." For example, as Afrocentrists argue, the presentation of Egypt as a black civilization and as the fountainhead of Greek civilization is necessary to the centering of black students in an alien white world. For pluralists, however, such a presentation would lead to a retrograde Balkanization and politicization of the curriculum, as each of America's many racial and ethnic group could insist on a favorable inclusion of its history. American society, the world's most successful experiment in pluralism, would eventually lose its integrative properties. Thus Ravitch writes:

Pluralism is a positive value, but it is also important that we preserve a sense of an American community—a society and a culture to which we all belong. If there is no overall community with an agreed-upon vision of liberty and justice, if all we have is a collection of racial and ethnic cultures, lacking any common bonds, then we have no means to mobilize public opinion on behalf of people who are not members of our particular group. We have, for example, no reason to support public education. If there is no larger community, then each group will want to teach its own children in its own way, and public education ceases to exist.[77]

These arguments, however, are rejected by some proponents of what is disputably described as a "particularistic multiculturalism." Public education, they argue, has not served the interests of women and persons of color; it has never been pluralist.

The various multicultural education proposals display concerns about the biased nature of most textbooks on history and in social sciences. Arthur

Schlesinger Jr., a critic of the Afrocentric approach to multicultural education, himself writes: "American history was long written in the interests of white Anglo-Saxon Protestant males."[78] This constitutes an admission that the curriculum is Eurocentric, which is a critical tenet of Afrocentric writings. Where "pluralists" draw the line is the moment that "particularists" claim that schools victimize students of color by not presenting accurate images of their ancestors. The allegation of victimization is not just historical or confined to African Americans. In Afrocentric and antiracist writings, it is argued that all persons of color are victimized by the virulent racism that has operated throughout the last five hundred years of world history, and continues to dominate U.S. history and social science textbooks. Multicultural education must remedy this condition, not maintain Eurocentrism and monoculturalism under the guise of cultivating a "common culture."

The issue of the relationship between the history-social studies curriculum and social cohesion is especially emphasized in the multicultural education reform favored by historians Ravitch and Schlesinger, and others. This brings them into sharp conflict with the advocates of Afrocentric and antiracist education reforms. The conflict surfaces in "an exchange" on multiculturalism between Ravitch and Asante; it is interesting for what it illustrates about standards for argument assessment in intellectual exchanges. Asante's writings manifest a vigorous advocacy of the distinctiveness of black social thought, Afrocentricity, and multicultural education.[79] Ravitch's works on American history and education span over two decades.[80] Significantly, Asante and Ravitch both claim to be committed to pluralism. Their dispute pertains to its relationship to equality, the role of "history" in the development of students' self-esteem, the status of the common culture, and the extent of Eurocentrism and racism in the curriculum.

On the face of things, the issues are "political." The pluralist approach to multicultural education steers clear of notions of racial and ethnic victimization. Terms such as *racism, sexism, Eurocentrism*, and *oppression* do not hold a central place in this approach. Its sponsors suggest a more inclusive curriculum that reflects and celebrates America's growing diversity. However, they argue that within the recognition of this diversity, there must also be a consolidation of national cohesiveness and cross-cultural harmony. This is to be achieved primarily through the use of textbooks that give pride of place to third world civilizations and the contributions of women and people of color to U.S. history. Thus pluralist education reformers seek to enhance cultural diversity, without divisiveness, accentuate different cultures and experiences without threatening the glue that holds the these cultures together. Ravitch argues that because America is already a multicultural society, what multicultural education should do is emphasize the *unum* in *E pluribus unum*, one common culture out of the many. As she writes: We are a multicultural people, but also a single nation knitted together by a common set of political and moral values. In the education that we provide to our students, how do we reconcile our pluribus and our unum? How do we ensure that education promotes pluralism not particularism?[81] Her answer: curriculum reform that emphasizes unity within diversity. Reform should proceed in the direction of recognizing America's diversity *and* unifying its various cultures. Therefore, it should stress common experiences, ideals, and commitments.

Proponents of the pluralist conception of multicultural education argue for a curriculum of inclusion not as a remedy for racism and sexism, but because of the increasing racial and ethnic diversity in the United States and as a corrective to a tradition of marginalizing certain experiences. The curriculum must also reflect recent demographic developments that change the racial and ethnic composition of schools and society. Moreover, if stereotypical images and prejudice are to be diminished among future adult citizens, all students need to be made aware of various contributions to history and civilization and of different aspects of "the American experience." Students, then, are to be inducted into a multicultural reinterpretation of history and culture. Various cultures, parts of the overall American culture, are to be presented fairly, that is, without racial and ethnocentric biases either way. In short, cultural pluralism is already a salient feature of American society. It simply needs to be more firmly institutionalized, especially in history and social science courses.

Ravitch describes the Afrocentric conception of multicultural education as an excessive centrism whose implementation would be harmful to the educational interests of African-American students. It is also unnecessary, she claims, for American society boasts a comparatively pluralistic culture in terms of its tolerance of diversity. There are no official or unofficial statutes that ordain the superiority of a particular culture or prohibit groups from expressing their cultures. On the contrary, there is an overt separation of state and culture, and no group's culture is favored. The Afrocentric approach to multicultural education seeks to break with a hallowed tradition of pluralism; it pursues sociopolitical goals that are not at all related to either cultural freedom or educational excellence. Asante, in turn, describes Ravitch's recommendations as: "not multiculturalism at all, but rather a new form of Eurocentric hegemonism."[82] However, in defending "pluralist multiculturalism," Ravitch describes Afrocentric multiculturalism as "particularistic," while Asante charges that Ravitch's pluralist multiculturalism is a "redundancy"—because plurality is already implied in multiculturalism—and particularistic multiculturalism an "oxymoron." On the other hand, Ravitch insists that an Afrocentric education cannot be advocated under the banner of multiculturalism because multiculturalism, by definition, cannot be centered on any racial or ethnic group.

The prospect of coexistence between the centrist and pluralist approaches to multicultural education is remote, for the latter favors an "ethnic additive multiculturalism" in which European-origin contributions to U.S. politics and culture form the core curriculum. On the other hand, "Afrocentrists" propose a curriculum in which the Afrocentric perspective on events is at the center of the educational experiences of black students. Disdaining the label "particularists," they charge that it is the so-called pluralists who are "monoethnic" and "centrist." However, for pluralists, *their* and the Afrocentric approaches are not of comparable scholarly caliber. Afrocentrists, argue their critics, construct a myth of a dominant, white, male, Eurocentric education, and demonize Western civilization in order to slip in an Afrocentric worldview that has no credibility except the dubious promise to improve black students' self-esteem. Pluralists further contend that the factual inaccuracies in Afrocentric writings on Egyptian history are egregious and their recommended texts for history-social science instruction lack even the pretense of scholarly neutrality. The teaching of history cannot be a process of inculcating worship of ancestors. Afrocentrists counter with the claim that the history being taught makes black students worship Europe, forcing them to embrace a Eurocentric worldview and disrespect black civilizations. Advocates of the pluralist approach counter by denying that Western and English intellectual traditions are the racist and Eurocentric demons they are made out to be by Afrocentrists. Indeed, Diane Ravitch insists that appreciation of these traditions is crucial to an understanding of America's democratic institutions and civic culture. These traditions, then, cannot be ejected from schools simply because their institutional operation has not yet been extended to all citizens.

Advocates of a pluralist approach to multicultural education would deny that the centralizing of Western traditions in the curriculum implies a downgrading of other traditions. These must also be taught, but America's European cultural roots embody Greek democratic ideals, and the Enlightenment legacies of rationalism, individual freedom, equality, and universalism, which are the foundation of civil society. This does not imply that non-Western civilizations do not contain, or did not contribute to the presence of, these legacies. Some non-Western traditions ought surely to be included in the curriculum, but a distinction must be maintained between inclusion and replacement. Western culture is irreplaceable, because the core U.S. culture derives from Western traditions. If this feature of U.S. education is not maintained, it would be very difficult to make a case for public education. What should be added to the curriculum, however, is courses that stress the significance of all contributions to the history and development of cultural pluralism in the United States.

In keeping with their commitment to education as a means of fostering national cohesion, "pluralist" allege that Afrocentricity is part of the same project of de-Americanization expressed in the "Eurocentric" curriculum in which African Americans are presented as people from Africa. By defining African Americans as an African people, Afrocentrists implicitly deny them their place in U.S. society as full-fledged Americans. Ravitch suggests that a self-fulfilling cycle of self-segregation results from the Afrocentrists' insistence that African Americans identify with ancient Egypt: "If children are taught that their real identity must be found on another continent or in a vanquished civilization, they may suffer an intense sense of marginalization."[83] The inculcation of Afrocentricity leads to a conviction of not being centered in America and to a resignation from the pursuit of American education. African-American educational failures are then attributed to white racism, not to the de-Americanizing and de-centering effects of Afrocentricity. These pluralist criticisms of Afrocentricity, however, are inaccurate for failing to recognize that Afrocentricity is a logical outcome of racial socialization. Pluralists are caught up in the contradiction of endorsing the classification of students as white and black and rejecting its logical outcome—Afrocentric demands for a curriculum that "centers" black students. On the other hand, if, as Afrocentrists insist, educational success depends on a racial-ethnic centering and a fit between racial-ethnic identity and curriculum content, which explains why "white" students overachieve, how would an Afrocentric curriculum benefit white students? Because these students are already at the center of the curriculum, and are thereby spiritually enriched, would Afrocentric reforms not decenter and impoverish them? White students should, therefore, be expected to oppose these reforms, which Afrocentrists could cite as evidence of racism. Ultimately, "white" texts and students would have to be ejected from public schools where they are in a minority, or "black" students placed in Afrocentric schools. In other words, some of the effects of an Afrocentric curriculum would be separate curricula for black and white students in certain schools.

Pluralist and Afrocentric approaches to multicultural education share the practice of racially classifying persons and regionally demarcating culture and civilization. Afrocentrists go further and ascribe ownership of knowledge to "races"; they then raise the following questions: Whose knowledge is to prevail in the curriculum? Why are white knowledge and white perspectives on black history being fed to black students? Their "pluralist" critics ask: Why should the European roots of U.S. society be disparaged or rejected? How can the society be described as white supremacist, given its democratic structure and its unique tolerance of cultural differences? How can it be said that there is not a common American culture, given an obvious consensus among U.S. citizens on the rule of law, respect for individual rights, and the ideal of equality? Afrocentrists, on the other hand, claim that Western values clearly fail black students. Pluralists respond that the failure is neither complete nor permanent, that U.S. society may be partially flawed, but its many virtues are traceable to its Western heritage. Significantly, however, neither camp questions the classical anthropologists' legacy of racial classification. A "race" is merely reconceptualized as a "culture," or assumed to have a culture, and because culture is conceived as the axis of social relations, it may be politically defined and used as a ground rule for intellectual exchanges. For example, an argument or criticism can be dismissed as "culturally biased." Thus "pluralists" reject Afrocentric proposals, pointing to the damage they would do to the common American culture. Afrocentrists, in turn, condemn so-called pluralist proposals as an attempt to maintain Eurocentric hegemony. Within this type of evaluations, the divergences between pluralist and centrist approaches to multicultural education are conceived as unresolvable political disagreements. However, it may be argued that the disagreements are philosophical, or epistemological. Their source is a theory of knowledge that recommends a focus on persons and the real world in the assessment of arguments. Thus the "culture" and politics of participants in intellectual exchanges and their (mis)representations of "reality" are cited to validate or invalidate arguments. Because grasping the true nature of the real world is not achieved and because an infinite number of moral and political attributes of persons can be alluded to, a state of gridlock emerges and prevails in the pluralist-Afrocentrist exchanges over multicultural education.

Globalist and Rational-Humanist Approaches to Multicultural Education

As indicated, some advocates of multicultural education seek a specific revamping of the curriculum, especially history, social science, and humanities courses, which are said to be based not on scholarly criteria but on Eurocentric, monocultural, and sexist canons. These canons allegedly vitiate studies of the experiences of women and persons of color. Their removal would contribute enormously to the eradication of stereotypical images, prejudice, and discrimination. However, a larger political issue is also at stake, for ignorance of the cultures and experiences of ethnic groups is fertile ground for the emergence of organizations and leaders seeking scapegoats. Because a multicultural curriculum would inoculate the population against the appeal of hate-mongers and bigots, it represents America's only hope for decreasing intolerance, bigotry, and hate crimes. Ultimately, it will lead to a general appreciation of America's cosmopolitan culture and better equip Americans for contacts with people from Asia, Africa, the Middle East, and Latin America. U.S. schools need a multicultural curriculum to increase its citizens' understanding of a progressively smaller world.

Proponents of globalist multicultural education make similar points about the present curriculum's inadequacies.[84] However, they regard multicultural education as a thrust toward not so much interracial and interethnic as human unity and harmony. As defined by Jesus Garcia and Sharon L. Pugh: "In its full complexity, then, *multiculturalism* implies the cultivation of a global view of human affairs. Paradoxically, perhaps, this expanded view of multiculturalism places primary emphasis on the individual and on the importance of individual decisions regarding all issues concerning the welfare of humankind."[85] Sponsors of this approach to multicultural education, and this term is sometimes used interchangeably with multiculturalism, argue that because of an increasing global interdependence, U.S. students need to know much more about world cultures, world literature, and world history. It follows that schools should develop a curriculum that centralizes world history, geography, and cultures. Such a curriculum would transcend the limitations of a multicultural education that restricts itself to racial and ethnic experiences in the United States. James Lynch's criticisms apply to most multicultural education programs. He writes: "Moreover, multicultural education has also over-emphasized differences (and anti-racist education more so), and has consequently augmented social category salience or "categorization," when it should have been stressing those things that unite humanity, the similarities and commonalities, thereby seeking to achieve "de-categorization."[86] Lynch advocates a globalist multicultural curriculum as a remedy for the parochialism in the contemporary curriculum that breeds not only cultural but also geographic illiteracy, and indifference to the fate of others in the world. In any case, and this is one of the criticisms of E.D. Hirsch's notion of cultural literacy, such literacy should include knowledge not only of the works of Shakespeare, Milton, and Dante but also Meso-American, African, and Asian philosophers and poets. This conception of multicultural education is grounded in a concern with the human condition; which may well be the necessary foundation of a strategy to protect the planet from the ravages of competition among "the different."

As the globalist-multicultural argument continues, there are many cultures not only in the United States but also the world. Indeed, the different cultures in the United States are extensions, through migration, of world cultures. An adequate multicultural education must reinforce the links between internal and global cultural variations. Otherwise, the parochialism within U.S. education will not be diminished. The purpose of multicultural education would be to promote not diversity but critical thinking about diversity as well as awareness of human similarities within differences. Lynch's advocacy of multicultural education pursues an integration of humanist and rationalist themes. His definition of multicultural education might be considered unobjectionable by most advocates of multicultural education: "For, ideally, multicultural education can be considered as the initiation of children into critical-rational acceptance of cultural diversity and the creative affirmation of individual and group difference within a common humanity."[87] Appeals for social justice, an end to oppression, a recognition of the humanity of women, people of color, gays, and the handicapped, and a simultaneous endorsement of critical thinking also grace the writings of some advocates of multicultural education.[88] On the face of it, then, multicultural education is not inconsistent with a rationalist-humanist perspective on society.

On the other hand, it is from a rationalist-humanist perspective that John I. Goodlad criticizes multicultural education:

Up till now, multicultural education has been too much dual cultural education. . . . Multiculturalism must be seen to embrace the whole of humankind. From a strategic point of view, this maturing of multicultural education through cooperative pluralism represents an opportunity of joining with other groups and other movements designed to assist the human race to live together in understanding, appreciation, and peace.[89]

The dualism that both Lynch and John I. Goodlad reject refers to the binary racial and gender categories—black people and white people, men and women—used in multicultural educational advocacies. Their remedy is use of a more inclusive classification—humankind.

From a rationalist-humanist perspective, multicultural education reforms could address the implications of a human identity for social relations. Such reforms would seek to further discussions of: (1) how relations among the early settlers, Native Americans, and Africans would have unfolded had they possessed identities exclusively, or primarily, as members of humankind; (2) the reasons for the absence of such an identity in the fifteenth-century and, indeed, the twentieth-century intellectual environment; (3) social scientists' construction of the history of humankind as gender, racial, ethnic (national, regional, and religious), and class, but not as *human* relations and *human* conflicts; (4) the dominance of a group, as opposed to a universalistic, conception of culture in social studies; and (5) the role of self-classification in acts of discrimination and violence. In this context, some related questions that are not generally asked about education and social change are: why has rational-humanism not taken root in educational organization and social studies? Is its absence related to a conception of human nature as intrinsically imperfect, flawed at its genesis, irrational, and damned—these being natural states that education cannot remedy? Can a rational-humanist perspective take root in a society with an official, media, and schools' bombardment of the student and general population with not a vision of their humanness, but gender, racial and ethnic differences? Why are both formal and informal educational experiences so bereft of a human perspective, and does this lacuna explain the lack of trust in human reasoning? It may be necessary to "center" such a perspective in the curriculum, if reasoning is to be regarded as relevant to the understanding of how human experiences, relations, and conflicts come to be regarded as racial and cultural.

Is the rationalist-humanist approach to multicultural education integrationist? Christine Sleeter and Carl Grant might respond affirmatively, arguing that it falls under the "human relations approach" to multicultural education.[90] Their summary contrasts two approaches to multicultural education:

1.   the Single Group Studies Approach in which the presentation of the experiences of oppressed groups is integrated into social sciences as separate departments of racial, ethnic, and women's studies, and

2.   the Human Relations Approach, which is integrationist and inculcates principles and methods of bridging differences.

Lynch and Goodlad do recommend a rationalist-humanist curriculum transformation, but they would not necessarily agree that their perspective is "integrationist," for the idea of integration derives from a dualism that they reject. A rational-humanist approach would not seek to foster integration among "whites" and "people of color." Rather, it would promote discussions of these categories within rational principles of argumentation and evaluation. In delineating this critical-rational approach to cultural diversity, Lynch writes of multicultural education as: "a process conducted according to explicit, rational evaluative criteria: an ethical process, celebrating both diversity and unity, social differentiation and cohesion, stability and deliberate, systematic and evaluated change according to explicit yardsticks, themselves the subject of critical discourse."[91] Lynch's argument is that the advocacy of multicultural education has uncritically accepted certain categorizations, ignored cultural similarities, and has not been attentive enough to the need to develop students' critical thinking skills. These arguments foreshadow the development of "critical multiculturalism" by scholars, such as Barry Kanpol, Peter McLaren and Henry Giroux. Their contributions are assessed in Chapter 3, while the issue of compatibility between multicultural education and critical thinking is analyzed in Chapter 4.

The Controversy over Cultural Values

The thesis that the United States is a multiracial and multicultural society is endorsed by both "pluralist" and "centrist" multicultural education proponents. The former, however, aim simply at increasing awareness of different racial and ethnic experiences through celebrations of cultural diversity. In their view, multicultural education is a means of generating an appreciation of the historical fact of cultural pluralism as well as understanding and harmony among all racial and ethnic groups. All Americans need to be reminded of what they share, as Americans—a common culture. Other scholars conceive multicultural education as a "centering" vehicle for achieving cultural regeneration and improving students academic performance. Still others recommend a revamping of more than just textbooks in order to achieve social justice. Their proposed reforms focus on the entire organizational structure of schools, and are designed to achieve to explicit sociopolitical objectives. For example, antisexist and antiracist advocacies of multicultural education, whose theoretical affiliations are analyzed in Chapter 2, militantly challenge what is conceived as mainstream "racist," "sexist," and "ethnocentric" textbooks in social sciences as well as the underrepresentation of black and female faculty in educational institutions.

The diversity of the recommendations indicates that the various advocates of multicultural education are by no means in agreement on its purpose. Their objectives are significantly conflicting: increased cultural awareness, prejudice reduction, appreciation of differences and diversity, raising the self-esteem of students of color, egalitarian social reconstruction, world peace, awareness of human similarity, and so on. However, four areas of consensus stand out among the divergent schools of thought. The protagonists endorse the practice of racial classification, affirm the concept of cultural pluralism, agree that sexism and racism operate within U.S. society, and present cultural values both as a remedy for education's ills and a standard for evaluating multicultural educational proposals themselves.

One of the multiculturalists' arguments is that the cardinal mission of public schools is to develop a set of values and commitments among students. However, some insist that "students of color" should be centered in their own African and Latin American cultural values, while pluralists propose an immersion into U.S. culture, especially its European-origin values of individual freedom and democracy. Pluralists' criticisms of Afrocentricity are echoed in *The Devaluing of America*.[92] Its author, William Bennett, does not address the core of Afrocentric education reform—a proposal for an inclusion of African-centered values in schools—but criticizes the Afrocentric rejection of Western values. Bennett also recommends the cultivation of "moral literacy" to ensure social order, a recommendation that is endorsed by other leading Republicans, such as Alan Keyes, Rush Limbaugh, and Newt Gingrich, who writes: "Our civilization is based on a spiritual and moral dimension. It emphasizes personal responsibility as much as individual rights. Since 1965, however, there has been a calculated effort by cultural elites to discredit this civilization and replace it with a culture of irresponsibility that is incompatible with American freedoms as we have known them."[93] This recommendation of family and religious values as a remedy for social dislocation complements the Afrocentric call for an infusion of African-centered values and ancient images of black dignity as the means of regenerating African-American self-esteem and the academic performance of students. What appears to separate the disputants is the Afrocentrists' objection to Western civilization being presented as civilization as such, and to the "monoethnic" focus of the curriculum. However, both sides present values as the ultimate standard for evaluating propositions. Each justifies its arguments with reference to its own values—Afrocentric, Latinocentric, Western, family, Christian, and American-national—without noticing the implicit infinite regress of mutual objections to values.

Bennett's arguments in *The Devaluing of America* raise, but do not address, the general problem of the relationship between ethical concerns and logical reasoning and their individual significance for explaining human action. Yet he argues that moral values are the key to a stable community and social order, and that they are best inculcated in the early years through the family and churches. Bennett further claims that the post-1960's collapse of America's urban civilization began with the government becoming a surrogate parent of families in the inner cities. The antidotes are an end to these surrogate activities, a more powerful role for the church in the community and a reorientation of values among inner-city families. Nevertheless Bennett does not ask the question: how are these values acquired? This is because he avoids consideration of the role of reasoning in human behavior. *The Devaluing of America* thereby fails to explain how, or why, specific moral values are chosen. Nor does it present evidence that, between the 1960s and 1990s, the religiosity of the underclass dramatically declined. Hence the social dislocations from the 1960s—exploding violence, drug abuse, welfare dependency, teenage and single parentage, and disrespect for the law—cannot be attributed to religion's diminished influence. By implication, an infusion of religious values in schools would not remedy these social pathologies. But more significantly, Bennett's analysis is highly selective in its focus on moral values. The moral degeneracy of the "overclass"—exposed in, for example, Charles Derber's *The Wilding of America*—is not at all scrutinized.

In keeping with their emphasis on the pivotal role of values in human affairs, both Bennett and Afrocentrists propose an infusion of moral values—Christian and Afrocentric, respectively—in schools. However, neither addresses the condition responsible for the choice, assimilation, rejection, or acting out of values. Both propose that it is the function of schools to teach what to think rather than how to reason about what is thought. Chapter 4 addresses the conceptions of knowledge, learning, and schooling that undergird multicultural and values education. Suffice it to note here that one criticism of the proposal that schools should teach moral values would be that such a goal harbors dangers of a forced homogeneity and indoctrination. For example, which Christian or Afrocentric values should be selected? Any selection could be interminably challenged on grounds of cultural and political biases in educators' values.

Schools should cultivate students' ability to reason about the values they embrace. If the values presented in textbooks are an issue, a principle could be agreed upon that textbooks should be selected according to the logical quality, clarity, and consistency of their justifications for the values they present.

Despite the contrasting objectives in Bennett's and the Afrocentrists' proposals, they appear to have reached a consensus on a fundamental philosophical issue—the nature of human beings. Values, they claim, are the axis of the human personality and social life. "Values matter most." Yet the teaching of values itself cannot generate standards for the assessment of value claims. Reasonable standards must be used to decide which values are "good," or more desirable than others. Values may be foundational, but their adoption cannot be divorced from reasoning and standards for assessing reasoning. It would follow that educators should concentrate on not teaching values, as such, but how to reason about and assess them. Such a goal would promote curriculum development for the cultivation of students' reasoning and empathic abilities, including a commitment to binding standards for argument assessment. Even if "good" values are indeed at the core of responsible behavior, their adoption is inseparable from reasoning about values. In neglecting consideration of reasoning, the proponents of values education ignore the implications of and fail to justify their project.

Analytical and Practical Limitations of Multicultural Education

As indicated, some multicultural education advocates propose the cultivation of a common American culture. Others seek to nurture cultural differences, infuse non-Western perspectives in the curriculum, present the historical truths about Asian, African, and Latin American civilizations, prepare students for participation in social transformations, and cleanse the images and self-images of specific groups. This last objective seems innocuous enough. However, it may be argued that more accurate and positive textual representations of women, for example, do not necessarily mean a positive image for *women of color*. The assumption that such textual representations would alter attitudes is flawed, insofar as the negative and inaccurate images themselves are a result of already-held attitudes. Finally, insofar as it is admitted that persons can regard themselves as members of many groups, why should a particular ethnic group membership be singled out for emphasis in education? How inclusive of group experiences can the curriculum be without schools becoming group processing institutions?

In 1993, a committee at the University of Oregon proposed the curriculum's inclusion of courses on race, racism, and the experiences of persons of color. One amendment to the proposal included a suggestion that Jewish experiences also be included. The ensuing clamor included charges and countercharges of racism and anti-Semitism, and an assault on one faculty member. Dinesh D'Souza's *Illiberal Education* and Richard Bernstein's *Dictatorship of Virtue* draw attention to multicultural education's accompanying conflicts over speech codes, political correctness, and culture wars. Two underlying issues deserve mention. First, with each dispensation for a particular "culture," there emerge appeals for other dispensations. Second, the experiences of so-called racial and ethnic groups are so intertwined that any particular history involves references to other racial and ethnic groups. And the nature of these references has to be tested for their positive or negative views on other groups. Any multicultural education course could be charged with moral defaults in its presentation of a group's experiences, or with ignoring some group's "oppression." Can a multicultural education with a humanistic focus offer a way out of what promises to be unending ethical cross-examinations and accusations?

The Association for Supervision and Curriculum Development (ASCD) Multicultural Education Commission offers a definition of multicultural education as:

a humanistic concept based on the strength of diversity, human rights, social justice, and alternative life choices for all people. It is mandatory for quality education. It includes curricular, instructional, administrative, and environmental efforts to help students avail themselves of as many models, alternatives and opportunities as possible from the full spectrum of our cultures.[94]

This definition of multicultural education appears unobjectionable. However, its breadth makes multicultural education synonymous with a liberal arts education, without the customary emphasis on the humanities. Some educators might also object to the hint of political militancy in the reference to human rights and social justice, and the bland allusion to "cultures" would certainly draw objections from a few cultural anthropologists. Nevertheless, do the references to humanism in the multicultural literature constitute an appeal for the curriculum's inclusion of a human perspective on social relations? Underlying the thicket of diverse multicultural education reforms, there is a hint of a common end-product—a global human awareness founded on respect for differences, and opposition to exploitation and oppression. Can such an end-product be realized without sustained analyses of theories of values, knowledge, and differences? Relatedly, does the curriculum need an infusion of cultural awareness, or more analysis of the ethical, epistemological, and logical issues raised in social studies? Should the principle underlying inclusiveness be cultural, or theoretical? Or should it be political, as advocates of *multiculturalism* insist?

In apparent disregard for the troubling questions surrounding multicultural education, legislators and school administrators have been singularly impressed by its advocacy. In 1973, Congress passed the Ethnic Heritage Act, which outlined a policy on ethnic studies and provided federal funds for teacher training in multicultural curriculum development. During this same decade, the American Association of Colleges for Teacher Education (AACTE), the National Council for Accreditation of Teacher Education (NCATE), the National Council for Social Studies, and the Association for Supervision and Curriculum Development developed programs, prescriptions, and standards for multicultural education reforms. Writing in Annual Editions, *Multicultural Education, 95/96*, James A. Banks reports that a similarly intense interest in multicultural education now grips certain legislators, educational administrators, and teachers. Banks applauds the processes through which "multicultural education is moving down the road toward academic legitimacy and institutionalization. Signs of vitality are the establishment of required multicultural teacher education courses in a large number of colleges and universities, the proliferation of multicultural education textbooks."[95]

State legislators in Nebraska, Oregon, Louisiana, California, Alabama, and others have also endorsed and allocated funds for spawning multicultural education programs in secondary and postsecondary institutions. For example, the New Jersey Department of Higher Education has funded a multicultural education project that seeks to:

(1) bring multicultural and gender-balanced scholarship to the attention of New Jersey educators; (2) identify exemplary program models in multicultural education both locally and nationally; (3) provide a forum for dialogue among New Jersey educators interested in multicultural scholarship, research, and pedagogy; (4) strengthen, revise, and/or introduce courses across the curriculum that reflect multicultural perspectives; and (5) encourage and support research in multicultural studies.[96]

In various educational institutions, students, teachers, and administrators are being institutionally supported to attend conferences, symposia, and workshops on multicultural education. Side by side with its increasing popularity, multicultural education programs have drawn sharp criticisms.[97] Critics claim that multicultural education textbooks lack scholarly stature and are only marginally related to the teaching of history, social and natural sciences, and the purposes of education. Such have been the criticisms leveled at the Portland Baseline Essays, a major Afrocentric textbook, the Rainbow Curriculum that was endorsed by New York School Board President Joseph Hernandez, and the Los Angeles Unified School District's multicultural education workshops for teacher trainees.

How should teachers respond to the differences students bring to the classroom? In responding to this question, advocates of multicultural education suggest that teachers accommodate these differences, even nurture and use them as a basis for instruction in whatever discipline. The argument is that students' identities are important to them and teachers should respect them. These appear to be eminently empathic and laudable suggestions, but they raise thorny issues for the teaching profession, if a different angle of vision is adopted. The questions could be: What should be done with the *similarities* in identities and experiences that students bring to schools? Should teachers endorse differences and so mimic media and official practices of indoctrination into awareness of racial-ethnic differences? In his evaluation of multicultural education classes for teacher trainees in the Los Angeles Unified School District, G. Williamson McDiarmid concludes that the two-week program failed to alter teacher attitudes.[98] The failure pertains to the status of generalizations. To avoid stereotyping, teachers should not pre-define an individual student as a representative of a group. However, this is unavoidable within the principle of paying attention to certain differences. This principle leads to categorization based on the attribution of group characteristics to the individual student. Teachers committed to multicultural education will be hard pressed to avoid regarding an individual student as a representative of cultural characteristics that are attributed to the group of which the student is said to be a member.

A key assumption within multicultural education is that, because students bring different identities and experiences to classrooms, they are committed to maintaining them. A second assumption is that a given student represents a particular culture. Yet, on multicultural education's own terms, the student may be bicultural, transcultural, or multicultural, and eager to be regarded by teachers as just a learner, or as a human being. In this context, genuine respect for what students bring to classrooms can be expressed by teachers who adhere to the following strictures:

1. Regard students as individual human beings whose minds are to be nurtured with your guidance.

2. Treat students' beliefs about identities respectfully, but suggest that they must be justified according to agreed-upon criteria.

3. Do not identify yourself racially, culturally, or sexually without offering a similar justification and pursuing the implications of that identification.

4. Present the social theories out of which identities are constructed, and show that they are not natural and eternal but changing and contextual.

5. Discuss the possibility that identity-flexibility is critical to surviving in changing environments.

These guidelines would avoid charges of indoctrination and stereotyping; they are far more internally consistent, coherent, and pedagogically sound than the recommendations in the multicultural education advocacy. For example, in multicultural education proposals, teachers are advised variously: ignore differences, tolerate differences, bridge differences, respect differences, celebrate differences, nurture differences, include different perspectives in the history-social sciences curriculum, centralize these perspectives, present more information about people of color, accurate information about people of color, and present knowledge that is free of racist, sexist, and Eurocentric distortions. These recommendations necessarily lead to disputes over relevant and significant differences, positive images, and the meanings of sexism, racism, and Eurocentrism. Virtually any general claim about a "race" can be interpreted as stereotypical or racist. The suggestion that certain textbooks be replaced or rewritten to present positive images of women and people of color appears laudable. However, such replacements are themselves bound to be subjected to accusations of Eurocentrism, bias, ethnocentrism, sexism, and racism, for these terms are open to a wide variety of conceptual specifications. As revealed in the pluralist-Afrocentric dispute, some multicultural education recommendations are themselves designated Eurocentric and racist.

The following criticisms highlight significant analytical shortcomings in multicultural education both as a concept and a set of reform proposals:

1. Multicultural education relies on a conception of single cultures, a conception of culture that is most analytically problematic. "Culture" is pivotal to multicultural education. Yet the concept, and it is rich with variations, is nowhere systematically analyzed by advocates of multicultural education. Indeed, it is enigmatic that some advocates point accusing fingers at Western traditions, while practically applauding eighteenth- and nineteenth-century Western scholarship on race and culture.

2. Advocates of multicultural education endorse the traditional anthropologists' conception of single-group culture to facilitate the construction of innumerable regional, racial, generational, and sexual cultures. Some offer arbitrary, moral judgments of certain "cultures" as oppressed, dominant, and Eurocentric. But all fail to justify their rejection of a conception of culture that stresses the symbolic homogeneity of human creativity and the transcultural potential of individuals. In this sense, multicultural education is not so much divisive as analytically underdeveloped.

3. Advocates of multicultural education endorse the concept of racial differences, while insisting that drawing attention to racial differences in IQ test results, for example, is racist.

4. Proponents of multicultural education suggest that the remedy for prejudice is more favorable information about racial and ethnic groups, rather than the development of reasoning abilities that process information. While the recommendation of a "critical pedagogy" seeks to remedy this shortcoming, it remains an undeveloped aspect of the new multiculturalisms discussed in the following chapters.

5. In their omnipresent references to others as white students and black students, multicultural education's advocates assign students to gender, racial, and ethnic categories without consultation with students or consideration of their wishes and expectations. They also intensify awareness of racial-ethnic differences as part of their effort to liberate students from oppression. They then protest against the discrimination that results from this intensified awareness of differences, and recommend more multicultural education.

6. Multicultural education is grounded in an education model that contains what Paulo Freire calls a "banking concept" of teaching in which students are given information about cultural differences and the past, rather than taught how to reason about conceptions of history, differences, and similarities.

7. Certain approaches to multicultural education introduce highly disputable theses on the existence of racism, sexism, Eurocentrism, and homophobia as facts, rather than arguments mired in controversies in the social sciences.

8. In its specification of outcomes such as changed intergroup attitudes, the social reconstructionist approach to multicultural education would transform schools into institutions for behavior modification in which certain groups are deemed intrinsically innocent (women, the poor, and people of color) and others guilty by definition. Thus the infusion of multicultural education should be expected to exacerbate awareness of gender, racial, and ethnic differences, which will then be cited as proof of the need for more multicultural education.

9. Sponsors of multicultural education ignore one of the behavioral implications of their demand for cultural inclusiveness—a multiplication of such demands—and the

consequences of a rejection of demands that, for example, Arab-American and Jew-ish-American cultures, perspectives, and experiences be included in the curriculum.

10. Advocates of multicultural education do not recommend remedial courses on "the culture of violence" often said to be prevailing in American society, even though it is violence that profoundly affects the life-conditions of those they consider to be oppressed.

11. Because of the amorphousness and unspecified status of its basic conceptual catego-ries, such as whites, culture, diversity, inclusiveness, oppression, Eurocentric, and students of color, multicultural education proposals are evaluatively elusive. They slide surreptitiously between education reform for better teaching and learning to education reform for eradicating racism, classism, sexism, homophobia, handicap-ism, ableism, and so on, in society. In effect, multicultural curriculum reform should be distinguished from multicultural education as social reconstruction, and mul-ticulturalism.

12. The evolution of multicultural education into multiculturalism is unavoidable, and the latter, in insisting that schools be part of a project of liberation, would generate irremediable divisions among teachers.

13. Conceptually and programmatically, multicultural education is in virtual disarray. The case has yet to be made that it can deliver on its promises, and that it is not a means of perpetual differences-accentuation, despite the "good intentions" of its ad-vocates.

Nonetheless, a certain caveat must be appended to these criticisms of multicul-tural education. A movement that has captured the interest and often the enthusi-astic support of such a vast number of educators must contain a kernel of virtue. This virtue is its embryonic but convoluted quest for a human perspective.

Advocates of multicultural education claim to be representing specific groups, which suggests that multicultural education is a program for the devel-opment of special interests in educational institutions. However, some of its pro-ponents would deny such a description, arguing that multicultural education is not for people of color only and that it addresses universal concerns. The idea of inclusiveness seeks to enlarge the reach of education, both qualitatively and quantitatively, to include those whose humanness had been hitherto denied. Multicultural education, then, constitutes a nascent humanization of American education and social relations. Henry Louis Gates Jr., himself critical of Afrocentrism, writes:

To reform core curriculums, to account for the comparable eloquence of the African, the Asian and the Middle Eastern traditions, is to begin to prepare our students for their roles as citizens of a world culture, educated through a truly human notion of the "humanities," rather than—as Mr. Bennett and Mr. Bloom would have it—as guardians at the last fron-tier outpost of white male Western culture, the keepers of the master's pieces.[99]

These remarks could be interpreted as a suggestion that the humanities should be presented as human achievements, that they must be shorn of their racial and gender interpretations. By implication, multicultural education is not a move-ment for minorities; it threatens only those who define themselves as irrevocably "white," and exclude "others." In this context, the questions that must be posed to Gates and others who abjure "race" and continue to endorse blackness and African Americanness are: What explains the persistence of this contradiction? Should these racial and racial-cultural denominations not also be shown to be pieces of the master's ideological pieces?

If racial categorization is a way of dehumanizing persons, stripping the concept of culture of racial admixtures represents a project of human restitution. It is a project that is endorsed in Molefi Asante's qualification of the nature of Afrocentricity: "Afrocentricity is not anti-White; it is however, pro-human. Further, the aim of the Afrocentric curriculum is not to divide America, it is to make America flourish, as it ought to flourish."[100] This confession, that the goal of Afrocentric education reform is to create a flourishing America in which black Americans participate on equal terms with white Americans, may testify to good Afrocentric intentions. However, it does not set well with Asante's racial denunciations of criticisms of Afrocentric proposals. A pro-human perspective would identify these critics as human beings in pursuit of knowledge and truth, however much their pursuit may be influenced by what they conceive as their interests. This appears to be the direction of Asa Hilliard's perspective on multicultural education. Hilliard suggests that the purpose of multicultural education is to propagate truth about the "human record" and develop critical sensibilities through the pluralization of the educational environment. As he writes: "The primary goal of a pluralistic curriculum is to present a truthful and meaningful rendition of the whole human experience. Ultimately, if the curriculum is centered in truth, it will be pluralistic, for the simple fact is that human culture is the product of the struggles of all humanity, not the possession of a single racial or ethnic group."[101] But for its implicit endorsement of the idea of racial or ethnic group, these remarks are profoundly pro-human and revolutionary; they register a break with the idea of single, group cultures and affirm the notion that culture is singularly human. Hilliard should further recognize that human culture merely has infinite variations—just as there are innumerable variations of the human anatomical form—and that "white people" and "black people" are simply human beings who have been imputed, and who impute, a racial collective essence to their individual selves.

Some advocates of Afrocentricity advance a mission of humanization, demonstrating that their activism represents an albeit convoluted protest against the dehumanization of human beings in the name of "race." In this sense, even Diop's writings—hailed as the philosophical and theoretical foundations of Afrocentricity—present a glimmer of transcultural, human perspective. His studies of the ancient past fall, indeed, within the tradition of earlier racial classifiers, such as François Bernier, Johann Blumenbach, and Arthur de Gobineau. He agrees that Greece was a "white" civilization, but insists that. Ancient Egypt was a Negro or black civilization, that Greek and Roman civilizations owe much to Egypt's, that Egypt was, in turn, colonized and culturally nurtured by Ethiopia, and that, indeed, there were complex interactions among the ancient civilizations of West Africa, Nubia, Axum, Kush, Asia, and Egypt. It follows, then, that no race, nation, or continent can claim a culture or a civilization, that racial and regional-cultural boundaries are inapplicable to human creativity. Migratory flows, as well as reciprocal, creative influences and interpenetrations within human achievements deny the possibility of racial and cultural boundary construction. So-called whites should not be proud of Greece, and so-called blacks need not celebrate Ancient Egypt as theirs. In Diop's words: "Now, to avoid a false judgment, there is no particular glory to be drawn from placing the cradle of mankind in Africa, because this is only a fact of chance; if physical conditions of the planet had been different, the origin of humanity would have been elsewhere."[102] If human beings could conceive the idea of celebrating their "rise to civilization," including their stumbles, studies of *human* history, and *human* civilization, would become central to the history-social studies curriculum. Diop might have approved. Indeed, within some reconsiderations of theories of human nature, history, culture, and knowledge, William Bennett, Diane Ravitch, and Arthur Schlesinger Jr. on the one hand, and James A. Banks, Christine Sleeter, Asa Hilliard III, and Molefi Asante on the other might agree on the intellectual standards necessary to resolve their disputes.

NOTES

1.   See Education Commission for the States, *Action for Excellence: A Comprehensive Plan to Improve Our Nation's Schools* (Denver, Colorado: ECS, 1983); Twentieth Century Fund Task Force on Federal Elementary and Secondary Education Policy, *Making the Grade* (New York: Twentieth Century Fund, 1983); U.S. Commission on Excellence in Education, *A Nation at Risk: The Imperative for Education reform* (Washington, D.C.: U.S. Government Printing Office, 1983); Henry A. Giroux, *Theory and Resistance in Education: A Pedagogy for the Oppressed* (Westport, Conn. Bergin and Garvey, 1983); Diane Ravitch, *The Schools We Deserve: Reflections on the Educational Crisis of Our Times* (New York: Basic Books, 1985); Jonathan Kozol, *Illiterate America* (New York: Doubleday, 1985); Frank Smith, *Insult to Intelligence: The Bureaucratic Invasion of Our Classrooms* (New York: Anchor House, 1986); Allan Bloom, *The Closing of the American Mind* (New York: Simon and Schuster, 1987); Harriet Tyson-Bernstein, *America's Textbook Fiasco: A Conspiracy of Good Intentions* (New York: The Council for Basic Education, 1988); Henry Giroux, *Border Crossings: Cultural Workers and the Politics of Education* (New York: Routledge and Kegan Paul, 1992); Rebecca A. Martusewicz and William M. Reynolds (eds.), *Inside Out: Contemporary Critical Perspectives in Education* (New York: St. Martin's Press, 1994); Christine E. Sleeter, *Multicultural Education as Social Activism* (New York: State University of New York Press, 1996). Other influences are the criticisms of education voiced by "radical educationists" in the 1970s. See Tom Christoffel, David Finkelhor, and Dan Gilbarg (eds.), *Up against the American Myth* (New York: Holt, Rinehart, Winston, 1970), Chapter 3; Paulo Freire, *Pedagogy of the Oppressed* (New York: Herder and Herder, 1971); Harry Braverman, *Labor and Monopoly Capital* (New York: Monthly Review Press, 1974); Martin Carnoy, *Education as Cultural Imperialism* (New York: David McKay, 1974); Samuel Bowles and Herbert Gintis (eds.), *Schooling in Capitalist America* (New York: Basic Books, 1976).

2.   See M.D. Stent, W.R. Hazard, and H.N. Rivlin (eds.), *Cultural Pluralism in Education: A Mandate for Change* (New York: Appleton-Century-Crofts, 1973); Wil-

liam A. Hunter, *Multicultural Education through Competency-Based Teacher Education* (Washington, D.C.: American Association of Colleges for Teacher Education, 1974); National Council for the Social Studies, *Curriculum Guidelines for Multiethnic Education* (New York: Anti-Defamation League of B'nai B'rith, 1983); Frances E. Kendall, *Diversity in the Classroom: A Multicultural Approach to the Education of Young Children* (New York: Teachers College Press, 1983); F. Rodriguez, *Education in a Multicultural Society* (New York: University Press of America, 1983); Maurice Craft, *Education for Cultural Pluralism* (Philadelphia: Falmer Press, 1984); James Boyer, *Multicultural Education: Product or Process?* (Kansas City, Mo.: Kansas Urban Education Center, 1985); Christine E. Sleeter and Carl A. Grant, "An Analysis of Multicultural Education in the United States, *Harvard Educational Review* 57, no. 4 (November 1987), pp. 421-444; and *Making Choices for Multicultural Education: Four Approaches to Race, Class, and Gender* (Columbus, Ohio: Merrill, 1988); Diane Ravitch, "Diversity and Democracy: Multicultural Education in America," *American Educator* 14, no 1 (Spring 1990), pp. 16-20, 46-48; and "Multiculturalism: E Pluribus Plures," *The American Scholar* 59 (Summer 1990), pp. 337-354; James A. Banks and Cherry A. McGee Banks (eds.), *Multicultural Education: Issues and Perspectives* (Boston, Mass.: Allyn and Bacon, 1989); Hilda Hernandez, *Multicultural Education* (Columbus, Ohio: Merrill, 1989); P.G. Ramsey, E.B. Vold, and L.R. Williams, *Multicultural Education: A Source Book* (New York: Garland, 1989); James S. Friederes (ed.), *Multiculturalism and Intergroup Relations* (Westport, Conn.: Hugette Labelle, 1989); Carl A. Grant and Christine E. Sleeter, *Turning on Learning: Five Approaches for Multicultural Teaching Plans for Race, Class, Gender, and Disability* (Columbus, OH: Merrill, 1989); Etta R. Hollins, Joyce E. King, and Warren C. Hayman, *Teaching Diverse Populations: Formulating a Knowledge Base* (New York: State University of New York Press, 1994).

   3.   Donna M. Gollnick and Philip C. Chinn, *Multicultural Education in a Pluralistic Society*, 2nd. ed. (New York: Merrill, 1990), pp. 255-256.

   4.   Francis J. Ryan, "The Perils of Multiculturalism: Schooling for the Group," *Educational Horizons* 71, no. 3 (Spring 1993), p. 135.

   5.   See Diane Ravitch, *The Great School Wars, New York City, 1805-1973: A History of the Public Schools as Battlefields of Social Change* (New York: Basic Books, 1974); Nathan Glazer, "A New Word for An Old Problem: Multicultural 'School Wars' Date to the 1840s," in Annual Editions, *Multicultural Education 95/96* (Guilford, Conn.: Dushkin, 1995), pp. 74-77.

   6.   In opposition to the practice of defining an ethnic group through culture, anthropologist Frederik Barth writes: "It is important to recognize that although ethnic categories take cultural difference into account, we can assume no simple one-to-one relationship between ethnic units and cultural similarities and differences. The features that are taken into account are not the sum of 'objective' differences but only those which the actors themselves regard as significant." "Introduction," in Frederik Barth (ed.), *Ethnic Groups and Boundaries: The Social Organization of Culture Differences* (Boston: Little Brown and Co., 1969), p. 14. Elsewhere, however, Barth writes: "there are discrete groups of people i.e., ethnic units to each culture" (p. 9). For an informative analysis of the ramifications of ethnicity, see Ronald Reminick, *Theory of Ethnicity: An Anthropologist's Perspective* (Lanham, Md: University Press of America, 1983). The culture concept also resurges most prominently in postmodernist analyses of social relations. See, for example, Pierre Bourdieu, *Reproduction in Education, Culture and Society* (London: Sage, 1990). In this sense, postmodernism is not temporally postmodern, unless nineteenth-century anthropology's exaltation of culture also represents postmodernism. But see Chapter 3 below for an analysis of postmodernism's modernity.

7.   See Stent, Hazard, and Rivlin (eds.), *Cultural Pluralism;* Robert Rothberg, *The Mixing of Peoples: Problems of Identity and Ethnicity* (New York: Greylock, 1978); James Parker, *Ethnic Identity* (Washington, D.C.: University Press of America, 1983); Arthur M. Schlesinger Jr., *The Disuniting of America* (Knoxville, Tenn: Whittle Communications, 1991), Chapter 1; Glenn C. Altschuler, *Race, Ethnicity, and Class in American Social Thought 1805-1919* (Arlington Heights, IL: Harlan Davidson, 1982), Chapter Two.

8.   Franz Boas, *Race and Democratic Society* (New York: J.J. Augustin, 1945), p. 37.

9.   George W. Stocking Jr., "Introduction: The Basic Assumptions of Boasian Anthropology," in George W. Stocking Jr. (ed.), *The Shaping of American Anthropology, 1883-1911: A Franz Boas Reader* (New York: Basic Books, 1974), pp. 18-19.

10.   Vernon J. Williams Jr. *Rethinking Race: Franz Boas and His Contemporaries* (Lexington, Kentucky: The University Press of Kentucky, 1996), p. 5.

11.   Franz Boas, "The History of Anthropology," in Stocking (ed.), *The Shaping*, p. 24. See also Franz Boas, *Race, Language and Culture* (New York: Macmillan, 1948); Melville J. Herskovits, *Franz Boas: The Science of Man in the Making* (New York: Charles Scribner's Sons, 1953).

12.   See Horace Kallen, *Culture and Democracy in the United States* (New York: Boni and Liverwright, 1924); and *Cultural Pluralism and the American Idea* (Philadelphia, Penn.: University of Pennsylvania Press, 1956). For a restatement of cultural pluralism in postmodernist language, see Giroux, *Border Crossings.*

13.   H. Prentice Baptise Jr. and Mira Baptise, "Developing Multicultural Learning Activities," in Carl A. Grant (ed.), *Multicultural Education: Commitments, Issues, and Applications* (Washington, D.C.: ASCD, 1977), p. 106.

14.   ASCD Multicultural Education Commission, "Encouraging Multicultural Education," in Grant (ed.), *Multicultural Education*, p. 3.

15.   Ibid.

16.   AACTE Commission on Multicultural Education, "No One Model American," *Journal of Teacher Education* 24, no. 4 (Winter 1973), p. 264.

17.   See Arthur Jensen, *Genetics and Education* (New York: Harper and Row, 1972). For a late 20th-century echo of Jensen's arguments, see Richard J. Herrnstein and Charles Murray, *The Bell Curve: Intelligence and Class in American Life* (New York: The Free Press, 1994).

18.   Francesco Cordasco, *The Equality of Educational Opportunity* (Totowa, N.J.: Littlefield, Adams and Co. 1973), p. 6.

19.   James A. Banks, "Multicultural Education: Progress and Prospects," *Phi Delta Kappan* 75, no. 1 (September 1993), p. 24.

20.   James A. Banks, "Multicultural Literacy and Curriculum Reform," *Educational Horizons* 60, no. 3 (Spring 1991), p. 137.

21.   Gerald Pine and Asa Hilliard III, "Rx for Racism: Imperatives for America's Schools," *Phi Delta Kappan* 71, no. 8 (April 1990), p. 598.

22.   Geneva Gay, "Ethnic Minorities and Educational Equality," p. 177. See also Geneva Gay, "Building Cultural Bridges: A Bold Proposal for Teacher Education," in Annual Editions, *Multicultural Education, 95/96* (Guilford, Conn.: Dushkin, 1995), pp. 34-40; Sonia Nieto, *Affirming Diversity: The Sociopolitical Context of Multicultural Education* (New York: Longman, 1992); Christine E. Sleeter (ed.), *Empowerment through Multicultural Education* (New York: State University of New York Press, 1991).

23.	James Banks, "Imperatives in Ethnic Minority Education," in Julius Menacker and Ervin Pollack (eds.), *Emerging Educational Issues: Conflicts and Contrasts* (Boston: Little, Brown and Co., 1974), p. 185.

24.	Linda McCormick, "Cultural Diversity and Exceptionality," in Norris G. Haring and Linda McCormick (eds.), *Exceptional Children and Youth: An Introduction to Special Education,* 5th ed. (Columbus, Ohio: Merrill, 1990), p. 75.

25.	Baptise and Baptise, "Developing," p. 105.

26.	See *National Review*, "Special Issue on Multiculturalism," February 21, 1994.

27.	See Wolfgang Welsch, "Transculturality—the Puzzling Form of Cultures Today," *California Sociologist* 17-18 (1994-1995), pp. 19-39.

28.	For texts representative of an Afrocentric perspective, see Yosef ben-Jochanan, *Africa, Mother of Civilization* (Chicago: Black Classic Press, 1971); Cheikh Anta Diop, *The African Origin of Civilization* (New York: Lawrence Hill and Co., 1974); George G.M. James, *Stolen Legacy* (San Francisco, Calif.: Julian Richardson Associates, 1976); Chancellor Williams, *The Destruction of Black Civilization: Great Issues of a Race from 4500 B.C. to 2000 A.D.* (Chicago: Third World Press, 1976); Maulana Karenga, *Introduction to Black Studies* (Inglewood, Calif.: Kawaida Publications, 1982); Ivan Van Sertima, *African Presence in Early America* (New Brunswick, N.J.: Transaction Books, 1987); Molefi Asante, *Afrocentricity* (Trenton, N.J.: Africa World Press, 1989), and *Kemet, Afrocentricity and Knowledge* (Trenton, N.J.: Africa World Press 1990). For trenchant criticisms of Afrocentric readings of ancient history, see Frank M. Snowden, "Bernal's 'Blacks,' Herodotus, and Other Classical Evidence," *Arethusa Special Issue* (Fall 1989), pp. 83-93; David H. Kelly, "Egyptians and Ethiopians: Color, Race, and Racism," *The Classical Outlook* (Spring 1991), pp. 77-82; Molly M. Levine, "The Use and Abuse of Black Athena," *American Historical Review* 97, no. 2 (April 1992), pp. 440-463; Robert Palter, "Black Athena, Afro-Centrism, and the History of Science," *History of Science* 31, (1993), pp. 228-287; Mary Lefkowitz, *Not Out of Africa: How Afrocentrism Became an Excuse to Teach Myth as History* (New York: Basic Books, 1996). For doubts about a causal relationship between self-esteem and academic success, see Dennis Kelly, "High Self-Esteem Doesn't Ensure Academic Success," *USA Today*, January 10, 1991. Alfie Kohn, "The Truth about Self-Esteem," *Phi Delta Kappan* 76, no. 4 (December 1994), pp. 272-283.

29.	Camille A. Clay, "Campus Racial Tensions: Trend or Aberration?" *Thought and Action* 5, no. 2 (Fall 1989), p. 26.

30.	Geneva Gay, "Curriculum Design for Multicultural Education," in Grant (ed.), *Multicultural.* p. 97.

31.	Cameron McCarthy and Michael Apple, "Class, Race, and Gender in American Educational Research: Toward a Nonsynchronous Parallelist Position," in Lois Weis (ed.), *Race, Class, and Gender in American Education* (New York: State University of New York Press, 1988), p. 19. See also Freire, *Pedagogy;* Carnoy, *Education.*

32.	See Yehudi O. Webster, *The Racialization of America* (New York: St. Martin's Press, 1992), Chapter 1.

33.	Stephan Thernstrom, *The Other Bostonians: Poverty and Progress in the American Metropolis, 1880-1970* (Cambridge, Mass.: Harvard University Press, 1973), p. 218.

34.	See August Meier, Elliot Rudwick, and Francis L. Broderick (eds.), *Black Protest in the Twentieth Century* (Indianapolis, Ind.: Bobbs-Merrill, 1965); Harold Cruse, *The Crisis of the Negro Intellectual: From its Origins to the Present* (New York: William Morrow, 1967); Raymond F. Betts (ed.), *The Ideology of Blackness* (Lexington, Mass.: D.C. Heath and Co., 1971); Raymond L. Hall, *Black Separatism in the United*

States (Hanover, N.H.: University Press of New England, 1978); Sterling Stuckey, *Slave Culture: Nationalist Theory and* the *Foundations of Black America* (New York: Oxford University Press, 1987); Wilson J. Moses, *The Golden Age of Black Nationalism, 1850-1925* (New York: Oxford University Press, 1978); William H. Watkins, "Black Curriculum Orientations," *Harvard Educational Review* 63, no. 3 (Fall 1993), pp. 321-338.

35.   Asante, *Afrocentricity*, p. 43.

36.   Molefi Asante, "The Afrocentric Idea in Education," *Journal of Negro Education* 60, no. 2 (Spring 1991), p. 171.

37.   Molefi Asante, "Multiculturalism: An Exchange," *The American Scholar* 60 (Spring 1991), p. 270.

38.   See Alphonso Pinkney, *The Myth of Black Progress* (Cambridge: Cambridge University Press, 1986); Janet Dewart (ed.) *The State of Black America 1990* (New York: National Urban League, 1991); National Urban League, *The State of Black America 1994* (New York: AG Publishing, 1994).

39.   Jon M. Spencer, "Trends of Opposition to Multiculturalism," *The Black Scholar* 23, no. 2 (Winter-Spring 1993), pp. 4-5.

40.   Gerald Early, "The Anatomy of Afrocentrism," in Center for the New American Community, *Alternatives to Afrocentrism* (New York: The Manhattan Institute, 1994), p. 12.

41.   Pine and Hilliard III, "Rx for Racism," p. 595.

42.   Asante, "The Afrocentric Idea in Education," p. 172.

43.   Molefi Asante, "An Afrocentric Curriculum," *Educational Leadership* 49, no. 4 (December 1991-January 1992), p. 29.

44.   See Diop, *African Origin of Civilization* and Chiekh Anta Diop, *The Cultural Unity of Black Africa* (Chicago: Third World Press, 1978); Ivan Van Sertima (ed.), *Great African Thinkers* Vol. 1. (New Brunswick: Transaction Books, 1987); Asante, *Afrocentricity*. Frances Cress Welsing, *The ISIS Papers: The Keys to the Colors* (Chicago: Third World Press, 1991).

45.   Cheikh Anta Diop, *Civilization or Barbarism: An Authentic Anthropology* (New York: Lawrence Hill, 1991), p. 3.

46.   Arthur de Gobineau, cited in Michael D. Biddiss, *Father of Racist Ideology: The Social and Political Thought of Count Gobineau* (New York: Weybright and Talley, 1970), pp. 112-113.

47.   Arthur de Gobineau, in *Gobineau: Selected Political Writings*, edited with an introduction by Michael D. Biddiss (London: Jonathan Cape, 1970), pp. 134-135.

48.   What Martin Bernal calls "the Aryan Model" is exemplified in Gobineau's writings. According to Bernal, this model asserts whiteness, Westernness, and white Western exclusivity and superiority over its counterparts and was applied by many eminent scholars to the comparative study of ancient civilization s. See Martin Bernal, *Black Athena: The Afroasiatic Roots of Classical Civilization: Vol I, The Fabrication of Ancient Greece* (New Brunswick, New Jersey, Rutgers University Press, 1987). See also David Goldberg, *Racist Culture: Philosophy and the Politics of Meaning* (Cambridge: Blackwell, 1993*)*.

49.   See Diop, *Civilization*, pp. 2-3, 16-17.

50.   Diop, "Origin of the Ancient Egyptians," in Van Sertima (ed.), *Great African Thinkers*, pp. 53-54

51.   Diop, *Civilization or Barbarism*, p. 65.

52.   Ibid., p. 11.

53.   See Michael Banton, *The Idea of Race* (Boulder, Colo.: Westview Press, 1977); Michael Banton and Jonathan Harwood, *The Race Concept* (New York: Praeger

Publ., 1975); F. James Davis, *Who Is Black?: One Nation's Definition* (University Park, PA: Pennsylvania State University Press, 1991); Audrey Smedley, *Race: The Evolution of a Worldview* (Boulder, Co.: Westview Press, 1993); Pat Shipman, *The Evolution of Racism: Human Difference and the Use and Abuse of Science* (New York: Simon and Schuster, 1994); L. Luca Cavalli-Sforza, Paolo Menozzi, and Alberto Plazza, *The History and Geography of Human Genes* (Princeton, N.J.: Princeton University Press, 1994).

54. Naomi Zack, *Race and Mixed Race* (Philadelphia: Temple University Press, 1993), p. 169.

55. See Thomas Gossett, *Race: The History of an Idea in America* (New York: Schocken Books, 1965); Michael Banton, *Racial Theories* (Cambridge: Cambridge University Press, 1987); Banton and Harwood, *The Race Concept.*

56. Asante, *Afrocentricity,* p. 95.

57. Ibid., p. 97. .

58. Clinton M. Jean, *Behind the Eurocentric Veils: The Search for African Realities* (Amherst: University of Massachusetts Press, 1991), p. 66.

59. Ibid., p. 68

60. Asante writes of anthropologists: "The limits of their own knowledge were defined by the sociocultural realities of the anthropological profession, one of the most highly Eurocentric disciplines." "Afrocentricity and Culture," in Molefi Kete Asante and Kariamu Welsh Asante (eds.), *African Culture: The Rhythms of Unity* (Westport, Conn.: Greenwood Press, 1985), p. 3.

61. Frank M. Snowden Jr., "Whither Afrocentrism?" *Georgetown* (Winter 1992), p. 7.

62. Jean Genet, *The Blacks: A Clown Show*, trans. Bernard Frechtman (New York: Grove Press, 1960).

63. See Melville J. Herskovits, *The Myth of the Negro Past* (Boston: Beacon Press, 1958); Stuckey, *Slave Culture.*

64. See Albert Murray, *The Omni Americans: New Perspectives on Black Experience and American Culture* (New York: Outerbridge and Dienstrfrey, 1970); Stanley Crouch, *The All-American Skin Game, or, the Decoy of Race: The Long and the Short of It* (New York: Pantheon, 1995).

65. George A. Levesque, "Black Culture, the Black Esthetic, Black Chauvinism: A Mild Dissent," *The Canadian Review of American Studies* 12, no. 3 (Winter 1981), p. 276.

66. Cornel West, *Race Matters* (Boston: Beacon Press, 1993), p. 4. West is not alone in this simultaneous disavowal and endorsement of racial classification. This contradiction surfaces in most writings on "race relations." It amounts to saying: "Race is nonsense, even nonexistent, but the black race must be mobilized for liberation from white racism and oppression."

67. Ibid.

68. Ibid.

69. Asante, "Afrocentricity and Culture," in Molefi Kete Asante and Kariamu Welsh Asante (eds.), *African Culture: The Rhythms of Unity* (Westport, Connecticut: Greenwood Press, 1985), p. 5. By contrast, Kwame Anthony Appiah writes: "The position that there is something unitary called African culture that could thus be summarized has been subjected to devastating critique by a generation of African intellectuals. But little sign of these African accounts of African culture appears in the writings of Afrocentrism." "Europe Upside Down: Fallacies of the New Afrocentrism," *Times Literary Supplement* (February 12, 1993), p. 25. See also, Ali Mazuri and Tobi Levine (eds.), *The Africans* (New York: Praeger, 1986).

70.   Anne Wortham describes how, in reviewing her book, *The Other Side of Racism*, Asante charges her with being ignorant of African history. "Restoring Traditional Values to Higher Education: More Than 'Afrocentrism,'" *The Heritage Foundation* (February 22, 1991), pp. 1-16

71.   See Molefi Asante, *The Afrocentric Idea* (Philadelphia: Temple University Press, 1987).

72.   Ravitch, "Multiculturalism: E Pluribus Plures," p. 339.

73.   Ibid., p. 341.

74.   See Diane Ravitch, "Diversity and Democracy."

75.   History-Social Science Curriculum Framework and Criteria Committee, *History-Social Science Curriculum Framework for California Public Schools Kindergarten through Grade Twelve* (Sacramento, Calif: California State Board of Education, 1988), p. 5.

76.   See *Newsletter on Intellectual Freedom* 40, no. 5 (September 1991), p. 154.

77.   Ravitch, "Multiculturalism: E Pluribus Plures," p. 353.

78.   Schlesinger, *Disuniting*, p. 24.

79.   See Molefi Asante, *Rhetoric of Black Revolution* (Boston: Allyn and Bacon, 1969); *Contemporary Black Social Thought: Alternative Analyses in Social and Behavioral Science* (Beverly Hills, Calif.: Sage Publications, 1980); *The Afrocentric Idea;* and *Kemet, Afrocentricity and Knowledge*.

80.   See Diane Ravitch, *The Great School Wars, The Schools We Deserve: The Troubled Crusade: American Education, 1945-1980* (New York: Basic Books, 1983), and "A Culture in Common," *Educational Leadership* 49, no. 4 (December 1991-January 1992), pp. 8-11.

81.   Ravitch, "Diversity," p. 47.

82.   Asante, "Multiculturalism," p. 270.

83.   Ravitch, "Diversity" p. 47. Ravitch's point is similar to that made by Julia Kristeva regarding the "foreigner" in *Strangers to Ourselves*, trans. Leon S. Roudiez (New York: Columbia University Press, 1991). Kristeva asks: "Can one be a foreigner and be happy?" Her affirmative answer is significantly qualified: "Such happiness is, however, constrained, apprehensively discreet, in spite of its piercing intrusion, since the foreigner keeps feeling threatened by his former territory, caught up in the memory of a happiness or a disaster—both always excessive" (p. 4). For Afrocentrists, African Americans are foreigners in the U.S. Their happiness lies in ancient Egypt. Disaster was born in slavery and a Eurocentric education. Like Afrocentrists, Kristeva is doubtful that the foreigner can be happy. She contemplates the foreigner's anguish in constructing a mythical past and an imaginary home: "as he seeks that invisible and promised territory, that country that does not exist but that he bears in his dreams, and that must indeed be called a beyond" (p. 5).

84.   See James Lynch, *Multicultural Education in a Global Society* (New York: Falmer Press, 1989); Kenneth Tye (ed.), *Global Education: School Based Strategies* (Orange, Calif.: Interdependence Press, 1990); Erich Martel, "Multiculturalism, Not Afrocentrism for D.C. Public Schools," *Journal of the Educational Excellence Network* 10, no. 2 (February 1991), pp. 44-48.

85.   Sharon L. Pugh, Jesus Garcia, and Sonia Margalef-Boada, "Global Dimensions of Diversity: Taking Multiculturalism Beyond National Boundaries," unpublished manuscript, School of Education, Indiana University, Bloomington, 1991, p. 3. Cited in Jesus Garcia and Sharon L. Pugh, "Multicultural Education in Teacher Preparation Programs: A Political or an Educational Concept?" *Phi Delta Kappan* 74, no. 3 (November 1992), p. 218.

86.   Lynch, *Multicultural Education in a Global Society,* p. ix.

87.   James Lynch, *The Multicultural Curriculum* (London: Batsford Academic and Educational Ltd., 1983), p. 15.

88.   For example, James Banks writes: "Teachers should help students to become critical thinkers who have the knowledge, attitudes, skills, and commitments needed to participate in democratic action to help the nation close the gap between its ideals and its realities." James A. Banks, "The Canon Debate: Knowledge Construction and Multicultural Education," *Educational Researcher* 22, no. 5 (June-July 1993), p. 6. Asa Hilliard III writes: "We say that the search for truth is one of the highest goals for students. To foster it, we must facilitate in students the assumption of a critical orientation." "Why We Must Pluralize the Curriculum," *Educational Leadership* 49, no. 4 (December 1991-January 1992), p. 13. Massimo Calabresi reports that in an African Heritage 101 course at Harlem's City College, Professor Jeffries told students: "The idea is to get you to be critical thinkers." "Skin Deep 101," *Time* (February 14, 1994), p. 16.

89.   John I. Goodlad, from a speech at the Center for Educational Renewal, University of Washington, 1986, cited in Pamela L. Tiedt and Iris M. Tiedt, *Multicultural Teaching: A Handbook of Activities, Information, and Resources* (Boston: Allyn and Bacon, 1990), p. 1.

90.   See Sleeter and Grant, *Making Choices;* Grant, "So You Want to Infuse Multicultural Education into Your Discipline?"

91.   Lynch, *The Multicultural Curriculum,* pp. 15-16.

92.   William Bennett, *The Devaluing of America: The Fight for Our Culture and Our Children* (Colorado Springs, Colo.: Focus on the Family Publishing, 1992).

93.   Newt Gingrich, *To Renew America* (New York: Harper/Collins, 1995), p. 7. For similar sentiments, see Alan Keyes, *Masters of the Dream* (New York: William Morrow, 1995); Rush Limbaugh, *See, I Told You So* (New York: Pocket Books, 1993).

94.   ASCD Multicultural Education Commission, "Encouraging Multicultural Education," p. 3.

95.   See James A. Banks, "Multicultural Education as an Academic Discipline," in Annual Editions, *Multicultural,* p. 58.

96.   National Congress of Black Faculty Newsletter, "New Jersey Multicultural Studies Project" (Spring 1993), p. 2.

97.   See John Leo, "A Fringe History of the World," *U.S. News and World Report* (November 12, 1990), pp. 25-26; Paul Gray, "Whose America?" *Time* (July 8, 1991), pp. 13-17; Thomas Sowell, *Inside Education: The Decline, the Deception, the Dogmas* (New York: The Free Press, 1993); Ryan, "The Perils"; Gary K. Clabaugh, "The Cutting Edge: The Limits and Possibilities of 'Multiculturalism,'" *Educational Horizons* 71, no. 3 (Spring 1993), pp. 117-119; Richard Bernstein, *Dictatorship of Virtue: Multiculturalism and the Battle for America's Future* (New York: Knopf, 1994); Schlesinger, *Disuniting*; Dinesh D'Souza, *Illiberal Education: The Politics of Race and Sex on Campus* (New York: The Free Press, 1991); Irving Howe, "What Should We Be Teaching?" *Dissent* (Fall 1988), pp. 477-479; and "The Value of the Canon," *New Republic* (February 18, 1991), pp. 40-47; Fred Siegel, "The Cult of Multiculturalism," *New Republic* (February 18, 1991), pp. 34-40. For criticisms of the Portland Baseline Essays—an Afrocentric contribution to curriculum reform—see Bernard Ortiz de Montellano, "Multicultural Pseudoscience: Spreading Scientific Illiteracy among Minorities," *Sceptical Inquirer* 16 (Fall 1991), pp. 46-50. Center for the New American Community, *Alternatives to Afrocentrism.*

98.   See G. Williamson McDiarmid, "What to Do about Differences? A Study of Multicultural Education for Teacher Trainees in the Los Angeles Unified School District," *Journal of Teacher Education* 43, no. 2 (March-April 1992), pp. 83-93.

99.   Henry L. Gates, "Whose Canon Is It, Anyway?" *New York Times Book Review,* (February 26, 1989), p. 45.

100.   Asante, "The Afrocentric Idea in Education," p. 179.

101.   Hilliard III, "Why We Must Pluralize the Curriculum," p. 13.

102.   Cheikh Anta Diop, "Civilization or Barbarism: An Authentic Anthropology," in Van Sertima (ed.), *Great African*, p. 173.

2

Multiculturalism: Egalitarian Social Reconstruction through Education Reform

As demonstrated in Chapter 1, multicultural education has a number of versions that embody contrasting goals, recommendations, and programs. Nevertheless, despite comparatively frequent recommendations for its infusion in educational institutions, the concept itself is rarely examined at its points of construction. Sohan Modgil et al. allude to this absence of basic research on multicultural education as follows:

> The very term is without an agreed definition, and the implementation of the concept appears to depend largely upon the standpoints of individuals, whether they take an assimilationist, cultural pluralist, or anti-racist approach . . . multicultural education has no clear-cut meaning; the term has blind alley implications which not only take us away from moral and social realities, but direct us towards conceptual confusion.[1]

It is this "conceptual confusion" that is manifest in confessions of support for cultural pluralism and multicultural education by Arthur Schlesinger Jr., Lynne Cheney, Diane Ravitch, Molefi Asante, and James Banks, side by side with mutual denunciations of proposals. The troubling question is: What should be included in a multicultural curriculum? The various recommendations indicate not so much the absence of a clear-cut meaning of multicultural education as the presence of a vast number of competing meanings. As Patricia L. Francis writes: "Clearly, the development of multicultural education has been characterized by many conceptual shifts in a short period of time. It is not surprising, then, that this educational approach means different things to different people."[2] However, there is more than mere discovery of many meanings at stake. No advocate of multicultural education or multiculturalism has attempted to explain the reasons for the plethora of conceptions, definitions, meanings, and perspectives. Nevertheless, an understanding the chameleon like character of multicultural education is surely crucial to any decision on its implementation. Second, as a concept, a discipline, an educational ideal, or a set of practices, multicultural education is bound to be conceptually variegated, but at what point do these variations cease to be part of the "discipline?" When does a particular approach to diversity not come under the conceptual umbrella of multicultural education? These issues can be explored through analysis of an internal-developmental aspect of multicultural education.

The Evolution from Multicultural Education to Multiculturalism

A closer scrutiny of the variety of multicultural educational perspectives and objectives reveals a progression through specific propositions on culture, schooling, social problems, and social change. This progression extends from the initial goals of multicultural education—curriculum transformation for appreciation of different cultures, consolidation of the common culture, and improving the educational performance of black students—to curriculum reorganization to build the self-esteem of all "students of color," to the inclusion of group cultures, experiences, and perspectives in the curriculum, and school restructuring for equalization of educational opportunities. However, if equality and cultural pluralism are inseparable, multicultural education should be more far-reaching. As Joan Lester, executive director of the Equity Institute, writes of a phase in multicultural education's implementation:

The third stage of multicultural change involves cracking open the (often unintentionally) restrictive policies and structures. Examples: Admissions policies. Partner benefits. Grievance policies and mechanisms. Sexual harassment policies. Calendars and holiday policies. Performance evaluations (including both the issue of "standards" and whose norms they represent, and how to make leadership on multicultural concerns a criterion). Tenure line appointments as opposed to non-tenure lines. Joint appointments. Pay equity. Appointment and promotions committee membership (e.g. full professors only, therefore mostly male and white, so it represents a non-diverse committee evaluating diverse candidates).[3]

Some critics might argue that these measures are far removed from the goal of introducing students to the ramifications of cultural pluralism, that they go beyond the goals of cultural infusion and differences-appreciation. On the other hand, prominent proponents of multicultural education, such as James Banks, Carl Grant, Christine Sleeter, and Sonia Nieto, would insist that cultural pluralism is inconceivable without an assault on the prejudices, discrimination, sexism, racism, and inequality that permeate hiring practices in educational institutions. For these authors, an affirmation of diversity is inseparable from not only the curriculum's inclusion of students' cultures and experiences, as well as the perspectives of women, people of color, and other "oppressed" groups but also the reconstruction of schools to empower students and teachers toward social reconstruction. They make the case that, once the monocultural and Eurocentric biases that permeate schooling are ejected, other processes of inclusion should follow, until schools are transformed into purposively egalitarian institutions. This conception of multicultural education is a far cry from a mere insistence on cultural pluralism in schools. By incorporating concepts of oppression, power, equity and equality into multicultural education, these scholars present an agenda for teacher and student empowerment as well as antisexist, antiracist, antihomophobic, and egalitarian social transformations.[4]

The promotion of multicultural education as a strategy for attaining equality of educational opportunities, student and teacher empowerment, and social reconstruction is a specific, 1980s development. It combines the egalitarian and antidomination themes in black liberationist and feminist writings and the radical criticisms of education presented in works such as Samuel Bowles and Herbert Gintis, *Schooling in Capitalist America* (1976), Paulo Freire, *Pedagogy of the Oppressed* (1971), and Martin Carnoy, *Education as Cultural Imperialism* (1974). Multicultural education is to be inclusive of all oppressed groups as part of a struggle for "social justice"; it is not only about changing the curriculum to include differences or celebrate diversity. Rather, it is about initiating an integrated and systematic reorganization of educational institutions to challenge political and cultural domination. These developments and increments represent the concept of multiculturalism—a project for egalitarian social reconstruction.

In the early conception of multicultural education, curriculum reforms represent a means of achieving cultural pluralism and tolerance. Some of the subsequently added objectives are: diversity celebration, and identity affirmation, and an improvement of self-esteem in order to improve the academic performances of "students of color" (Afrocentricity and Latinocentricity). In multiculturalism, curriculum reforms and school reorganization are meant to change the opportunity and power structures within schools and society. These divergences imply that an interchangeable use of "multicultural education" and "multiculturalism" indicates an unawareness of the analytical cross-currents in the literature.[5] However, matters are not helped by an oscillation—in the works of some scholars, for example, Carl Grant, Christine Sleeter, and James Banks—among goals of (1) cultural pluralism, (2) equalization of educational opportunities, (3) teacher empowerment, (4) student mobilization for liberationist sociopolitical activism (5) a gay, black, women's, third world, and anti-Eurocentric cleansing of educational institutions, and (6) overall social justice.[6]

The various perspectives within multicultural education and multiculturalism are branches of the same tree of cultural pluralism. However, some of these branches are so intertwined with other trunks of knowledge—the critical theory of the Frankfurt School, postmodernist theses on differences, power, culture, and knowledge, radical feminism, the liberation pedagogy of Paulo Freire, and a Gramscian conception of ideology—that they constitute separate and distinct formations. Thus emerge insurgent, resistance, and critical multiculturalisms that propose *school reorganization* against all forms of political and cultural domination.[7] What is distinct about these developments is their rejection of a mere celebration of differences and of multiculturalism as a project for cultural equality in schools. Theirs is pursuit of social revolution through teachers' recognition of themselves as transformative intellectuals within sites of cultural politics and struggles—the schools.

Within the advocacies of critical and insurgent multiculturalism other perspectives on education reform are often described as conservative multiculturalism, corporate multiculturalism, difference multiculturalism, and academic multiculturalism.[8] These qualifications prolong the disputes among multiculturalism's advocates and detractors, but they also reflect specific, analytical additives. For example, advocates of "insurgent multiculturalism" and "critical multiculturalism," such as Henry Giroux, Peter McLaren, and Barry Kanpol, embrace aspects of the liberation pedagogy of Paulo Freire, postmodernism, and the "critical theory" of the Frankfurt School.[9] However, these additives are largely absent from the writings of James Banks, Carl Grant, Christine Sleeter, and Sonia Nieto who present multicultural education as education for social activism and egalitarian social reconstruction. Nevertheless, a common goal of justice for "women" and "people of color" and appeals to teachers to become involved in social transformation enjoin the works of these authors. On the other hand, significantly, Henry Giroux, Peter McLaren, and Barry Kanpol espouse multiculturalism not multicultural education, and they oppose the "essentialization" of racial differences.

In the 1960s, proponents of multicultural education, including James Banks and Carl Grant, focused on the cultural-educational problems facing "black" Americans. Two decades later, their multicultural educational proposals show evidence of an inclusion of other populations. They now argue that multicultural education should include racial as well as gender and class experiences, and that empowered teachers should prepare students for social reconstructionist activism through the adoption of "critical pedagogy" and an infusion of antioppression themes in the curriculum. This agenda involves not only curriculum transformation, but also changes in the schools' personnel, faculty and staff development programs, and teacher-student relations. In justifying these recommendations, multiculturalism's advocates point to the increasing presence of people of color and different cultures in schools and the pervasiveness of sexism, homophobia, and racism in both schools and society. Behind all this, they claim, lies a hegemonic, white, male, heterosexual culture that resists diversity, inclusiveness, and change. The schools' monoculturalism and the society's racist and sexist patterns of exclusion must be countered. In the words of Peter McLaren: "The sociohistorical dynamics of race, class, and gender domination must never be left out of the education for social struggle or take a back seat to the sociology seminar room."[10] A "critical pedagogy" is recommended to enable students to deessentialize their identities and contextualize them in power, politics, and theory. This recommendation radically deviates from a multicultural education that involves mere diversity affirmation and respect for differences.

The developmental trajectory of multicultural education is recognized by Carl A. Grant, who himself publishes widely in the field. Grant suggests that there are five "approaches" to multicultural education:

1. Teaching the Exceptional and Culturally Different. This approach does not challenge the overall cultural and social structures. It merely identifies special populations that might be in need of cultural enrichment programs.

2. The Human Relations Approach, which is integrationist and inculcates principles and methods of bridging differences.

3. The Single Group Studies Approach in which the presentation of the experiences of oppressed groups is integrated into social sciences as separate departments of racial, ethnic, and women's studies.

4. A Multicultural Approach to Education, which promotes cultural pluralism and racial-ethnic equality.

5. An Education that is Multicultural and Social Reconstructionist (EMC-SR).[11]

Grant contrasts the "Multicultural Approach to Education" and "Education that is Multicultural and Social Reconstructionist," arguing that one limitation of the former is that "curriculum is organized around the contributions and perspectives of different cultural groups."[12] On the other hand:

The Education that is Multicultural and Social Reconstructionist Approach extends the previous approaches and teaches students to analyze social inequality and oppression by helping them develop skills for social action. This approach promotes social structural equality and cultural pluralism and prepares students to work actively toward equality for all peoples.[13]

Here it is clearly stated that the purpose of the EMC-SR approach to multicultural education is not only to increase students' sensitivity to cultural differences, but also motivate them to recognize and act on patterns of disempowerment, discrimination, and deprivation.

The oscillation between multicultural education and multiculturalism is well illustrated in the works of James A. Banks, who writes: "Multicultural education is also a process whose goals will never be fully realized. Educational equality, like liberty and justice, are ideals toward which human beings work but never fully attain. Racism, sexism, and handicapism will exist to some extent no matter how hard we work to eliminate these problems."[14] Here multicultural education is conceived as a strategy for eradicating certain social problems. However, Banks also suggests that multicultural education is an offshoot of ethnic or multiethnic studies.[15] It marks a transition from a focus on race to ethnicity, from racial studies to ethnic studies. Its goal is the development of ethnic literacy, which would be achieved through an introduction of various ethnic perspectives into the curriculum as equally sound worldviews.

Should multiculturalism not be divested of a concern with issues of racial oppression and racial justice? After all, such a concern does essentialize racial differences. This question indicates a latent divergence between the proposals of

James Banks, Geneva Gay, Christine Sleeter, and Carl Grant and the multiculturalism advocated by Peter McLaren and Barry Kanpol, who are critical of
"difference multiculturalism."[16] Kanpol and McLaren do express solidarity with
the struggles of oppressed racial groups, but they also insist that racial identities
and experiences must not be separated from theoretical significations and shifting power relations. Black people are, in poststructuralist terms, merely linguis-
tically signified others. Racial differences are neither pregiven, nor anterior to
oppression. On the other hand, sponsors of multicultural education treat racial
groups as preexistent phenomena upon which a historical oppression was imposed. Nevertheless, as will be argued in Chapter 3, critical multiculturalism is
profoundly ambivalent, even self-contradictory, on the question of racial differences.

Antisexist Education Reform and Radical Feminism

As indicated, one of the analytical foundations of multiculturalism is the
claim that America is a multiracial and multicultural society. Some of its advocates insist, however, that the society also operates not only on Eurocentric and
racist, but also on classist and sexist principles, and that it is the majority-
minority, women, who are the main victims.[17] As the argument goes, in schools,
patriarchal structures serve male interests and thereby psychologically disempower women. The chosen textbooks are produced mainly by males and are either biased or inimical to the interests of women. The solution is the adoption of
antisexist and nonsexist principles of curriculum construction. This curriculum
reform would proceed in the direction of focusing on women's experiences, increasing the number of female faculty, and selecting the works of female authors
as course textbooks.[18] Once the transformation of the "canonical" or traditional
curriculum is achieved, organizational, political, legal, and behavioral transformations would follow.

A key assumption within antisexist proposals is that it is educational institutions, not the economy, that represent sites of struggle for a sexually egalitarian
social order. It is initially in schools that the experiences of women are caricatured and girls disempowered. The texts used in social science and humanities
courses either demean women or fail to portray them as active, creative shapers
of human civilization. Thus the identity, motivations, and expectations of female
students are distorted and marginalized Emerging from this alien educational
environment, they necessarily, subsequently become socioeconomic undera-
chievers. These arguments underlie the thrust for and antisexist curriculum; they
derive from certain strains in feminist writings, writings that are themselves part
of an overall gender theory of social relations.

The gender theory signifies reproductive organs to classify human beings
into males and females, and characterizes social relations as sexual relations or
relations grounded in "sexual politics."[19] In this theory, the principal historical
actors, if not antagonists, are males and females. Some proponents of the gender

theory argue that male and female behavior and destinies are determined by their respective, god-created natures. This argument represents a naturalist variant of the gender theory, and Rosemarie Tong's description of the "conservative" position captures its basic propositions:

When conservatives say that biology is destiny, they mean that (1) people are born with the hormones, anatomy, and chromosomes of either a male or a female; (2) females are destined to have a much more burdensome reproductive role than are males; (3) males will, other things being equal, exhibit "masculine" psychological traits (for example, "assertiveness, aggressiveness, hardiness, rationality or the ability to think logically, abstractly and analytically, ability to control emotion"), whereas females will, other things being equal, exhibit "feminine" psychological traits (for example, "gentleness, modesty, humility, supportiveness, empathy, compassionateness, tenderness, nurturance, intuitiveness, sensitivity, unselfishness"); and (4) society should preserve this natural order, making sure that its men remain "manly" and its women "womanly."[20]

These claims go beyond a mere comment on the nature of men and women; they constitute a set of basic propositions on human behavior, history, and social order based on an assumption of natural gender differences. In classifying persons into males and females and locating their behavior and experiences in a biologically determined social order, these propositions form an overall theory of social relations.

In the women's liberationist variant of the gender theory, a pervasive sexism is generally advanced as the cause or explanation of women's subordination. Although there is considerable dispute as to the precise origin of sexism—nature's sexual dimorphism, men's nature, capitalism, historical developments, unconscious drives—it is usually defined as beliefs, attitudes, or policies that subordinate or justify the subordination of women.[21] This inclusion of cognitive, behavioral, and social structural referents means that, like the concept of racism, sexism has a multitude of denotations. In women's liberationist writings, the term *sexism* is used as a referent of ideas, beliefs, and practices, a description of attitudes, behavior, and policies, an identification of social conditions, an explanation of male behavior, and a moral accusation. Women are presented as a historically victimized group, and feminist writings are offered as part of a project for women's liberation. Thus women's liberationist feminism may be distinguished from the naturalist perspective on women's experiences that regards "the woman question" as an issue long ago settled by the natures of man and woman. For example, according to Kazem Alamdari, at the Fourth UN World Conference on Women in Beijing in 1995: "Some Islamic countries, including Iran and Sudan, supported by conservative Christian coalitions suggested replacing 'equality' with 'equity.' This suggestion was based on the thesis that because men and women are naturally, biologically different, as created by divine intervention, they must accept the sexual division of labor, obligations, responsibilities, and roles. Vatican and Islamic representatives argued that women's place in society reflects their biological characteristics."[22] It is this naturalist perspective that is deemed "right wing" and "conservative" by advocates of women's liberation, and some have challenged its concomitant divine ordination.[23]

In the naturalist perspective, women's experiences do not unfold along a trajectory of male misdeeds and oppression. Women are claimed to be naturally different from, not victims of, men. The two sexes were made different by *divine ordinance* or *nature's decree*; their physical differences are complementary, and accompanying socioeconomic differences are therefore inevitable, not something against which women should protest. If women need to be liberated at all, it is from the illusion that they are oppressed in the family and other institutions. These arguments are strongly opposed by advocates of women's liberation, for whom women are indisputably objects of male domination. However, a concrete identification of the victimizers of women has proven to be extraordinarily difficult. A variety of candidates surface as explanations of women's oppression: men's beliefs, sexist beliefs that are held by both men and women, men's nature, sexual discrimination, sexual roles, a scarcity of resources, capitalism, subliminal patterns of sexual repression, woman's reproductive attributes, and a patriarchal culture. As implied by the development of gender-class combinations, these explanations are not necessarily complementary. Nevertheless, despite the absence of a positive identification of the causes of women's oppression, and the definitional amorphousness surrounding the term *sexism*, antisexism has emerged as a call for resistance and struggle against the oppression of women. What remains unclear, however, is whether "sexism" can legitimately perform so many analytical functions—a description of beliefs, attitudes, policies, and behavior, a referent of gender inequalities, an accusation against men, and an explanation of women's oppression—and what is not considered is whether the identification of men as victimizers and women as victims is itself not sexist.

The gender theory of social relations retains a powerful presence in the intellectual environment. Its classificatory criteria are appropriated by media, educators, political representatives, and parents to structure institutions and socioeconomic policies with an overall gender socialization. Masculinities and femininities, boys and girls, and subsequently men and women are created in delivery rooms, nurseries, and kindergarten. The newborn are immediately sexually identified, according to their sexual organs, and, in the words of sociologist Jessie Bernard, enter "blue and pink worlds" of distinct genders.[24] In *The Lenses of Gender,* Sandra Lipsitz Bem demonstrates how three "lenses"—male-centeredness, gender polarization, and biological essentialism—shape socialization, sell-perceptions, social policies, and prescriptions for social change.[25] Through official, customary, and educational appropriations of the classificatory criteria of the gender theory, human beings are categorized according to their reproductive organs. Some "feminists" regard the conceptualization of sexual attributes as natural properties that divide the human species into males and females as a form of biological essentialism. Women and men, they argue are social constructs, not nature's products.

In feminist writings that reject the essentialization of gender differences, the concept of social construction is used to focus on the gendering of experiences, that is, on gender identities and women's situation as a consequence of sexual power-differences, which lead to the imposition of biologically based identities, coercive role-allocation, and discrimination. One of the points made by those writers who deem gender a social or cultural construct is that gender distinctions derive from an analytical procedure. Specific classificatory criteria are applied to signify certain differences and construct "males" and "females." The process is described by Cynthia Epstein: "Consider the kind of analysis that focuses on distinctions between the sexes. Human reason makes it possible to make categories of discrete things and events in nature and in social life. Developing concepts that group things and events is economical and practical. But, as we know, people often treat concepts as real even though in fact they are only representations of real things."[26] The categories male and female are representations developed in order to understand certain biological processes, map observations, and engage in specific practices; they are not produced by nature, but by human beings attempting to conceptualize their observations. It follows that there is no logical necessity or foundation for the claim that sexually classified processes, situations, and relationships are natural, or real. Indeed, Epstein's assertion that concepts represent "real things" faces the insurmountable difficulty of conceptually mirroring a nonconceptual "real world."[27] Alternatively, classifications could be analyzed as extensions of other concepts, which are representations of meanings derived from, and governed by, rules of language use. "Male" and "female" would then be regarded as bipolar categories or images specific to a theoretical signification of certain biological attributes; they are not depictions of real objects, in the sense of things existing beyond a theoretical order.

The notion of social constructionism grounds classifications in changing social structural relations. It is manifest in androgynous and poststructuralist feminist perspectives that challenge any intrinsic social significance or scientific basis of male-female differences. According to Chris Weedon, in poststructuralist feminism, biological differences "do not have inherent 'natural' or social meaning. Their meanings, which are far from uniform, are produced within a range of conflicting discourses, from medicine and sociobiology to radical feminism."[28] The "conflicting discourses" that generate various conceptions of maleness and femaleness are echoed in disputes within feminist writings. The analytical elusiveness of their objects of study—women's experiences—results in a multiplicity of competing feminisms, such as liberal, radical, Marxist, lesbian, black, postmodern, victim, differences, Chicana, cultural, structuralist, positive, Christian, and so on.[29] Not all feminisms seek to achieve women's liberation. It is advocates of women's liberationist feminism who suggest that women, because of their gender, are especially oppressed, either by men (radical feminism), men in conjunction with capitalism (socialist feminism), or capitalism (Marxist feminism). Their objectives vary through women's specific rights as homemakers, sexual equality, separatism, and the destruction of patriarchy. Advocates of radical feminism, especially, emphasize that men are the dominant gender and that their domination produces pervasive socioeconomic disproportions between the sexes. In this male-dominated world, women are said to be especially victimized by an unequal distribution of power, and violence.

In what is generally regarded as a path-breaking exposition of radical feminism, *The Dialectic of Sex: The Case for Feminist Revolution*, Shulamith Firestone makes a sustained case for conceiving Marxism and Freudianism as fore-
runners of feminism.[30] Such a reading of feminism's history equates the concepts of class conflict and group conflict. However, in Marx's analysis of capitalist development, class conflict is identified as a manifestation of conflicting
interests derived from different relations to the means of production and exploitation. By contrast, group conflict derives from competition over scarce resources. This concept is well developed in Georg Simmel's notion of the intrinsically conflict-ridden nature of social relations. The foundation of the conflict
perspective in sociology properly belongs not to Karl Marx's but to George
Simmel's writings.[31] As Randall Collins notes: "Modern conflict theory began
early in the twentieth century with the work of Georg Simmel (1908) which was
revived and systematized 50 years later by Lewis Coser (1956)."[32] Radical feminism appropriates arguments from conflict theory to construe history as an unfolding conflict between two groups—men and women. Men emerge victorious
from this conflict, as discernible in the global system of patriarchy.[33] Antisexist
education reform pursues a specific transformation of the curriculum in order to
empower women and eradicate their oppression. It develops on the core radical
feminist tenet that women are disempowered and victimized by men in what is
essentially a patriarchal society. Some of its immediate goals are curriculum
transformations that positively revamp the images of women in history and society, and gender parity in hiring policies, remuneration, and promotion in the
Academy. Once women become empowered in educational institutions, and
male-based scholarship ceases to be privileged, the entire patriarchal social order
could be abolished.

Various intellectual legacies are expressed in the competing perspectives on
women's experiences within women's liberation feminism. Radical feminism
itself is by no means a homogeneous school of thought, and cannot be claimed as
women's perspective or a perspective unique to female writers. Many "males"
espouse feminism, which has its share of writers, called conservatives, who
identify nature's invisible hand operating in gender experiences. In *The Woman
Question in Classical Sociological Theory*, Terry Kandal conducts an extensive
review of "thirteen male classical sociologists" who concede the existence of the
political and economic subordination of women and suggest various measures
for women's emancipation.[34] Their legacies survive, as divergent and competing
intellectual traditions, in a variety of feminist analyses of women's experiences
that do not share descriptions and explanations. For example, advocates of traditional or "conservative" feminism conceive the sexual division of labor as not
male dominance but a natural expression of essential differences between men
and women; it, therefore, repudiates the idea of women being oppressed by men.
For "Christian" and "positive" feminists, women's liberation, if it is to mean
anything at all, must mean the promotion of women's identification with the
roles of wife, mother, and homemaker. Representatives of these perspectives on
women's experiences will surely ask for a voice in a multicultural curriculum.

Antisexist education represents a project seeking the abolition of the oppression of women and the construction of a sexually egalitarian social order. Utilizing certain arguments from the radical feminist perspective on women's experiences, its sponsors ask: How are women to be liberated from their disempowerment? They answer: an antisexist curriculum transformation, an educational program for women's liberation that would supplement antidiscrimination laws. This answer meets three sets of objections. First, the radical feminist focus on women's oppression requires considerable justification, given that the categories men and women are regarded as untenable by advocates of poststructuralist and postmodernist feminism. Second, if education reforms are to be grounded in explicitly sociopolitical objectives, their implementation is bound to be stalled by those who do not share these objectives. Finally, if schools are to be training grounds for sexual-egalitarian social reconstruction, those opposed to such egalitarianism should be allowed to stake their claims on the curriculum, faculty recruitment, and codes of conduct. Other political perspectives on women's experiences must also be given "voice" in the curriculum. And so the so-called Right also advances recommendations for education reform: a curriculum based on family values, prayer in schools, more discipline among students, and the ejection of multiculturalism. In the confrontations between the "Left" and the "Right" schools become not sites for social transformation but locations of "culture wars" that educators—those most professionally qualified to resolve disputes—cannot resolve. Their contributions, too, will be politically evaluated.

Antiracist Education Reform

In terms of its analytical roots and conceptual structure, antiracism is a complex phenomenon; it reflects a particular moralizing tendency in studies of relations between "blacks" and "whites"—a tendency denounced in Shelby Steele's *The Content of our Character*—and a related egalitarian thrust of "modern liberalism."[35] It is also grounded in a racial classification of persons and the thesis that racist beliefs and practices permeate schools and society. Antiracism, then, represents a particular kind of extension of racial studies. It predates but is related to the Boasian challenge to the naturalists' thesis that cultural and social inequalities reflect superior and inferior racial endowments.[36] Anthropologists from the Boasian school had deemed this thesis "racist" and mounted a sustained campaign against it.[37] They argued that because all cultures are relatively equal, races are also equal. Antiracist education reform extends certain claims about race and culture into the educational sphere. Overall, it is grounded in the following arguments: (1) Schools should function to equalize opportunity; (2) Because all cultures and their knowledges are equal and autonomous, single cultures should be equally represented in the curriculum; and (3) Because the dominant culture is racist, the curriculum must be divested of racist texts, practices, and influences. Otherwise, it would be a case of equal educational opportunities being denied to "students of color," for these students cannot perform equally well in a racist school environment.

Most studies of so-called race relations present racism as an explanation of the behavior of "white people."[38] It is generally presented as a morbid mental state, an irrational belief system, or an institutionalized condition of discrimination that may be rooted in economic conditions and class considerations. The authors of three best-selling books on "race relations"—Cornel West, *Race Matters*; Andrew Hacker, *Two Societies, Separate and Unequal*; and Derrick Bell, *Faces at the Bottom of the Well*—insist that racism is rampant in American society. Their allegation echoes a proposition that is dramatically expressed by former Congresswoman Shirley Chisholm:

America is a racist nation. Indeed, racism is so universal in this country, so widespread and deep-seated, that it is invisible because it is so normal. Yes, the central issue of mid-20th century America has been, and still is, racism. Racism has accounted for more than physical segregation and discrimination in obtaining the basic necessities of life, jobs, housing, and education. It is the most evil, pervasive, and systematic destruction of personality, the negation of one's humanity.[39]

The Kerner Commission also charged racism with the responsibility for both ghetto-formation and the urban riots of the 1960s: "What white Americans have never fully understood—but what the Negro can never forget—is that white society is deeply implicated in the ghetto. White institutions created it, white institutions maintain it, and white society condones it. White racism is essentially responsible for the explosive mixture which has been accumulating in our cities since the end of World War II."[40] Even "conservative" and "liberal" writings on race relations admit to the operational presence of racism in American society.[41] It is undeniably there, they agree, but "black people" can and should deal with it by strengthening and mobilizing the positive values in the black community.[42]

The idea of racism's pervasiveness has acquired the status of a canon in American intellectual life; it may be voiced without fear of opposition or a request for its substantiation. Among the voluminous writings on race relations, it is indeed a rarity to discover any questioning of the argument that American society is racist, that is to say, morally diseased. Because schools are reflections of political decisions, their curriculum, personnel decisions, and pedagogic practices are necessarily affected by America's endemic racism. As Frances E. Kendall writes: "Racism is one of the most crippling diseases from which this country suffers. It affects each of us, whether we are white or red, yellow, black, or brown, oppressor or oppressed. Education can be a powerful force in the struggle to eliminate racism."[43] How can schools be organized to rid U.S. society of the scourge of racism? This leads to a second question that is of equal strategic importance: Which racism? For Kendall's claim that racism affects all races implies that "blacks," too, can be racist. On the other hand, this claim is opposed by two leading advocates of antiracist education. According to Gerald Pine and Asa Hilliard: "Racism is a mental illness characterized by perceptual distortion, a denial of reality, delusions of grandeur (belief in white supremacy), the projection of blame (on the victim), and phobic reactions to differences. A colonizer may be racist, but a victim cannot be so."[44] For these authors, racism is a malaise affecting white people only. "Black racism" is simply prejudice against the oppressors, and thus may be explained as a function of "white racism," something of an oxymoron. Blacks do not have power, and so cannot be racists. This defense, however, simply moves the issue to one of racism's many meanings.

Antiracist education draws its rationale from writings that conceive racism as a referent of prejudiced white beliefs and attitudes, which have institutional effects that generate a wide range of social problems. This usage of the concept of racism, as an explanation of behavior and social conditions, marks a peculiar development in studies of "race relations." In early nineteenth-century treatises, biologically inferior attributes were a common explanatory category of the Negro's immoral and uncivilized nature, while from the second half of the twentieth century, the morally inferior attribute of whites—their racism—is cited as an explanation of their behavior. Thus the concept of racism was negatively value loaded. In *The Retreat of Scientific Racism*, Elazar Barkan observes that: "The use of 'racism' as a derogatory neologism was first recorded in English in the 1930s."[45] However, David T. Goldberg dates this emergence in 1940, with the publication of Ruth Benedict's *Race, Science and Politics*.[46] In most texts on race relations, the term *racism* depicts the beliefs and actions of "white people," and the consequences. It functions as an accusation and an explanation. In the last instance, it is the analytical equivalent of the naturalists' claim that blacks are biologically inferior and that this inferiority explains their socioeconomic underdevelopment. These various usages are conjoined within a general racial theory whose centerpiece is classification by anatomy to observe white and black people.

In studies of so-called race relations, whether the emphasis is placed on black inferiority or the moral deficiencies of whites, racial classification is retained. Indeed, these studies are extensions of the early anthropologists' and biologists' treatises on racial constitutions and destinies in which race is analyzed as a thing produced by nature. As Roxanne Doty writes: "Race is taken as a given, a real and self-evidently neutral fact. When race is defined it is as an independent variable that interacts with other variables to produce certain outcomes, e.g., discrimination and stratification problems."[47] This givenness of "races" is present in most social studies texts, government publications, and media reports on social problems. It *is* what makes race a social construct, so that social scientists, political representatives, and journalists cannot then claim that they study and comment on race because it is a social construct. What this claim on social constructionism obscures is the act of racial classification—the generation of racial selves.

Usage of the concept of racism as an explanation is inseparable from the racial classification of persons. Anthropologist Terrence Epperson makes the point that scholars of race relations utilize Locke's fact-value distinction, on the basis of which race is described as a fact, and racism a value. Epperson writes:

The conception of race as an innate, distinct, and natural attribute of the human condition is grounded in John Locke's empiricism. Locke's concept of "normal essence" provided a mechanism whereby a single attribute such as race could be defined as "essential" for the definition of humanity. Within the empiricist fact/value dichotomy race is reified as a fact and racism is viewed as a value. It therefore seems possible to write a history of racism without questioning the category of race.[48]

An essentialism born of Lockean empiricism rules antiracist education. The racial classification of persons is not challenged as a possibly illegitimate practice. Its endorsement is necessary for criticizing the moral failings of "white people" and promoting racial equality. So-called whites and blacks are treated as biological or social facts, and their experiences are explained as outcomes produced by their natures. There is a parallel between the badges of Negro biological inferiority and white moral deficiency. The white race is as bad, that is, "racist," as the black race is inferior. Race-blaming and race-hating rule a roost that is empty of criticism of racial classification.

Villains and victimizers are indispensable to antioppression political activities. Thus racist motives are imputed to "whites," over and above their confessions of innocence, and "blacks" are portrayed as their innocent victims.[49] The plays and ploys involved in the tragicomic processes of ascribing racial guilt and innocence are well described in Shelby Steele's *The Content of Our Character*. In the struggle for power, "whites" and "blacks" are selected to represent guilt. The race between black and white intellectuals is to ensure that guilt sticks to the other race. Their conversation could proceed thus:

You whites believe that blacks are biologically inferior. This proves that you are racists, morally stunted beings. We blacks are historically morally advantaged precisely because of the disadvantages heaped on us, and are best qualified to judge, if not lead, this nation.

You blacks must divest yourselves of your racial paranoia and self-righteousness. Stop playing the politics of race, for it demoralizes your race and infuriates us, whites.

And so emerges the stalemate that underlies observations of "bad" and "worsening" race relations, as well as sporadic predictions of fires next time.

All studies of "race relations" reflect on the natures of so-called black people and white people and their moral qualifications to be just, judge, lead, succeed, or integrate. The accusation of racism is meant to disqualify "whites," to discredit whatever they say, and silence their evil voices. A "white" who generalizes about black people may be called a racist. However, a "black" who suggests that all whites are racist is not deemed a racist. As racial liberationists would insist, whites are racist because they cannot escape their evil nature, just as blacks are naturally inferior, as the naturalists would have it. More significantly, blacks cannot be racist, for they lack power. This claim shifts the definition of racism from prejudiced beliefs and attitudes to power-contextual decisions.[50] Blacks are comparatively powerless and hence incapable of being racists. This description of the political status of blacks may be said to be inaccurate. How can a people that created the civil rights movement, a movement, as

Stanley Crouch insists, whose tenets and tactics were imitated in Eastern Europe and China, be said to not have power?

The claim that blacks are powerless and, therefore, free of racism merely serves to maintain racism's selective applicability—that is, to whites only. As Philip Perlmutter and Walter Williams write:

For years now, black "leaders" have been pretending that all the problems of black people can be attributed to white racism. Libraries, bookshelves and newspaper offices are crammed with tomes explaining what black people are, what they think, why they have problems, and what government can do to lead them out of the wilderness. Much of this material is now considered sacred. To question it—or worse, to criticize it—leaves one open to harsh attack. If he's lucky, the critic may be called an insensitive clod, or perhaps a political reactionary. If he is less fortunate, he'll be called a racist, or in the case of a black, an Uncle Tom.[51]

However, in the torrent of moral-political condemnations, the application of racism to whites only is necessarily challenged. Some "whites" are allegedly anti-racist, and even powerless "blacks" are shown to have racist beliefs.

Anne Wortham in *The Other Side of Racism,* the authors of *The Color Complex*, and more recently Dinesh D'Souza in *The End of Racism* insist that blacks can be as racist as whites.[52] And so discoveries of "white racists" and "black racists," and mutual denials of being racist, prevail. These discoveries are reminiscent of medieval and Salem witch-hunts, for the denial of being a racist can itself be cited as proof of racism—a subconscious racism, institutional racism, symbolic racism, or racism in denial. The accused simply cannot escape or avoid punishment. However, what is burned, or drowned, are clarity and logical reasoning in argument exposition. The plethora of definitions of racism, its usage to describe the nature of persons, as well as to accuse, and to explain indicate a profound, conceptual hyper-inflation of the term. A term so all-inclusive and so unfalsifiably applied must be meaningless and, therefore, a hindrance to conclusive discussions. The fact that eminent scholars and political representatives continue to endorse the thesis that racism permeates U.S. society reflects a lack of commitment to deep thought and analytical integrity and a moralistic blame-seeking ethos in the intellectual environment. It also indicates that there was a need for critical thinking in schools a generation if not centuries ago.

As indicated, the charge of racism is generally laid at the feet of one "race," that is, applied to the comments, beliefs, attitudes, and behavior of "white people," but not those of "black people." This is because racism is an analytic feature of the liberationist variant of the racial theory. Its sponsors agree that persons may be classified as "white people" and "black people" on the basis of certain anatomical attributes. By imputing negative psychological-moral characteristics to "white people," those who are committed to equality for "black people" conclude that "white people" are racists. Proof of racism is found in the discovery of prejudiced white beliefs about blacks. The term *racism* identifies these beliefs, which are allegedly manifest in negative attitudes, behaviors, and policies that exclude resources from black people. However, because beliefs evolve and operate within personality types, political systems, social structures, and economic contexts, the concept of racism acquires myriad psychological, economic, institutional, and social-structural qualifications. It is used to identify a variety of mental states, policies, and social conditions: racial ideas, belief in these ideas, racial attitudes, oppressive policies, discriminatory behavior, and social inequalities. Each meaning attempts to capture the state of the white mind, as it manifests itself in statements, behavior, policies, and institutions. Thus racism is presented as the axis upon which turn all relations between white people and people of color. "White behavior" is the operationalization of racist beliefs, and "black behavior" is a reaction to it. The entire society must be deemed racist, white supremacist, or institutionally racist.

Even if racist beliefs are not voiced by "white people," institutional racial discrimination and power imbalances may be cited to prove their existence. Thus the black experience may be regarded as an effect of "institutional racism," which is a racism that does not require the expression of, or consciousness of having, racist beliefs. In *Black Power*, Stokely Carmichael and Charles Hamilton utilize elements of Talcott Parsons' institutionalist perspective to present racism as an impersonal, bureaucratic, and institutional force.[53] They argue that the individual prejudices and motives of whites are not relevant to the analysis of the black experience. What matters is whether the effects of white actions hurt blacks. This institutionalist conception of racism seals the fate of all whites as racists, whether they know or admit to it. Thus no refutation of racism's existence and operation is possible. Any action by a "white" can be designated racist. But the same may be said of the actions of a "black," unless it is assumed that "blacks" are intrinsically morally superior to "whites." And if whites *are* a morally inferior race, surely they should be separated or exterminated, as is voiced in certain quarters. However, is this not what was once said, and is still being said, of "blacks" in other quarters? Thus antiracism is often deemed an inverted form of racism, whose multiplicity of meanings again comes to the fore.

The term *racism* functions as description, explanation, and accusation, but its most frequent usage is as a form of denunciation of "white people," their statements, beliefs, and actions. Inevitably, it is similarly applied to "black people," history, and all social relations. As indicated, this usage reflects the adoption of a racial theory of social relations, a theory involving the classification of persons according to their anatomical attributes and making moral judgments on their natures: Negroes are biologically inferior, and Caucasians are morally flawed. It is the adoption of this theory that leads to the search for the nature of races. A focus on racial characteristics constitute its causal or explanatory component. Usage of the concept of racism to describe or explain social phenomena merely indicates location with the racial paradigm.

In an indirect criticism of moral denunciations of white people, Gary Howard, executive director of REACH, a national curriculum and staff development program focusing on multicultural education, bemoans the absence of positive images for his fellow whites: "it sometimes becomes difficult for us as white people to feel good about our own history. Where do we turn to find positive images for ourselves and our children?"[54] Howard protests against his fellow whites adopting the cultures of the oppressed races, and recommends that they search for their own cultural roots in Europe. White Americans should cease their adoption of minority cultural expressions, cease being "wannabees." Minority cultures are useful, however. As Howard continues: "But with a little help from our friends in other cultures even white folks can learn to dance again, as we once did among the great stone circles of ancient Europe."[55] Unlike persons of color, white people cannot dance. In REACH's staff development programs, these would be the sort of statements used in multicultural education workshops to combat stereotyping and racism.

References to human beings as white people and black people are part of an intellectual tradition of anatomical reductionism and differentiation; they belong to the blunders of a bygone biology. But the early biologists need not be described as whites or Europeans. They were but human beings who unreasonably assumed that *their* anatomical attributes represent generic human attributes that are so distinct as to make them a separate race; they went on to classify other persons as nonwhites—Negroes, colored people, red people, yellow people, and brown people. Some of these classifiers further proclaimed that "nonwhites" are biologically inferior by divine design. Certain entrepreneurs and legislators utilized these arguments in justification of their commercial and political activities; they may even have believed in them. And so policies of conquest, enslavement, exclusion as well as socioeconomic and political relegation were justified in racial terms. Studies of black people, their history, experiences, and culture, blossom out of this tradition of identifying persons as races. Legislative edicts on "race relations" and antiracism further extend the racial theory of social relations. The schools' adoption of antiracist proposals constitutes a yet further incorporation and consolidation of racial classification in educational institutions.

In emphasizing the racial-cultural specificity of students and teachers, antiracist education inexorably drifts toward the proposal that black students need schools, curricula, teaching methods, and texts produced by members of their own race. Molefi Asante's remarks come close to nostalgia for the good old days of segregated schools: "Of course segregation was legally and morally wrong, but something was given to black children in those schools that was just as important in some senses as the new books, better educated teachers, and improved buildings of this era. The children were centered in cultural ways that made learning interesting and intimate."[56] White teachers cannot "center" black students; they have not had the black experience, and, of course, are unacquainted with black culture. By implication, "black teachers" cannot teach "white students." Judging by the tenor of the opposition to multiculturalism, some educators are outraged at these suggestions.[57] For, despite being qualified to attend to the development of logical reasoning competencies, teachers are being evaluated according to a criterion that has no logical foundation. As antiracist education takes hold, the issue of the "race" of students and teachers must polarize educators. It is a polarization that has no potential for resolution, for white teachers may be categorized as essentially racist, and black teachers will be accused of "playing the race card." To avoid this schism, should teachers not simply refuse to refer to themselves or their students as white or of color?

Disputes among "races" necessarily end in gridlock, if not violence, for the endorsement of racial classification necessarily affects the disputants, and racial motives are imputed to them. This imputation can reach the level of suspicion of a conspiracy to destroy "my race." More to the point, racial classifications are without logical justification. They were born in a context of a search for a natural basis for certain policies and are maintained by official fiat, educational practices, and racial liberationist projects. Hence discussions of racial experiences and relations are trapped in vicious circles of denunciation and rejection. By implication, unless social scientists and educational authorities pay more attention to the cultivation of critical thinking, logical reasoning, and rational communication, so-called blacks and whites will be eternally quarreling about each other's racism and intelligence. The persistence of particular, racially classified social problems and periodic spates of violence will be taken as proof of either white racism or black biological or cultural deficiency. The fact that centuries of racial name-calling, denunciation, and violence have not led to an abandonment of racial classification indicates a peculiar commitment to maintaining the illogical. Educated within schools that marginalize instruction in sound reasoning, political representatives, business leaders, journalists, educators, and the lay public are unable to recognize the absurdity of racially classifying persons.

The antiracist strand of multiculturalism is inconsistent with its own claim that whites are racist, for it follows that there should be no appeals to white teachers and administrators, unless it is assumed that some whites escape their racist nature and culture. If so, some blacks are not victims of racism, and surely can do without an antiracist curriculum. The antiracist mission—the removal of racism from the curriculum and society—is misplaced, for the racism being challenged is a misnomer, "the ghost in the machine" of racial classification. The insoluble nature of disputes over what is or is not racism testifies to the moral-political purpose of its usage. Racism is an analytically useless concept, unless it is defined as racial classification of persons. Hence it is not a question whether white people are racist or not. What must first be established is that it is justifiable to refer to persons as "white people" and "people of color." It is not that human beings have not been and are not being maimed by specific decisions in legislatures and boardrooms. The issue is whether racial explanations and descriptions of these decisions are accurate or relevant to remedial purposes.

A curriculum that promotes racial distinctions cannot eliminate stereotyping and discrimination, for it would consolidate racial identities, racial generalizations, and the in-group out-group distinctions that underlie discrimination. Even after exposure to positive features of "cultures of color," "white" students would point to the superior features of white culture in order to maintain *their* self-esteem. In any case, if "nonwhites" are despised, so, too, their cultures. Despite being informed about the richness and glories of ancient black civilizations and individual "black" intellectual excellence, students who are unable to think critically could still regard blacks as biologically and culturally inferior. Nevertheless, more generally, persons should not be officially characterized as "white students" and "students of color," if a priori categorizations of others and nepotism at a variety of levels are to be avoided. People who are convinced that they are "white" will be largely indifferent toward the suffering of "persons of color." These persons will, in turn, engage in antiracist protests that castigate whites and demonize their identity. As "white" people become fearful and angry, they intensify their exclusion of "persons of color." Proponents of antiracist education follow up with more demands for antiracist education, and so on, and so on. An alternative to antiracist education, which is developed in chapter four, may be mentioned. Let the curriculum prioritize the development of students' analytical, reasoning, and empathic abilities. With these abilities, students would could conclude that the incoherence of the idea of white and black people makes nonsense of the notion of racial-cultural superiority; they may even arrive at another conclusion—probably dear to the heart of most teachers and parents—that corporate and political leaders should reconstruct a whole of range of economic and social policies on prenatal care, child care, Headstart, school funding, welfare, health care, employment, teacher preparation, and access to college within an overarching goal of creating "a learning society."

Social Theories Underlying the Multicultural Agenda: Racial Theory

Economist John Maynard Keynes is immortalized more for his interventionist recommendations for economic policy than his contribution to philosophy. However, some of his remarks in *The General Theory of Employment Interest and Money* testify to an acute awareness of the relationship between ideas and action:

the ideas of economists and political philosophers, both when they are right and when they are wrong, are more powerful than is commonly understood. Indeed the world is ruled by little else. Practical men, who believe themselves to be quite exempt from any intellectual influences, are usually the slaves of some defunct economist.[58]

Exception may be taken to the proposition that ideas rule the world, for then it may be asked: what rules ideas, and what is their relationship to economic interests? These are Karl Marx's questions. He would add further that the ruling ideas are the ideas of the ruling class. Keynes' second proposition, that particular philosophical theories or arguments underlie the most "practical" recommendations, must stand, even if only on the strength of philosophy's composition—metaphysics, epistemology, ethics, and logic—and determinate links with social sciences.[59]

Arguments within the advocacy of multiculturalism are particularly expressive of ethical and epistemological issues—addressing "oppression" and the nature of knowledge, respectively. Other disciplinary legacies in multiculturalism are the constructs of early biological sciences, manifest in unqualified usages of anatomical classifications, and a Herderian perspective in anthropology that observes single cultures and equates them with biologically or otherwise-identified groups. Thus culture and knowledge are placed in a variety of separate contain-ers—white, female, black, gay, and so on. Apart from these connections with classical anthropology, which is analyzed below, there are distinct analytical affinities between multiculturalism and what may be called postcontemporary sociological theories—gender, racial, ethnic and class constructions of social relations. Although analytically related to them, these theories are beginning to displace classical (the writings of Spencer, Comte, Marx, Durkheim, and Weber) and contemporary (functionalist, symbolic interactionist, and conflict perspec-tives) sociologies, in the wake of the social and political ferment of the 1960s and 1990s. A reflection of the growing interest in gender, race, ethnicity, and class is that in 1994 more than three hundred members of the American Socio-logical Association supported a proposal for the establishment of a new section entitled "Race, Gender, and Class." The authors of the proposal argue that these modalities underlie many social problems in contemporary society, that they are interconnected, and that their study is essential if one is to do "good sociology": "If we don't understand what is happening today, we will again be out of touch with the real world, which is too bad for a sociologist!"[60] Post-1960's, libera-tionist gender, racial, ethnic, and class perspectives in social studies, often inac-curately designated "liberal," have coalesced under the rubric of multicultural-ism. Their practitioners necessarily embrace the postmodernist emphasis on differences and localization of knowledge.

Multiculturalism represents solutions for problems of racial oppression and inequality. However, it is important to recognize that these problems are discov-ered only through usage of racial classification. It is possible to observe social problems such as poverty, deviance, violence, and unemployment, and concep-tualize them as class or human problems. The discovery of racial oppression is theory-specific, and it is expressed forcefully in Pan-Africanist writings.[61] Thus Pan-Africanism extends a racial theory of social relations that comprises ana-tomical and cultural descriptions of persons and social phenomena, explanations of racial relations, and remedies for similarly described problems. This theory shares its type of classificatory criteria with gender and ethnic theories, and this facilitates the combination of concerns with gender, cultural, and racial oppres-sion under the rubric of multiculturalism.

Figure 2.1 below presents analytical features of gender, racial, ethnic, and class theories. The first column depicts general analytical components of social theories: classificatory criteria, causation, identification of victims, proof struc-tures, and prescriptions for problems identified. Subsequent columns disclose the specific analytic components of gender, racial, ethnic, and class theories. These theories embody explanatory concepts such as racism, sexism, ethnocentrism, and capitalism. However, because the persons assigned to groups are also in-volved in other relations, explanations of their experiences can make reference to cultural, psychological, and political variables. As a result, explanations, sub-explanations, and combinations of explanations of gender and racial experiences proliferate—class, race-class, race-gender-class, gender-class, and so on.

Figure 2.1
Social Theories (GREC)

	GENDER	RACIAL	ETHNIC	CLASS
Criteria of classification	Anatomical	Anatomical	Cultural	Economic
Explanation	Sexism	Racism	Ethnocentrism	Capitalism
Object of victimization	Women	Non-whites	Non-WASPS	Working class
Stratification	Male power	White power	WASP domination	Ruling class
Proof structure	Reality	Reality	Reality	Reality
Solutions within the racial theory*	Legal reforms	Legal reforms	Pluralism	Socialism

*Genocide, repatriation, reparations, segregation, separatism, affirmative action and anti-discrimination laws, black power, black capitalism, racial awareness training, miscegenation, multiculturalism, acculturation, assimilation.

Explanations of race relations and solutions for racial problems are developed in two broad variants of the racial theory—naturalist and liberationist—and liberal, Marxist, conservative, cultural nationalist, fundamentalist, separatist, social Darwinist, sociobiological, Eugenicist, and white supremacist perspectives. In the naturalist variant, it is argued that social inequalities reflect superior/inferior biological attributes, while the liberationist variant explains inequalities in terms of specific mind-sets—prejudice, cultural biases, and racism—which are often analytically linked with class, power, and capitalism.[62] The thesis that there are biologically based disparities in group aptitudes is central to the naturalist variant of the racial theory. Nature is given a causal status, and natural attributes, for example, "genes," and "intelligence" are held responsible for behavior and social conditions. As sociologist John Macionis notes:

This naturalist view of human behavior was also adapted to explain how entire societies differed from one another. Centuries of world exploration and empire building brought Western Europeans into contact with people whose customs, manners, and mores differed markedly from their own. They readily attributed these differences to biological characteristics rather than to cultural diversity.[63]

Adhering to a conception of nature as a First Cause, some eighteenth- and nineteenth-century social philosophers presented, first, a biological determination of behavior, and then a correlation among biological attributes and behavior, culture, and civilization. Insofar as some civilizations were perceived as superior to others, biologically defined groups, or races were also regarded as superior and inferior. Once this correlation was established, and it dominated much of nineteenth-century writings on history and society, something called "race" became an explanation of global historical developments and individual behavior. The tradition continues in multitudes of studies of race relations, racism, and racial experiences.

The analytical foundation of these studies is a racial classification of persons, but the classification is carried out unreflexively, as if it "mirrors" nature, or the real world. It is this unreflexiveness that underlies what some scholars refer to as an essentialization of racial differences. Essentialization takes place through a practice of racial classification that is justified by the claim that "races" are phenomena existing in "the real world" and therefore, in the words of Diana J. Fuss, "transhistorical, eternal, and immutable essences."[64] What is not generally observed about essentialization is that it derives from a realist theory of knowledge that presents concepts and classifications as a reflection of elements of reality. Thus the terms *blacks* and *whites* are conceived as descriptions of actual persons and therefore not in need of rigorous definitions. This realist epistemology serves not only to avoid conceptual specifications but also to obscure certain social scientific practices. Societies are said to have races and racial problems, not official policies of racial classification whose propagation resonates in popular racial expressions, identities, and policies favoring one's own kind. Thus even those scholars who purport to be pursuing the eradication of racial oppression consolidate the idea of essential racial differences; they thereby continue the early biologists' project of locating races in "the real world," that is, an entity separate from their practices.

In the naturalist tradition, not just biological characteristics, but irrevocably inferior biological characteristics, are cited to explain past as well as contemporary social relations. A general theory of historical development and social change was developed in which a white race emerged as superior in every possible way. Many modern scholars designate these naturalist writings as "racist," but this moral-political description is not a substitute for an analysis of the intellectual conditions that led to the construction of racial differences and the usage of "race" to explain the course of human history. Cedric Robinson's remarks capture the distinguishing features of the "race sciences" that emerged from naturalist writings:

For more than two hundred years, the objective of the ensemble of race sciences and their subdisciplinary adjutants (for example, comparative politics) was to secure fixed taxonomies, stable racial-historical and gender identities which, in turn, could be composed into a natural sociology of hierarchy. The primary colors of race—white, black, yellow, red, brown—coordinated with an Aristotelian construction of sex differences, were to be arranged in a descending order of humanity thus justifying social privileges at home and abroad.[65]

But what must also be conceded is that the writings of abolitionists, Pan-Africanists, and racial egalitarians form an opposed, *but still racial*, analysis of history and social relations. Such writings are also part of "race sciences." The racial classification is simply appropriated and then given a specific moral twist: whites are guilty, blacks are innocent victims. As Kwame A. Appiah writes of Pan-Africanism: "The idea of the Negro, the idea of an African race, is an unavoidable element in that discourse, and these racialist notions are grounded in bad biological—and worse ethical—ideas, inherited from the increasingly racialised thought of nineteenth-century Europe and America."[66] W.E.B. Du Bois' "the problem of the twentieth century is the problem of the color line" is an extension of the racial theory, and indeed Appiah discovers a deep-seated ambivalence in Du Bois' writings on racial experiences. For Appiah, the early Pan-Africanists fostered "extrinsic racism."[67] In opposition to the naturalists, however, their project is the liberation of the black race.

Racial liberationist writings proclaim a purpose of freeing the black race from white domination. Strategies for achieving this objective find expression in a gamut of activities: legal protests, the formation of investigatory bodies, lobbying, political party and trade union organization, street demonstrations, moral appeals, and ultimately the 1960's civil rights movement. This movement gave spurt to the Mexican-American civil rights movement and was subsequently joined with proclamations for women's liberation, and Native-American liberation. In this same period a militant genre of multicultural education emerged as one of many projects for achieving equality among racial and ethnic groups. Its advocates' observations of educational marginalization, cultural colonialism, and political domination were subsequently applied to a variety of other "oppressed" groups to form multiculturalism. Both multicultural education and multiculturalism, then, are adjuncts of liberationist variants of gender, racial, and ethnic relations. The various perspectives within these variants cite sexism, racism, ethnocentrism, and combinations of sexism, racism, and capitalism as the cause of socioeconomic deprivation among "women" and "people of color." These explanations can be contrasted with naturalist writings in which it is asserted that black people are genetically and therefore also intellectually inferior to white people, and women to men. This is said to be a natural state of affairs, and hence social inequalities between men and women, as well as black and white people, are unalterable through legislation and social policies. Unequal natural attributes separate the two races and sexes. Naturalist propositions on races can be found especially in a stream of late nineteenth-century treatises on biology and history, in pamphlets from the Ku Klux Klan and the White Aryan Resistance League, and in books by contemporary scholars such as Arthur Jensen, Michael Levin, Richard J. Herrnstein, and Charles Murray.[68]

In *The Bell Curve,* Herrnstein and Murray, who advocate a "conservative multiculturalism" in recognition of distinct racial cultures and ethnic group inequalities, write: "It is possible to look forward to a world in which the glorious hodgepodge of inequalities of ethnic groups—genetic and environmental, permanent and temporary—can be not only accepted but celebrated."[69] Herrnstein and Murray present a combination of eugenicist and sociobiological arguments to form their main thesis that, according to most studies of racial intelligences, there is a clear black-white difference in IQ. They then pose the question: Is the difference genetically or environmentally based, or do both contribute? In all probability, they respond, genes do play some role, but in regard to the combination of genes and environment, the authors remain "resolutely agnostic."

Racial classification is obviously central to the discovery of racial IQs, but there are objective and subjective, or self-referential, modes of racial classification. In the former, races are identified by an observer on the basis of the presence of certain anatomical attributes. Herrnstein and Murray confess to an avoidance of this mode:

We frequently use the word *ethnic* rather than *race,* because race is such a difficult concept to employ in the American context. What does it mean to be "black" in America, in racial terms, when the word black (or African-American) can be used for people whose ancestry is more European than African? How are we to classify a person whose parents hail from Panama but whose ancestry is predominantly African? Is he a Latino? A black? The rule we follow here is to classify people according to the way they classify themselves. The studies of "blacks" or "Latinos" or "Asians" who live in America generally denote people who *say* they are black, Latino, or Asian—no more, no less.[70]

This passage both forms and, because of its fallacies, destroys the foundation of the entire edifice of the construction of black-white differences in IQ. First, it is illegitimate to base IQ studies, that purport to be identifying hereditary patterns, on how respondents classify themselves, for, objectively, they may belong to different "races" from the ones they claim. Second, Herrnstein and Murray's choice of the self-referential mode is inconsistent with their conclusion on genetically determined IQs. The racial classification must be genetic, if the conclusion—a genetically based IQ difference—is to hold.

Third, if "race is such a difficult concept to employ in the American context," why are the experiences and intelligences of different races—black people and white people—being studied? To suggest, as the authors do in the above passage, that racial classification is unreliable, and then go on to measure and compare the intelligence of races indicates an inability to recognize self-contradiction. This trait is particularly prevalent among persons with limited cognitive capacities. Fourth, to demonstrate their methodological consistency Herrnstein and Murray must present questionnaires indicating that all the research subjects were specifically asked to classify themselves racially, and the responses to that request. Then the whole enterprise would be seen to be absurd, given the researchers' admission that "race is a difficult concept to use in the American context." Finally, Herrnstein and Murray's choice to "use the word ethnic rather than race" is a case of jumping out of the frying pan into the fire. The allocation of persons to an ethnic group is as controversial as allocation to a racial group, and Herrnstein and Murray should at least comment on the implications of their choice.[71] They choose to use the term *ethnic* rather than *race*, but offer conclusions on racial groups and racial intelligences; they compound this analytical indiscretion by citing IQ test results that identify and select black and white people not according to how these people designate themselves but observationally, or objectively—that is, according to skin color, facial form, and hair type.

The comparative intelligence of objectively identified white and black people was tested, and it was concluded that black people are genetically inferior. The flaw in this conclusion, however, is that unless the selection of persons was made according to genetic criteria, as in the alleged basis of intelligence, the disparity in intelligence cannot be attributed to genes. *The respondents must be genetically selected.* However, in the construction of racial intelligences, the children were not selected according to their genes. They were selected and tested because they looked black and white to the researchers. Genetically, the black children may have been "white," and the white children "black." But how many white or black genes make a person white or black? An absurd one-drop rule is implicit in *The Bell Curve's* research. But the analysis fails to identify black people and white people; it does not demonstrate the existence of racial intelligence. In other words, the book contains no evidence of "black-white difference in IQ," although there may be, in the authors' words, "human variation in intelligence." *The Bell Curve* dissolves the idea of racial or ethnic intelligence.

An identification of black and white intelligences is as invalid as an opposition between genes and the environment, nature and nurture. Indeed, as the authors of *The Bell Curve* claim: "The debate about whether and how much genes and environment have to do with ethnic differences remains unresolved."[72] But the reason for the unresolved nature of the debate is that the quantification of influences, unlike performances on tests, is stymied by the interactive relationship between genes and the environment. Measuring their relative impact on the distribution of cognitive capacities remains the bane of psychometric studies. The environment is so nuanced that it is not identical for any two persons, and an its relationship with a genetic constitution is interactive. That is to say, the environment circumscribes the way genes express themselves, and genes set limits on the impact of environmental conditions.

Genes do not operate independently of the environment. How, then, can their influence be measured? Herrnstein and Murray's claim that cognitive ability is about forty to eighty percent genetically determined must be speculative. And indeed they (must) disclaim this calculation: "As of 1994, then, we can say nothing for certain about the relative roles that genetics and environments play in the formation of the black-white difference in IQ."[73] Is this a statement for certain? Underlying Herrnstein and Murray's claims and disclaimers is a flawed naturalist tradition, which the authors designate as "classicist." Its central postulate is that there is a measurable and unalterable core of human cognitive ability that is differentially distributed among individuals and groups. Herrnstein and Murray argue that this general factor holds the key to the understanding of unequal achievements among human beings. However, in analyzing and comparing the performances of human beings, the influence of the environment must also be considered. It is here that comparisons of performances on IQ tests enter treacherous territory, for, given the existence of genetic differences, no environment is the same for any two human beings. This means that there can be no generalized measurement of environmental influence or measurement of general intelligence.

By further implication, it is not that "nothing for certain" can be said of "the relative roles that genetics and environments play in the formation of the black-white difference in IQ." Rather, it can be said that the difference in performance on IQ tests is environmental-genetic and so does not reflect the intelligence of races, which are biological entities (descriptions). Some individuals repeatedly score less than others on certain tests. These individuals do not represent a race. Each individual's performance reflects an innate ability that creates a unique environment that, in turn, impacts that ability's evolution and expression. Thus intelligence is conceived by Howard Gardner as a "bio-psychological potential" with multiple variations, and for psychologist Robert Sternberg, it is a set of dynamic and interrelated components.[74] Intelligence, then, is multidimensional and developmental. By contrast, the naturalistic conception of intelligence used in *The Bell Curve* presents it as singular, unalterable, and static in order to fit the idea of race.

The authors trace a general intelligence factor to natural endowments, thereby analytically isolating intelligence from the environment. However, because intelligence is only observable as it unfolds in environments, its identification in nature and separation from nurture are unwarranted. Indeed, the entire nature-nurture controversy is based on a false distinction, since the natural basis of intelligence is itself a product of nurturing. Thus it is significant that the concept of nature remains unspecified in *The Bell Curve*. It is this omission that underlies the discovery of its numerous fallacies.[75] Its "conservative multiculturalism" simply invokes nature to construct racial genes that determine social destinies. These racial genes, however, remain as elusive as environmentally unaffected intelligences.

While *The Bell Curve's* "conservative multiculturalism" operates with unclearly specified naturally endowed races and ethnic groups, and thereby justifies "racial" inequalities, advocates of "insurgent multiculturalism" and "critical multiculturalism" decry such inequalities and protest against the essentializing of racial-ethnic identities in Left-liberal writings.[76] However, they themselves essentialize gender, racial, and ethnic identities, for the struggles of "people of color" and "women" are conceived as representations of the real, not strategies developed in theoretical structure. Not considered is the possibility that the essentializing of racial and gender identities and differences lies in a realist analysis in which classifications are conceived as referents of "reality" and theories an attempt to reflect reality. This "classical" thought-reality dichotomy lies at the center of much of social studies.[77] In this context, critical multiculturalism remains an extension of certain, unexamined theses in anthropology, sociology, and philosophy.

NOTES

1.   Sohan Modgil, Gajendra K. Verma, Danka Mallick, and Celia Modgil (eds.), *Multicultural Education: The Interminable Debate* (London: Falmer Press, 1986), p. 5.

2.   Patricia L. Francis, "A Review of the Multicultural Education Literature," *Race, Gender and Class* 2, no. 2 (Winter 1995), p. 51.

3.   Joan S. Lester, "Stages in the Diversity Process," *Black Issues in Higher Education* 10, no. 4 (January 27, 1994), pp. 64-65.

4.   For representative works, see Grant and Sleeter, *Turning on Learning*; James A. Banks, "Multicultural Education: Development, Dimensions, and Challenges," *Phi Delta Kappan* 75, no. 1 (September 1993), pp. 22-28; Sonia Nieto, *Affirming Diversity*; Giroux, *Theory*, and *Border*; David Theo Goldberg (ed.), *Multiculturalism: A Critical Reader* (Oxford: Blackwell, 1994); Amy Gutmann (ed.), *Multiculturalism: Examining the Politics of Recognition* (Princeton, N.J.: Princeton University Press, 1994); Barry Kanpol and Peter McLaren (eds.), *Critical Multiculturalism: Uncommon Voices in a Common Struggle* (Westport, Conn.: Bergin and Garvey, 1995).

5.   Brian M. Bullivant regards multiculturalism and multicultural education as "two approaches to cultural pluralism." "Culture: Its Nature and Meaning for Educators," in James Banks and Cherry A. McGee Banks (eds.), *Multicultural Education: Issues and Perspectives* (Boston: Allyn and Bacon, 1989), p. 27. Some authors do not make such a distinction, however. For example, Diane Ravitch uses these terms interchangeably in "Diversity and Democracy"; "Multiculturalism: An Exchange," *The American Scholar* 60 (Spring 1991), pp. 272-276; and "Multiculturalism: E Pluribus Plures." Another reason for maintaining a distinction is that, among others, Barry Kanpol, Henry Giroux, and Peter McLaren declare themselves to be advocates of multiculturalism, not multicultural education. Indeed, these authors rarely, if ever, use the latter term.

6.   See James A. Banks, "Multiethnic Education and the Quest for Equality," *Phi Delta Kappan* 64, no. 2 (1983), pp. 582-585; Sleeter (ed.), *Empowerment through Multicultural Education*; Sleeter and Grant, *Making Choices for Multicultural Education*.

7.   See Kanpol and McLaren (eds.), *Critical*; Goldberg (ed.), *Multiculturalism*.

8.   See Goldberg (ed.), *Multiculturalism*; Kanpol and McLaren (eds.), *Critical*.

9.   See Giroux, *Theory*; Peter McLaren, "White Terror and Oppositional Agency: Toward a Critical Multiculturalism," in Goldberg (ed.), *Multiculturalism*, pp. 45-74.

10.   McLaren, "White Terror," p. 63.

11.   See Grant, "So You Want to Infuse Multicultural Education into Your Discipline?"

12.   Ibid., p. 22.

13.   Ibid.

14.   James A. Banks, "Multicultural Education: Characteristics and Goals," in Banks and Banks (eds.), *Multicultural Education*, p. 3.

15.   See James A. Banks, Multiethnic Education: *Theory and Practice* (Boston: Allyn and Bacon, 1988), pp. 178-179. Banks sees many goals for multicultural education: egalitarian social change, prejudice reduction, content integration, equity pedagogy, greater epistemological sophistication in natural and social science courses, and general student empowerment. Banks, "Multiethnic Education and the Quest for Equality," pp. 582-585; and "Multicultural Education: Development, Dimensions, and Challenges."

16.   McLaren writes: "Identity based on 'sameness' and identity based on 'difference' are forms of essentialist logic." McLaren, "White Terror," p. 53. What does this imply for McLaren's self-confessed "white" identity? It should be noted, however, that the analyti-

cal status of essentialism is not made clear. Indeed, McLaren nowhere in his text defines essentialism or identifies its flaws. Essentialism is simply denounced, by innuendo.

17.   See Patricia Hill Collins, "Toward a New Vision: Race, Class, and Gender as Categories of Analysis and Connection," *Race, Gender and Class* 1, no. 1 (Fall 1993), pp. 25-46; Margaret Andersen and Patricia Hill Collins (eds.), *Race, Class and Gender: An Anthology* (Belmont, Calif.: Wadsworth, 1995); Jean Belkhir, Suzanne Griffith, Christine E. Sleeter, and Carl Alsup, "Race, Sex, Class and Multicultural Education: Women's Angle of Vision," *Race, Gender and Class* 1, no. 2 (Spring 1994), pp. 7-34; Jean Belkhir, "Multicultural Education: Race, Gender, and Class. Rethinking the Introductory Textbook in the Academic Disciplines," *Race, Gender and Class* 2, no. 2 (Winter 1995), pp. 11-38.

18.   See Banks and Banks (eds.), *Multicultural Education*; James A. Standifer, "The Multicultural, Nonsexist Principle: Why We Can't Afford to Ignore It," *Journal of Negro Education* 56, no. 4 (1987); pp. 471-474; Lois Weis and Michelle Fine (eds.), *Beyond Silenced Voices: Class, Race, and Gender in United States Schools* (Albany, N.Y.: State University of New York Press, 1993).

19.   See Gloria Steinem, *Moving beyond Words* (New York: Simon and Schuster, 1994); Marilyn French, *The War against Women* (New York: Summit Books, 1992); Susan Faludi, *Backlash: The Undeclared War against Women* (New York: Crown Books, 1991); Andrea Dworkin, *Woman Hating* (New York: E.P. Dutton, 1974); *Letters from a War Zone* (New York: Lawrence Hill, 1993); Daphne Spain, *Gendered Spaces: Sex Discrimination Against Women* (Chapel Hill: N.C.: University of North Carolina Press, 1992).

20.   Rosemarie Tong, *Feminist Thought: A Comprehensive Introduction* (Boulder, Colo.: Westview Press, 1989), p. 3.

21.   See Paula S. Rothenberg (ed.), *Racism and Sexism: An Integrated Study* (New York: St. Martin's Press, 1988), Part 1.

22.   Kazem Alamdari, "The Beijing Conference: a Testimony for Women's Achievements and Reshuffling of Global Alliances," *California Sociologist* 17-18 (1994/1995), p. 84. For extensions of the naturalist perspective on women's experiences, see Phyllis Schlafly, *The Power of the Positive Woman* (New York: Arlington House, 1977); George Gilder, *Men and Marriage* (Gretna, L.A.: Pelican 1986); Arianna Stassinopoulos, *The Female Woman* (New York: Random House, 1973).

23.   See Andrea Dworkin, *Right Wing Women* (New York: Perigee Books, 1983); Rebecca Klatch, *Women of the New Right* (Philadelphia: Temple University Press, 1987); Pamela J. Conover and Virginia Gray, *Feminism and the New Right: Conflict over the American Family* (New York: Praeger, 1983).

24.   See Jessie Bernard, *The Female World* (New York: The Free Press, 1981).

25.   See Sandra Lipsitz Bem, *The Lenses of Gender: Transforming the Debate on Sexual Inequality* (New Haven, Conn.: Yale University Press, 1993).

26.   Cynthia Fuchs Epstein, *Deceptive Distinctions: Sex, Gender, and the Social Order* (London: Yale University Press, 1988), p. 11.

27.   See Richard Rorty, *Philosophy and the Mirror of Nature* (Princeton, N.J.: Princeton University Press, 1979).

28.   Chris Weedon, *Feminist Practice and Poststructuralist Theory* (Oxford: Basil Blackwell, 1987), p. 127. See also Claire M. Renzetti and Daniel J. Curran, *Women, Men and Society* (Boston: Allyn and Bacon, 1992), Chapters 1, 2 and 3; Andrea Dworkin, *Our Blood: Prophecies and Discourses on Sexual Politics* (New York: Harper and Row, 1976), Chapter 9.

29.   See Tong, *Feminist;* Maggie Humm (ed.), *Modern Feminisms: Political, Liter-ary, Cultural* (New York: Columbia University Press, 1992).

30.   See Shulamith Firestone, *The Dialectic of Sex: The Case for Feminist Revolution* (New York: Bantam Books, 1970), Chapter 1.

31.   See Georg Simmel, *Conflict and the Web of Group Affiliations* (New York: The Free Press, 1955).

32.   Randall Collins, *Theoretical Sociology* (New York: Harcourt Brace Jovanovich, 1988), p. 119.

33.   For elaborations of the concept of patriarchy, see de Beauvoir, *The Second Sex;* Millet, *Sexual Politics;* Zillah Eisenstein, "Some Notes on the Relations of Capitalist Patriarchy," in Zillah Eisenstein (ed.), *Capitalist Patriarchy and the Case for Socialist Feminism* (New York: Monthly Review Press, 1979), pp. 41-55; Juliet Mitchell, *Women: The Longest Revolution* (New York: Pantheon Books, 1984); Mary Daly, *Gyn/Ecology: The Metaethics of Radical Feminism* (Boston: Beacon Press, 1978). For "empirical" evidence against the thesis of a patriarchal social order, see Warren Farrell, *The Myth of Male Power* (New York: Simon and Schuster, 1993). For criticisms of "victim femi-nism," see Camille Paglia, *Vamps and Tramps: New Essays* (New York: Vintage Books, 1994).

34.   See Terry R. Kandal, *The Woman Question in Classical Sociological Theory* (Miami: Florida International University Press, 1988).

35.   See Zbigniew Brzezinski et al. (eds.), *The Relevance of Liberalism* (Boulder, Colo.: Westview Press, 1977); Lyman Tower Sargent, *Contemporary Political Ideolo-gies: A Comparative Analysis,* 7th ed. (Chicago: The Dorsey Press, 1987).

36.   See Franz Boas, *The Mind of Primitive Man* (New York: Macmillan, 1966); and *Race, Language and Culture.*

37.   See Herskovits, *Franz Boas;* Stocking Jr. (ed.), *The Shaping.*

38.   See Robert E. Park, *Race and Culture* (New York: The Free Press, 1950); E. Franklin Frazier, *Race and Culture Contacts in the Modern World* (New York: Alfred Knopf, 1957); Thomas Sowell, *Race and Culture: A World View* (New York: Basic Books, 1994); Michael Omi and Howard Winant, *Racial Formation in the United States: From the 1960s to the 1990s,* 2nd. ed. (New York: Routledge and Kegan Paul, 1994).

39.   Shirley Chisholm, "Foreword," in D.G. Bromley and C.F. Longino Jr. (eds.), *White Racism and Black Americans* (Mass.: Schenkman Publications Co., 1972), p. 18.

40.   Otto Kerner, *Report of the National Advisory Commission on Civil Disorders* (New York: E.P. Dutton & Co., 1968), pp. 2 and 10.

41.   See William J. Wilson, *The Declining Significance of Race: Blacks and Chang-ing American Institutions* (Chicago: University of Chicago Press, 1978); Bruno Leone (ed.), *Racism: Opposing Viewpoints,* rev. ed. (San Diego, Calif.: Greenhaven Press, 1986); Glenn C. Loury, *One by One from the Inside Out: Essays and Reviews on Race and Responsibility in America* (New York: The Free Press, 1995); Keyes, *Masters.*

42.   See Dinesh D'Souza, *The End of Racism* (New York: Simon and Schuster, 1995). D'Souza claims that the charge of racism is overdone. He offers anecdotal evi-dence that blacks, too, are racist, and presents "a cultural deficit model" to account for the variety of pathologies that plague "blacks."

43.   Kendall, *Diversity in the Classroom,* p. 1. See also Nieto, *Affirming,* Chapter 3; Pine and Hilliard, "Rx for Racism"; Christine E. Sleeter, "White Racism," in Annual Editions, *Multicultural Education 95/96* (Guilford, Conn.: Dushkin, 1995), pp. 70-73.

44.   Pine and Hilliard, "Rx for Racism," p. 595. This conception of racism is not an isolated one. In *Dictatorship of Virtue,* Richard Bernstein notes that the Milwaukee pub-lic school system distributed a brochure in which racism is defined as follows: "Racism is

a mental illness of some groups of persons/institutions induced by greed and fear that systematically oppresses another group of people by suppressing their history/truth, their culture, their identity, and their speech and by controlling their socialization, their education, and their wealth, and by means of unjust laws enforces segregation/apartheid thereby giving credence to the notion of genetic superiority of oppressors." *Dictatorship,* p. 193.

45.   Elazar Barkan, *The Retreat of Scientific Racism: Changing Concepts of Race in Britain and the United States between the World Wars* (Cambridge: Cambridge University Press, 1992), p. 3.

46.   Goldberg, *Racist Culture,* p. 3. See also Kenneth Leech, "'Diverse Reports' and the Meaning of 'Racism,'" *Race and Class* 28, no. 2 (Autumn 1989), pp. 82-88.

47.   Roxanne Doty, "The Bounds of 'Race,' in International Relations," *Millennium* 22, no. 3 (Winter 1993), pp. 448-449.

48.   Terrence Epperson, "The Politics of Empiricism and the Construction of Race as an Analytical Category," *Paper Presented at the 116th Annual Spring Meeting of the American Ethnological Society,* Santa Monica, California, April 14-16, 1994.

49.   Shelby Steele charges that discussions of race relations are characterized by imputations and denial of racial guilt in struggles for power: *The Content of Our Character: A New Vision of Race in America* (New York: St. Martin's Press, 1990).

50.   See Carmichael and Hamilton, *Black Power;* Raymond Franklin and Solomon Resnick, *The Political Economy of Racism* (New York: Holt, Rinehart and Winston, 1973). Robert Blauner writes of racism as "an historical and social project aimed at reducing or diminishing the humanity . . . of the racially oppressed." *Racial Oppression in America* (New York: Harper and Row, 1972), p. 84. Richard Bernstein cites the University of Cincinnati's booklet *Combatting Racism on Campus: A Resource Book and Model for the 1990s*: "Racism is the power individuals and groups of one race use to systematically oppress those of another race. The power bases through which this oppression takes place are government, corporations, educational systems, and other institutions such as churches and the judicial system." *Dictatorship,* p. 191.

51.   Philip Perlmutter and Walter E. Williams, "Racism Is No Longer Prevalent," in Leone (ed.), *Racism: Opposing Viewpoints,* p. 149.

52.   See Anne Wortham *The Other Side of Racism: A Philosophical Study of Black Race Consciousness* (Columbus, Ohio: Ohio State University Press, 1977); Kathy Russell, Midge Wilson, and Ronald Hall, *The Color Complex: The Politics of Skin Color among Blacks* (New York: Harcourt Brace Jovanovich, 1992).

53.   Compare Leon H. Mayhew (ed.), *Talcott Parsons on Institutions and Social Evolution: Selected Writings* (Chicago: University of Chicago Press, 1982) and Carmichael and Hamilton, *Black Power.*

54.   Gary Howard, "Whites in Multicultural Education: Rethinking Our Role," *Phi Delta Kappan* 75, no. 1 (September 1993), p. 40.

55.   Ibid., p. 41.

56.   Molefi Asante, "An Afrocentric Curriculum," *Educational Leadership* 49, no. 4 (December 1991-January 1992), p. 29.

57.   See Bernstein, *Dictatorship.*

58.   John M. Keynes, *The General Theory of Employment, Interest and Money* (New York: Harcourt, Brace and World, 1935), p. 383.

59.   For a review of some of the epistemological issues in social studies, see below, Chapter 3.

60.   Jean Belkhir, "Revised Proposal for a New Section: Gender, Race, and Class," *Race, Gender and Class* 2, no. 2 (Winter 1995), p. 7.

61.   See Moses, *Golden Age*; Watkins, "Black Curriculum Orientations"; Frederick Dunn, "The Educational Philosophies of Washington, DuBois, and Houston: Laying the Foundations for Afrocentrism and Multiculturalism," *Journal of Negro Education* 62, no. 1 (1993), pp. 24-34.

62.   For analysis of both variants of the racial theory, see Webster, *The Racialization of America*, Chapter 1.

63.   John J. Macionis, *Society: The Basics* (Englewood Cliffs, N.J.: Prentice-Hall, 1992), p. 54.

64.   Diana J Fuss, "'Essentially Speaking': Luce Irigaray's Language of Essences," in Nancy Fraser and Sandra Lee Bartky (eds.), *Revaluing French Feminism: Critical Essays in Difference, Agency, and Culture* (Bloomington, Ind.: Indiana University Press, 1992), p. 94.

65.   Cedric Robinson, "Ota Benga's Flight through Geronimo's Eyes: Tales of Science and Multiculturalism," in Goldberg (ed.), *Multiculturalism*, p. 390.

66.   Kwame Anthony Appiah, *In My Father's House: Africa in the Philosophy of Culture* (New York: Oxford University Press, 1992), p. 13.

67.   Ibid.

68.   See Jensen, *Genetics and Education;* Michael Levin, "Responses to Race Differences in Crime," *Journal of Social Philosophy* 23, no. 1 (Spring 1992), pp. 5-29; Herrnstein and Murray, *The Bell Curve.*

69.   Charles Murray and Richard Herrnstein, "Race, Genes and I.Q.—An Apologia," *New Republic* (October 31, 1994), p. 37.

70.   Herrnstein and Murray, *The Bell Curve*, p. 271.

71.   See Reminick, *Theory of Ethnicity;* Fred Matthews, "Cultural Pluralism in Context: External History, Philosophic Premises and Theories of Ethnicity in Modern America," *Journal of Ethnic Studies* 12, no. 2 (Summer 1984), pp. 63-79.

72.   Herrnstein and Murray, *The Bell Curve*, p. 270.

73.   Murray and Herrnstein, "Race, Genes and I.Q.," p. 34.

74.   See Robert Sternberg, "Instrumental and Componental Approaches to the Nature and Training of Intelligence," in Susan F. Chipman et al. (eds.), *Thinking and Learning Skills, Vol. 2: Research and Open Questions* (Hillsdale, N.J.: Lawrence Erlbaum Associates, 1985), pp. 215-244; Howard Gardner, *Multiple Intelligences: The Theory in Practice* (New York: Basic Books, 1993).

75.   See Russell Jacoby and Naomi Glauberman (eds.), *The Bell Curve Debate* (New York: Random House, 1995).

76.   See Kanpol and McLaren (eds.), *Critical*; McLaren, "White Terror," pp. 45-74.

77.   For key arguments within various types of realism and pragmatism, see William Outwaithe, *New Philosophies of Social Science: Realism, Hermeneutics, and Critical Theory* (New York: St. Martin's Press, 1988); Ernest R. House, "Realism in Research," *Educational Researcher* 20, no. 6 (1991), pp. 2-9; Peter K. McInerney (ed.), "The Twenty-ninth Oberlin Colloquium in Philosophy," *Philosophical Studies* 61, nos. 1-2 (February 1991); Cleo H. Holmes, "Notes on Pragmatism and Scientific Realism," *Educational Researcher* 21, no. 6 (August-September 1992), pp. 13-17.

3

Multiculturalism: An Assessment of Its Analytical Foundations

He who still, in the manner of the Reformation man, combats and crushes other opinions with defamations and outbursts of rage betrays clearly that he would have burned his opponents if he had lived in another age, and that he would have had recourse to all the methods of the inquisition if he had been an opponent of the Reformation.

> —Friedrich Nietzsche, *Human, All Too Human: A Book for Free Spirits*

As indicated in Chapter 2, multiculturalism is much more complex than a literal reading of the term suggests. As a series of educational proposals, it embodies strategies for attaining prejudice reduction, cultural pluralism, equality of educational opportunity, group empowerment, equality, and liberation from oppression. Multiculturalism, then, is said to represent both opposition to injustice and a prospect for democratic renewal. In substantiation of their arguments for linking education reforms and social change, advocates of multiculturalism present the following criticisms of educational institutions and practices and the social order:

(a) Dead white males, or Eurocentric and patriarchal ideas, dominate the educational institutions. Because schools utilize curricula centered on white male culture and Western civilization, the accomplishments and creations of women and people of color as well as those of past and present third world civilizations are marginalized, falsified, and caricatured.[1]

(b) A specific group of living white males dominates political, economic, and cultural arrangements. This ruling group establishes educational practices that not only perpetuate various patterns of discrimination against others on grounds of race, gender, and cultural differences, but also exclude the experiences and knowledges of the subjugated.[2]

For advocates of insurgent multiculturalism, domination is manifest especially in schools, which are virtual sites for the production of meaning, identities, and culture. Henry Giroux's remark captures both the theme of domination and the socially reconstructive thrust within multiculturalism: "Third, the existing cultural transformation of American society into a multiracial and multicultural society structured in multiple relations of domination demands that we address how schooling can become sites for cultural democracy rather than channeling colonies reproducing new forms of nativism and racism."[3] In Giroux's analysis, schools represent ideological factories that produce the beliefs and policies necessary for the reproduction of domination. Their organizational structure mirrors patterns and practices of sexism, racism, ethnocentrism, classism, and cultural domination. Nevertheless, schools harbor prospects for social transformation. Because knowledge and power are both integrated and unstable, the schools' reproduction of domination and oppression is not permanently secured. While their main function is the legitimation of knowledge and specific political and economic relations, they also activate forms of critique and resistance that could generate democratic social renewal.[4]

Consistent with the vast reach and breadth of its goals, multiculturalism contains a variety of qualifications and tendencies: mainstream, radical, critical, insurgent, conservative, liberal, Left-liberal, resistance, difference, and encyclopedic. Robert Stam and Ella Shohat, who advocate a "radical" multiculturalism, write: "The concept of multiculturalism is, admittedly, open to various interpretations and subject to diverse political force fields; it has become a slippery signifier onto which diverse groups project their hopes and fears."[5] The slippery quality of multiculturalism makes its general refutation susceptible to a counter-criticism of demolishing a strawman. That is to say, the refutation can be accused of ignoring arguments advanced by a particular version of multiculturalism. On the other hand, criticisms of particular arguments can be repudiated by noting that the criticisms address only a specific version of multiculturalism. To avoid such reprisals against this text, this chapter will explicate weaknesses in both the general concept of multiculturalism and its particular expressions.

The writings of Peter McLaren, Barry Kanpol, Henry Giroux—advocates of critical, insurgent, and resistance multiculturalism—and James A. Banks, Carl Grant, Christine Sleeter, and Sonia Nieto are most representative of multiculturalism. However, their contributions both overlap and diverge at significant instances. Certain themes in critical multiculturalism and insurgent multiculturalism are echoed in the works of Banks, Grant, Sleeter, and Nieto: critical pedagogy, teacher empowerment, school reorganization for social transformation, cultures as political formations, and equality, representation, and justice for oppressed groups. On the other hand, in deploying the notion of border cultures, proposing an understanding of the similarities within differences, and advocating a "de-essentializing" of differences by identifying their historical specificity and political vicissitudes, McLaren, Kanpol, and Giroux implicitly contest the approach to differences endorsed by Banks, Grant, Sleeter, Nieto, and others.[6] These divergences are embodied in two broad species of multiculturalism—one that presents different racial and ethnic groups as biological and historical-cultural givens, and an antiessentialist, critical, or resistance multiculturalism that seeks to "problematize" and "rewrite" differences by locating them in specific political practices and historical-cultural contingencies. It will be demonstrated, however, that this attempt at differences deconstruction is subverted by a necessary accentuation of differences in order to liberate "oppressed groups."

Overall, this chapter will demonstrate the following analytical-logical weaknesses in multiculturalism:

(1) simultaneously endorsing and rejecting specific ground rules for intellectual exchanges and standards for argument assessment, and equating moral-political denunciations of arguments with their refutation;

(2) presenting an incomplete analysis of the concept of power, relative to its analytical salience in the advocacy of multiculturalism;

(3) lack of clarity regarding the differences between ethical and factual claims, which is manifest in the presentation of the assertion that women and people of color are victims of oppression as a factual claim;

(4) presenting a conception of culture that dissolves it into an infinite number of microcultures and at the same time as a political formation;

(5) endorsing anatomical (gender and racial) classifications without consideration of arguments refuting such classifications; and

(6) utilizing fragments of postmodernism, without addressing their relativistic implications, ambivalence, and self-contradictions.

Multiculturalism comes of age on a wave of decentering, poststructuralist, deconstructionist, and postmodernist salutations to: cultural heterogeneity, discontinuity, fragmentation, and power-knowledge. Armed with certain postmodernist claims, its advocates argue that because the social world is characterized by differences, relations of domination and cultural diffusion, knowledge is an intrinsically political and culture-specific phenomenon. Thus any attempt to claim a neutral status for knowledge would be guilty of complicity in domination. Multiculturalism, as education reforms that integrated themes of differences, power, oppression, represents an "insurrection of subjugated knowledges."[7]

Multiculturalism and Knowledge

Most studies in the philosophy of social sciences highlight the philosophical moorings of social sciences, indicating their reliance on distinctions between theoretical and empirical, ideology and truth, as well as mutual allegations of positivism, empiricism, realism, idealism, rationalism, and materialism.[8] The often decisive presence of these categories in social studies indicates that social scientists are profoundly indebted to philosophy for their means of evaluating knowledge. Advocates of multiculturalism are no exception; they draw on certain postmodernist criticisms of the totalizing, masternarratives and foundational certitudes of the Enlightenment, metaphysical philosophy, and modernity to challenge contemporary educational practices.[9]

Jean-François Lyotard's *The Post-modern Condition: A Report on Knowledge* is generally considered the seminal work on postmodernism, although, as Kwame Anthony Appiah points out, postmodernism's meanings are as varied as Thomas Kuhn's "paradigm." Hence other scholars could lay claim to postmodernist seminality and instantiation.[10]   Indeed, postmodernism is also generally traced to the works of Nietzsche, Wittgenstein, Foucault, Deleuze, Derrida, and Jameson, which come into their own as embryonic disruptions of metanarrative legitimation. It is Lyotard's conception of postmodernism that is most visible in multiculturalism, whose rejection of "canons" mirrors his definition of postmodernism as "incredulity toward metanarratives." Metanarratives are in disarray, as evidenced in the plurality of artistic and architectural expressions. Postmodernists register objections to the totalizing ethos of metanarratives, their pretensions at universality, and their vitalist claims—(the end of) history, God's will in action, the Spirit's unfolding, an articulation of a clash between the relations of production and productive forces, reality in motion—that suppress differences and thereby facilitate domination, tyranny, and terror. However, the postmodern age of representation is not a negation of modernity, but its apogee, not its antithesis so much as its present and future. Lyotard writes:

I define *postmodern* as incredulity toward metanarratives. This incredulity is undoubtedly a product of progress in the sciences: but that progress in turn presupposes it. . . . The narrative function is losing its functors, its great hero, its great dangers, its great voyages, its great goal. It is being dispersed in clouds of narrative language elements—narrative, but also denotative, prescriptive, descriptive, and so on.[11]

Lyotard's question is, given the death of metanarratives and the presence of epistemological heterogeneity, where is the legitimation of knowledge to be found? Jurgen Habermas' communicative rationality based on a consensus on rational rules is rejected for violating "the heterogeneity of language games." It is these essentially sovereign and incommensurate language games that define the postmodern. Any consensus would have to be arbitrary or authoritarian. A player can only observe specific epistemological practices.[12]

The postmodern condition is one of a legitimation crisis, but it is also a state of creative pluralist ferment, and an "agonistic" language game that prescribes playful linguistic fights in order to revolutionize discourse.[13]   In Lyotard's analysis, the concept of postmodern is denotative, descriptive, and prescriptive. It is descriptive and prescriptive in that presents an alternative to the Enlightenment's teleological conceptions of history and subject.[14] By contrast, the postmodern artist should not seek to mirror the real world, but imagine and invent the undeclared.[15] Postmodern language games must be antirealist, for "the realization of the fantasy to seize reality" bespeaks terror. It must also be antihistoricist, against Orphic mirrors of a predestined reality, such as the Enlightenment's

Reason, or the marches of Hegel's Spirit, Marx's historical materialism, Durkheim's division of labor, and Weber's rationalization.

At the center of Richard Rorty's *Philosophy and the Mirror of Nature*, there is a rejection of philosophy's attempts to grasp reality in thought, that is, its treatment of "reality" as if it is not itself a conceptual element of thought. If this attempt to mirror reality is modernist, modernism precedes the Enlightenment, for it is discernible in the ancient philosophers' questions: What is the nature of the real? What is the nature of human beings? What is the relationship between human beings (subjects) and the real world, that is, objects external to subjects? For these philosophers, the answers to these questions would provide the foundation for the discovery of truth. Descartes' foundation was the self, the ego, which is the only certitude and, therefore, the fitting starting point for the evaluation of all knowledge. But the self—as Hume, Kant, Feuerbach, Marx, Weber, Freud, and others subsequently demonstrated—is a complex substance comprising reason, emotions, unconscious urges, economic interests, values, traditions, and normative influences; and the objectification of "reality" through its separation from language and its integration with "signs" are challenged by many philosophers, from the Greek dialecticians to Edmund Husserl, Ferdinand Saussure, and William Quine.[16] Against Richard Rorty's claim, then, it can be noted that philosophy is not unified in an insistence that it mirror the world. It is a particular epistemological current—realism—that harbors such pretensions, and its analysis requires the dissemination of other epistemological currents throughout educational institutions.

In postmodernist readings of the course of knowledge, a dominant narrative is identified and it is argued that this narrative has collapsed in its efforts at legitimation. This collapse means that all "language games" are relatively equal. Each seeks to legitimate the rules of its own game, to stamp its knowledge with an aura of authority. Knowledge, then, is a subjective, political, and cultural phenomenon. The Enlightenment itself is a set of language games, and its emphasis on reason need not be taken as a universal dictum. Arguing that the idea of objective knowledge is a mythical legacy from the Enlightenment, Tom Bridges writes: "Thus, the immediate consequence of the demise (in our collective contemporary common sense) of Enlightenment universalism is the demand that all discourses and truth claims be culturally identified and located."[17] The myth of objectivity, Bridges argues further, is often a cover for the propagation of the views of the powerful and the marginalization of views that are different.

Advocates of multiculturalism propose abandoning the idea of objective knowledge, and inclusion of knowledge of, or by, groups defined by cultural differences. The flaw in this argument, however, is that it invites arbitrary and authoritarian decisions as to what counts as knowledge of or by women, people of color, gays, youth, and the disabled. Moreover, if anatomy and culture are to be criteria for this inclusion, they can also function as standards for exclusion. Critics of particular arguments can allude to, not their logical quality but an author's gender, racial, or ethnic background. In the end, the only valid knowledge would be that produced by deracialized, degendered, and decultured beings. Differences would have to disappear.

The implications of the rejection of the Enlightenment's universalism do not bode well for processes of argument assessment or for the oppressed groups championed by multiculturalism. While the debate continues about the Enlightenment's responsibility for Jacobin Terror and the nonfulfilment of the egalitarian and democratic promises in the French Revolution, the American Revolution, and modernity, there is virtual consensus that it expresses a leap from faith in God's will and priestly fiats to trust in human reason. As a historian of the Enlightenment, Ernst Cassirer, writes:

> The eighteenth century is imbued with a belief in the unity and immutability of reason. Reason is the same for all thinking subjects, all nations, all epochs, and all cultures. From the changeability of religious creeds, of moral maxims and convictions, of theoretical opinions and judgments, a firm and lasting element can be extracted which is permanent in itself, and which in this identity and permanence expresses the real essence of reason.[18]

Enlightenment thinking is not coldly rational and amoral. It was their trust in human intelligence that led the *philosophes* to conclude that freedom and justice are desirable states and that war is an evil initiated by men bereft of good sense.[19] Voltaire strove to make a necessary connection between logic and ethics: "People who believe in absurdities are in danger of committing atrocities."[20] In other words, unfounded, illogical beliefs are ineluctably expressed in violence, for they stymie verbal conflict resolution, and can be maintained only through nonverbal action.

For the Enlightenment's protagonists, reason is the centrifugal force of human existence as well as the remedy for its ailments. Through the use of reason, with which all are endowed, the human experience can be studied as *human* wills in action, consensual codes of conduct established, and liberty, fraternity, and equality realized.[21] Voltaire took reason's sovereignty in the direction of searing satires against dogma, superstition, and self-contradictions. These are obstacles to progress in that they prematurely terminate intellectual exchanges, and in the ensuing epistemological vacuum, anything goes. Or rather, violence moves into the epistemological emptiness produced by dogmatism, superstition, and self-contradiction. The persecution of witches and heretics, enslavement, the Terror, genocide in the New World, world wars, the Holocaust, Stalin's Gulag, U.S-Soviet surrogate wars in the "third world," and global malnutrition side by side with billion-dollar stockpiles of weaponry—these are testimonies to beliefs in absurd ideas, continuations of a "march of folly," to use Barbara Tuchman's phrase."[22] In this sense, the philosophes' singular failure was in not amplifying the antimony between reason and violence or proposing a universal pacifism. Nevertheless, Voltaire came close. In a letter to Rousseau, he opines: "Great crimes are committed by great ignoramuses."[23] Ignorance, dogma, and superstition are the only enemies of human beings, and their antidote is sound reasoning. This remedy is radically different from faith in God, or goodness, for its justification appeals to standards that can be used to question any authority. Reason is

the great demystifier and equalizer and thus the foundation of liberty and fraternity.

The Enlightenment had its detractors. They objected to its humanism and
logocentrism, arguing that reason is not above the mutations of history, passion,
and politics, that its meaning varies, and it often proves itself impotent. This attempt to disempower and de-universalize reason is echoed in postmodernism and
multiculturalism, which explains their proponents' attachment to racial and gender differentiation. To de-universalize reason is to make it possible to identify
human beings by the shapes and colors of their bodies and claim that "blacks"
and "women" cannot reason, or that they reason differently from their counterparts. Make reasoning culture-specific, in the name of differences, and conclusive standards for argument assessment disappear in a welter of cultural relativist
righteousness. Inevitably, in constructing and evaluating arguments, anything
goes and anything does not go. Thus the status quo is maintained, and it is this
implication that leads Jurgen Habermas to conclude that postmodernism reflects
a resurgence of neoconservatism.[24]

In postmodernism, all alleged universal and objective discursive representations are products of nonuniversal and subjective agencies. What does this imply
for the recognition of flawed reasoning in intellectual exchanges? The postmodernist depiction of knowledge as "heteromorphous" (Lyotard) *does* present a
standard for evaluating such exchanges. It is a standard, however, that generates
perpetual reprisals, for it can be described as an expression of postmodernism's
specific, cultural location. In turn, this description can also be culturally located.
The postmodernist standard must have, but cannot acquire, the consensual status
necessary for participants in language games to decide how to play, or what
counts as contributions to the game. The assertion that knowledge is culture-
specific cannot be itself culture-specific, if it is to be a standard. But what would
justify an application of a principle of exceptionalism? Culture? Surely not.
There are no acultural standards, if all standards are culture-specific. Why, then,
would postmodernists engage in intellectual exchanges at all? They know, in
advance, that unresolvable disagreements will result from intellectual exchanges,
for rules are but arbitrary, localized choices; they develop arguments within
syntactical and logical rules, and claim that these rules cannot be used to evaluate the arguments. Intellectual disputes, then, are to be in perpetual stalemate. Is
this conclusion not a prelude to violence, a condition laid at the feet of Enlightenment philosophers? Violence lurks in the postmodernist rejection of the possibility of dispute resolution through the use of rules or intellectual standards. In
critical multiculturalism, the rejection is accompanied by an ascription of moral
privilege—multiculturalism is a representation of the oppressed—and appeals to
political authorities for protection against particular speech acts.[25] Administrative
and punitive arms of the state—the executive committee for managing the affairs
of the bourgeoisie (Marx)—are called upon to protect oppressed "cultures."

Certain advocates of postmodernism present the notion of an intrinsic cul-
ture-boundness of knowledge as a counter to the modernist view of knowledge as
a reflection of objective conditions. M. Fox and D. Ward characterize the con-

trast between its cultural-epistemological foundation and the objectivism of Western science as follows:

> The Western scientific heritage is founded upon an epistemological system which prizes the objective over the subjective, the logical over the intuitive, and the empirically verifiable over the mystical. The methods of social scientific examinations of cultures are thus already value-laden; the choice to examine and understand other cultures by these methods involves a commitment to certain values such as objectivity. . . . Scientific discourse has a privileged place in Western cultures, but the discourses of myth, tradition, religion, and mystic insight are often the dominant forms of thought and language of non-Western cultures.[26]

As the argument goes, knowledge is not produced in decontextualized and de-subjectivized spaces, but rather within a milieu of cultural, ideological, and political differences. It follows, then, that it may be divided into segments such mainstream and transformative. Multicultural knowledge is transformative, and multiculturalists become "transformative intellectuals," to use Henry Giroux's phrase. This distinction between mainstream and transformative knowledge is further developed by James A. Banks who constructs five types of knowledge—personal/cultural, popular, mainstream academic, transformative, and school, and argues for the inclusion of "transformative academic knowledge" in the curriculum as a counter to "mainstream academic knowledge." The questions to be answered in deciding what is to be part of the curriculum are: Whose side is the knowledge on? Whose interests does it represent? However, a third question could be added: What cultural traditions are reflected in "transformative academic knowledge?"

A closer analysis of this type of knowledge would reveal that it is a feature of the liberationist variant of gender and racial theories of social relations, specifically, radical and victim feminisms, and the cultural nationalist perspective on "the black experience." Banks concedes as much in writing:

> Transformative academic knowledge challenges the facts, concepts, paradigms, themes, and explanations routinely accepted in mainstream academic knowledge. The transformative research methods and the theory that have been developed in women's studies since the 1970s constitute, in my view, the most important developments in social science theory and research in the last 20 years.[27]

Banks regards the works of Aristotle, Shakespeare, Dante, and Chaucer as "mainstream academic knowledge," while the writings of Henry Louis Gates, Houston Baker, T. Amott and Julie Mathaei, Jacqueline Jones, Shirley Geok-lin Lim, Mayumi Tsutekawa, Terry McMillan, and Margarita Donnelly represent "transformative academic knowledge." Significant for their absence are the works of "authors of color" such as Kwame Anthony Appiah, Thomas Sowell, Linda Chavez, Shelby Steele, Anne Wortham, and critics of "victim feminism" such as Camille Paglia and Carol Tavris. Nevertheless, these authors surely challenge mainstream academic writings on "race relations" and "women's experiences." Limitations of space cannot be an explanation of the fact that not a single representative of libertarian scholarship found a place in Banks' catalogue of transformative scholars.

It is not skin color, quality of scholarship, or culture that determines one's place in the two types of knowledge identified by Banks. Indeed, Banks' criteria for distinguishing between mainstream and transformative scholarship are not clearly specified. For example, it is not clear why Shakespeare is "mainstream," if, as Peter Brier demonstrates, Shakespeare's works contain some of the strongest, independent, and autonomous female characters to be seen on stage.[28]   Indeed, given the level of arbitrariness in the selection of "transformative scholars," transformative academic knowledge may be said to be defined only by Banks' notion of social transformation. Thus *the multiculturalists' demand for diversity and inclusion of the voices of the different is not an appeal for gender, racial, and ethnic inclusiveness as such.* It is not the writings of any woman or person of color that are to be included in the multicultural curriculum. Rather, female authors and writers of color are to be selected on the basis of the transformative quality of their works, a quality to be identified by the advocates of multiculturalism. The potential for arbitrariness and nepotism is overwhelming, for there are no explicitly stated standards for deciding which writers challenge mainstream knowledge and which do not. This leaves the selection of textbooks, tests, and teachers open to perpetual challenges and disagreements. Those female authors, teachers, and authors of color whose views are not regarded as "transformative" (by the most vocal advocates of multiculturalism?) may find themselves excluded from the curriculum. Multiculturalism thereby replicates the exclusionary practices of its antagonist, monocultural education.

For its advocates, multiculturalism is an antidote to the monoculturalism prevailing in schools, a monoculturalism that reflects the arrogance of Eurocentrism. Western knowledge contains an erroneous self-image as the pinnacle of human intellectual achievements as well as flawed assumptions about its own origin, non-Western cultures, and forms of knowledge. In a word, it is an expression of Eurocentrism, which Sandra Harding depicts as: "a cluster of assumptions, central among which are that peoples of European descent, their institutions, practices and conceptual schemes, express the unique heights of human development, and that Europeans and their civilization are fundamentally self-generated, owing little or nothing to the institutions, practices, conceptual schemes, or peoples of other parts of the world."[29] advocates of multiculturalism generally recommend the inclusion of transformative knowledge in the curriculum, arguing that it would be a radical breakthrough for education and social transformation. Banks goes beyond this, however, and proposes the establishment of multicultural education as an academic discipline in its own right.[30]   If Banks' works on multicultural education are any indication, this discipline would retain the gender, racial, and ethnic categories prevailing in social studies. It follows that, insofar as these categories are central to history, anthropology and sociology, multicultural education is but a continuation of traditional social sciences. It presents the same gender, racial, and ethnic classifications that are embedded in eighteenth- and nineteenth-century biological, anthropological, and sociological writings, and *arguments refuting these classifications are systematically excluded from all advocacies of multiculturalism*. In effect, multiculturalism remains an extension of particular "Western" theories of human experiences, history, and social relations. Adoption of its recommendations would not constitute a rupturing of the current social studies curriculum. On the contrary, it would strengthen a curriculum already replete with Black, Ethnic, and Women's Studies Departments, as well as countless courses and research programs on gender, racial, and ethnic experiences.

Multiculturalism cannot be said to be a transcendence of "Western knowledge," for it propagates the same racial divisions and conception of culture that were constructed within nineteenth-century physical and cultural anthropology. Its sponsors' claim to be making a sharp break with mainstream knowledge is inconsistent with the obvious connections between their proposals and what may be called classical racial studies. In *Race in North America: Origin and Evolution of a Worldview*, Audrey Smedley demonstrates how anthropology's discovery of races was regarded as a major scientific breakthrough in the nineteenth century. Its racial classifications influenced a number of classical anthropologists and sociologists, and were used to develop an authoritative racial worldview that permeated educational institutions up to the late nineteenth century and was continued in "the sociology of race relations" developed in the early twentieth-century Chicago School of Sociology.[31] To this day, racial classification remains a deeply-entrenched practice among sociologists.

Certain classical sociologists and anthropologists—Herbert Spencer, Karl Marx, Emile Durkheim, Max Weber, Johann Blumenbach, and Edward Tylor—not only endorsed the categories white and Negro, but also provided key concepts for the development of symbolic interactionist, structural functionalist, and conflict perspectives in sociology as well as cultural and communication studies. The following remarks by Henry Louis Gates Jr. come close to a recognition of multiculturalism's intellectual lineage: "There's no denying that the multicultural initiative arose, in part, because of the fragmentation of American society by ethnicity, class, and gender. To make it the culprit for this fragmentation is to mistake effect for cause."[32] Multiculturalism may be not guilty of the *initial* fragmentation of U.S. society by ethnicity, gender, and class, if that is indeed an accurate portrayal of the society. However, by virtue of its systematic stress on racial, gender, and ethnic differences it certainly consolidates the fragmentation.

The multiculturalists' pursuit of liberation from male, white, European, intellectual hegemony reflects certain radical feminist arguments, as well as black and Hispanic cultural nationalist perspectives that are deeply indebted to "classical" works on gender, race, and culture. These arguments and perspectives are not, as James Banks suggests, more relevant to "cultural and political realities" than "mainstream scholarship." Rather, it is the advocates of multiculturalism who utilize specific conceptions of knowledge, gender, race, and culture to conceive events as gender and racial "realities." Pioneer proponents of liberal, radical, socialist, and Marxist feminisms often express their debt to the writings of John Stuart Mill, Karl Marx, Max Weber, and Sigmund Freud. The debates among feminists and black liberationists implicitly and explicitly utilize the rules of logic developed in Aristotle's *Organon*. No deep understanding of the concepts of power, conflict, social constructionism and class can be reached without an examination of the writings of Georg Simmel, Emile Durkheim, Karl Marx, Max Weber, and Alfred Schutz. All variants of multiculturalism are closely affiliated to these "classical" sociologists. The paradigm twist, and contradiction, in the idea of multicultural inclusiveness is that the race and gender of certain scholars—"dead white males"—are cited to justify their exclusion from a multicultural curriculum.

It follows that James Banks' distinction between his "transformative" advocacy of multicultural education and "Western traditionalists" is inaccurate and void. More inaccuracies follow, as Banks further describes the Western traditionalists as "fearful" but "highly organized," and "well-financed." Does this mean that their arguments are invalid? Is tradition, by definition, bad? Given that Banks elsewhere asserts that "multicultural education itself is a thoroughly Western movement," should not his advocacy of it be conceived as part of the Western tradition? Isn't he himself, therefore, a "Western traditionalist? Banks' nonconsideration of the implications of his own remarks could be explained as follows: In neglecting philosophy, social science departments rob their graduate students of the intellectual tools necessary to resolve the logical and epistemological issues raised in social studies. These students grow into scholars more prone to present negative descriptions of arguments than analyze them within specific intellectual standards. Dismiss an argument by pasting a "negative" adjective onto it, without demonstrating any flaws in the argument that warrant that adjective. That is the most common form of argument analysis in multicultural education advocacies. To focus on the structure of arguments would be to recognize the necessity and viability of universal standards for argument assessment. Advocates of multiculturalism, however, deny the applicability of such standards.

Behind the multiculturalists' practice of dismissal by negative description and imputation, there is a traditional subject-object conception of knowledge in which knowledge is defined as a product of human subjects contemplating real objects. This grounding of knowledge in the real world facilitates its identification with particular kinds of persons, interests, positions, and power-relations. As James Banks writes:

Multicultural education, as conceptualized by the major theorists in the field, is a form of transformative academic knowledge. . . . Transformative scholars, unlike mainstream scholars, assume that knowledge is not neutral but is heavily influenced by human interests; that all knowledge reflects the social, economic, and political relationships within society, and that an important purpose of transformative knowledge is to help citizens improve society.[33]

It is paradoxical that while claiming to be distancing multicultural education from mainstream knowledge, Banks offers a definition of knowledge as "the way a person explains reality" and experiences.[34] This definition replays the Lockean thesis of the mind as a mirror and ideas as reflections of reality. For Banks, these ideas belong to persons who are themselves mired in social reality. Thus ideas reflect interests and values that are ultimately expressive of gender, racial, ethnicity, and class positions. It follows, then, that all arguments cannot be evaluated with the same standards. Standards cannot be neutral. For example, Eurocentric standards cannot be applied to arguments for multicultural education, for this would be to impute a questionable universality and neutrality to these standards.

There are two self-nullifying implications of the multiculturalists' denial of the neutral quality of standards for evaluating knowledge. First, is this denial itself neutral and of universal value? The answer cannot be affirmative, since all knowledge is said to reflect individuals' values. If their denial, which is itself knowledge, is not neutral, it can be rejected for being as partisan as Eurocentrism. Second, their claim is analytically incomplete. The reasons for designating knowledge as "Eurocentric" are not made clear. What can it mean to say that an idea is Eurocentric? Taken literally, the term *Eurocentric* means centered in Europe, and placing an argument in Europe's center does not amount to its evaluation. "Eurocentric" is a geographical description, which could be variously analyzed within specific perspectives in cartography. Nevertheless, if "Eurocentric" is metaphor indicating that things originating from Europe are negative, what are the implications for Molefi Asante's use of the English language? Does it make his arguments Eurocentric? Asante's claim that Eurocentrism is objectionable because of its pretensions to universality itself makes a claim for a universal recognition of the nonuniversal nature of Eurocentric knowledge. As critics of postmodernism insist, the postmodernist rejection of metanarrative itself produces and requires a metanarrative. [35]

The conclusion that universal standards of knowledge are impossible constitutes a judgment on all knowledge. Its metanarrative status has two significant implications. First, advocates of multiculturalism cannot object to the proposition that universal standards are necessary for decisions on an argument's plausibility. Second, they must agree that transformative knowledge is necessarily constructed, and to be evaluated, within standards accessible to all discursive participants. The issue of the neutrality or nonneutrality of these standards is irrelevant. Indeed, no producer of knowledge need claim that knowledge is neutral or nonneutral. What knowledge producers must pursue is a consensus on standards for knowledge evaluation. There could be a common agreement, for example, that claims that are implicitly or explicitly absurd must be abandoned. Otherwise, there would be no common conclusions that could be drawn from intellectual exchanges.

Some advocates of multiculturalism claim that interests and power underlie the production and possession of knowledge. It is not just that knowledge is power, but that it is the powerful who decide what constitutes knowledge, and their decision is based on their interests. This may be a plausible proposition, depending on how power and interests are defined, but it has no implication for the validity of the given knowledge. Disclosing the political and cultural conditioning, or determination, of thinking does not render the *knowledge* produced invalid. Knowledge is thought organized according to specific rules and normative obligations. Even if power and knowledge are intrinsically related, as Foucault and Lyotard claim, this relationship does not warrant a given producer of knowledge claiming an exemption from standards of knowledge-evaluation such as accuracy, clarity, logical consistency, and analytical depth. Nevertheless, an intrinsic relationship between power and knowledge is not demonstrated in Lyotard's text, which correlates not power and knowledge, per se, but a specific conception of power, and knowledge. Lyotard's critical question is: Who produced the knowledge? The producer is then located in an institution that is deemed expressive of power, for example, the state, the university, and media. The knowledge thereby becomes state knowledge, university knowledge, media knowledge, and so on. This linking of knowledge and institutions constitutes power-knowledge. But it begs the question of the nature of power, for it is yet to be demonstrated that power resides in any of these institutions. However, there are more pertinent objections to the Lyotardian and Foucauldian power-knowledge connection.

Lyotard's question—who produced the knowledge—implicitly endorses the thesis that knowledge is produced by subjects. However, this endorsement is inconsistent with his opposition to modernism and its irrepressible realities. As he writes: "Modernity, in whatever age it appears, cannot exist without a shattering of belief and without discovery of the "lack of reality" of reality, together with the invention of other realities. . . . Within the tradition of the subject,. . . this contradiction develops as a conflict between the faculties of a subject, the faculty to conceive of something and the faculty to "present" something."[36] Modernity breeds impenetrable layers of reality and endless realities engendered by the gazes of subjects. In its epistemological expression, all ideas are reflections of "real" or external objects as perceived by different subjects.[37] But to centralize subjects in cultural and power relations and, through this, localize "narratives" is to present knowledge as the product of subjects' interrogating reality that has "a lack of reality" precisely because of the presence of subjects. The collapse of reality necessarily follows the grounding of knowledge in subjects and reality. The knowledge, too, self-obliterates. Linking it with "power" does not alter its fate.

In postmodernist readings/writings, a knowledge producer as a socially grounded subject is identified. This subject, as a bearer of a culture structured in power relations, is centered in the knowledge-production process. In this sense, postmodernism is peculiarly modernist, for it reproduces the subject-object conception of knowledge that characterizes "modern" (allegedly beginning with Descartes) philosophy. Postmodernism merely extends modernism by pushing differences among subjects into an all-consuming relativism. However, if knowledge is not a product of a subject's contemplation of real objects, power and knowledge are not intrinsically related. In order to demonstrate that they are so related, power would have to be defined as an omnipresent feature of human interaction. All knowledge would be power-contextualized, including the claims about the intrinsic connections between power and knowledge. Nevertheless, so what, it may be asked? A demonstration of a power-knowledge connection does not provide a basis for refuting arguments; it is merely a locating of the origins of a given knowledge, not an exposé of inaccuracies and fallacies in arguments.

Multiculturalism's debt to the subject-object conception of knowledge is illustrated in its proponents' references to the biological and cultural attributes of authors—"European theorists," "writers of color" and "white academics."[38] James A. Banks makes the connection more explicit: "Multicultural theorists maintain that knowledge is positional, that it relates to the knower's values and experiences and that knowledge implies action. . . . Multiculturalists believe that in order to have valid knowledge, information about the social conditions and experiences of the knower are essential."[39] Positionality assumes that knowledge is produced by human subjects located in the real world and contemplating real objects to produce knowledge. It is further assumed that the background, attributes, and cultures of subjects may be correlated with the knowledge they produce. Thus a description of ideas expressed by subjects may allude to their gender, racial, ethnic, class, and political characteristics, and in evaluating arguments, allusions are made to motives, intentions, interests, as well as gender, regional, racial, and other attributes of the subject. If the subject is a "European," then "Eurocentric" can be applied to the knowledge that subject produces, and used as a reason for rejecting that knowledge. However, even if the subject is not "European," Eurocentric can still be applied to the ideas expressed by the subject because, for advocates of multiculturalism, "culture" and "interests" are organically linked to knowledge.

Any critic or criticism of multiculturalism may be said to be representing European culture, power, and interests, and thus, by an accusation of power-culture partisanship, criticisms of multiculturalism are neutralized. Or are they? Because a consensus on the criteria for identifying the nature of culture, power, and interests is ruled out, any social phenomenon may be deemed "multicultural." As indicated in previous chapters, some multicultural projects are unrecognizable as such, and discussions of their purposes are enmeshed in acrimonious exchanges. These projects are bound to be constructed and applied in an ad hoc, sporadic, transitory, and arbitrary fashion, for multicultural proposals are grounded in a realist conception of knowledge in which standards for evaluating ideas and proposals reside in "social reality," or the experiences of groups that are to be liberated from oppression. As James Banks advises: "We should teach students that knowledge is a social construction, that it reflects the perspectives, experiences, and the values of the people and cultures that construct it."[40] But, in the interest of intellectual diversity, should not students also be taught that social constructionism is but a particular and contested conception of knowledge, and that the cultural-experiential context in no way reflects on the validity of the knowledge constructed? Students could make their own choice of perspective after being made acquainted with philosophy's rich menu of epistemological traditions, such as realism, idealism, materialism, empiricism, positivism, rationalism, and postmodernism.

Multiculturalism's epistemological foundation derives from a subject-object conception of knowledge that necessarily leads to: (1) relativist disputes over the nature of the real world, and (2) moral-political evaluations and accusations, as the subjects-producers challenge each other's qualifications to make statements about the real nature of the real world: "I know some facts from the real world, or about what really happened in history, of which you are unaware. Hence you are ignorant," and your arguments false." An example of this tendency will be found in Molefi Asante's review of Mary Lefkowitz's *Out of Africa* in which Asante presents his "facts," describes Lefkowitz as "white," and "a novice in this arena," and places her work in an "Aryanist tradition" without demonstrating how this amounts to an inconsistency on Lefkowitz's part.[41] Asante elsewhere accuses both Anne Wortham and Diane Ravitch of ignorance of African history and the African-American experience.[42] These accusations are clear examples of argumentum ad hominem, and they illustrate a pattern in disputed interpretations of ancient records of the past. Some critics claim that Afrocentrists are themselves ignorant of European and African cultures, as well as Egyptian history, and do not know enough Greek and Western history to pass judgments on Europeans.[43] In the same vein, it could be said that Asante's response to criticisms of Afrocentricity continues a (black) racist and sexist tradition of dismissing white and black *female* authors as either morally corrupt or ignorant and that his version of Afrocentricity is irrelevant, since he is a middle-class professor whose life-style is far removed from that of the parents of "underachieving" African-American students. Surely education reform is too important for its analyses to be characterized by negative personal and political descriptions of authors' arguments.

Multiculturalism espouses a worldview and an epistemological grounding in certain aspects of social constructionism and postmodernism. It makes a metanarrative of racial differences, conceiving them as things in the real world. On the other hand, postmodernism, at least Lyotard's version, is antirealist. Hence it is not compatible with the treatment of racial and cultural differences as "real," and postmodernists, as Harvey Siegel lucidly demonstrates, cannot challenge a thesis on reason's foundational status without utilizing rational standards for evaluating arguments.[44] The modernist error—an error that Richard Rorty capitalizes on but does not correct with his assault on philosophy itself—lies in historicist and anthropocentric conceptions of reason.[45] Postmodernism's accusations against Enlightenment philosophy should be limited to the claim that certain Enlightenment thinkers, in zealously seeking to refute metaphysical certitudes, capitalized the term *reason* and gave it the status of history's generalissimo. Thus Reason's march could be portrayed as regionally and racially differentiated—in Greece, but not in Egypt— and temporally spasmodic, but climaxing in the Prussian state. This is Hegel's project of Ideational historicism. The exaltation of Reason facilitates the conclusion that maleness, Greece, the Enlightenment, or Hegel's philosophy itself represents Reason's apex, the human intellectual finale, modernity, or "the end of history." Critics of modernity protest against this anthropomorphic capitalization of reason, but this protest cannot be taken as a refutation of the Enlightenment's emphasis on human reasoning as the standard for assessing human experiences.

A redeeming feature of the Enlightenment is its endorsement of human *reasoning* as the standard for evaluating all knowledge. This implies that any anthropomorphic capitalization of Reason itself may be questioned within standards for evaluating reasoning. In other words, both modernity and postmodernity can be evaluated by the standards implicit in language use and communication. One necessary standard would be a recognition of a distinction between denunciation and refutation. An argument would not be valid, or invalid, because it is considered Greek, Aristotelian, Voltairean, Hegelian, modernist, or postmodernist. Any individual claim to be a unique and self-justified embodiment of Reason would be invalidated by the need to use universal standards to construct and evaluate that claim. No "race" possesses a monopoly on reason, not because every race reasons, but because the construction and evaluation of the claim to a monopoly assume the presence of certain intellectual standards through which it can be demonstrated that "race" is the product of unreasonable criteria of classification. Insofar as postmodernism represents arguments that reject universal standards of reasoning, it commits the error of relativizing all judgments.

Postmodernist arguments about the nature of knowledge attempt to integrate ethics and epistemology, to merge conceptions of justice and truth. The tendency is discernible in multiculturalists' attempt to reconstruct educational institutions and knowledge so that they serve the realization of ending oppression and securing justice. Truth is justice, ideas that lead to justice, or ideas that are opposed to exploitation and oppression. Hence oppressors cannot produce true knowledge. These assertions underlie the thesis that the knowledge produced by white males, or texts on civilization and culture written by whites are potentially racist and ethnocentric. Such knowledge is counterposed to Afrocentric and feminist knowledge, which is true by virtue of being geared toward emancipation of the oppressed. Women and people of color are innocent victims, as opposed to white European males, who are historical predators. These assertions are curiously fundamentally Christian in its demonization of white males. They transpose the Biblical characterization of man as intrinsically evil onto the male gender. Given that white males are evil, their ideas are inaccurate and untrue, that is, racist and sexist. "Racist" and "sexist" are accusations that discredit arguments and place the accusers in a position of moral and epistemological privilege. Women and "people of color" are morally unsullied by virtue of being victims. Therefore, the knowledge they produce is morally superior to white male knowledge. But, it must be asked, which women's knowledge?

The self-described feminist Andrea Dworkin, whom feminist Camille Paglia in *Vamps and Tramps* calls "a hypocrite," writes: "The discovery is, of course, that 'man' and 'woman' are fictions, caricatures, cultural constructs. As models they are reductive, totalitarian, inappropriate to human becoming. As roles they are static, demeaning to the female, dead-ended for male and female both. Culture as we know it legislates those fictive roles as normalcy."[46] Reflecting a growing rejection among feminists of the category woman, Linda Alcoff and

Elizabeth Potter write: "If the concept of woman has lost its analytical credibility, the concept of a universal human nature is even less credible."[47] In recognition of the difficulties in discovering an objective, or representative "woman" sociologists generally conclude that gender is culturally constructed.[48] The term *female* refers to naturally occurring biological attributes, while "woman" identifies a product of nurture, or socialization. Some of the early feminists even suggested that the imposition of womanhood on females is a suppression of the human ability to adopt various identities and sexualities. Developing on this theme, radical scholarship on "men" and "women" could unravel the process through which human beings become gendered. Instead, feminist scholarship is caught up in what Anthony Appiah refers to as a classic dialectic: "On the one hand, a simple claim to equality, a denial of substantial difference; on the other, a claim to a special message, revaluing the feminine 'Other' not as the 'helpmeet' of sexism but as the New Woman."[49] Feminism emerged out of the study of women's experiences, experiences assumed to be specific to women who are defined as essentially different from men. Its ambivalence reflects efforts to de-essentialize and deconstruct gender differences and still study or liberate women.

What certain arguments in poststructuralist writings indicate is that the category "women" is theoretically mediated, that is, it derives from certain classificatory criteria.[50] Because these criteria represent only a fraction of a person's attributes, women share some characteristics with nonwomen, and do not share others with other women. Thus it would be unjustifiable to claim that writings by certain "women" represent women, and no feminism may be said to be women's voice. Women do not have a voice, but an infinite number of voices that are not demonstrably in a determinate relationship to reproductive organs. As Jane Flax argues: "Any feminist standpoint will necessarily be partial. Thinking about women may illuminate some aspects of a society that have been previously suppressed within the dominant view. But none of us can speak for "woman" because no such person exists except within a specific set of (already gendered) relations—to "man" and to many concrete and different women."[51] Advocates of multiculturalism homogenize many different "concrete" persons into "women." These objects of study are then ascribed distinct experiences and interests that are allegedly different from men and represented by selected authors. In evaluating knowledge, attention is directed at the authors' gender, culture, or politics. This attention may privilege an author and prevent the refutation of arguments, or it may serve to discredit them. The practice is typified in bell hooks' remarks:

Reading much of the popular contemporary literature on race and racism written by men in this society, I discovered repeated instances that racism will never end. The bleak picture prophesied in these works stands in sharp contrast to the more hopeful vision offered in progressive feminist writings on the issue of race and racism. The writing is fundamentally optimistic even as it is courageously and fiercely critical because it emerges from concrete struggles on the part of diverse groups of women to work together for a common cause, forging a politics of solidarity.[52]

As in the traditional curriculum, the antiracist and antisexist strands of multiculturalism promote racialized and gendered subjects and knowledges, and reflect a certain philosophical presence in the curriculum. Specifically, a subject-object or realist conception of knowledge dominates the multiculturalism advocacy. It posits that: (1) ideas reflect both the real world (objects) and the values, attributes, interests, and experiences of subjects; (2) knowledge can be racially and culturally described; and (3) a person's race or gender is significant for the evaluation of the validity of that person's arguments. Concentrating on persons—their bodies, politics, and values—rather than the structure of arguments, multiculturalists pose the following question: Whose culture (knowledge) is in the curriculum, and whose interests does it serve? However, in turn, it may be asked: who is asking this question? What kind of culture and politics does he or she represent? The discussions are thereby taken into regressive relativist torrents, and, for want of intellectual standards for argument evaluation, the disputants drown each other in mutual accusations of moral-political complicity. Insofar as disputes over multicultural education and multiculturalism revolve around the issue of what is truth or valid knowledge, its advocacy requires forays into various theories of knowledge.

The curriculum needs not cultural inclusions but infusions of various philosophical traditions, but it is precisely philosophy that remains a curricular pariah. In *The Closing of the American Mind*, Allan Bloom bemoans the absence of philosophy in the curriculum and its dethronement by "political and theoretical democracy." Bloom's lament should not be taken to mean that philosophy is a panacea for education's problems. Rather, Joan Robinson's remark about economics applies equally to the study of philosophy: "The purpose of studying economics is not to acquire a set of ready-made answers to economic questions, but to learn how to avoid being deceived by economists."[53] First, greater attention to philosophy would be an antidote to the uncritical utilization of philosophical categories in social studies, and an aid to the recognition of conflicting theories of knowledge within specific arguments. Second, students would need to be cognizant of logical rules as well as ethical and epistemological assumptions, if they are to evaluate discussions of multiculturalism conclusively. In this sense, implementation of the multiculturalists' recommendations would be premature and ineffective relative to the goal of improving students' understanding of politics and culture.

Differences and the Practice of Racial Classification in Critical and Insurgent Multiculturalisms

Arguments for multiculturalism are organized around the concept of difference(s). Some celebrate differences as irrepressible cultural phenomena. Others offer a political celebration of differences as a means to the end of establishing justice and democracy. For example, advocates of critical multiculturalism attempt to deconstruct differences, expose their volatility, historical pliability, and at the same time forge their connections with power and political struggles. Their efforts thereby constitute a legitimation and further cultivation of specific differences, reflecting Henrietta Moore's claim:

Difference exerts an uncanny fascination for all of us. Contemporary social and cultural theory exhibits an obsessive concern with issues of differences, and such is the malleability of the term that almost anything can be subsumed under it. The passion for difference seems to be linked to its unspoken and under-theorized pair, "the same" or "sameness."... Deciding on differences is one way of delineating identities. Difference(s) from others are frequently about forming and maintaining group boundaries. The brutal and bloody nature of this maintenance work is everywhere in evidence.[54]

Define a difference as a rupturing of an anticipation, a perceptual break with an expectation of continuity. Difference is, therefore, synonymous with a disruption of cognitive uniformity; it is recognition of rupture of expectation. Julia Kristeva writes of the different: "The foreigner comes in when the consciousness of my difference arises, and he disappears when we all acknowledge ourselves as foreigners, unamenable to bonds and communities."[55] The expectation is of sameness, and its falsification is expressed in this fictive event: "Look, a white man," shout some children in an African village. He, being "white," in turn, saw "blacks." In those sightings, there were nonrecognition through recognition of rupture, "otherization," and classification. As Kristeva continues: "the sense of strangeness is a mainspring for identification with the other, by working out its depersonalizing impact by means of astonishment."[56] To observe difference is to classify, for example, noticing a different race, racial classification, a different sex, gender classification—as in doing race, doing gender, racing, and gendering. These are acts of bodily boundary creation and identity construction.

Advocates of multiculturalism endorse the construction of oppositional identities based on anatomical differences. In critical multiculturalism, these differences are conceptualized as cultural and political phenomena in order to construct social relations along a trajectory of cultural-political domination and struggles. This construction is crucial to the mission of attaining power and justice for oppressed groups. As in Marx's transcendental dialectic of class struggle, cultural differences are recognized as only strategically pertinent. Thus insurgent and critical versions of multiculturalism are allegedly antiessentialist, that is, deconstructive of differences and attentive to their dialectical intertwining with similarities. Henry Giroux writes:

Fourth, an insurgent multiculturalism must challenge the task of merely re-presenting cultural differences in the curriculum; it must also educate students of the necessity for linking a justice of multiplicity to struggles over real material conditions that structure everyday life. In part, this means understanding how structural imbalances in power produce real limits on the capacity of subordinate groups to exercise a sense of agency and struggle. It also means analyzing specific class, race, gender, and other issues as social problems rooted in real material and institutional factors that produce specific forms of inequality and oppression. This would necessitate a multicultural curriculum that produces a language that deals with social problems in historical and relational terms, and uncovers how the dynamics of power work to promote domination within the school and the wider society.[57]

Insurgent multiculturalism takes aim at the opportunity and power structures in schools, as they impinge on equality for women, people of color, homosexuals, and the handicapped. It holds no brief for a celebration of cultural differences, and points to differences only as a means of exposing how power operates and empowering those defined as different. Its advocates, then, aim explicitly at egalitarian social reconstruction, seeking the eradication of power imbalances as well as inequality of opportunity, discrimination, and group subordination.

The critical and insurgent versions of multiculturalism represent a set of educational-organizational solutions to specific social problems: Eurocentrism, racism, sexism, homophobia, prejudice, discrimination, and educational underachievement. Persons of color, homosexuals, women, the handicapped, or "the physically challenged," and "third world people" are defined as oppressed cultural groups that are being excluded from power within educational institutions and the larger society. Differences, then, are maintained, but they are taken to a plateau of cultural politics, to sites of legitimation, resistance, and renewal. Indeed, culture itself is reconceptualized as a political formation. For example, Henry Giroux makes innumerable definitional references to culture. It is a magisterial modality that weaves its way through history; it is also a set of group peculiarities and a determinant of behavior.[58] However, these specifications of culture border on the unintelligible. "Politics" could replace "culture" without any alteration of the meaning of the sentence. And, if culture and politics are synonymous, what does this imply for Giroux's advocacy of "a theory of cultural politics?"

Insurgent multiculturalism is cultural only to the extent that it has an affinity with certain cultural pluralist tenets described in Chapter 1. The affinity, however, is tenuous, for insurgent multiculturalism utilizes the culture concept to wage war against hegemonic and oppressed perspectives and the monocultural politics of schooling. In conceiving culture as a form of "empowerment for collective action, self-reproduction, and struggle" against oppression, proponents of insurgent multiculturalism argue that appreciation of differences cannot be an end in itself, but the starting point for challenging cultural hegemony and attaining more comprehensive objectives, such as group solidarity, social justice, and overall social reconstruction. Recognition of diversity is not self-justified. Danny Weil, former director of multicultural studies at the Center for Critical Thinking at Sonoma State University, writes: "Understanding diversity is to understand diversity of thought, action, and conditions relative to pressing social and institutional power structures. It is to understand the logic of thinking, from the point of view of gender groups, gays, the aged, the disabled, newly arrived immigrants, people of color, and economically disadvantaged social classes."[59] Weil argues for a curricular incorporation of diverse cultural perspectives in order to combat the "Eurocentric monopolization of thought" that vitiates education. Through a critical multicultural literacy, students can liberate themselves from sociocentric prejudices and come to appreciate the richness and strengths of a diverse society. Such literacy would enable students to challenge not only their beliefs and assumptions, but also the social arrangements that perpetuate oppression and injustice.

In their focus on social arrangements that generate differences, advocates of critical multiculturalism challenge "difference multiculturalism" by identifying the historical conjunctures through which differences are constructed. They call for a "politics of signification" that denotes how differences are configured and re-configured through power-knowledge. Thus the concept of differences is strategically located in a politics of resistance and opposition. In opposition to conservative multiculturalism that "biologizes" differences, liberal multiculturalism's denial of their existence, and Left-liberal multiculturalism which essentializes them, critical multiculturalism locates differences within discursive and political agendas. Its analysis of differences unfolds within the construction of a critical pedagogy, liberationist praxis, and resistance.

Peter McLaren takes particular aim at the "liberal multiculturalists" "pluralists" and their notion of a common culture as well as the Left-liberal multiculturalists who "esssentialize cultural differences." McLaren writes:

From the perspective of critical multiculturalism, the conservative and liberal stress on sameness and the left-liberal emphasis on difference is really a false opposition. Identity based on "sameness" and identity based on "difference" are forms of essentialist logic: in both, individual identities are presumed to be autonomous, self-contained, and self-directed. Resistance multiculturalism doesn't see diversity itself as a goal, but rather argues that diversity must be affirmed within a politics of cultural criticism and a commitment to social justice. It must be attentive to the notion of "difference." Difference is always a product of history, culture, power, and ideology. Differences occur between and among groups and must be understood in terms of the specificity of their production.[60]

Differences, like experiences, are not theoretically and politically innocent. Specific practices of signification and conflicts over representation and meanings are implicated in their production, as is evident in the periodic re-furbishing of categories: Negroes, coloreds, blacks, Afro-Americans, and African Americans.

It follows from critical multiculturalism's opposition to the essentializing of differences that Afrocentric, Latinocentric, and antisexist demands for an inclusion of different voices in the curriculum are unacceptable. After all, inclusion of the different is not necessarily their empowerment; it may merely leave them ensconced in traditional patterns of domination. Thus critical multiculturalism is critical of Left and Left-liberal multiculturalism. Is it critical enough, though? The answer must be negative, for its advocates continually double-back into an endorsement of the idea of white people and black people. Henry Giroux writes:

Multiculturalism in this sense is about making whiteness visible as racial category; that is, it points to the necessity of providing white students with the cultural memories that enable them to recognize the historically and socially constructed nature of their own identities. In part, this approach to multiculturalism as cultural politics provides white students with self-definitions upon which they can recognize whether they are speaking from within or outside privileged spaces.[61]

So, whites have cultural memories that must be invoked to demonstrate the social construction of whiteness. What is not noticed is that "race" is being merged with "culture," and students remain "white" and "of color." Giroux's analysis continues modernity's focus on bodies and racial blood-lines. Does this multiculturalism qualify as antiessentialist or deconstructive?

Critical multiculturalism's allocation of bodies (equated with persons) to races and genders is central to its goal of eradicating the marginalization of cultural groups in the curriculum, educational institutions, the economy, and the power structure. As the argument goes, multicultural transformations of education will bring about significant educational benefits—socioeconomic mobility, genuine democratic structures, a decolonization of social thought—for women, gays, the handicapped, and people of color. If justice is to be realized, some form of empowerment of "people of color" must be established in educational institutions, and multiculturalism is the intellectual agent of this empowerment. In the words of Kris Gutierrez:

Multiculturalism is a new paradigm of race relations, a new concept of the proper relations between ethnic groups and races and is a reflection of the post-World War II challenge by people who have been marginalized and colonized. The ethnic and discriminated races have challenged the assumption of the inherent superiority of European cultures and have demanded the elevation of their cultures to equal those of Europe or white America.[62]

Guttierez makes explicit what Giroux and McClaren prefer to gloss over— critical and insurgent multiculturalisms are elements of a tradition of racial liberationist studies and struggles. Women, the poor, Hispanics, homosexuals, and the disabled are brought into the fray on the grounds that they, too, are oppressed cultures and so these multiculturalisms aspire to realize what Marxism could not for the working class—a mobilization, but not unification, of the exploited, disenfranchised, and oppressed.

The goal of racial and cultural equality is central to what Peter McLaren calls liberal and Left-Liberal multiculturalism, and the radical feminist perspective within the gender theory of social relations provides the key arguments for women's empowerment and gender equality. Critical multiculturalism continues this pursuit of justice for "persons of color," "women," and other oppressed people. But what its advocates do not recognize is that the demand for justice, a demand that reaches into the Enlightenment and Socrates' ruminations, becomes an ethical universal, a metanarrative. As Lyotard writes: "Justice as a value is neither outmoded nor suspect. We must thus arrive at an idea and practice of justice that is not linked to that of consensus."[63]   Is this not, on Lyotard's terms, a "modernist" argument?   It seeks to persuade readers to struggle for universal justice. The "we" is consensual. Or is it? For Lyotard's method is "agonistic"— fight in the sense of playing and not playing only to win. Lyotardian postmodernism is (not) dead serious.

Reason versus Racial Theory, Racial Classification, and Races

Critical multiculturalism emerges out of a specific appropriation of some of Lyotard's epistemological and ethical claims. Lyotard's embryonic antirealism is ignored, but his assault on reason and exaltation of differences is affirmed. Kenan Malik was moved to align postmodernism's metanarrative of differences with a tradition of racial theorizing:

The irony in the postmodern embrace of difference is that, for all its radical rhetoric, its hostility to universalism mirrors that of racial theory. Postmodern and poststructuralist theories regard Enlightenment universalism as imbricated with the categories of race. In reality, nineteenth century racial theory was as hostile to Enlightenment universalism as is contemporary poststructuralism. Racial theorists despised what they regarded as the abstract universalism of Enlightenment thinkers which they believed denied, and even undermined, the concrete reality of human differences. In its stead racial theorists embraced the relative and the particular.[64]

Critical and insurgent multiculturalisms reproduce the anatomical classifications of classical anthropology that still prevail in social studies. The categories women, blacks, Latinos, and minorities are advanced as referents of real persons, although allusions are made to their socially constructed status. Despite their endorsement of the postmodernist emphasis on the contextual underside of all knowledge, advocates of critical multiculturalism do not construe women, blacks, whites, gays, and the handicapped as theoretically contextual knowledge. Rather, these categories are presented as observable features of the real world. In effect, advocates of critical and insurgent multiculturalism impute a metatheoretical, ontological status to the categories whites, blacks, men, gays, and the handicapped and at the same time protest against the essentialization of differences.

It may be thought that this analytical error is not particularly serious. But it must be considered in conjunction with the insurgent multiculturalists' commitment to social justice and a "critical citizenry," and their criticisms of official ideological manipulation. In the construction of oppressed women and blacks, Giroux et al. give no consideration to certain feminists' depictions of gender differences as "fictions," "deceptions" and "fabrications," or to the argument that the characteristics that distinguish "whites" from "blacks" are so analytically problematic as to render these objects empirically unidentifiable. The categories blacks and whites are not sufficiently clear to be the basis of transformative intellectual praxes. Genuinely transformative knowledge would pose questions such as: Are racial categories being constructed according to objective criteria or by self-reference? Given that oppression, exploitation, and domination must be universal phenomena, why are these particular bodies being singled out for remedial attention? Can "black people" be identified? Consider Theodore Allen's observations:

According to Virginia law in 1860, a person with but three "white" grandparents was a Negro; in 1907, having no more than fifteen out of sixteen "white" great-great grandparents entitled one to the same classification; in 1910, the limit was asymptotic: "every person in whom there is ascertainable any Negro blood [was to] be deemed a colored person." as of 1983, the National Center for Health Statistics was effectively following the 1910 Virginia principle by classifying any person as black if either of the parents was black. At the same time, in Texas the "race" classification was determined by the "race" of the father. . . . In 1970, "racial" classification became the subject of hard bargaining in the Louisiana state legislature. The Conservatives held out for 1/64, but the "more enlightened" opposition forced a compromise at 1/32 as the requisite proportion of Negro forebears, a principle that was upheld by the State's Supreme Court in 1974.[65]

As indicated in the preceding chapter, criticisms of the criteria of classification that underlie observations of diversity in U.S. society have grown into a significant body of knowledge. Enigmatically, the scholars characterized and self-characterized as radical feminists, Afrocentrists, antiracists, conservatives, and liberals choose to ignore the literature that exposes a number of analytical shortcomings and conceptual inaccuracies in the allocating of persons to groups on the basis of certain anatomical, cultural, and economic differences. These categories intrude into discussions of multiculturalism, for the participants themselves are racially, sexually, and culturally classified. Because such classifications engender reciprocal imputations of corresponding identities and interests, discussions of multiculturalism have acquired the flavor of confrontations between representatives of "women," "whites," "Jews," "men," and "persons of color." For example, Peter McLaren writes: "When people of color attack white ground rules for handling disputes, or bureaucratic procedures, or specific policies of institutional racism, these are necessary oppositional acts."[66] McLaren's demonization of "whiteness," is unbounded. Whiteness, he claims, is an ideology and a social construct that is "parasitic on blackness." Blackness emerges as a noble, innocent, and morally privileged condition. No reasons are given for this oppressive and exploitative behavior of whites, except their racist nature, for reason is not significant in human affairs. Rather, "race" is.

Racial explanations of behavior derive from the racial descriptions produced by a specific theoretical mediation. If persons are identified as white people and black people, accounts of their behavior must be pursued in racial attributes. Not reasoning processes, but racial beliefs, motives, and interests are discovered and examined. Once reasoning processes are disdained, ethical judgments can be applied to racial motives and behavior. "Whites" or, for that matter, "blacks" can be accused of bearing malevolent intentions. This imputation of perverse intentions serves a specific purpose in intellectual exchanges. It represents a form of dehumanization that confers moral and epistemological privileges on the accuser. Because the accused are being labeled diseased, deviant, and corrupt, they are not qualified for membership in a moral community, and their speech is intellectually discredited. Thus the accusation of racism deprives "white people" of their humanness and invalidates their voice. They must prove that they are not racist before their speech becomes acceptable.

One way out of the regressive disputes over who is racist and what is racism is to recognize race and racism as inseparable analytical categories. Races are a product of racial classification, and race(ism) refers to a racial classification of persons. In other words, racial classification is itself a racist practice. This definition is not morally evaluative of statements, persons, or actions. Rather, it identifies an implicit or explicit action of allocating a person to a racial group on the basis of certain anatomical attributes. According to this definition, the claim that white people are racists is racist, because it classifies persons as "white people." Etymologically speaking, to describe a human being as a white, or a person of color is racist. Racism is any allocation of persons to races. To call whites or blacks racists implicitly endorses the idea of white and black people; it is, then, an act of racism. To write of the victimization of "persons of color" amounts to racism. To formulate policies and laws on "race relations" is racist.

The definition of racism as racial classification is not morally or politically evaluative, and its adoption would terminate its usage to silence disputants and foreclose discussions. It refers to not persons, but the practice of racial classification. This practice assigns a person to a race on the basis of selected anatomical attributes. For example, the skin color, hair type, and facial form of persons are used to distinguish them from other human beings with whom they may share innumerable other characteristics. Hence racial classification may be said to be a form of anatomical reductionism. It categorizes the whole person on the basis of a few anatomical attributes, placing a variety of individuals and social beings into a single phenotypical category, a race. Human beings are simply reduced to some of their anatomical characteristics. What antiracists ignore is the policy and behavioral implications and the absurdity of racial classification. Historian Wilson Moses comments on the practice of racial classification as follows:

Another point to remember is that the classics of the Afrocentric tradition, which argued that the ancient Egyptians were black, were written at a time when "one drop of Negro blood" was enough to make anyone a Negro. Even today, this insane reasoning remains the basis for classifying appreciable numbers of people as "black" despite their blue eyes and blond hair.[67]

It is this "insane reasoning" that underlies discussions of race relations and policies for improving race relations. Sensible policies cannot be constructed around flawed classifications. All policies for better race relations are bound to fail, for racial categorization—the placing of same-race persons in groups—leads to in-group and out-group orientations and expectations, as well as discrimination for members of the given category. That is to say, "white people" discriminate for white people. This discrimination will be conceived as "discrimination against" by those not belonging to the category of white people. Clearly "good" race relations are no race relations, and no race relations are inconsistent with the racial classification of persons.

Why are the categories black people and white people endorsed by legislatures, activists, academic bodies, and advocates of antiracist education, despite myriad refutations of "race" in the biological and anthropological literature and the obvious discrimination that results from racial classification? How can educational institutions, media, legislative bodies, publishing houses, social scientists, virtually the entire intelligentsia, continue to endorse the absurdity of racial classification? One answer is premised on a thesis that formal education plays a significant role in the refusal to abandon a practice that is riddled with illogicalities and undesirable consequences. Because educational inputs do not cultivate sensitivity to logical rules and consistent reasoning, the concept of race is disdained side by side with references to black people and white people, which are used interchangeably with African Americans and Euro-Americans, respectively. Were reasoning and analytical skills cultivated in schools, this contradiction would not pass unnoticed, and white people and black people would be recognized as "biological misnomers." It would be deduced that human relations are not plagued by either race or racism. Rather, it is the practice of racial classification—the census, academic, and media references to persons as black people and white people on the basis of their skin color and facial form—that continually heighten awareness of racial differences and lead to discrimination for and against. Racial classification may be said to be the canon of social studies and multiculturalism one of its reverberations.

Despite voluminous refutations of the notions of black and white races, or black and white people, social scientists, political representatives, and journalists continue to offer racial descriptions of social phenomena. Henry Louis Gates Jr. points to a certain contradiction in speech on "race":

Race, as a meaningful criterion within the biological sciences, has long been recognized to be a fiction. When we speak of "the white race" or "the black race," the Jewish race," or "Aryan race," we speak in biological misnomers and, more generally, in metaphors. Nevertheless, our conversations are replete with usages of race which have their sources in the dubious psuedosciences of the eighteenth and nineteenth centuries.[68]

But what is the status of "black literature" and "colored folks?" Are they not extensions of the biological misnomer—a black race? Do they not prolong the existence of biological misnomers in social consciousness? Twentieth-century discourse on human experiences and literary creations need not utilize psuedo-scientific ruminations.

Most textbooks on race relations contain a generally brief admission that racial classification is an unscientific practice. At the same time they offer a variety of explanations of the experiences of races—black people and white people. This contradiction is generally glossed over with the claim that race is a "social reality." However, it is studies, reports, and policies on "race relations" and "racial" experiences that consolidate the idea of race and reinforce perceptions of race as a social reality. Michael Omi and Howard Winant's remarks are typical: "U.S. society is racially both more divisive and more complex today than at any previous time in its history. Racial theory must address this reality."[69] Is it not possible that the constant theorizing about race creates that so-called reality? Typical, too, is the authors' self-contradiction and tautology: "We have argued that race has no fixed meaning, but is constructed and transformed sociohistorically through competing political projects, through the necessary and ineluctable link between the structural and cultural dimensions of race in the U.S."[70] Race has no "fixed meaning," but is "transformed by . . . dimensions of race in the U.S.!" How can *race* be transformed through cultural dimensions of *race*?

The concept of race represents an identification of certain anatomical attributes not persons. "Race" is not problematic, if it is so conceived. What is problematic is the allocation of persons to races and the criteria of classification used to do so. What is thoroughly logically flawed is the practice of describing persons as members of races. Because race is an identification of certain attributes, to claim that it is a social problem goes beyond the bounds of coherence. The popular observation—America has a race problem—makes no sense. Are there problems between the races? No. Black and white people or black and white races are yet to be identified accurately. Is American society plagued with racism? No. Poor reasoning, which leads to the identification of persons as members of races. Under the guise of dealing with racism, multiculturalism's advocates classify persons racially and thereby intensify awareness of differences and different treatment of the different. These phenomena are then cited to substantiate the proposition that multiculturalism is the remedy for racial oppression.

Multiculturalism propagates and consolidates racial classification, promoting a practice of lumping a wide variety of different individuals into groups of "African Americans," "Hispanics," "Asian Americans," and "Native Americans," and homogenizing them all into "people of color." What its advocates do not notice is that there are innumerable skin colors, lip sizes, and nose shapes among persons classified as black people.[71] Some persons who are classified as black in the United Kingdom are officially regarded as Caucasian in the United States. The official and unofficial racial classification system in the United States and Brazil makes a mockery of skin color as the decisive criterion of race membership.[72] In both societies, a person can be anatomically "white" but officially "black," and vice versa. Why, then, do media commentaries continue blandly to refer to people as blacks and whites? And it is not just journalists, but also presidents, vice presidents, members of Congress, and educators that disseminate nonsensical racial categories. Donald Muir charges that social scientists are also miseducating students about "race":

One of the scandals of the twentieth century has been the general failure of the scientific community to publicly disavow the concept of physiological "race," a causal taxonomic scheme that first appeared in biology two and a half centuries ago. Although the ambiguities of this typology forced biologists and geneticists to abandon it during the last half century, little effort was made to educate the public. Social, behavioral, and applied scientists, on the other hand, continue to report research findings about race without bothering to define it. Both practices, one of omission, and the other of commission, have allowed race to endure as a major component of the public mind.[73]

Racial classification remains an arbitrary accentuation of specific anatomical differences; it should be taken not as a representation of things in nature but as part of a "system of nomenclature."[74]

In attempting to construct "races," eighteenth-century naturalists sought to follow up on their systematic classifications of elements in nature; they failed, however, to demarcate definite racial types within the human species. Nevertheless, as Theodore Allen demonstrates in *The Invention of the White Race*, the results of their efforts were adopted by politicians, entrepreneurs, and publicists who stressed hierarchical differences among the human species to justify certain political and economic decisions. White and black attributes were concocted and used to explain behavior and historical developments, and justify policies. These concoctions are as chimerical as they are popular; their official utilization has been so systematic that even "transformative intellectuals" adopt racial identities and "see" racial oppressors and victims.

Overall, justifications for multiculturalism are replete with affirmations of racial, ethnic, and gender classifications that are generally glossed over with the claim that "women" and "people of color" are socially constructed and a social reality. Nevertheless, the idea of social constructionism, as advanced by Peter Berger and Thomas Luckmann's *The Social Construction of Reality*, was deployed precisely to combat references to social reality as a thing out-there that sociologists analyze.[75] Social constructivism is not a form of methodological realism. By redirecting a focus on social practices, Berger and Luckmann asked sociologists not to hide their classificatory preferences behind the perceptions of the subjects being studied, or assume that there is an agreement on these preferences. Such procedures would be an expression of "bad faith" on the part of sociologists. As Peter Berger writes in *Invitation to Sociology*:

The sociologist . . . should know the acrobatics by which the actors have gotten into their costumes for any particular role, and this should make it very hard for him to give ontological status to the masquerade. The sociologist ought, therefore, to have difficulties with any set of categories that apply appellations to people—"Negroes," "whites," "Caucasians," or, for that matter, "Jews," "Gentiles," Americans," "Westerners." In one way or another, with more or less malignancy, all such appellations become exercises in "bad faith," as soon as they are charged with ontological implications. Sociology makes us understand that a "Negro" is a person so designated by society, that the designation releases pressures that will tend to make him into the designated image, but also that these pressures are arbitrary, incomplete and, most importantly, reversible.[76]

When social scientists present findings about black people and white people, they are not just recording popular perceptions, for the dissemination of their findings may itself be the basis of these popular perceptions. In other words, the findings of social scientists are part of the construction of social reality, not a reflection of it. In the context of social constructionism, social scientists' claim that their remarks and studies on racial and ethnic relations represent the real world should be regarded as an expression of professional irresponsibility.

The fact that identities are social constructed does not imply that sociologists can refuse to engage in conceptual clarification, or to examine official and institutional policies that generate racial and gender self-identifications. On the contrary, social constructionism prompts the question: By what criteria are whites, women, and people of color identifiable, and are these criteria stable, intelligible, and internally consistent? Social constructionism also facilitates recognition of a distinction between usage and the endorsement of racial-ethnic and gender categories. Gender and racial categories may be deployed for analytical purposes, but they do not have to be endorsed by social scientists. Endorsement takes place when these categories are taken as representations of "real" people. As such, it introduces the very essentialism and reification that social constructionism opposes.

References to social constructionism, as a justification for claiming that race is socially real, face the difficulty of deciding which of the many divergent conceptions of blacks reflects the real world. The criteria of racial classification simply do not justify allocating persons—who possess innumerable biological attributes—to fixed and exclusive races. Thus racial classificatory competition continues within genetic, regional, cultural, and anatomical markings. A recent study of the geographic distribution of genes is rich with demonstrations of the specious status of anatomical classification into races.[77] Nor is there any "empirical" confirmation of a general acceptance of the categories "black" and white." As the demand for a new census category for "multiracials," or "racially mixed people" indicates, many citizens oppose the bipolar racial classification based on skin color that the Census Bureau has adopted.[78] The Bureau does not publicize the number of respondents who write "human" or "other" on their forms, or those who refuse to identify as members of races and ethnic groups. Such respondents are silenced, for they resist the officially imposed racial and ethnic identities. Multiculturalism continues this silencing of different voices. If it had been about including silenced voices, its advocates would have been proposing that the curriculum include texts that refute gender, racial, and ethnic classifications. Had it been a movement dedicated to laying bare the arbitrary and inconsistent status of differences-construction, its protagonists would have been in the forefront of an exposé of official racializing and gendering practices.

The Culture Concept and Realism

As indicated, advocates of critical multiculturalism distance their project from those versions of multiculturalism that pursue the celebration of cultural differences. Terence Turner's remarks make explicit critical multiculturalism's opposition to mere diversity affirmation and identity politics:

Critical multiculturalism seeks to use cultural diversity as a basis for challenging, revising, and relativizing basic notions and principles common to dominant and minority cultures alike, so as to construct a more vital, open, and democratic common culture. . . . In sharp contrast to critical multiculturalism is that of cultural nationalists and fetishists of *differences* for whom *culture* reduces to a tag for ethnic identity and a license for political and intellectual separatism.[79]

Advocates of critical multiculturalism take issue with both the essentialization of differences expressed in difference multiculturalism and traditional anthropology's conception of culture. For Turner, anthropology has proven itself irrelevant to "the multiculturalist project of education reform and, more broadly, to social political and cultural transformation."[80] As a corrective, he advises anthropologists to cease to be bystanders in the historical struggle for cultural democracy.

Turner's broadside against anthropology assumes that anthropologists operate within a single definition of culture. This is an inaccurate assumption, for there are sharp contrasts among the definitions of culture offered by the founders and practitioners of the discipline. For example, Edward Tylor's much-cited definition signals culture as an intrinsically human property: "Culture or Civilization, taken in its wide ethnographic sense, is that complex whole which includes knowledge, belief, art, morals, law, custom, and any other capabilities and habits acquired by man as a member of society."[81] Here "man" represents the human species, and "culture," the creations, practices, and inheritances of members of that species. By contrast, other anthropologists utilize a conception of *single cultures to construct groups and their own individual cultures*. The usage is exemplified in Alfred Kroeber and Clyde Kluckhohn's remarks:

Confusion both on the part of some anthropologists and of certain critics of anthropological work has arisen from lack of explicit clarity as to what is encompassed by culture. Some anthropologists have described culture as if culture included only a group's patterns for living, their conceptions of how specified sorts of people ought to behave under specified conditions. . . . In our opinion, as we have indicated earlier, culture includes both modalities of actual behavior and a group's conscious, partly conscious, and unconscious designs for living.[82]

Kroeber and Kluckhohn, after reviewing some one hundred and sixty definitions of culture, endorsed a definition that focuses on human group rather than the human species as a group. It is this tendency that has had the greatest influence on contemporary usage of the culture concept, especially as culture became a means of national identification and group mobilization from the mid-twentieth century.

The observation of specific symbols, values, and material artifacts to identify a single culture, or group culture has two significant weaknesses. First, it is based on an assumption that the observed phenomena are not part of a universal pattern of symboling, and are therefore not a distinct, single culture but variations on (human) culture. This comment echoes Wolfgang Welsch's critical analysis of the concept of single cultures.[83] Welsch argues further that the concepts of interculturality and multiculturality follow in the wake of eighteenth century philosopher Johann Herder's notion of single cultures where culture is defined as an inner sphere that differentiates groups of people. A second and major weakness in the construction of groups according to cultures is that it begs the question of group identification. An observer notices cultural differences and, on this basis, identifies different "groups." It is the observer, then, that takes the concept of cultural differences into the field, so to speak. These differences cannot be subsequently invoked as empirical instances that demonstrate the existence of different groups. Individuals may share "culture" without belonging or regarding themselves as belonging to a group.

The complexity of the culture concept reflects its purpose of construction—the explanation of behavior, and its prominence in social studies cannot be overstated. From the late nineteenth century, "culture" functioned as means of repudiating naturalists' biological explanations of behavior, as well as their correlations of behavior and biological attributes. Some anthropologists, and later the Boas School of Anthropology, insisted that the plasticity of human capabilities and the enormous variations in customs, habits, mores, values, beliefs, and behavior invalidated the claims of the biological determinists. It was argued that culture not biology determines behavior, and it defines the human personality. All human beings, unlike other animals, are bearers, practitioners, and products of culture. This universalistic conception of culture gradually lost its influence as a result of geographic excursions, colonial incursions, and attention to the myriad differences in human behavior. It is in this context that Carl Grant noted that anthropologists generally prefer to study "how humans differ from animals and how humans differ from each other."[84] Once it was agreed that culture determines behavior, it was but a short step to claim that different behaviors reflect different cultures. Grant suggested an alternative focus on human similarities. However, this alternative is yet to be pursued, even by Grant himself, who continues to advocate a multicultural education mired in notions of racial differences and multiple cultures.

Another alternative would be focus on neither "empirical" differences or similarities, but on the various conceptions of culture and how these conceptions of culture themselves shape identities, expectations, and interactions. For example, although culture is generally conceived as a phenomenon that an individual or a group could possess, it is also defined generically, that is, as *human* symbol construction and utilization. As anthropologist Leslie White writes: "All culture (civilization) depends upon the symbol. It was the exercise of the symbolic faculty that brought culture into existence and it is the use of symbols that makes the perpetuation of culture possible. Without the symbol there would be no culture, and man would be merely an animal, not a human being.[85] White's writings on culture draw attention to the specific, symboling quality undergirding human practices and experiences. His conceptions of culture leave open the possibility of observing variations on that symboling quality. By contrast, in the conception of culture popularized from the mid-twentieth century, these variations are construed as (single) cultures in themselves. Particular material objects, practices, values, beliefs, achievements, and behavioral patterns are selected and deemed "culture." These entities are then associated or located within an otherwise-defined group—a race, a class, a generation, a gender, or a nation—to form racial culture, middle-class culture, youth culture, "womanculture," and American culture, respectively. The national culture—American culture, for example—is then depicted as a macroculture comprising a multiplicity of microcultures.[86] But representatives of any of the microcultures can claim distinctiveness, autonomy, and educational rights.

Critical multiculturalism's observation of cultural differences is used to identify groups—"blacks," "Latinos," and "white students." The cultural differences within each of these groups is ignored, for critical multiculturalism's observation follow official lines of racial-ethnic demarcation. It also shares certain core classifications with difference multiculturalism, and its "commitment to social justice" is identical to difference multiculturalism's objective—the liberation of "women" and "persons of color." Peter McLaren's assertion that differences do not exist independently of history, culture, and power can also be found in the writings of James Banks, Christine Sleeter, Carl Grant, and Molefi Asante, who would be regarded as advocates of "difference multiculturalism. "[87] Critical multiculturalism's propositions, then, are not consistent. Its advocates proclaim a goal of de-essentializing racial and cultural differences, and simultaneously reinforce these differences in order to sharpen group awareness of injustice and oppression.

The transformation of the oppressed into oppositional agencies is the goal of both critical and difference multiculturalisms as their advocates express their resolve to eradicate racism, sexism, injustice and inequality. This objective defines critical and difference multiculturalisms as moral-political protests requiring, then, an immoral Other—white people, white males, and white culture. This demonization of whiteness is possibly therapeutic for "whites" who deem themselves "liberal" on race relations—"I am white but not a racist." It may also gratify some "blacks" as Shelby Steele claims in *The Content of Our Character*—who pursue power and favors from "whites" through guilt ascription. In both difference multiculturalism and critical multiculturalism, "whites" are morally denounced, politically essentialized as the historical enemy of "people of color," and not given their humanness. The question not asked is: Can their humanness be denied without a consequence of increased "white terror" and self-created black dehumanization?" "Whites" are surely not going to take their dehumanization lying down, and "blacks" will increasingly being to sound like the white racist they allegedly abjure. A radical criticism of difference multiculturalism would assert that those characterized as white people, women, and people of color are human beings constituted as different groups within the specific "forms of signification" provided by racial and gender theories of social relations. It would dispense entirely with these forms.

A perspective critical of difference multiculturalism would identify the theoretical inputs that racialize and genderize differences and persons. It would recognize that anatomical differences do not justify allocating *human beings* to races and genders. It would identify the specific gender and racial theories of history and society that suggest this allocation, and the official and academic practices that realize it. In the context of a purpose of de-essentializing is differences, questions that might be pursued are as follows: Does the practice of racial classification produce clearly defined and recognizable races? If culture is defined as the artifacts, beliefs, and values of groups, would not many, many cultures be discovered? For, as James Stuart Olson writes: "In short, shifting combinations of race, nationality, language, culture, and religion organized ethnic life in America, creating hundreds of culturally independent communities."[88] Should they all be present in the curriculum? But each cultural community may contain sub-communities. As Jane Flax writes: "Only recently have scholars considered the possibility that there may be at least three histories in every culture—'his,' 'hers,' and 'ours.'"[89] His and her cultures may be divided further along class, ethnic, regional, and racial lines, and these may also be combined to produce innumerable types of cultures, histories, and knowledges. Schooling would collapse under the weight of the effervescence of cultures.

Like the early racial-cultural classifiers, advocates of multiculturalism utilize a concept of single cultures that accommodates the idea of separate "races" and "groups." By implication, an operational multicultural curriculum would be steeped in arbitrariness and disputes. Would such a curriculum be achieved when there are: (1) courses on the vast number of different "cultures" in society; (2) courses on history and society from different cultural perspectives, including those of "gays," "gangs," and polygamists; (3) courses that are sympathetic to "oppressed" cultures; (4) courses that omit the so-called canons of mainstream culture; or (5) courses designed to examine the ramifications of the thesis that there are many cultures? As matters stand, advocates of multicultural education may be said to be monocultural, in that they exclude a variety of conceptions of culture. Their chosen conception of culture merely serves to make differences ineradicable and insurmountable features of culture, which serves to further cultural struggles.

By depicting these groups as having conflicting interests, culture is reconstituted as a site of resistance and struggle. Thus Danny Weil defines culture as: "[The] unique manner by which diverse groups of human beings organize and actualize their physical and mental lives in dialectical confrontation with biological survival, oppression, resistance, and the struggle for human dignity, self-determination, and fulfillment."[90] This definition of culture centralizes conflicts and political struggles as part of demonstrating that knowledge is essentially linked with practices and struggles. Two observations could be made about Weil's conceptions of culture. First, it is circular. What makes groups diverse? Their cultures. What makes their cultures different? Their diversity. Are these groups diverse because of cultural differences, or are the differences noted after these "diverse" groups were observed? If so, what drew attention to the persons comprising a group in the first place? Second, the definition is incoherent. Its underlying premise is that culture is not a politically neutral category because knowledge is not a politically neutral category. But, by implication, political neutrality is itself not politically neutral.

Similar Differences and Different Similarities

Human beings possess both similarities and differences, and an emphasis on either must be justified. Thus observation of cultural differences cannot be an end in itself. There are also cultural similarities to be considered. Indeed, cultural differences are embedded in human similarities. It is *similar* human beings that are being compared to discover their cultural differences. But how different are we—"we" being the human beings classified as American citizens? Consider the following claim as an "empirical" observation:

We are one of the most diverse societies in the world, a polyglot nation teeming with differences—racial differences, language differences, religious differences, regional differences, and differences in sexual preferences. The key to our cohesion and survival as a nation is the cultivation of respect and tolerance for and appreciation of our differences.

This passage appears to be a reasonably accurate and morally laudable description of American society. However, another empirical description of U.S. society could be as follows:

We are one of the most homogeneous societies in the world, a society replete with credal, attitudinal, and behavioral similarities—pursuit of money as a means of happiness, fear of violence and willingness to engage in preemptive violence, mistrust of human nature, allegiance to a deity, a concern with racial and ethnic differences, belief in the power of education to foster progress, committed to individualism and democratic values, and optimistic regarding both personal and social developments.

These passages implicitly demonstrate the arbitrariness of the multiculturalists' accentuation of differences. Why is there not a similar emphasis on similarities? But that is not the critical issue either. The critical issue is our mutual dependency. *Not differences but dependencies should be the watchword of education reform for a world growing smaller.* As Martin Luther King Jr. writes: "We are caught up in an inescapable network of mutuality, tied to a single garment of destiny."[91] He might have added that, precisely because of our differences, we are bound together in a seamless web of dependencies.

What should also be obvious from the above passages is that differences, like similarities, are in the mind's eye of the observer. It is human beings who must choose to stress either their differences or their similarities. Indeed, it is because of the common status of being human that differences can be perceived. Hannah Arendt's remarks capture this condition: "In our human sameness, lies our differences. Plurality is the condition of human action because we are all the same, that is, human, in such a way that nobody is ever the same as anyone else who ever lived, lives, or will live."[92] It is up to human beings to choose whether to emphasize their differences or their similarities. Those who regard themselves as *indelibly* white, female, Hispanic, Native American, and so on have already made their choice. The rest should choose in light of projected consequences and events in Rwanda, India, Somalia, Yugoslavia, and the Middle East.

Human beings make the choice to notice either their differences or their similarities. However, either choice should be justified, for there are some noteworthy implications. Who is different from whom, and on what basis is a prototype selected? It is frequently observed that women are different from men, and that blacks are different from whites. By implication, "men" and "whites" provide the comparative standards. But, it may be asked of these observations, so what? What are the purposes and policy implications of the observation that women are different from men? Women are also similar to men. But men *are* different from women, it may be insisted; they generally possess larger and stronger musculature, for example. However, these differences pale into functional insignificance in specific circumstances. Were physical strength not prized, large muscles would not be a glorified standard, and similarities in musculature rather than differences would be noticed. The point is that because any observation of differences is contextual, its purpose must be made explicit. Explicitness of purpose may be demanded of any observation of similarities among human beings, for example, self-awareness, the capacity for symbolic representation and self-reflexiveness, empathy, conscience, and needs that are perceptually linked to the future.

Multiculturalism's celebration of differences is most pertinent to the functioning of a market economy whose purpose is the production of commodities. The cultivation of differences facilitates the thrust and processes of competition. Thus governments should be expected to sponsor multiculturalism in schools. It is no threat to the market economy; indeed it nurtures the distinct in-group/out-group identities that are often called upon to compete and wage war. Henry Giroux seems particularly unaware of the complicity between "the discourse of differences" and market exigencies, in arguing: "Difference is important both as a marker for including specific forms of knowledge into the curriculum and as a basis for developing a pedagogy that takes seriously the notion that students read the world differently, that they produce knowledge and categories of meaning that must be understood if they are to be inserted into, rather than outside of, the process of teaching and learning."[93]   Giroux's assumption that "students read the world differently" requires considerable clarification and justification. Differently from whom or what?   Indeed, are not the ideological mystifications prevailing in both schools and mass media the source of students' reading of the world?   If so, students do not have specific forms of knowledge, although they may hold beliefs of unjustified ideas about "other groups" and social phenomena.

Can a pedagogy be "critical" that takes students' interpretations of events for granted?   Are teachers of mathematics and physics expected to conform to and confirm students' beliefs about numbers and energy? are the differences students bring to the classroom not partly a result of an "ideological" cultivation of differences?   Unlike the official practice, however, Giroux's cultivation of differences is couched in a language of resistance to cultural domination. Yet his writings contain no critical analysis of the sites—the Census Bureau, public policies, academic studies, and media reports on race relations—where racial and cultural differences are constructed. Like much of nineteenth-century anthropology, Giroux's "discourse of differences" collaborates with legislatures in the project of constructing and magnifying in-group and out-group identities. His writings celebrate perhaps the most salient claim within arguments for multiculturalism—U.S. society harbors profound racial and cultural differences. The contentious issue, however, is what is the purpose of noticing these differences, given that the society also contains equally profound racial and cultural similarities?   This is the question implicitly raised by Barry Kanpol's advocacy of "a mutual pedagogy that crosses the boundaries of differences into a terrain of similarities and solidarity without understanding our similarities within our differences public school educators, as well as radical academics, have little to cling to in terms of alleviating the frustrations of intersecting race, class, and gender relations."[94]   Kanpol does not substantiate his claim that racial, class, and gender relations are intersecting, nor his assertion that differences "precede" similarities. Nevertheless, it should be obvious that U.S. students and citizens bear a host of similarities: beliefs in God, an after life, family, and democracy, loyalty to country, the necessity of money, the unacceptability of violence, and the sovereignty of the individual. Do teachers not also have a duty to emphasize these similarities?

Multiculturalism is necessarily silent on human similarities. Its basic classifications testify to its status as an extension of liberationist variants of gender and racial theories. These theories enjoy a canonical status in political and intellectual life, not to mention governmental endorsement. Multiculturalism, then, is neither "transformative" nor a challenge to "mainstream knowledge." It is a discourse that, to quote Henry Louis Gates Jr., "remains entrapped within the presuppositions of the discourse it means to oppose, enacts a conflict internal to that 'master discourse.'"[95] Indicating its derivation from a realist theory of knowledge and being, multiculturalism's advocates present the categories—blacks, women, gays, the handicapped, Latinos, and whites—as observable persons, and ignore the definitional problems surrounding these categories. Conceiving these categories as reflections of reality, they present gender, racial, and ethnic oppression, domination, and injustice as indisputably existing conditions, as if this makes their descriptions immune to evaluation within intellectual standards, and unrelated to the logical structure of the arguments in which they are couched. Their reliance on a realist theory of knowledge that leads to the marginalization of standards such as clarity, accuracy, and logical consistency in description and argument exposition. However, this marginalization necessarily generates dogmatic and relativist disputes over differences in observations.

Any theorist can claim that a personal observation of reality, for example, oppression, is relatively autonomous and cannot be successfully challenged by any other's observation. Reality has to be observed and mere observations do not present standards for dispute resolution. Hence no person's observation of reality can be said to be decisive. Thus disputes over the nature of the "real" social world can only be shunted into personal and political denunciations and accusations. Consider some of the questions that are raised by critics of multiculturalism: Are women and people of color *really* oppressed, and by whom? What is (the actual nature of this) oppression? Which women's experiences are to count as oppression? These questions indicate that the multiculturalists' proof of oppression lies in observations of oppression, and challenges to their observations are met with charges of racism, sexism, and partisanship for the "oppressor."

A way out of this state of infinite analytical regress is to conceive situations and experiences as events signified within a given theoretical arrangement. No experiential claim could then be said to represent reality, defined as extra-theoretical conditions. As Peter McLaren writes:

Since all experience is the experience of meaning, we need to recognize the role that language plays in the production of experience. You don't have an experience and then search for a word to describe that experience. Rather language helps to constitute experience by providing a structure of intelligibility or mediating device through which experiences can be understood. Rather than talking about experience, it is more accurate to talk about "experience effects."[96]

Critical multiculturalism, then, is critical of any multiculturalism that takes experiences as theoretically unmediated, "foundational" events. However, McLaren does not confront the deconstructive implications of his "criticalist" position, as he declares his empathy for "real people who suffer," that is, blacks, women, and Latinos. In critical multiculturalism, the experiences of certain races and a certain gender remain foundational conditions.

What "critical pedagogists" should notice is that experiences of oppression are racialized and gendered only through the endorsement of theories of race and gender. These theories deserve to be present in the curriculum, but as theoretical structures, not as representations of reality, for that would be to claim a monopoly purchase on the world, which, by implication, leaves no space for other theories. The exclusion of other voices begins precisely with a claim to be presenting the way the world really is. And challenges to this claim that share its epistemological position merely lead to interminable disagreements over the correspondence between empirical data and the real world. It is on this regressive slope that multiculturalism's disputes slide. Its advocates present gender, racial, ethnic, and class experiences as "real," in the sense of being independent of criteria of classification, assumptions, and conceptions of social causation.

In their wholesale rejection of "Western philosophy" and simultaneous appropriation of realist epistemology, critical pedagogists and multiculturalists ignore an epistemological tradition that conceives "reality" as simply a concept used in a particular theory of knowledge to construct a foundation for truth. The problem is that reality cannot be conceived as an external object that theory grasps or reflects, for a theoretical appropriation of the real cannot be ascertained. Paraphrasing Roy Bhaskar's perspective on realism, Ernest House writes:

Theory is not in a relation of correspondence with reality and does not mirror reality. To provide an explanation is not to provide a mirror of events, a subtle but important distinction. Theory attempts to explain events, and the explanation may be adequate or inadequate. Theory must confirm to standards of adequacy established within particular substantive disciplines.[97]

Bhaskar does argue for a nonnaive realism, which posits that the world can be known through and only through descriptions. The descriptions, however, do not reflect the world, but conceptual arrangements which must be logically consistent. If reality cannot be conceptually mirrored, then, descriptions of gender, racial, ethnic, and class experiences do not reflect real conditions; they are simply intellectual constructs. In proclaiming otherwise, advocates of critical multiculturalism render unchallengable the racial and gender differences discovered by "modernist" sciences and propagated by official institutions.

Multiculturalism's Oppression and Power versus Alienation and Commodification

As if in opposition to Marx's discovery of bipolar class interests and concentrated bourgeois power, advocates of multiculturalism describe society as mired in relations of group domination and oppression—of women, gays, the handicapped, and persons of color. They further recommend that the experiences and perspectives of women, persons of color, and the poor should be included in the curriculum as a means of democratizing education and empowering the oppressed. These arguments are well developed in the writings of Paulo Freire, whose influence on the theorists of insurgent and resistance multiculturalism is generally acknowledged.[98]

The analyses of culture, schooling, and liberation developed in the writings of advocates of insurgent and critical multiculturalism partially echo the Freirean construction of a pedagogy for emancipatory social change. However, it should be noted that what these "multiculturalists" adopt from Freire's *Pedagogy of the Oppressed* is not its implicit recommendation of nonviolence, and its explicit proposal of love for humankind, but its dialogical pedagogical remedy for education's failures, its emphasis on different cultures, and its thesis of an endemic oppression in society that stifles both learning and liberation. The first sentence in Chapter 1 of Freire's work *Pedagogy of the Oppressed* states: "While the problem of humanization has always, from an axiological point of view, been humankind's central problem, it now takes on the character of an inescapable concern."[99] In other words, the development of a human-species consciousness is now an ethical imperative. Can such a consciousness be developed within an a priori allocation of persons to groups and identification of some as oppressors and oppressed? Freire continues: "Dehumanization, which marks not only those whose humanity has been stolen, but also (though in a different way) those who have stolen it, is a *distortion* of the vocation of becoming more fully human."[100]

One of the features of Freirean educational philosophy is its grounding in a universalistic conception of being—humankind. Nevertheless, Freire's work is analytically flawed at two levels. First, its conception of oppression is incomplete, circular in its dependency on unspecified conceptions of "exploitation" and "violence." Second, "oppressors" are not accorded membership of the human family. Freire defines oppression thus:

Any situation in which "A" objectively exploits "B" or hinders his and her pursuit of self-affirmation as a responsible person is one of oppression. Such a situation in itself constitutes violence, even when sweetened by false generosity, because it interferes with the individual's ontological and historical vocation to be more fully human. With the establishment of a relationship of oppression, violence has *already* begun.[101]

Oppression, elsewhere depicted as "overwhelming control," precedes violence, but is also defined by violence, which Freire nowhere specifies. On this analytical basis, Freire divides human beings into oppressors/oppressed, manipulators/manipulated, violators/victims, and cultural invaders/invaded.

Throughout Freire's analysis, "oppressors" are morally maligned, and Freire expresses no confidence in the possibility of their rehabilitation, but he admits that they are also caught up in a system of dehumanization. However, he appeals to and seeks to organize only the oppressed, in order to usher in an ethos of humanization. And this selection of the oppressed as agents for the realization of a fully human social order is also morally based. They are chosen simply because theirs is a life of suffering and disempowerment. Freire writes:

This, then, is the great humanistic and historical task of the oppressed: to liberate themselves and their oppressors as well. The oppressors, who oppress, exploit, and rape by virtue of their power, cannot find in this power the strength to liberate either the oppressed or themselves. Only power that springs from the weakness of the oppressed will be sufficiently strong to free both.[102]

Power has corrupted the oppressors, and makes them incapable of initiating humanization. But why should it not corrupt the oppressed also, either in the process of struggle against the oppressors or after the process is complete? By not attending to this issue, Freire fails to substantiate his implicit assertion that suffering and disempowerment ennoble their bearers. Faith prevails or takes the place of reasoned analysis.

In Freire's *Pedagogy of the Oppressed*, the oppressed are, like Rousseau's "noble savage" or Marx's morally pure proletariat, originally unsullied beings corrupted by "bourgeois ideology" (read culture in Freire and Giroux). But while the young Marx proposes philosophy as the means of the proletariat's intellectual emancipation, Freire recommends a cultural transformation:

Cultural synthesis is thus a mode of action for confronting culture itself, as the preserver of the very structures by which it was formed. Cultural action, as historical action, is an instrument for superseding the dominant alienated and alienating culture. In this sense, every authentic revolution is a cultural revolution.[103]

Educators are to be the torchbearers of cultural revolution, or, as Henry Giroux conceives them, "transformative intellectuals" utilizing schools for resisting oppression. The question is, however, will the "oppressors" stand idly by while educators engage in their acts of revolutionary transformation? Surely to describe certain persons as oppressors—"dominant elites," "cultural invaders," and "capitalists"—and announce an intention to destroy their system of privileges will lead to their demolishing of all attempts at a liberating and revolutionary education. Thus Freire's recommendation may be said to be strategically counter productive. If adopted, the self-proclaimed educator-revolutionaries and transformative intellectuals would achieve their own marginalization. However, they would revel precisely in this fate, for the oppressors' crushing of the revolution in education proves the existence of a system of oppression. The revolution is doomed to fail, but the educator-revolutionary knowingly settles for being a martyr in pursuit of power for the oppressed.

The concepts of culture, power, and domination play pivotal roles in expositions of multiculturalism that integrate oppression, political struggles, and education. Freire's representation of education as an "insurgent" cultural politics is an example that is echoed in some of Henry A. Giroux's writings. Indeed, the concept of culture as a political formation is pivotal to arguments in Giroux's *Theory and Resistance in Education: A Pedagogy for the Opposition,* and *Border Crossings*. For Giroux, there are many cultural expressions, all unfolding in the context of power:

In the most general sense, culture is constituted by the relations between different classes and groups bounded by structural forces and material conditions and informed by a range of experiences mediated, in part, by the power exercised by a dominant society . . . culture is constituted as a dialectical instance of power and conflict rooted in the struggle over both material conditions and the form and content of practical activity.[104]

Here multiculturalism is a form of resistance to the schools' legitimation of certain relations of power, privilege, and domination; it directs attention to group differences only in order to forge a radical understanding of political domination Nevertheless, Giroux's overall thesis is that power does not reside in a centralized monolithic system. Rather, it is a ubiquitous feature of social relations, and both its origin and conditions of existence inhere in practices within educational institutions. As the strategic-intellectual representative of subjugated groups, multiculturalism must expose and challenge the legitimation and reproduction of power relations that result in structural inequities and domination. It must not be part of either the liberal emphasis on diversity or the radical endorsement of differences structured in dominance. Rather, it should seek to create agencies of social transformation in educational institutions, which is precisely where knowledge is produced and legitimated.

For Christine Sleeter and Carl Grant the process of challenging the power structure and empowering the oppressed begins with a demonstration of connections among power, knowledge, and interests:

One exercises power when one desires a certain state of affairs and acts to bring it about. Power requires desire, interest, or passion; a vision of a state of affairs which is desirable or attractive and which differs from the current state of affairs; and the ability to act in a way that is sufficiently potent and informed to achieve what one desires. . . . Knowledge is central to power. . . . Knowledge that empowers centers around the interests and aims of the prospective knower.[105]

In positing a connection between power and knowledge it becomes plausible to conceive intellectual exchanges as confrontations between power players. Critics of multiculturalism can be accused of pursuing power or seeking to retain power. James Banks writes:

Despite its impressive successes, however, multicultural education faces serious challenges as we move toward the next century. One of the most serious of these challenges is the highly organized, well-financed attack by the Western traditionalists who fear that multicultural education will transform America in ways that will result in their own disempowerment.[106]

Here multicultural education is described as a form of knowledge opposed to the status quo, and therefore being attacked by the superior force of "traditionalists." However, as a beleaguered combatant in a struggle on behalf of the powerless and oppressed, it becomes morally superior to the attacks of the traditionalists.

Although the analysis of power in advocacies of multiculturalism is presented as a description of actual patterns of domination in society, it represents a peculiar combination of certain Marxist claims about power and ideology, the pluralist conception of power advanced by Max Weber, and the notion of the ubiquity of power that is articulated in the writings of Michel Foucault and Jean-François Lyotard.[107] While Foucault insists that in modern society there is a general phenomenon of bourgeois domination, he, like Weber, disdains the Marxist thesis that power is centralized in a class or in the state:

Power . . . is never localised here or there, never in anybody's hands, never appropriated as a commodity, or piece of wealth. Power is employed and exercised through net-like organizations. And not only do individuals circulate between its threads; they are always also in the position of simultaneously undergoing and exercising power.[108]

This conception of power resembles both Talcott Parsons' conception of power as a "generalized capacity" to secure obligations, a circulating mechanism, like money, and Marx's insistence that the bourgeoisie is both in power and under the power of the laws of capitalist development. Because individuals are merely instances of the articulation of power, Foucault is not interested in who wields power, their intentions, or their strategies. Such "labyrinthine" imponderables are to be avoided in favor of an "analytics of power," "the *how* of power." He writes: "My problem is rather this: what rules of right are implemented by the relations of power in the production of discourses of truth?"[109] Power is not mere repression, an original right, ideology, or a hostile engagement of forces, not a Leviathan, or the state. Power is an epistemological condition of action, for decisions are rooted in convictions of production and possession of truth.

For Foucault, because the possession of truth activates individuals, power and the legitimation of knowledge are inseparable: "There can be no possible exercise of power without a certain economy of discourse of truth which operates through and is the basis of this association. We are subject to the production of truth through power and we cannot exercise power except through the production of truth."[110] This paradoxical declaration gains its status from being an equivocation, for "power" is being conceived in different senses—as outcome and as a process. Nevertheless, it does demonstrate that Foucault's project is radically different from Lyotard's for whom: "knowledge and power are simply two sides of the same question: who decides what knowledge is, and who knows what needs to be decided?"[111] Advocates of multiculturalism claim Foucault's focus on institutional practices, but embrace Lyotard's power-knowledge connection to ask: Who wields power? They answer: white males. Where are the "mechanisms of power?" They endorse Foucault's reply: in schools—institutional processes of cultural-political subjugation and knowledge legitimation. Multiculturalism draws on Lyotard's and Foucault's linking of knowledge and power, and is also indebted to Weber's coupling of power and hostile wills.

Foucault's (and Weber's) presupposition of power's existence in all social relations imitates the Hobbesian-Nietzschean ontology of human nature as a will to power. Foucault, however, denies any connection with the Hobbesian project, and offers six "methodological precautions" that are reminiscent of Weber's objections to Marx's monolithic and economistic conception of power and class action.[112] Weber delimits power by defining it as a projected outcome: "'Power' (*Macht*) is the probability that one actor within a social relationship will be in a position to carry out his own will despite resistance, regardless of the basis on which this probability rests."[113] Power is contextual and relational, and its pursuit is not merely a function of economic interests.

True to his method of rigorous conceptual demarcations, Weber offers other qualifications of power. The exercise of power may be part of a striving after social honor. Power may even be valued as an end in itself. This last conception of power as an essential human attribute comes close to Hobbes' conception of man as a power-seeker in perpetual motion.[114] It is also reminiscent of Nietzsche's will to power and Hegel's conception of man as a historical pursuer of recognition, a thesis developed in Francis Fukuyama's *The End of History and the Last Man*. Within the thesis that men perpetually "struggle for recognition," social relations are conceived as results of the interaction of wills to power and resistance to power. As Weber writes: "All conceivable qualities of a person and all conceivable combinations of circumstances may put him in a position to impose his will in a given situation."[115] For Weber, domination is a characteristic feature of social relations as actors struggle to realize their often conflicting interests using the most rational means at their disposal. However, domination is only a probable outcome, for the putatively dominated may voluntarily obey, or resist.

Weber's analysis of power, as action based on a clash of wills, makes reference to a wide range of conditions: the state, violence, forms of authority, the discharging of duties, the human pursuit of domination and honor, obedience, and resistance to domination. What is not usually recognized is Weber's equivocal use of the term *power,* and the notion of conflicting interests that underlies his reference to competing wills. In Weber's analysis, power performs triple duty—as an immanent, human urge to dominate, a calculation of outcomes within a specific balance of forces, and a set of means, whether charismatic, administrative, or coercive. These various usages of "power" allow Weber to suggest that actors pursue power, exercise power, and use the means of power to dominate, or to realize interests that are not necessarily economic. The means of power constitute a discrete amount of resources whose possession raises the probability of an individual or group dominating another. But individuals may comply or resist so that to have *more power* is not necessarily synonymous with having power *over*. For example, the use of force to ensure compliance implies both an absence of legitimacy and the presence of conflicting interests. Such interests are so significant that in order to substantiate a proposition that a relationship of power exists between A and B, it would be necessary to focus on decision making processes and underlying interests.

These themes surface in the debate between "pluralists" and "elitists," a debate that Steven Lukes reviews in *Power: A Radical View*. Lukes concentrates on the relationship between power and "real" interests to demonstrate certain inadequacies in the one-dimensional (pluralist), two-dimensional (elitist), and functionalist approaches to power.[116] For Lukes, power is an intrinsically evaluative and "essentially contestable" concept. It is also inseparable from some conception of conflicting interests:

power may or may not be a form of influence—depending on whether sanctions are involved; while influence and authority may or may not be a form of power—depending on whether a conflict of interests is involved. Consensual authority, with no conflict of interests, is not, therefore, a form of power. . . . A exercises power over B when A affects B in a manner that is contrary to B's interests.[117]

Because expressions of interests unfold in complex sociopsychological conditions, Lukes qualifies interests as "subjective," and "objective," and "real," and identifies two related limitations in the pluralist and elitist analyses of power. First, they illegitimately ignore the relationship between power and interests. Second, they focus on "actual, observable conflict" without recognizing that there may be no overt or covert conflict between A and B *precisely because power is in operation*. The conflict can be "latent," that is, congealed "in a contradiction between the interests of those exercising power and the real interests of those they exclude."[118] A may be said to be exercising power over B if A's decisions prevent B from perceiving interests whose realization would not be beneficial to A.

Lukes' "alternative" analysis situates power in a context of a clash between A's interests and B's real interests, namely, B's preferences, if B had unhindered access to alternative information and choices. Power, then, is also exercised when individuals are brainwashed or ideologically manipulated to the extent that they cannot construe their "real interests." Lukes' conceptualization of power and real interests, then, could be extended into an analysis of "the marketplace of ideas," ideology, and education; it also turns Bacon's dictum knowledge is power—on its head: Knowledge is the *antidote* to power. This claim also underlies multiculturalist assertions about white male knowledge, hegemony, and patriarchy, as well as their proposals on curriculum transformation. Women and people of color are to have their knowledges inscribed in the curriculum as part of their empowerment and assault on patriarchal and Eurocentric domination.

The multiculturalist assertion that white men are dominant, have power over, or more power than women and people of color implies the existence of mutually exclusive interests among these actors. These interests, however, remain unspecified in the advocacies of multiculturalism. However, can such interests be identified? For, despite the mutual criticisms voiced by their self-characterized representatives, men, women, persons of color, and whites may all be said to be engaged in a common, human pursuit of life, liberty, and happiness, which could be understood as economic security and nonviolent social relations. It may also be argued that the technological, intellectual, and economic resources at the disposal of the human species can deliver these outcomes. The conflicts among these groups over resources deemed "scarce" may, therefore, be regarded as false in the sense of not being in their "real interests," and the outcomes of these conflicts certainly do not reflect human aspirations.

A Marxian Alternative to Multiculturalism?

Following Lukes' analysis, it may also be claimed that it is the self-styled representatives of "oppressed" women and people of color who exercise power over them, for these representatives deny these groups access to knowledge of the Marxian tradition that demonstrates how decommodification can achieve the above-mentioned outcomes. What multiculturalists pursue—cultural equality and equal access to the purchasing of commodities—is inimical to the *human* interests of those classified as women and people of color. Other related inadequacies in multiculturalists' claims about power are as follows: (1) no presentation of the interests of men, women, whites, and persons of color, how these interests are in conflict, or which interests are in conflict—subjective, objective, or real; and (2) no demonstration of how knowledge of the history and achievements of women and people of color would rupture white male power. These weaknesses reflect the fact that the idea of specific, racial and gender interests confronts the same difficulties as biological compartmentalizations of the human species into races and genders. The thesis that white men have power over women and people of color remains as incomplete as the overall project of establishing biological types of human beings.

Lukes' "radical" criticisms of one-dimensional approaches to power are reminiscent of elements of Marx's analysis of political economy. For Marx, the substance of social processes is an antagonism between classes. Fueling this antagonism, however, is a specific mode of production dominated by the bourgeoisie, who, nevertheless, are themselves dominated by the laws of capitalist development: "To prevent possible misunderstanding, a word. I paint the capitalist and the landlord in no sense couleur de rose. But here individuals are dealt with only in so far as they are the personifications of economic categories, embodiments of particular class-relations and class-interests."[119] Power, then, is not a zero-sum resource possessed by groups in conflict. The bourgeoisie rules, collectively, only in the sense that it invests more heavily, through means of violence and ideology, in maintaining the status quo. But its collective dominance is constrained by individual decisions that produce economic anarchy, social disruptions, and modes of resistance. Ultimately, however: "Society can no longer live under this bourgeoisie, in other words, its existence is no longer compatible with society."[120] The "sway of the bourgeoisie" is incompatible with social stability and progress. Thus the bourgeoisie proves itself unfit to be the ruling class and is powerless to forestall revolutionary uprisings.

For Marx, what Steven Lukes describes as "real interests" would be human needs shorn of bourgeois ideological manipulation and intellectual infestations. These needs are in conflict with the exigencies of capitalist commodity production, in which the means of life are commodities, and human creative impulses are reduced to processes of buying and selling labor power. Marx's definition of labor power is eminently humanist and universal: "By labour-power or capacity for labour is to be understood the aggregate of those mental and physical capabilities existing in a *human being*, which he exercises whenever he produces a use-value of any description."[121] In conditions of buying and selling labor power, all human beings experience a multidimensional alienation—from the product of their labor, from one another, from their "species-being," and from creative life activities. Above all, within wage labor, human beings experience a perennial anxiety about (future) access to the means of life. As Marx writes: "An immediate consequence of the fact that man is estranged from the product of his labor, from his life activity, from his species being, is the estrangement of man from man. . . . What applies to a man's relation to his work, to the product of his labor, and to himself, also holds of his relations to the other man and to the other man's labor."[122] It is this estrangement of (generic) men that finds expression in the false consciousness of class, race, and gender. Nevertheless, Marx suggests that among these forms of alienation, only the working class can attain the revolutionary consciousness necessary for the progression of human speciation.

The ultimate objective of the proletarian revolution is decommodification through, first, the abolition of wage labor. This would pave the way for the removal of the pervasive economic insecurity that capitalist commodity production engenders. As David Harvey writes: "Capitalism, in short, is a social system internalizing rules that ensure it will remain a permanently revolutionary and disruptive force in its own world history. If, therefore, 'the only secure thing about modernity is insecurity,' then it is not hard to see from where that insecurity derives."[123] Marx's scathing analysis of wage labor and money indicates an opposition to the commodification of human experiences that is exemplified in the economic insecurity of not only the working class. The accumulative rollercoaster unleashed by capitalist commodity production also imprisons the bourgeoisie in a perpetual state of anxiety over prices and profits.[124]

What is clearly central to Marx's analysis of capitalist development is a critique of social relations dominated by commodities. It is not men, or even classes, but capitalist commodity production that dominates social relations. As Marx writes in the preface to *A Contribution to the Critique of Political Economy*:

In the social production of their existence, men inevitably enter into definite relations, which are independent of their will, namely relations of production appropriate to a stage in the development of their material forces of production. . . . The bourgeois mode of production is the last antagonistic form of the social process of production—antagonistic not in the sense of individual antagonism, but an antagonism that emanates from the individuals' social conditions of existence.[125]

Neither men nor whites have power over others. Rather, all agents within bourgeois relations of production are held in the sway of the antagonisms and vicissitudes of commodity production.

Multiculturalism cannot be presented as being affiliated with Marx's analysis of social relations. Indeed, it is antagonistic with this analysis. It highlights cultural relations and disassociates them from the buying and selling of labor power. It is not without significance that "class" is only cursorily mentioned by its advocates who appeal to other forms of false consciousness—gender, racial, and ethnic identities. These identities are false in the sense of not only being symptoms of specific political economic and intellectual conditions but also in the sense of lacking possibilities for human emancipation. Agitation on behalf of women and people of color merely heightens white male self-identities. By contrast, Marx assumed that agitation on behalf of the working class can lead to de-commodification and the withering away of the state that are preconditions for universal economic security and nonviolent social relations.

What gives multiculturalism an appearance of radical and revolutionary thrusts is its self-description as the voice of the oppressed and disempowered. However, as demonstrated above, neither oppression, power, or for that matter, culture is adequately analyzed. Nowhere in the advocacies of multiculturalism is there any sustained analysis of the literature on these core concepts. Because its sponsors prioritize the liberation of culturally defined groups, they delink power and economic relations, and present a noneconomic conception of power that Foucault abjured: "One can understand nothing about economic science if one does not know how power and economic power are exercised in everyday life."[126] Utilizing the zero-sum conception of power advanced in the debate between "pluralists" and "elitists," advocates of multiculturalism pay no attention to its subsequent modifications and criticisms in the writings of political scientists, sociologists, and philosophers, including Foucault, who expose certain ambiguities in the proposition that power is a thing unequally divided among groups.[127] These criticisms raise an entirely different set of questions, such as: Do white men have more power than women and people of color, or power *over* them? Do white men use their power to subjugate, deliberately and exclusively, women and people of color, or is this subjugation an unintended consequence of their actions? Is there an economic structure that dominates the considerations and actions of white males? Do white men possess power, authority, or influence? Is it men or, as socialist feminists suggest, certain classes among men that wield power?[128] Are all white men equally dominant over women and people of color? Are some white men not also dominant over other white men? How, then, is gender significantly related to domination? These questions have led to various attempts to combine racial, gender, and class analyses.[129] On the other hand, such combinations rob each of its analytical determinacy and necessarily render class indistinguishable from gender or race.[130]

Marx's argument that with the concentration and centralization of capitalist production, workers would subsequently create a monolithic class opposition to the encroachments of capital suffers serious gaps in logical entailment. The concrete identification of classes encounters similar subjective-objective obstacles as in the "invention" of races. Thus Marx's conception of class, nowhere adequately defined in his writings, has been exhaustively pilloried, most significantly by Max Weber, Weberian sociologists, and Althusserian Marxists.[131] They demonstrate that Marx's propositions and prognosis on the revolutionary potential of the working class are replete with analytical deficiencies. What stands out, however, is Marx's insistence that the working class should not be deluded by appeals for national solidarity. Indeed, in Marx's writings, national and racial classifications have no determinate relationship with wage labor and alienation, and are of no analytical significance. These classifications are part of theories of history and social relations that are parallel and competitive with Marx's analysis. The bourgeoisie are neither white, nor male. Members of the working class neither Irish, nor English. They may be made to regard themselves as such as part of maintaining intra-working class competition—a condition of capitalism's reproduction. As Marx writes: "The essential condition for the existence, and for the sway of the bourgeois class, is the formation and augmentation of capital; the condition for capital is wage-labor. Wage-labor rests exclusively on competition between the laborers."[132] Thus Marx maintained a focus on class relations, unlike his contemporaries such as Arthur de Gobineau and Johann Blumenbach, who specialized in constructing separate races and cultures and charting their conflicting relations in history.

Despite references to "the capitalist marketplace" and "the growing disparity between rich and poor," and an insistence on resistance and transformation through education reform, the advocacy of multiculturalism does not address the political economy of educational delivery. David Goldberg notes: "Cultural theorizing in the name of multiculturalism, as I argued earlier, has suffered the poverty of avoiding, if not effacing, political economy."[133] Sporadic allusions to commodity relations do not save critical multiculturalism from failing to criticize the relations of production underlying power relations. Peter McLaren offers the following incisive comments:

What Weber missed was the incorporation of all areas of public and private life into the money economy. There exists no autochthonous and monolithic space of pure culture or uncontaminated identity—everything has been commodified. . . . We are, all of us, subjects of capital—the *point d'appui* between wage relations and commodity relations, with commodification representing the hinge between the future and the past.[134]

However, Weber did not miss the commercialization of the world that accompanies Western capitalism. He simply did not regard it as being as significant as the historical rationalization/bureaucratization of the world. What many "Marxists" and "revolutionary educators" miss, however, is the centrality of the concept of commodity production to Marx's analysis of capitalist society.

The first two sentences in Chapter 1 of *Capital* announce: "The wealth of those societies in which the capitalist mode of production prevails, presents itself as 'an immense accumulation of commodities,' its unit being a single commodity. Our investigation must therefore begin with the analysis of a commodity."[135] As if in opposition to Marxian political economy, multiculturalists centralize culture and cultural oppression and depict society as an accumulation of cultural exchanges. These significations stand in contrast to a conception of social relations as structured around commodified exchanges fetishized and naturalized by "bourgeois" theories, for example, Hobbesian and Malthusian notions of a flawed human nature and insurmountably scarce natural resources. The multiculturalists' refusal to analyze commodity relations underlies their honorific references to ideology, class, and exploitation. Their avoidance of Marxian political economy diverts attention from a major objective of schooling—the transformation of students into commodity hucksters. Students' passive opposition to this commodification of their aspirations is expressed in "crises" in the classroom. However, they cannot demand *learning* from their teachers without an understanding of why they ask themselves: How much money will I make after my time in school? They can hardly become change agents opposed to oppression, if their major concern is acquiring skills and information in order to capitalize on labor market opportunities. The critical pedagogists' goal of ideological demystification requires students' being committed to knowing as an end in itself, and to learning as a joyful part of being, not a means of obtaining a livelihood. Such commitments are stymied by the official construction of schools to serve the economy, the commercialization of knowledge, and the resulting inability of some students to pay for education. The disempowerment of students and teachers begins with the commodification of their educational aspirations, but the advocacy of education's decommodification is beyond the analytical reach of cultural politics.

Multiculturalism and Ground Rules of Discourse

Discussions of multiculturalism necessarily involve rules and standards for the assessment of arguments. However, in general, such standards are not made explicit. Denunciations of multiculturalism as a threat to American society, its cohesiveness, and its stability permeate the writings of its opponents.[136] Because these criticisms do not concentrate on the philosophical—logical, ethical, and epistemological—ramifications of the arguments for multiculturalism, it is tempting to suggest that political denunciations have usurped the place of intellectual standards for argument evaluation because of the comparative absence of instruction in philosophy in schools.[137] However, a mere introduction of philosophy in schools would not necessarily remove personal and political accusations from intellectual exchanges. For some scholars, who were themselves schooled as philosophers, are not averse to political denunciations. This is illustrated in David Goldberg's remarks:

By contrast, the primary unifying assumption of the motley crew who argue against multiculturalism—of William Bennett, that philosopher-educator turned drug czar and now guardian of the nation's virtues, of William Buckley, Linda Chavez and Lynne Cheney, Arthur Schlesinger in his analysis of the "disuniting of America," Saul Bellow, Allan Bloom, and the like—is one of the sociopolitical and cultural necessity of homogeneity.[138]

A "motley crew" indeed! Any crew member could respond with a denunciation of Goldberg's self-confessed "Jewish," liberal promotion of multiculturalism. Such a response, however, would affirm a principle that the ethnicity, gender, or politics of authors constitutes valid reference points in the evaluation of their works. In the ensuing politicized and personalized forms of intellectual exchanges, "liberal" and "conservative" armies would emerge to further marginalize sound language use and reasoning.

Advocacies of multiculturalism contain implicit and explicit recommendations on how the proposals themselves are to be evaluated as knowledge. However, the implicit and the explicit are not consistent. The implicit recommendation is that the logical structure of arguments should be decisive for their affirmation or invalidation. On the other hand, the explicit counsel suggests evaluation through examination of the political representations in arguments. The underlying premise is that power, politics, and knowledge are inseparable. As Danielle Flannery writes in defense of a "postmodernist conception of multiculturalism":

In critical postmodernism, while persons must speak from their own histories, collective memories, and voices, they must also simultaneously challenge the grounds on which their knowledge and power are constructed and legitimated. . . . Critical implies that all human interactions, including the theoretical text of learning that supports the teaching/learning exchange, must be viewed as political. This means not contributing to or sustaining the alienation and oppression of people or groups.[139]

The thesis that structures of power and knowledge are implicated in all human expressions may be accurate. However, by itself, it does not provide criteria for evaluating the validity of a given argument. Indeed, it leads to an infinite regress, as disputants may continuously interrogate the structures of power and politics implicated in their arguments, including the interrogation itself. An eternal, epistemological free-for-all would prevail, as they probe each other's culture and political interests to produce arguments that require further probings.

The standards for argument assessment presented by advocates of multiculturalism refer to an author's political position, culture, and interests in order to dismiss and affirm arguments. The underlying assumption is that knowledge is produced by a subject to whom references may be made as part of evaluating the knowledge. Thus an invalidation of arguments can be pursued through descriptions of the subject-producer as Eurocentric, ethnocentric, racist, sexist, Western, traditionalist, mainstream, middle-class, right-wing, homophobic, and conservative. Nevertheless, it is not only multiculturalism's advocates who endorse this practice. Rush Limbaugh confesses to being a "conservative," and comments on multiculturalism as follows:

It is my conviction that the people who concocted multiculturalism and are now trying to institute a multicultural curriculum in New York are basically miserable. And rather than look at their own responsibility in this, or try to find solutions that involve a change in attitudes, they simply blame institutions. They blame America. So multiculturalism . . . is the tool of revenge of many who have failed to assimilate and fit into mainstream American life.[140]

Of course, in response, Limbaugh could be called an "ultra-conservative," a "right-wing fanatic," "the most dangerous man in America," a "sexist," and a "racist" seeking to blame the victims of racism and sexism.

Once the act of negative political-moral description is initiated, it is invariably reciprocated, and disputes become trapped in endless recriminations. For example, on November 29, 1993, at Kean College in New Jersey, Khalid Abdul Muhammad, a minister in the Nation of Islam, voiced some remarks about, inter alia, Jews, the Pope, and homosexuals.[141] In subsequent media discussions, some of Muhammad's remarks on Jews were described as "intemperate," "ignorant," "racist," and "anti-Semitic." Noticeable among them were demands for the "denunciation" of Muhammad, not for an exposé of the flawed reasoning and inaccurate premises underlying his claims. Reasoning was side-stepped by both sides, and the pattern of negative descriptions of persons and arguments also prevails in discussions of multicultural education and multiculturalism.

In exchanges between representatives of different schools of thought on education reform, political characterizations of arguments and of the persons offering arguments surface repeatedly as apparent forms of refutation. For example, Henry Giroux's *Border Crossings* and *Theory and Resistance in Education* present numerous, moral-political characterizations of the arguments of other scholars.[142] It is not clear, however, whether terms such as reductionist, essentialist, traditional, and liberal automatically disqualify arguments. Giroux also accuses "traditional," "liberal," and "radical" perspectives on education of "silences" and "erasures," but these omissions are significant only in relation to Giroux's project of education for social emancipation. Hence they are not evidence of flaws in these perspectives. In recognition of the acceptability of "erasures," Giroux fails to mention *his* "erasures" of: (1) the discussions of definitions of culture in the anthropological literature; (2) discussions of class, in the Marxian sense of relationship to the means of production; (3) the pluralist-elitist debate over power; (4) critical reviews of the conception of domination that "radical and critical educators" utilize; (5) criticisms of the practice of racial classification; and (6) standards of argument assessment. These issues are significantly related to Giroux's own remedial proposals, for they impinge on the conceptual foundations of his entire analysis.

Standards for argument assessment are required for the success of Giroux's advocacy of a "critical pedagogy," for the term *critical* is intrinsically evaluative.[143] Critical pedagogy seeks to sharpen the analytical and reasoning skills of students so that they challenge patterns of oppression and domination, and feel empowered to pursue change. Thus Giroux must affirm that sound reasoning is essential to social transformation, and that its practice requires usage of standards of argument assessment. On the other hand, by virtue of his omission of such standards, Giroux is obliged to unleash a barrage of moral accusations at political Others. For example, in defending "a politics of cultural differences," Giroux, takes issue with: "conservatives such as Allan Bloom, E.D. Hirsch, Diane Ravitch, Pat Buchanan, and Senator Jesse Helms," without specifying the standards used to describe these persons as "conservatives" and whether their conservatism means their arguments are invalid.[144] Diane Ravitch, for example, is charged with dehistoricizing and depoliticizing the idea of culture, attempting to "silence or marginalize the voices of those who have traditionally been excluded," glossing over dominant configurations and utilizing "the language of desperation and extremism."[145] But these remarks appear to be themselves desperate and extreme political condemnations. Were they to be reciprocated as such, the debate over cultural politics would reach a stalemate and oppressed women and blacks (sic) would be no wiser on how to end their oppression. In effect, Giroux's arguments are eminently "conservative," and ultimately they are silenced by their own inconsistencies.

The construction of political Others and denunciation of their writings also surface in *The Graywolf Annual Five: Multicultural Literacy*. The editors, Rick Simonson and Scott Walker, write that Allan Bloom's *The Closing of the American Mind* is an appeal

for the revival of a conservative system of education utterly out of date with contemporary cultural and political realities . . . a "lack of" a book that complains of contemporary America's lack of values, our educational system's lack of purpose, and the average American's lack of vision, lack of understanding, and lack of knowledge. Bloom seems to long for a Reaganesque return to simpler times, when men were men, when we all—meaning white folk more than colored, meaning more men than women—learned the 3-R's by way of the certain classic texts, in our little schoolhouses on the prairies.[146]

These descriptions exemplify the patterns of denunciation and rejection that characterize the advocacy of multiculturalism. Opponents invariably reciprocate, and the logically flawed arguments from both sides are neither perceived, corrected, nor abandoned.

The participants in discussions of multicultural education/multiculturalism generally equate refutation—a demonstration of logical deficiencies in an argument—and denunciation, which is a mere condemnation of an argument. The exchange over multicultural education between Molefi Asante and Diane Ravitch, in particular, demonstrates the illegitimacy of this equation. In his analysis of Ravitch's criticisms of "particularist multiculturalism," Molefi Asante comments: "Few whites have ever examined their culture critically. . . . A considerable number of white educators and some blacks have paraded in single file and sometimes in concert to take aim at multiculturalism. "[147] Asante also adds that the notion of a particularist multiculturalism is "an oxymoron." This assessment is accurate and sufficient to cause Ravitch's ultimate self-correction. Asante's other remarks, however, do not serve the purpose of a conclusive exchange; they are not relevant to the issue—whether knowledge of ancient Egypt's history is indispensable to African Americans' self-esteem and educational success.

Asante's analysis of his critics' claims remains in a denunciatory vein. In arguing against Ravitch's criticisms of Afrocentric proposals, Asante questions Ravitch's educational credentials: "What is at issue is her own educational background. Does she know classical Africa? Did she take courses in African American studies from qualified professors? Those who know do not question the importance of Afrocentric or Latino infusion into the educational process.[148] On the other hand, Kwame Anthony Appiah comments: "A final irony is that Afrocentrism, which is offered in the name of black solidarity, has, by and large, entirely ignored the work of African scholars other than Diop. . . . Molefi Asante has written whole books about Akan culture without referring to the major works of such Akan philosophers as J.B. Danquah, William Abrahams, Kwasi Wiredu, and Kwame Gyekye."[149] These Afrocentric omissions derive from a politicized conception of knowledge that simultaneously endorses and abjures standards of consistency and evidentiary adequacy. What underlies the Afrocentrists' neglect of African cultures and philosophies is a political usage of (knowledge of) the past. What matters is not so much the complexities of African history and cultures as the production of knowledge to serve the purpose of restoring black self-esteem and liberating the race from deprivation and discrimination. Nevertheless, as evidenced by their criticisms of Eurocentric inaccuracies, advocates of Afrocentricity agree that flawed ideas lead to ineffective policies and therefore cannot liberate the oppressed. There is, then, a crucial reason for the development of a consensus on standards for deciding which ideas are flawed.

Disputes over multiculturalism follow a standard polarization into "Right" or conservatives, and "Left" or liberals. However, this polarization is eminently avoidable; it is not a necessary feature of intellectual life. Specifically, the classifying of arguments as left-wing and right-wing reflects an overall neglect of the humanities, especially philosophy, in educational institutions. This is not to suggest that an infusion of philosophy would resolve all disputes, but rather that its nonconsideration robs disputants of concepts that could aid in the resolution of their disputes, especially since the disputants invariably use terms such as truth, experience, reality, facts, and values. Bereft of awareness of the philosophical roots and implications of propositions involving these terms, the disputants are dragged into the murky waters of political evaluations.

For those who claim to be on the "Right," multicultural education is a kind of stealth affirmative action, while the "Left" is alarmed that a struggle against sexism, racism, homophobia, and ethnocentrism meets opposition. Gary Howard, director of a National Curriculum and Staff Development Center, chides the opposition to multicultural education: "Underlying both the denial and the hostility is a deep fear of diversity. . . . The same fear is dressed in more sophisticated fashion by Western traditionalists and neoconservatives who campaign against multicultural education. They fear the loss of European and Western cultural supremacy in the school curriculum."[150] Nevertheless, to accuse critics of being afraid is hardly a refutation of their criticisms, and even so, the fear is understandable, for justifications of multicultural education and multiculturalism are often couched in terms that make dead and living whites inveterate enemies of the rest of humanity.

Much of the "conservative" opposition is not so much to multicultural education, defined as respect for cultures, as to demands for proportional racial representation in faculty and textbook selection and equality of educational outcomes. What generates fears from these "conservatives" is multiculturalism's theme of biological and historical demonization—the presentation of white males and "western" traditions as the source of all forms of disempowerment, marginalization, oppression, and economic victimization. On the other hand, it is not only "conservatives" who are concerned about multicultural education. For example, while defending multiculturalism, Christine Sleeter cautions:

As educators increasingly ask how race and ethnicity should be thought about, and as the teaching profession becomes increasingly White, I am very concerned that the ethnicity paradigm will increasingly guide interpretations of differential attainments and multicultural curricula as presented in schools. In the process, racial diversity will be reinterpreted within the symbolism of Euro-American ethnicity.[151]

These remarks reclaim the notion of the specific conditions facing "blacks"; they register alarm that this specificity would be lost, if the "ethnicity paradigm" were to displace a racial interpretation of events. Sleeter is concerned that "White" teachers, focusing on ethnic relations, will marginalize recognition of racial inequalities in educational achievements.

The fears and concerns of both the "Left" and the "Right" pertain to two sets of issues that are embodied in the following question: How should diversity (gender, racial, ethnic, class) be addressed, and discrimination remedied, in educational institutions and society? There is a mutual agreement that diversity and residues of discrimination are "social facts," but contrasting perceptions of the degree of gender, racial, ethnic, and class discrimination and hence how it is to be remedied. What vitiates their analyses and exacerbates their disputes is inattention to the implications of classifications, conceptual analysis, and the distinction between ethical and factual aspects of arguments.[152] For the advocates of multiculturalism, the level of discrimination experienced by women, people of color, and gays amount to oppression. However, this charge of oppression is not accompanied by the necessary examination of conceptions of ethical conduct. Is discrimination a knowingly morally wrong action, its consequences, intended or unintended, or the right action in given circumstances? Can it be said that women, people of color, and gays emotionally oppress whites, males, and heterosexuals by frequently accusing them of oppression? Second, the classifications that are central to multiculturalism—women, whites, and people of color—have been confounded by a variety of studies in genetics, sociology, and anthropology. Finally, the arguments for and against multiculturalism remain inconclusive, for neither camp addresses the conflict between the implicit (logical rules) and the explicit evaluative standards (moral-political denunciations) being used in their exchanges. On the other hand, can advocacies and evaluations of multiculturalism move beyond moral-political accusations, given that they are both grounded in political-moral conceptions of schooling and the social order?

Disagreements with a moral claim within multiculturalism lie at the root of the opposition it faces. For advocates of multiculturalism, their claim of oppression and domination represents facts. For their critics, however, these descriptions are value-loaded categories—a rhetorical feature of "liberal" challenges to the common culture. Nevertheless, the resulting stalemate indicates an epistemological presence, for because of an endorsement of the thesis that their arguments represent the way the world is, neither side takes the dispute into the field of conceptual analysis. The stalemate could be resolved by an agreement to pursue the clarification of concepts, probe disputed assumptions about the nature of knowledge, observe certain intellectual standards in argument exposition, and strive for a consensus on ground rules of intellectual exchange. The arrival at such a consensus does not imply that there will be an absence of disagreements. On the contrary, even more profound disagreements may emerge. However, the difference will be that their origin and processes of resolution will be identifiable. The pursuit of agreement must take precedence over expressions of disagreements in order to resolve disagreements.

If the purpose of intellectual exchanges is the resolution of disputes, there are some significant requirements for the achievement of an agreement on ground rules for such exchanges. First, participants in intellectual exchanges would have to conceive the objective of discourse as bringing minds together to resolve human problems, and as a process of enlarging areas of agreement, one of conflict resolution, not conflict generation. The existence of disagreements cannot be presupposed, since that presupposition itself generates disagreements. Second, propositions cannot be said to be representations of reality and/or human subjects, for then the question can be posed: Whose representation is to prevail? Disagreements reflect an adherence to different forms of signification and language use, not aspects of the real world or intrinsically subjective affiliations.

The protracted disputes over multiculturalism testify to a specific feature of the curriculum—the comparative absence of courses in reasoning, philosophy, and the philosophy of social sciences. Such courses would have alerted students—and ultimately graduate students, scholars, political representatives, and journalists—to the significance of rational codes of conduct in what Jurgen Habermas calls communicative action:

> If we assume that the human species maintains itself through the socially coordinated activities of its members and that this coordination has to be established through communication—and in certain central spheres through communication aimed at reaching agreement—then the reproduction of the species also requires satisfying the conditions of a rationality that is inherent in communicative action.[153]

Habermas makes the case that rationality, defined as an amenability to criticism and rules, is intrinsic to communicative action and decision making. Indeed, rationality and universality are at the core of communicative action. They are present in language use itself, in the offering of reasons for claims, and the pursuit of persuasion through intersubjective understanding.

Communicative action consists of "speech acts" oriented toward mutual understanding and agreement. Human beings think and talk their way into disagreements. At the same time, they engage in further discourse to resolve these disagreements, which are, in effect, disputes over validity claims. In order to achieve a state of resolution, Habermas recommends that speakers and listeners strive for an "ideal speech situation," which would be characterized by revelations of assumptions, purposes, and premises underlying claims, and their examination within specific ground rules:

> Registering a *validity claim* is not the expression of a contingent will; and responding affirmatively to a validity claim is not merely an empirically motivated decision. Both acts, putting forward and recognizing a validity claim, are subject to conventional restrictions, because such a claim can be rejected only by way of criticism and can be defended against a criticism only by refuting it. One who opposes directions is referred to existing [*geltende*] regulations and not to the mere fact of penalties that can be expected

if they are not followed. And one who doubts the validity of the underlying norms has to give *reasons*.[154]

By implication, certain claims are ruled out, for example, claims that silence critics in advance, that utilize double standards, or that implicitly refute themselves. As Habermas writes: "only those speech acts with which a speaker connects a criticizable validity claim can move a hearer to accept an offer independently of external forces."[155] The regulations in speech acts, then, provide the basis for drawing conclusions regarding the validity or invalidity of arguments. A consensus on the meaning and significance of rules and regulations generates mutual understanding and obviates the need for coercion, which is antithetical to rational communication. Thus the ideal speech situation requires a consensus on the intellectual standards to be used to evaluate assumptions, purposes, premises, and implications.

One of the implications of Habermas' analysis of communicative action is that arguments cannot be regarded as the product of a human subject contemplating a real world. No one's ideas can be said to represent "reality," for then that knowledge would be uncriticizable. An argument or proposal cannot be deemed "unrealistic," or refuted by showing its lack of conformation with a "real" object. Claims on reality, as a defense against criticisms, or a rebuttal of another argument, are illegitimate, for listeners would be unable to criticize arguments that claim to reflect, or represent, reality. Such references seek an epistemological privilege for the arguer. Because they self-classify as "truth," they silence criticisms, in advance, and explicitly preclude the possibility of refutation.

On the other hand, claims on reality are implicitly self-refuting, for, unless prevented by force or authority, listeners can also stake claims on reality, arguing for their epistemological superiority and factual reprsentativeness. Thus the entire set of speech acts would run aground on multiple realities and subjective perceptions. Intellectual exchanges would have no means of closure, and decisions would be arbitrary and idiosyncratic. Such communication cannot fulfill the human project of self-reproduction. Without consensual rules for evaluating thinking, there is no conclusive communication. An absence of a commitment to communicative rationality would be reflected in political condemnations of arguments, imputation of political motives, and castigation of a person's politics, often by innuendo. Nevertheless, if the purpose of discourse is to reach understanding and agreement, proponents and opponents would do well to strive for an "ideal speech situation." Such a purpose would involve the deployment of ground rules and the evaluation of arguments in terms of their clarity, depth, and logical consistency.

In *The Postmodern Condition,* Lyotard challenges two key assumptions in Habermas' analysis of communicative rationality: that consensus is the goal of discourse, and that "it is possible for all speakers to come to agreement on which rules or metaprescriptions are universally valid for language games when it is clear that language games are heteromorphous, subject to heterogeneous sets of pragmatic rules."[156] There are four objections to this assertion. First, it confuses

actuality and potentiality. The fact that language games are actually heteromorphous does not in any way imply that, potentially, all speakers cannot agree on
the rules of a particular game. Second, no game is possible without a recognition
of concepts of same and difference—a feature, then, that must be shared by all
games.

Third, Lyotard agrees that some consensus on rules is necessary. His caveat
is that this consensus need not be universal: "any consensus on the rules defining
a game and the "moves" playable within it *must* be local, in other words, agreed
on by its present players and subject to eventual cancellation."[157] This caveat is
based on a misunderstanding of "universal" in Habermas analysis. For Habermas, rules are to be discursively universal, that is, binding on those localized in
the Diskurs. Second, Lyotard's rejection of Habermas' assumption of consensus
as the goal of discourse is not refutation. He writes: "consensus is only a particular state of discussion, not its end. Its end, on the contrary, is paralogy."[158]
By paralogy Lyotard understands the production of tension, instability, and subversion of "normal" paradigms. Neither Habermas nor Lyotard can know the
motives of players as they enter dialogue, whether they are pursuing consensus,
persuasion, or conflict. What can be said, however, is that both paralogy and
consensus are part of discursive processes, that without rules paralogy would be
unidentifiable, and that paralogy often signifies hidden rule-changes, a break-
down, or the absence of consensus on rules.

If it is agreed that criteria of argument assessment must accompany intellectual exchanges, some ground rules may be sketched. They may be described
as Lockean, for they echo his proposition that *laws*, not men, should govern,
with the caveat that there must be a consensus on the rules, that is, the consent of
those being governed by the rules. The following ground rules are proposed for
consideration.

First, *arguments not the persons voicing them, should be evaluated.* Indeed,
no connection may be pursued between a speaker's moral-political motives and
the arguments advanced. Such a connection cannot validate or invalidate the
arguments, for motives are imputed, not discovered, and they have no validative
bearing on the arguments. This rule avoids the ad hominem fallacy.[159]   Arguments are expressed by, *they are not of, persons*; they are embodied in analytically related classifications, premises, and implications. If arguments are evaluated as an expression of a person's motives, or of a political view that is traceable to gender, racial, or class positions, their evaluation becomes caught up in
endless relativist disputes, as the gender, racial, and class attributes of the
evaluator can also be subjected to a similar evaluation. A given person could
respond as follows: If my gender, racial, political interests, or class attributes are
responsible for, or vitiate, my "position," then so do yours. Gridlock necessarily
results, and the disputants would be engaged in discourse in order not to engage
in discourse. By implication, moral-political evaluations of arguments are self-
contradictory.

Both advocates and critics of multiculturalism address the issue of the relationship among knowledge, gender, race, and culture in history and social

change. What they fail to do is lay out ground rules for intellectual exchanges and criteria for argument assessment. Their inattention to the conceptual structure and implications of arguments leads to the propagation of a variety of fallacies, particularly argumentum ad hominem, equivocation, and poisoning the well. The last is especially served by the terms *racism, ethnocentrism, sexism, and Eurocentrism,* which function to morally and politically discredit and disqualify speakers and so avoid consideration of the validity of their arguments. With but a few exceptions, advocates of multiculturalism respond to criticisms of their proposals with accusations of political bias. Some reports of campus debates indicate that to criticize multiculturalism is to be deemed Eurocentric, racist, and sexist, and some colleges have established speech codes that pertain to, not the intellectual quality of speech, but its moral-political character.[160]

The second ground rule suggests *a recognition of the difference between moral-political descriptions of an argument and a demonstration of its validity or invalidity.* Denunciations of persons, or pejorative descriptions of their claims as "liberal," "conservative," "racist," "antiwhite," "ethnocentric," and "Eurocentric" do not invalidate the claims. Rather, such descriptions can lead to an interminable process of mutual recrimination. This condition is illustrated in Molefi Asante's comments on Diane Ravitch's multicultural educational recommendations: "few whites have ever examined their culture critically" [161] Such remarks express a practice of racially identifying persons and using this identification as a means of discrediting their arguments. However, this practice is open to a reciprocation that leaves the dispute in an unresolved state. Ravitch *could* reply with a similar denunciation of Asante: "Some blacks have exploited white guilt over past and present discrimination. To hide their own racism, they stereotype all whites as racists, and jump on an oppression bandwagon in order to make whites feel guilty." Thus the Asante-Ravitch debate would stall on accusations of moral-political incorrectness and personal castigation.

Conclusive discussions require a consensus on ground rules. Once participants agree to exchange or analyze ideas, they must agree that denunciation, rejection, and repudiation are obstacles to discovering the soundness of their arguments. To *denounce* is to evaluate an argument morally or politically, or the person making the argument, for example: "That is nonsense, ridiculous, conservative, liberal, and so on." "You are a racist, or a sexist, a Marxist, etc." *Rejection* is an expression of disagreement with an argument, as in: "I don't agree with that." "I don't believe it." "That's only your opinion, position, or point of view." To *repudiate* is to reject an argument, giving as justification a personal experience or observation, for example, "I don't agree that men are sexist. I am a man, and I am not." Repudiation is a strong form of rejection; its weakness is that it is open to counterchallenges to one's personal evaluations: "Are you sure that you are a man?" "As a sexist, you are obviously in denial." The legitimation crisis in knowledge flows from the subject-object conception of knowledge, which, as was earlier demonstrated, postmodernism both refutes and affirms.

Patterns of denunciation, rejection, and repudiation lie at the root of accusations of bias, conservatism, and political correctness in speech. They are mani-

fest in Jurgen Habermas' accusing postmodernists of being harbingers of neoconservatism and Jean-François Lyotard impeaching modernists and defenders
of the Enlightenment for laying the foundation for terror.[162] Such exchanges indicate that the protagonists are refusing to evaluate arguments within consensual
intellectual standards in order to affirm or refute them. Applying the rule of
refutation, it would be noted that the postmodernist prescription, which suggests
that intellectual divergences be conceived as evidence of different language
games whose rules are incommensurable, does not clarify how language games
may be demarcated from one another? are their criteria of demarcation another
language game? The postmodernist conception of discourse, then, leads to an
infinite multiplication of language games, just as multiculturalism generates a
proliferation of cultures in political struggles. For their advocates, ideas are not
produced in a vacuum, and no rules can be neutral toward the real patterns of
domination existing in society, or the subjective context of discourse. All arguments are moral and political and therefore intrinsically biased. Yet the implication of this claim leads to a self-contradiction, for the claim itself must also be
regarded as moral and political, and hence biased. Why present a claim that is
intrinsically ineffective for resolving intellectual disputes, unless the purpose is
not to resolve the disputes? In this sense, intellectual conservatism—the perpetuation of inconclusive disputes—permeates both "Left" and "Right" analyses
of education and social change.

The third ground rule is that during discussions arguments must be either
affirmed or *refuted*. Affirmation is an endorsement of the validity of an argument. Refutation may be defined as a demonstration of self-contradictions, unwarranted premises, and incomplete or incoherent definitions of key terms in an
argument. The related processes of affirmation and refutation involve using intellectual standards to assess the reasoning involved in given arguments. In processes of affirmation/refutation, participants in discussions jointly pursue possible
flaws in the reasoning underlying their conclusions, inaccuracies in premises,
inconsistencies in implications, or ambiguities in the definitions of terms. Affirmation and refutation are two sides of a coin of discourse aimed at reaching
mutual agreement and understanding. Disputants would specify the intellectual
standards and ground rules that are to govern their intellectual exchanges. Such
specification is absent from the discussions of multiculturalism. What is powerfully present is a grounding of propositions in a taken-for-granted realist theory
of knowledge. Nevertheless, consideration of other theories of knowledge would
require considerable expansion of philosophy in all levels of schooling.

Can educational institutions that shunt the humanities aside, and by extension philosophy, prepare educators to deal with the logical, ethical, and epistemological ramifications of their disciplines? David Theo Goldberg's observation
should be well taken:

Disciplines appear, as contemporary nations do, more or less with modernity. Prior to the
seventeenth century, roughly, knowledge was pursued formally and legitimated in the
name of Philosophy. Distinctions were drawn within Philosophy. It is worth recalling
that until the nineteenth century the chair of Physics in the European university was

known as the chair of Natural Philosophy. Psychology, Sociology, Economics, Linguistics, and Anthropology were all carried out under the rubric of Philosophy, and by philosophers.[163]

If modernity is to be faulted, as Goldberg suggests, its failure can be traced to the separation of philosophy from the natural and social sciences and the creation of hard-and-fast disciplinary boundaries. Specialists emerged, randomly utilizing some of philosophy's basic concepts—experience, truth, reality, facts, empirical, reason, subjective, objective—to clinch arguments. A postmodernism that claims to be engaged in acts of philosophic restoration would be one that ruptures the professionalization and specialization that accompany modernity's commodification of knowledge.

It was through centuries of specialization that natural sciences, social sciences, and the humanities emerged as distinct fields of knowledge. In the process, the humanities, including philosophy and its focus on reasoning, were marginalized, giving way to more "practical" concerns. Nevertheless, logical rules proved to be irrepressible, which should be taken not as a tribute to Aristotle, but as a recognition of the need to evaluate reasoning, if human communication is to resolve disputes. Hence, advocates of multiculturalism implicitly appeal to reasonable standards to justify their explicit commitment to justice and their skepticism toward the Enlightenment. But this appeal is made side by side with the continuation of an ancient endeavor to disempower such standards in the name of subjective, cultural, and political contextualizations.[164] Can this and other contradictions in the postmodernist contextualization of knowledge empower groups? Would not the empowering of particular groups lead to attempts to empower other groups? Can justice, a necessarily universal condition, be established by groups in power? Drawing on neglected conceptions of learning, knowledge, and education, advocates of critical thinking education reforms pursue the empowerment of human beings through the development of their capacity for reflection on their thinking. Is an infusion of critical thinking concepts in the intellectual environment and schools the remedy for the crises in knowledge and education? It is to this question that the final chapter turns.

NOTES

1.   See Henry A. Giroux, "Insurgent Multiculturalism and the Promise of Pedagogy," in Goldberg (ed.), *Multiculturalism*, pp. 325-343.

2.   In his exposition of critical multiculturalism, Peter McLaren writes: "As we approach the year 2000, we increasingly are living simulated identities that help adjust our dreams and desires according to the terms of our imprisonment as schizo-subjects in an artificially-generated world. These facsimile or imitated identities are negotiated for us by financial planners, corporate sponsors, and marketing strategists through the initiatives of transnational corporations, enabling a privileged elite of white Euro-Americans to control the information banks and terrorize the majority of the population into a state of intellectual and material impoverishment." "White Terror," p. 45.

3.   See Giroux, *Theory*, Chapters 2, 4, and 6.

4.   Henry Giroux, "Series Foreword," in Kanpol and McLaren (eds.), *Critical,* p. x.

5.   Robert Stam and Ella Shohat, "Contested Histories: Eurocentrism, Multiculturalism, and the Media," in Goldberg (ed.), *Multiculturalism,* p. 299. Terence Turner's definition captures a general sentiment: "*Multiculturalism,* as a movement in support of the collective empowerment of all relatively disempowered culturally-identified groups, would entail such forces, including those of an overtly noncultural character such as economic exploitation and political repression." "Anthropology and Multiculturalism: What Is Anthropology That Multiculturalists Should Be Mindful Of It?" in Goldberg (ed.), *Multiculturalism,* pp. 423-424.

6.   See Kanpol and McLaren (eds.), *Critical;* Giroux, "Insurgent Multiculturalism." The goal of de-essentializing differences is implicitly and explicitly absent from the writings of James A. Banks, Carl Grant, Christine E. Sleeter, and Sonia Nieto, although these authors would argue that they recognize the socially constructed nature of gender and racial identities. What they do not appear to recognize is their own theoretical practices of as part of the social construction of .these identities.

7.   This phrase is taken from Michel Foucault, *Power/Knowledge: Selected Interviews and Other Writings 1972-1977* (New York: Pantheon, 1980), p. 81.

8.   S.C. Brown (ed.), *Philosophical Disputes in the Social Sciences* (Atlantic Highlands, N.J.: Humanities Press, 1979); Outwaithe, *New Philosophies;* John B. Thompson, *Studies in the Theory of Ideology* (Cambridge: Polity Press, 1984), Chapter 9. See also Peter Winch, *The Idea of a Social Science and Its Relation to Philosophy* (London: Routledge and Kegan Paul, 1971); Maurice A. Natanson (ed.), *Philosophy of the Social Sciences: A Reader* (New York: Random House, 1963); Robert S. Cohen and Mark H. Hartofsky, *Epistemology, Methodology and the Social Sciences* (Boston: Kluwer, 1983); David Theo Goldberg, "Introduction: Multicultural Conditions," in Goldberg (ed.), *Multiculturalism,* pp. 1-41.

9.   For postmodernist approaches to education, and critical thinking, see Bourdieu, *Reproduction;* McLaren, "White Terror"; Kanpol and McLaren, "Introduction: Resistance Multiculturalism"; Banks, "The Canon"; Henry A. Giroux and Stanley Aranowitz, *Postmodernism and Education* (Minneapolis, Minn.: University of Minnesota Press, 1991); Kerry Walters (ed.), *Re-thinking Reason: New Perspectives in Critical Thinking* (New York: State University of New York Press, 1995).

10.   Appiah, *In My Father's House;* Chapter 7. See also David Harvey, *The Condition of Postmodernity: An Enquiry into the Origin of Cultural Change* (Cambridge: Blackwell, 1990), Chapter 3.

11.   Jean-François Lyotard, *The Postmodern Condition: A Report on Knowledge* (Minneapolis, Minn.: University of Minnesota Press, 1993), p. 24.

12.   See Bourdieu, *Reproduction.* For a critical assessment of Bourdieu, see Jeffrey Alexander, *Fin de Siècle Social Theory: Relativism, Reduction, and the Problem of Reason* (New York: Routledge, 1995).

13.   Lyotard, *The Postmodern,* pp. 10-11.

14.   Ibid., p. 73.

15.   Ibid., p. 81.

16.   See Jonathan Barnes, *Early Greek Philosophy* (London: Penguin Books, 1987); William V. Quine, *Word and Object* (Cambridge, Mass.: Technology Press of MIT, 1960).

17.   Tom Bridges, "Postmodernism and the Primacy of Cultural Differences," *Inquiry: Critical Thinking Across the Disciplines* 9, no. 2 (March 1992), p. 40.

18.   Ernst Cassirer, *The Philosophy of the Enlightenment*, trans. Fritz C.A. Koelln and James P. Pettegrove (Princeton, N.J.: Princeton University Press, 1951), p. 6. See also Will and Ariel Durant, *The Age of Voltaire* (New York: Simon and Schuster, 1965).

19.   See Peter Gay, *The Enlightenment: An Interpretation, Vol. II, The Science of Freedom* (New York: Alfred A. Knopf, 1969), pp. 401-407.

20.   Voltaire, cited in Hans Askenasy, *Are We All Nazis?* (Secaucus, N.J.: L. Stuart, 1979), p. 52.

21.   In a defense of the Enlightenment, David Harvey notes: "Enlightenment thought . . . embraced the idea of progress, and actively sought that break with history and tradition which modernity espouses. It was, above all, a secular movement that sought the demystification and desacralization of knowledge and social organization in order to liberate human beings from their chains. . . . Doctrines of equality, liberty, faith in human intelligence (once allowed the benefits of education), and universal reason abounded." *The Condition*, pp. 12-13.

22.   Tuchman poses a significant question: "Why do holders of high office so often act contrary to the way reason points and enlightened self-interest suggests?" *The March of Folly* (New York: Ballantine Books, 1984), p. 4.

23.   Voltaire, letter to Rousseau, in Ray Ben Redman (ed.), *The Portable Voltaire* (New York: Viking, 1949), p. 496.

24.   See Jurgen Habermas, *The Philosophical Discourse of Modernity: Twelve Lectures*, trans. Frederick Lawrence (Cambridge, Mass.: MIT Press, 1987).

25.   See Paul Berman (ed.), *Debating P.C.: The Controversy over Political Correctness on College Campuses* (New York: Laurel Paperbacks, 1992); Bernstein, *Dictatorship*; Teachers for a Democratic Culture, "The State of Academic Freedom 1995," *Democratic Culture* 4, no. 2 (Fall 1995), pp. 6-35.

26.   M. Fox and D. Ward, "Multiculturalism, Liberalism, and Science," *Inquiry: Critical Thinking Across the Disciplines* 10, no. 4 (December 1992), p. 3.

27.   Banks, "Multicultural Education: Development," p. 26.

28.   See Peter Brier, *Howard Mumford Jones and the Dynamic of Liberal Humanism* (Kansas City, Mo.: University of Missouri Press, 1994).

29.   Sandra Harding, "Is Science Multicultural? Challenges, Resources, Opportunities, Uncertainties," in Goldberg (ed.), *Multiculturalism*, p. 346.

30.   See Banks, "Multicultural Education as an Academic Discipline."

31.   See Park, *Race*. Robert Faris, *Chicago Sociology, 1920-1932* (Chicago: University of Chicago Press, 1970); Joyce Ladner, *The Death of White Sociology* (New York: Vintage, 1970).

32.   Henry Louis Gates Jr., "Good-bye, Columbus? Notes on the Culture of Criticism," in Goldberg (ed.), *Multiculturalism*, p. 204.

33.   Banks, "Multicultural Education as an Academic Discipline," pp. 61-62.

34.   Banks, "The Canon," p. 5.

35.   For critical evaluations of postmodernism, see Christopher Norris, *What's Wrong with Postmodernism?* (Baltimore, Md.: Johns Hopkins University Press, 1993); Alex Callinicos, *Against Postmodernism: A Marxist Critique* (New York: St. Martin's Press, 1989); Harvey, *The Condition*, Chapter 6.

36.   Lyotard, *The Postmodern*, p. 77.

37.   For discussions of realism, see Roger Trigg, *Reality at Risk: A Defence of Realism in Philosophy and the Sciences* (Sussex: Harvester Press, 1980); Karl Popper, *Realism and the Aim of Science* (Totowa, N.J.: Rowman and Littlefield, 1983); George Levine (ed.), *Realism and Representation: Essays on the Problem of Realism in Relation*

to Science, Liberation and Culture (Madison, Wisc.: University of Wisconsin Press, 1993).

38.   See Christine E. Sleeter, "The White Ethnic Experience in America: To Whom Does It Generalize?"; *Educational Researcher* 21, no. 1 (January-February 1992), pp. 33-35; McLaren, "White Terror"; Henry A. Giroux, "The Politics of Insurgent Multiculturalism in the Era of the Los Angeles Uprisings," in Kanpol and McLaren (eds.), *Critical*, pp. 107-124.

39.   Banks, "Multicultural Education: Development," p. 23.

40.   James A. Banks, "Multicultural Education for Freedom's Sake," p. 33.

41.   See Molefi Asante, "Roots of the Truth: Repelling Attacks on Afrocentrism," *Emerge* 7, no. 9 (July-August 1996), pp. 66-70.

42.   See Molefi Asante, "The Afrocentric Idea in Education."

43.   See Martel, "Multiculturalism, Not Afrocentrism"; Mary Lefkowitz, "The Origins of Greece and the Illusions of Afrocentrists: Not Out of Africa," *New Republic* (February 10, 1992), pp. 29-36; and *Not Out of Africa.*

44.   Harvey Siegel, "On Some Recent Challenges to the Ideal of Reason," *Inquiry: Critical Thinking Across the Disciplines* 15, no, 4 (Summer 1996), pp. 2-16.

45.   See Rorty, *Philosophy*. But see also Cleo H. Holmes, "Notes on Pragmatism." For critical analyses of realism in philosophy and social sciences, see Dominique Lecourt, *Marxism and Epistemology: Bachelard, Canguilhem and Foucault,* trans. Ben Brewster (London: New Left Books, 1975); Gaston Bachelard, *The New Scientific Spirit* (Boston: Beacon Press, 1984); Sean Sayers, *Reality and Reason: Dialectic and the Theory of Knowledge* (Oxford: Basil Blackwell, 1985).

46.   Dworkin, *Woman Hating*, p. 174. See also Janet Sayers, *Biological Politics: Feminist and Anti-Feminist Perspectives* (London: Tavistock, 1982), Chapter 7.

47.   Linda Alcoff and Elizabeth Potter, "When Feminisms Intersect Epistemology," in Linda Alcoff and Elizabeth Potter, *Feminist Epistemologies* (New York: Routledge, 1993), p. 4.

48.   "Feminist" writings generally claim that gender is a fiction, a social construct, a deception, and a fabrication. These descriptions, however, are not necessarily consistent, and indeed their implications lead to "gender trouble": If gender is a fiction, what is the truth? If gender is a social constructed it can be deconstructed. But how can gender be deconstructed, if the categories men and women are treated as natural, real, or politically necessary portrayals? And if it is entire society that needs reconstruction for so-called men and women to embrace their humanness, can a focus on *women's* oppression contribute to this reconstruction? Should feminism not dispense with "women" and "men"? Some "feminists" have. See Juliet Mitchell and Ann Oakley (eds.), *What Is Feminism? A Re-Examination* (New York: Pantheon, 1986); Judith Lorber, *Paradoxes of Gender* (New Haven, Conn.: Yale University Press, 1994), Part 1. See also John Money and Patricia Tucker, *Sexual Signatures: On Being a Man or a Woman* (Boston: Little, Brown and Co., 1975); Sherry Ortnar and Harriet Whitehead (eds.) *Sexual Meanings: The Cultural Construction of Gender and Sexuality* (Cambridge: Cambridge University Press, 1981); Renzetti and Curran, *Women, Men and Society*, Chapters 1, 2, and 3; Dworkin, *Woman Hating,* Chapter 9; Epstein, *Deceptive Distinctions;* Carol Tavris, *The Mismeasure of Woman* (New York: Simon and Schuster, 1992); Ruth Bleier, *Science and Gender: A Critique of Biology and Its Theories on Women* (New York: Pergamon, 1984); Diana T. Meyers, "The Subversion of Women's Agency in Psychoanalytic Feminism: Chodorow, Flax, Kristeva," in Fraser and Bartky (eds.), *Revaluing French Feminism*, pp. 137-161.

49.   Appiah, *In My Father's House*, p. 30.

50.   See Judith Butler, "Contingent Foundations: Feminism and the Question of Postmodernism," *Praxis International* 11, no. 2 (1991), pp. 150-165; Fraser and Bartky (eds.), *Revaluing;* Ben Agger, *Gender, Culture and Power* (Westport, Conn.: Praeger, 1993); Margaret Ferguson and Jennifer Wicke (eds.), *Feminism and Postmodernism* (London: Duke University Press, 1994); Robyn Wiegman, *American Anatomies* (London: Duke University Press, 1995).

51.   Jane Flax, "Postmodernism," in Micheline R. Malson et al. (eds.), *Feminist Theory in Practice and Process* (Chicago: University of Chicago Press, 1989), p. 72.

52.   bell hooks, *Killing Rage: Ending Racism* (New York: H. Holt and Co., 1995), p. 6.

53.   Joan Robinson, *Collected Economic Papers,* cited in Peter Bauer, *Equality, the Third World and Economic Delusion* (Cambridge, Mass.: Harvard University Press, 1981), p. 213.

54.   Henrietta L. Moore, *A Passion for Difference* (Indianapolis, Ind.: University Press, 1994), p. 1.

55.   Kristeva, *Strangers to Ourselves,* p. 1.

56.   Ibid., p. 189. For an excellent analysis of the Simmelian roots of the sociological concept of the stranger, see Donald N. Levine, "On the History and Systematics of the Sociology of the Stranger," in William A. Shack and Elliot P. Skinner (eds.), *Strangers in African Societies* (Berkeley, Ca.: University of California Press, 1979), pp. 21-36.

57.   Giroux, "Insurgent Multiculturalism," p. 340.

58.   Giroux, *Theory,* Chapter 4. Giroux's analysis comes close to making the dominant culture an ideology, and vice versa. See also Goldberg (ed.), *Multiculturalism,* passim.

59.   Danny Weil, "Toward a Critical Multicultural Literacy," *Inquiry: Critical Thinking Across the Disciplines* 13, nos. 1-2 (February-March 1994), p. 15.

60.   McLaren, "White Terror," p. 53.

61.   Giroux, "The Politics of Insurgent Multiculturalism," p. 120.

62.   Kris D. Gutierrez, in Kris D. Gutierrez and Peter McLaren, "Pedagogies of Dissent and Transformation: A Dialogue about Postmodernity, Social Context, and the Politics of Literacy," in Kanpol and McLaren (eds.), *Critical* p. 139.

63.   Lyotard, *The Postmodern,* p. 66.

64.   Kenan Malik, "Universalism and Difference: Race and the Postmodernists," *Race and Class* 37, no. 3 (March 1996), p. 3.

65.   Theodore Allen, *The Invention of the White Race* (New York: Verso, 1994), pp. 27-28. See also Earl Conrad, *The Invention of the Negro* (New York: Paul Eriksson, Inc., 1966); Lawrence Wright, "One Drop of Blood," *The New Yorker* (July 25, 1994), pp. 46-55; Paul R. Spickard, "The Illogic of American Racial Categories," in Maria P.P. Root (ed.), *Racially Mixed People in America* (Newbury Park, Calif.: Sage, 1992), pp. 12-23; Marek Kohn, *The Race Gallery: The Return of Racial Science* (London: Jonathan Cape, 1995).

66.   McLaren, "White Terror," p. 61.

67.   Wilson J. Moses, "In Fairness to Afrocentrism," in Center for the New American Community, *Alternatives to Afrocentrism,* pp. 20-21.

68.   Henry L. Gates Jr., "Introduction: Writing 'Race' and the Difference It Makes," in Henry L. Gates, Jr. (ed.), *"Race," Writing and Difference* (Chicago: University of Chicago Press, 1986), p. 4.

69.   Omi and Winant, *Racial Formation,* p. 152.

70.   Ibid., p. 71.

71.   See Larry T. Reynolds and Leonard Lieberman, "The Rise and Fall of 'Race,'" *Race, Sex and Class* 1, no. 1 (Fall 1993), pp. 109-127.

72.   See Spickard, "The Illogic"; Kohn, *The Race*, Chapter 1.

73.   Donald E. Muir, "Race: The Mythic Root of Racism," *Sociological Inquiry* 63, no. 3 (August 1993), p. 339.

74.   See Cassirer, *The Philosophy*. According to Cassirer, Georges-Louis Buffon, himself a passionate naturalist, criticized "the father of zoology," Linnaeus, for confusing signs and what they signify, making real definitions of merely nominal ones (p. 78). Buffon's criticism is echoed in Lyotard's objection to any attempt to seize reality in thought. Lyotard, *The Postmodern*, pp. 73-77. The chief difficulty with the realist and naturalist claim to be describing nature is that then the classifications become beyond criticism.

75.   See Peter Berger and Thomas Luckmann, *The Social Construction of Reality: A Treatise in the Sociology of Knowledge* (New York: Doubleday, 1967).

76.   Peter Berger, *Invitation to Sociology: A Humanistic Perspective* (New York: Anchor Books, 1963), pp. 156-157.

77.   See Cavalli-Sforza et al., *The History and Geography of Human Genes*.

78.   See Root (ed.), *Racially Mixed*.

79.   Turner, "Anthropology and Multiculturalism," pp. 408-409. However, Turner's reconceptualization of culture still presents it as an analytical tool for establishing group boundaries, which is precisely the current social scientific usage of the concept. Thus Turner's claim that "multiculturalism remains essentially unconcerned with culture in any of its usual anthropological senses" is inaccurate.

80.   Ibid., p. 408.

81.   Edward Tylor, *Primitive Culture: Research into the Development of Mythology, Philosophy, Religion, Language, Art, and Custom* (New York: Brentano's Publishers, 1924), p. 1.

82.   Alfred Kroeber and Clyde Kluckhohn, *Culture, A Critical Review of Concepts and Definitions* (Cambridge, Mass.: Harvard University Peabody Museum of American Archaeology and Ethnology Papers, 1952), p. 162. Anthropologist George Stocking Jr. alludes to the mutations in usages "The concept of culture has since 1950 undergone an increasingly self-conscious reanalysis. Culture is now seen less in terms of inventories of material artifacts and concrete behavioral manifestations and more in terms of codes and rules, symbolic structures, and systems of meaning. Even so, the recent development of the concept can be viewed as a convergence of the Boasian 'pattern' and the Durkheimian 'structural-functional' theories of culture." p. 19.

83.   See Welsch, "Transculturality."

84.   Carl A. Grant, "Anthropological Foundations of Education That Is Multicultural," in Grant (ed.), *Multicultural Education: Commitments*, pp. 32-33.

85.   Leslie White, *The Science of Culture* (New York: Farrar, Straus and Cudahy, 1949), p. 33.

86.   See James Banks, *Multiethnic Education: Theory and Practice* (Boston: Allyn and Bacon, 1988).

87.   See Banks, "Multiethnic Education"; Sleeter (ed.), *Empowerment*. Asante, *Afrocentricity*.

88.   James Stuart Olson, *The Ethnic Dimension in American History*, vol. 1 (New York: St. Martin's Press, 1979), p. 17.

89.   Flax, "Postmodernism," in R. Malson et al. (eds.), *Feminist Theory*, p. 72.

90.   Weil, "Towards a Critical," p. 14.

91.   Martin Luther King Jr., "Letter to a Clergyman from Birmingham City Jail" (April 16, 1963).

92.   Hannah Arendt, *The Human Condition* (Chicago: University of Chicago Press, 1958), p. 8.

93.   Giroux, *Border*, p. 236.

94.   Barry Kanpol, "Multiculturalism and Empathy: A Border Pedagogy of Solidarity," in Kanpol and McLaren (eds.), *Critical*. p. 178.

95.   Henry L. Gates Jr., "Transforming the American Mind," paper presented at the Annual Meeting of the Modern Language Association, San Francisco, 1989, cited in Gutierrez and McLaren, "Pedagogies of Dissent," p. 128.

96.   McLaren, "White Terror," p. 55.

97.   House, "Realism," p. 5.

98.   See Paulo Freire, "Foreword," in Giroux, *Theory*, pp. ix-x.

99.   Freire, *Pedagogy of the Oppressed*, p. 25.

100.   Ibid., p. 26.

101.   Ibid., p. 37.

102.   Ibid., p. 26.

103.   Ibid., p. 161.

104.   Giroux, *Theory*, p. 163.

105.   Christine E. Sleeter and Carl A. Grant, "Mapping Terrains of Power: Student Cultural Knowledge versus Classroom Knowledge," in Sleeter (ed.), *Empowerment*, p. 50.

106.   Banks, "Multicultural Education: Development," pp. 27-28.

107.   See Max Weber, *The Theory of Social and Economic Organization* (Glencoe, Ill.: The Free Press, 1947), Chapters 1, 3, and 4, and *Economy and Society: An Outline of Interpretive Sociology. Vol. Two*, ed. Guenther Roth and Claus Wittich (Berkeley: University of California Press, 1978), Chapters 9 and 10-15.

108.   Foucault, *Power/Knowledge*, p. 98.

109.   Ibid., p. 93.

110.   Ibid., p. 92.

111.   Lyotard, *The Postmodern*, pp. 8-9.

112.   See Weber, *Economy and Society*, vol. 2, pp. 926-939, and *The Theory*, pp. 152-157.

113.   Weber, *The Theory*, p. 152. C. Wright Mills echoes Weber: "the elite are simply those who have most of what there is to have. . . . By the powerful we mean, of course, those who are able to realize their will, even if others resist it." *The Power Elite* (New York: Oxford University Press, 1959), p. 9.

114.   See Thomas Hobbes, *Leviathan* (New York: Collier, 1962), Chapter 10.

115.   Weber, *The Theory*, p. 153.

116.   See Steven Lukes, *Power: A Radical View* (London: Macmillan, 1974).

117.   Ibid., pp. 32-34.

118.   Ibid., pp. 24-25.

119.   Karl Marx, *Capital* (New York: International Publishers, 1977), p. 10.

120.   Karl Marx and Friedrich Engels, *The Communist Manifesto* (New York: Monthly Review Press, 1964), p. 24.

121.   Marx, *Capital*, p. 167.

122.   Karl Marx, *Economic and Philosophic Manuscripts of 1844* (New York: International Publishers, 1970), p. 114

123.   Harvey, *The Condition*, p. 107.

124.   Marx, *Capital*, Chapter 15.

125.   See Karl Marx, *A Contribution to the Critique of Political Economy* (New York: International Publishers, 1970), pp. 20-21.

126.   Foucault, *Power/Knowledge*, pp. 51-52.

127.   See Nelson Polsby, *Community Power and Political Theory* (London: Yale University Press, 1963); Robert Dahl, *Modern Political Analysis* (Englewood Cliffs, N.J.: Prentice Hall, 1963); Harold Lasswell and Abraham Kaplan, *Power and Society: A Framework for Political Theory* (New Haven, Conn.: Yale University Press, 1965); Peter Bachrach and Morton Baratz, "Decisions and Non-Decisions: An Analytical Framework," *American Political Science Review* 57, no. 2 (1963), pp. 633-642; Nicos Poulantzas, *Political Power and Social Classes* (London: New Left Books, 1973).

128.   See Eisenstein, "Some Notes"; Lise Vogel, *Marxism and the Oppression of Women: Toward a Unitary Theory* (New Brunswick, N.J.: Rutgers University Press, 1983).

129.   See Belkhir et al., "Race, Sex, Class"; Belkhir, "Multicultural Education."

130.   For an analysis of race-class combinations, see Webster, *The Racialization*, Chapter 4.

131.   See Nicos Poulantzas, *Classes in Contemporary Capitalism* (London: New Left Books, 1975); Erik O. Wright, "Class Boundaries in Advanced Capitalist Societies," *New Left Review* (July-August 1976), pp. 3-41; Frank Parkin, *Marxism and Class Theory: A Bourgeois Critique* (London: Tavistock, 1979); Erik O. Wright, "Varieties of Marxist Conceptions of Class Structure," *Politics and Society* 9, no. 3 (1980), pp. 323-370; Jean L. Cohen, *Class and Civil Society: The Limits of Marxian Critical Theory* (Amherst, Mass.: University of Massachusetts Press, 1982).

132.   Marx and Engels, *The Communist*, p. 24.

133.   Goldberg, "Introduction," in Goldberg (ed.), *Critical*, p. 30.

134.   Peter McLaren, in Gutierrez and McLaren, "Pedagogies," p. 130.

135.   Marx, *Capital*, p. 35. Elsewhere Marx writes: "But in bourgeois society the commodity form of the product of labor—or the value form of the commodity—is the economic cell form" (p. 8).

136.   See D'Souza, *Illiberal*; Rush Limbaugh, *The Way Things Ought to Be* (New York: Pocket Star Books, 1993); Bennett, *Devaluing*; Siegel, *The Cult*.

137.   See Matthew Lipman, Ann M. Sharp, and Frederick S. Oscanyan, *Philosophy in the Classroom* (Philadelphia: Temple University Press, 1980); Robert E. Proctor, *Education's Great Amnesia: Reconsidering the Humanities from Petrarch to Freud with a Curriculum for Today's Students* (Bloomington, Ind.: Indiana University Press, 1988).

138.   Goldberg, "Introduction," p. 20.

139.   Danielle Flannery, "Adult Education and the Politics of the Theoretical Text," in Kanpol and McLaren (eds.), *Critical*. pp. 154-156.

140.   Limbaugh, *The Way*, pp. 212-213.

141.   See Paul Berman, "The Other and the Almost the Same," *The New Yorker* (February 28, 1994), pp. 61-71.

142.   Henry Giroux's *Border Crossings* and *Theory* and *Resistance in Education* present numerous, moral-political characterizations of the arguments of other authors, not refutations of their arguments. Their arguments, then, still stand, unless Giroux conceives his characterizations as refutations. This, however, should be made clear.

143.   See Richard Paul, *Critical Thinking: What Every Person Needs to Know to Survive in a Rapidly Changing World* (Sonoma, Calif.: Foundation for Critical Thinking, 1992).

144.   Giroux, *Border*, p. 230.

145.   Ibid., pp. 234-235.

146.   Rick Simonson and Scott Walker, "Introduction," in Rick Simonson and Scott Walker (eds.), *The Graywolf Annual Five: Multicultural Literacy* (St. Paul, Minn.: Graywolf Press, 1988), p. 9.

147.   Asante, "Multiculturalism: An Exchange," p. 270.

148.   Ibid., p. 269.

149.   Appiah, "Europe Upside Down," p. 24.

150.   Howard, "Whites," p. 39.

151.   Sleeter, "The White Ethnic Experience," p. 35.

152.   See John Wilson, *Thinking with Concepts* (Cambridge: Cambridge University Press, 1963).

153.   Jurgen Habermas, *The Theory of Communicative Action: Volume 1, Reason and the Rationalization of Society,* trans. Thomas McCarthy (Boston: Beacon Press, 1981), p. 397.

154.   Ibid., p. 301.

155.   Ibid., p. 305.

156.   Lyotard, *The Postmodern*, p. 65.

157.   Ibid., p. 66.

158.   Ibid., pp. 65-66.

159.   For analyses of argumentum ad hominem, see Henry Johnstone Jr. "Philosophy and Argument Ad Hominem," *Inquiry: Critical Thinking Across the Disciplines* 12, nos. 3-4 (November-December 1993), pp. 25-29; S. Morris Engel, "The Five Forms of the Ad Hominem Fallacy," *Inquiry: Critical Thinking Across the Disciplines* 14, no. 1 (Autumn 1994), pp. 19-35. For a summary of informal fallacies, see Theodore Schick Jr. and Lewis Vaughan, *How to Think with Weird Things: Critical Thinking for a New Age* (London: Mayfield, 1995), Appendix.

160.   See Teachers for a Democratic Culture, "The State of Academic Freedom 1995."

161.   Asante, "Multiculturalism," pp. 269-270.

162.   See Lyotard, *The Postmodern*, pp. 46, 63-64, 66, 81.

163.   Goldberg, "Introduction," pp. 27-28.

164.   See Walters (ed.), *Re-thinking*.

4

Education Reform, Multiculturalism, and Critical Thinking

If you are planning for a year ahead . . . sow rice; if you are planning for ten years . . . plant trees; if you are planning for a hundred years . . . educate people.

—"Chinese wisdom," quoted by Richard G. Lillard in *American West*, January 1974.

The centrality of education to human civilization has been emphasized repeatedly from ancient to modern times. As a proposition, it surfaces among Egyptian, Assyrian, Greek, Roman, and medieval scribes, as well as during the Enlightenment, and in the writings of America's "founding fathers."[1] Plato's *Republic* places education as *the* governing institution, and as an overarching process that determines the caliber of thinking, moral inclinations, and all social relations. His narrative of prisoners unknowingly dwelling in a cave of shadows symbolizes powerful customary and cognitive fetters to enlightenment. Like Plato, some contemporary educators point to significant relationships among educational experiences and character formation, communicative capacities, the adoption of moral values, reasoning abilities, human behavior, labor productivity, social problems, and social change. Mind and society are inseparably connected. Hence because educational practices significantly shape the mind, they would have to be reformed, if social relations are to be transformed. This conclusion undergirds certain strands of multiculturalism and multicultural education; they represent education reform projects with objectives ranging from a celebration of diversity to the eradication of all forms of oppression and injustice in society. As such, they embody pungent criticisms of the organization, structure, and sociopolitical functions of schooling, and aspirations for particular kinds of social change.

Education: Critiques and Reforms

Advocates of multiculturalism, going beyond the contributions of proponents of multicultural education, draw on "critical theory," as well as radical educationists' exposé of the ideological function of schools, that is, their complicity in maintaining patterns of legitimation, cultural domination, and oppression.[2] Their criticisms form a triad of unfavorable assessments of schooling, the other two being adverse assessments from advocates of critical thinking, and reports of economically damaging educational failures. The former Chairman of Zerox Corporation and undersecretary of state for education during the Bush administration, David T. Kearns, writes:

America's public schools graduate 700,000 functionally illiterate kids every year—and 700,000 more drop out. Four out of five young adults in a recent survey couldn't summarize the main point of a newspaper article, read a bus schedule, or figure their change from a restaurant bill. A 1987 survey of 5,000 high school seniors in eight major cities produced equally dismal results. In Boston, 39% of the students couldn't name the six New England states; in Minneapolis-St. Paul, 63% couldn't name all seven continents; in Dallas, 25% couldn't identify the country that borders the U.S. to the south.[3]

Kearns' observations were made in the context of America's declining economic performances and decreasing global competitiveness. In stump speeches, Newt Gingrich makes repeated references to high school graduates who cannot read their diplomas, and eminent economists and business leaders often warn of the portentous economic consequences of a failing system of public education.[4]

Some responses to negative comparative evaluations of U.S. education suggest that, on the contrary, all is well with the functioning of schools that are woefully underfunded, that teachers are performing yeoman services under very difficult conditions, and that criticisms of K-12 schools are corporatist, biased, and methodologically flawed.[5] Evaluations of educational organization and outcomes are often deemed "political," and the interests, values, motives, and ideology of commentators scrutinized when responding to their comments. The controversy over the evaluation of assessments of schooling indicates that what is perhaps most inadequate about educational outcomes is that educators themselves cannot agree on how to evaluate the efficiency and effectiveness of schooling. This lack of agreement may be a reflection of divergent philosophies of education, but it is also fueled by nonconsideration of conceptions of rationality and intellectual standards for assessing arguments. Arguably, an agreement to utilize intellectual standards and focus on the elements of reasoning underlying arguments is the necessary first move in education reform.

What should be the end-product of educational processes? Many types of outcomes could be desired—political, ethical, rational, behavioral, cultural, and so on—but they must be ordered along some hierarchy of preferences and some may be mutually exclusive. It is here that contentious theories of knowledge, human nature, and human happiness come to the fore. According to advocates of critical thinking, the core purpose of education must be the perfecting of the human capacity to be rational, for reasoning processes define the conscious actions of human beings. Their criticisms of education are an extension of this Enlightenment perspective on the nature of homo sapiens sapiens. For example, Richard Paul, a prominent protagonist of critical thinking, regrets the schools' underdevelopment of students' reasoning.

Education, so called, is a classic example. No culture sees itself as indoctrinating its young or discouraging intellectual development. Each sees itself as concerned with education worthy of the name. The rhetoric of reason and objective learning is everywhere. Yet classroom instruction around the world, at all levels, is typically didactic, one-dimensional, and indifferent, when not antithetical, to reason.[6]

In a similar vein, Mary Kennedy, professor of education at Michigan State University, writes:

First, national assessments in virtually every subject indicate that although our students can perform basic skills pretty well, they are not doing well on thinking and reasoning. American students can compute, but they cannot reason through complex mathematical problems. They can write complete and correct sentences, but they cannot prepare arguments. Nor can they reason through scientific problems very well. . . . Moreover, in international comparisons, American students are falling behind . . . particularly in those areas that require higher-order thinking.[7]

In its September 20, 1993 issue, *Time* describes a survey commissioned by the Department of Education and carried out by a Princeton-based Educational Testing Service. The survey found nearly half of the U.S. adult population, some ninety million, lacking the literacy and numeracy skills for adequate functioning in a modern industrial society. The majority of respondents were unable to paraphrase passages or to perform simple arithmetic calculations.[8] Questions could be raised regarding the conceptions of reasoning, literacy, and numeracy used in the surveys as well as the methods ascertaining levels of competence. However, even within minimal standards, a consensus would be reached among educators that students' intellectual competencies could be dramatically improved and that the resources are available to achieve this.

Following up on the criticisms of educational delivery outlined in *A Nation at Risk* (1983), a 1989 educational summit, convened by President George Bush and attended by fifty state governors, criticized public schools for failing to provide the quality labor force that is vital for America's success in this age of global competition.[9] A second summit was held in 1996. Participants included representatives from the U.S. Chamber of Commerce, the Business Roundtable, and the National Alliance of Businesses, and they repeated the criticisms of schools. To remedy the schools' failures, they recommended that: (1) the administration of schools be privatized, or brought into partnership with both parents and the corporate sector; (2) teachers should be obliged to be more accountable; (3) classroom processes should be infused with modern technology; and

(4) that there should be national standards for instruction and the testing of educational outcomes. These recommendations differ significantly from those of "critical pedagogists" and advocates of critical thinking. The latter traces education's problems to a neglect of the foundational role of reasoning in learning, and the use of flawed theories of knowledge and literacy to guide the training of teachers and classroom practices. By contrast, focusing on the politics of education, critical pedagogists accuse schools of failing to sensitize students to the sociopolitical realities of discrimination, domination, and oppression. The three perspectives on education reform—corporatist, critical pedagogist, and critical thinking—not only share not only a dissatisfaction with outcomes, but also a suggestion that schools focus on the development of students' higher-order thinking skills.[10] What their sponsors do not analyze in any sustained fashion is the possibility that: (1) students would need entirely different attitudes to knowledge, learning, and the purpose of life, if they are to pursue the development of higher order thinking skills, and (2) the development of these skills is incompatible with what may be called an education model. In other words, the attitudinal outcomes of this model are inimical to the drive for perpetual learning that is necessary for social reconstruction, the new economy, and the cultivation of critical thinking.

Two models of education may be constructed from criticisms of educational practices—an education model and an educability model. The latter is explicit in the advocacy of critical thinking and philosophy in schools, and in Newt Gingrich's *To Renew America*. The education model, critically analyzed as "reproduction theories" in Henry Giroux's *Theory and Resistance in Education*, is pragmatist in philosophical orientation and characterized by a subservience of schools to political and labor market exigencies. Its typical properties are: (1) a marginalization of the analytical, reasoning, and empathic skills of students, (2) a politicization of curriculum design, and (3) a commodification of educational delivery. This last feature effectively limits citizens' access to educational institutions. Richard Paul notices a tradition:

Higher education was little better. It began in the 17th and 18th centuries in primarily upper class "seminaries," providing a classical education though not, of course, in the Socratic sense. Students were drilled in Latin and Greek and Theology. Inculcation, memorization, repetition, and forensic display were the order of the day. Not until the latter half of the 19th Century was higher education possible for someone not in the upper class, and then only at the new Land Grant Colleges . . . established to promote "education of the industrial classes in the several pursuits and professions in life."[11]

Prices and the possession of money ruled schooling; they determined the quality of and access to schools. This condition reveals the status of education as a commodity. As such, it can be made inaccessible to specific persons by either monetary prerequisites, or legislative indolence.[12] Because money is the key that unlocks school doors and the essence of commodity relations, criticisms of the system of denial of access to schools should begin with the questions: Need education be a commodity? What conditions make it so?

In *Capital*, Karl Marx characterizes a commodity as an object of utility whose physical or chemical qualities satisfies human wants. But this, he adds, is only an appearance. A commodity is actually a two-fold substance that congeals specific social relations; it is a product whose use value becomes "the form of manifestation, the phenomenal form of its opposite, value," and the basis of exchange value. Commodities are historically specific kinds of goods, use values produced and exchanged for the purpose of realizing exchange value. Thus "goods" and "commodities" are not equivalent. The production of commodities reflects a specific historical conjuncture. Marx writes: "The mode of production in which the product takes the form of a commodity, or is produced directly for exchange is the most general and most embryonic form of bourgeois production."[13] This mode of production heralds a progressive universalization of commodity production. As it advances, neither "culture," nor education escapes its self-sustaining, commodifying ethos.

Certain attitudinal outcomes of the education model—make money by any means necessary, learning is merely a prelude to earning—are initially conducive to the development of capitalist commodity production, but they become drastically limiting once a certain threshold of industrial development has been reached. This point is brought out by Newt Gingrich in *To Renew America*. Gingrich presents a brief, critical analysis of certain aspects of the education model, and writes:

In the Industrial Age, the education model has been a passive student dominated by an active teacher. The teacher is supposed to know (1) what is appropriate to teach and (2) when it is appropriate to teach it. Industrial Age education is segmented into curriculum blocks and most learning takes place inside a public building. The students' interests are subordinated to whatever the state or national system of experts decree. All students are assumed to learn at the same time and pace.[14]

Students must become autonomous learners, and this requires that learning be placed on a different motivational threshold. The learn to earn principle does not suffice in an age when the means of life are relatively cheaply available. As will be shown, however, Gingrich did not extend his critique of the education model in the direction of rejecting the commodification of educational delivery. Nevertheless, remarkably, a Republican Speaker of the House of Representatives, critical pedagogists, and advocates of critical thinking share a deep dissatisfaction with some features of the education model that characterizes the Industrial Age. Where they diverge, as Marx and Weber did in their analyses of the modern world, is in their characterizations of the modern age. It is not, some would argue, so much industrial as *capitalist*.[15]

Within the education model, higher education is produced as a commodity that commands different prices; it is accessible only to those who can afford it, in conjunction with their performance in secondary education. Thus access to higher education follows patterns of income differentiation and success in the lower phases of education. Both performance in and the quality of the lower phases of education are circumscribed by wealth and income. To all appearances,

K-12 public education is produced (funded) and offered as goods that are not paid for directly by the consumers. These goods do not appear to be commodities. However, insofar as its quality depends on what local schools can afford to pay for equipment, buildings, textbooks, and teaching, K-12 schooling is also commodified, and the tax-based system of funding together with residential qualifications guarantees that some consumers do not have access to the best-quality primary and secondary education.[16]

K-12 schools prepare students to become living commodities on sale in labor markets, or, as college students, buyers of higher education. Because education is conceived as an investment in the creation of "human capital," outcomes are monetarily measured and often explained in terms of what consumers bring to the market-place. Thus the schools' failures are deemed "dropouts," rather than "pushouts." The pushout phenomenon indicates that all consumers cannot buy the schools' goods or consume it productively. For example, although effective demand for higher education can be manipulated through fiscal policies, scholarships, tuition fees, loans, grants, and equal opportunity programs, certain failures are guaranteed by socioeconomic conditions. Forty-three percent of the nation's college students work full-time, which must negatively affect their academic performance. Moreover, learning begins prenatally, and so a child's success in school is inseparably linked to a range of experiences in homes and neighborhoods.[17] Thus academic performances and outcomes reflect and perpetuate prevailing patterns of income distribution and socioeconomic stratification. "Putting kids through college" reflects generational patterns of purchasing power. Low-income parents generally raise poorly educated offspring who become low-income workers who, in turn, become low-income parents. Barring stupendous efforts, then, some families will cyclically slide into the secondary and tertiary labor markets, or not find a place in them at all.

Education must be conceived as an integrated, socially structured process and, therefore, inseparably connected with institutions such as the family, legislatures, and the labor market. Hence education reform proposals must be attentive to the motivational effects of the price of higher education on students in the lower phases of schooling. Some students may reason as follows: "I know my family cannot afford college, so why should I try to be a 'good' student?" Indeed, in general, low-income parents are not able to purchase college education. Thus their higher education expectations for their offspring are stillborn. As Newt Gingrich writes: "Poor children enter school with inadequate preparation and are limited from day one. Too many children simply will never learn how to read or write. High school students are not learning the math and science they need to be competitive in the world market. Going to college has become an expensive ordeal that can permanently shatter a family's finances."[18] These children eventually become poorly educated parents that are intellectually unable to motivate or help their children to stay in school. Those who argue that the eradication of "inner city" problems should begin in the family should consider the proposition that every failed school child has a high potential for being a failure at parenting, and indeed, for early and single motherhood or fatherhood.

Many of the school's failures will seek to make do in the underworld and underground economy. As David Thompson notes:

There are large and growing numbers of young people in the United States who face severe economic and social consequences resulting from the failure to obtain an appropriate education. The consequences are striking, as in almost all instances there is a history of school failure and low achievement that can be linked to high rates of unemployment, underemployment, low wages and unfulfilled potential. [19]

The drift into the underworld is manifest in the overwhelming presence of "dropouts," illiterates, and functional illiterates among the prison population. The waste of resources and "human capital" is as avoidable as it is monetarily incalculable. However, it is testimony to the tolerance of contradiction in American intellectual life that, while political representatives agree that inadequate education underlies these "crimes," they recommend ever more Draconian wars on drugs, gangs, and prostitution in order to punish, rehabilitate, and eliminate "criminals," or cultural renewal. It is as if the commodity nature of education is not to be altered, even if it is recognized as the source of education's failures.

In the education model, money-making is presented as the ultimate objective of schooling. The following story from Newt Gingrich indicates that his "revolutionary" criticisms of the education model do not reach into its commodification of attitudes to learning: "One incident in Douglasville, Georgia, turned me into a revolutionary. At our initial briefing, one child at a housing project said, 'You are going to cheat us.' Amazed, the volunteers asked him what he meant. 'You'll get us to read all summer and then you won't pay us,' he said. This remark convinced me that the welfare state has to be replaced." [20] This is a strange conclusion and conversion. How is the welfare state responsible for a child's demand for money for an activity that should be inner-directed and self-rewarding? What Gingrich does admit is that this child was already told by volunteers in Gingrich's "Earning by Learning" project that learning is preparation for earning: "Basically, we encourage children to read by paying them. Volunteers visit housing projects once a week and counsel the children in their reading. They then offer the children two dollars for every book they read during the next month." [21] More generally, as part of preparing students for the world of work, throughout K-12, teachers and parents often advise them to "learn to earn." Some of those who graduate will pursue higher education as a means to the end of making money. In seeking to sell their knowledge and skills to employers and move progressively up occupational ladders in the primary labor market, students are constrained to package themselves more and more as commodities. This kind of preparation may appear harmless. However, it means that students' interest in learning is limited to their perceptions of its usefulness in the labor market, and it becomes difficult for teachers to persuade them of the value of the humanities. Such students can hardly be encouraged to take courses in philosophy, a main source of considerations of moral values. Many teachers, parents, and Gingrich's volunteers work against his vision of a morally reinvigorated "learning society."

Didactic and inflexible classroom practices are consistent with the limited goals set within the education model. Becoming educable is a comparatively slow process. Becoming trained is relatively instantaneous. Because educational outcomes are monetarily driven and pragmatically assessed, instruction is organized to fast-feed students with the information adjudged necessary for mastering certain techniques. Thus students are to be very frequently tested, and in assessing outcomes, the questions asked are: What do they know, and how can we measure the amount of knowledge, rather than, how can we assess their ability to reason and evaluate knowledge? In schools that embrace the education model, students begin to learn less and less, and retain precious little, for lasting learning and the development of problem solving skill take place only through reasoned assessment of information, deep conceptual understanding, cognizance of theoretical connections. When learning, or the cultivation of the mind ceases to be the mission of schools, a vicious circle of degeneration ensues. The less students actually learn in school, the more schools become like prisons, as well as seed-beds of conspicuous consumerist exhibitionism and deviant behaviors. Reportedly, one hundred and thirty thousand students bring guns to school each day. Students progressively lose their desire for being in school. Reportedly, three thousand drop out every day. Why stay in school? There are easier ways to make money.

It may be argued that education, conceived as preparation to make money, provides the most powerful incentive to attend and stay in school. On the other hand, such an incentive has severe limitations. Credentials do not guarantee success in the labor market in the short run, and their acquisition demands levels of self-discipline and domestic tranquillity that are missing from certain environments. Moreover, learning for earning can cease to be attractive, if the basic necessities are cheapened by technological and economic advances to such an extent that parasitic behaviors—voluntary homelessness, petty thievery, "going on welfare"—easily acquire those necessities. Thus, paradoxically, the subservience of schools to the economy ultimately weakens both schools and the economy. Examine the students that out-perform American students and their attitude to learning will be found to be a stark contrast to the monetary instrumentalism of U.S. students. Schools can be run like a business, but they would strain with the dilemma of treating students as both consumers and commodities at the same time. As James Moffett protests: "The government's conviction that business can show the schools how to set their house in order derives not only from a concern about the employability of the population but also from the old false analogy that running a school is like manufacturing and marketing commodities."[22] Perhaps it is precisely because of the denial of a place of promise for reasoning in schools that the nation that established the first system of mass public education in the world does not now recognize that it is necessary to move schooling from employability to educability.

The second property of the education model is a linking of curriculum development to political conditions and considerations. Hence educational inputs are not necessarily aimed at the development of students' analytical, reasoning, and empathic skills. What takes priority is the inculcation of specific identities, attitudes, and values—Christian virtues, patriotism, as well as regional, racial, and ethnic histories. This practice has two problematic effects. First, because values are separated from reasoned justification, their selection generates intrinsically inconclusive disputes, as is evident in the debates over multicultural education and multiculturalism. Second, in cultivating specific identities in schools, teachers are constrained to inculcate factual information about national, gender, racial, and ethnic experiences, rather than encourage students to discover how certain events acquire the status of being facts and experiences. Students then treat their gender, racial, and ethnic identities as sacrosanct precisely at the moment when identity flexibility and "transculturality" are demanded by migration currents and globalization. Disturbed by this identity rigidity and its concomitant intolerance of "others," some scholars develop multicultural remedies that further ossify gender, racial, and ethnic identities. What they might have done is theoretically situate gender, racial, and ethnic classifications, and cease propagating these classifications as aspects of the real world.

The first two properties of the education model—overall commodification and localized curricular politicization—result in (1) a systematic denial of certain persons' access to educational institutions; (2) teaching styles that spoonfeed students; (3) a top-down use of schools to accommodate various political and commercial objectives; and (4) classroom practices that seek to inculcate what to think rather than standards for evaluating thinking. Thus, as manifest in Newt Gingrich's learning by earning project, certain features of the education model are embraced by political representatives. The other property—the marginalization of analytical, reasoning, and empathic abilities—is periodically condemned for decreasing labor productivity and national economic competitiveness. Other socially destabilizing effects of the model—commercialized values and racialized identities as well as group discrimination and confrontations—are not recognized as effects by political representatives who are themselves products of schooling within that model. Outside of the education model, schools would promote rational discussions of theories of values, including the value of sound reasoning, and identity formation, not cultivate any particular identity. Because schools hold captive populations who are at the most impressionable phase of their lives, a school-cultivated identity becomes virtually indelible, and leads to nepotistic behavior during the allocation of resources. Thus accusations of discrimination and reverse discrimination become the order of the day among citizens. It would be no exaggeration to claim that an education model underlies the racial-ethnic spoils system and incompetence that plague human society.[23]

The third property of the education model is reflected in the pariah status of the humanities in the curriculum, side by side with a canonization of epistemological realism. A particular conception of human nature underlies this comparative ejection of literature, art, music, geography, philosophy, and languages from the curriculum. As the argument goes, realistically and pragmatically, schools cannot fundamentally alter a morally flawed and irrational human nature. At most, human beings, who are basically individualistic, competitive, materialistic, and possessive, can be taught how to adjust to the real world. Two educational-organizational consequences of this philosophical anthropological assumption are clear. First, schools will be realist socialization agencies catering to the development of "good" character through inculcation of values such as a Puritan work ethic, competitive attitudes, and a passion to consume not knowledge, but material objects.[24] Second, and relatedly, teachers will have precious little incentive to cultivate minds in a spirit of rational inquiry and love of learning. The primary classroom processes would be the transmission of information and attempts to memorize it. Some of the effects on students are predictable: diminished motivation to learn, an inability to reason soundly, think and act consequentially, communicate with empathy and conclusiveness, and examine arguments for their assumptions, and implications. Above all, the moral development of students will be stunted, for it is through examining a variety of other perspectives that students acquire the habit of moving beyond their own worldviews, and connecting their welfare to the well-being of others.

From the commercialization of students' aspirations and marginalization of their analytical, reasoning and empathetic capacities, a variety of moral and characterological disorders follow. Citizens become incapable of reasoning consequentially, or expressing a deep concern for others and their pain. The principle—the ends justify the means—should also be expected to be popular, and making money by any means necessary a preeminent goal. Those that are perceived as vulnerable—the uneducated, children, females, immigrants, senior citizens—will form a disproportionate part of the victims of violence and violations. Social relations come to resemble the Hobbesian image of rampant, violent individualism that Charles Derber describes in *The Wilding of America*. But the orgies of destructive and self-destructive behaviors do not lead to questions such as: If education continues to be money-driven, and educational failure explained as a reflection of individual, biological attributes and cultural practices, can the phenomenon of a burgeoning prison population, with all the potential for high levels of recidivism, be avoided? Can "democracy" and "the free market" survive the schools' noncultivation of reasoning and empathy?

Benjamin Barber's remarks capture the connections among critical thinking and civil discourse, liberties, and social relations.

The logic of democracy begins with public education, proceeds to informed citizenship, and comes to fruition in the securing of rights and liberties. We have been nominally democratic for so long that we presume it is our natural condition. . . . Among the several literacies that have attracted the anxious attention of commentators, civic literacy has been the least visible. Yet this is the fundamental literacy by which we live in a civil society. It encompasses the competence to participate in democratic communities, the ability to think critically and act with deliberation in a pluralistic world, and the empathy to identify sufficiently with others to live with them despite conflicts of interest and differences in character.[25]

A certain level of consequential reasoning is required to recognize that, in a society in which each individual represents a means of making money, each is obliged to look out for the other's interest. In other words, a society with a free market system of economic organization requires, especially high-order thinking skills and empathy from citizens who must be able to examine their assumptions critically, to consider the long-term consequences of actions, and to recognize and reject contradictions in their reasoning. These are precisely the attributes lauded by all shades of education reform proposals.

Most education reformers endorse the proposition that schools should foster the development of critical thinking skills. Yet this endorsement is not followed through with the application of critical thinking's intellectual standards to the disputes over education reform. Were this to be done, discussions of education reform would be approached as a process of entering a dialogue with another human being about the value of knowledge and how to evaluate and reshape ideas so that they become mutually agreeable intellectual constructs. It follows that the standards for evaluating ideas cannot be politicized or relativized. Educators cannot quarrel over how learning processes are to unfold; they will disagree, but these disagreements can be resolved through attention to intellectual standards and ground rules for argument assessment. When educators fail to utilize such standards and rules, they quarrel; tracing their disputes to moral and political motives, interests, and ideologies. As they quarrel, arguments are (un)settled by recourse to the personal, the traditional, and administrative interventions. Educators' verbal behaviors come to mirror exchanges in legislatures, to the detriment of both the teaching profession and students' learning.

It has been remarked that transforming education is as difficult as moving a cemetery, for schooling is inseparably intertwined with other aspects of the social structure such as employment/unemployment, income distribution, social conditions in neighborhoods, family structure, and access to health care, welfare, and public transportation facilities. Industrial, social, and economic policies can place insurmountable obstacles in the way of success in educational institutions. Anyone can go to school in America. However, success in schools can be thwarted by child hunger, lack of affordable child care, or pre-natally generated disabilities. Not everyone can want to go to school, go to a "good" school, or even stay in a school of choice. Thus, general educational deprivation is a feature of the education model; it represents an end-product of the commodification of education. What happens to those who cannot afford, or properly consume, schooling, those who are denied opportunities to enhance their human capacities? Policies of benign neglect are generally applied to these "failures." The functional illiterates, academically unprepared, and "dropouts" are expected to enter the secondary and tertiary labor markets. As their numbers increase, however, federal government and corporate attention is paid to sectoral losses in comparative international labor productivity. Yet the questions to be asked of the ad hoc, federal and corporate responses to "educational crises" are: What happens after "we catch up with the Japanese and Europeans?" Will not major social dislocations be initiated by those who cannot find employment in secondary and tertiary labor markets that are increasingly being exported to the third world, or being sated by such immigrants? How many prisons can be constructed before recidivism begins to imprison citizens in their own homes? Will this education model be retrenched and replaced with a system of noncommodified education from kindergarten through college?

Echoing Newt Gingrich's proposal in *To Renew America*, President Bill Clinton, in his State of the Union Address in January 1997, seemed to perceive the need for the decommodification of education. He proposed two years of "free" college education, provided that the student maintain a B grade point average. However, this proposal is but a minute step in the direction along which education reform should be proceeding. Gingrich and Clinton's concession to certain students, however, reflect an analysis that marginalizes the links among operational issue—national standards, teacher accountability, centralization/decentralization, and parental choice of schools—and the macro-purposes of education. In general, education reform proposals do not address the larger issues underlying the educational crises that have plagued the society from its inception—a self-perpetuating distrust of reason and human nature, the conviction that human beings are means, and residues of social Darwinism. It is these philosophical-anthropological orientations that maintain the education model and render radical education reforms stillborn. Nevertheless, the periodic alarms over decreasing test scores, labor productivity, and civic literacy, and increasing deviancy among youth indicate that the education model is a failure. It serves neither community, the economy, nor democracy. Indeed, it is destructive of them all, for it aborts the development of students' reasoning faculties. It follows that issues of choice, site-based school management, national assessment, multicultural education, and whether there should or should not be greater federal involvement in schooling should take a back seat to changes that can be implemented at any administrative level. First, disputants in the debate over educational reform must strive after a consensus on standards for argument evaluation, for without this consensus there is no rational basis for accepting or rejecting any particular reform proposal. Second, access to all phases of education must be decommodified. Third, the curriculum should be restructured within critical thinking conceptions of teaching and learning.

Critical Thinking: Assumptions, Definitions, and Infusion

As indicated, recognition of the value of critical thinking periodically graces the writings of contemporary corporate and political leaders, as they bemoan the state of education. The mission statements of many colleges include the recommendation that courses and instructional methods be restructured in order to develop students' critical thinking abilities. This recommendation extends a long-standing tradition. Advocacies of reflective and self-corrective thinking can be found in the Socratic dialogues as well as the writings of Voltaire, Francis Bacon, and J.S. Mill, as well as John Dewey in the early twentieth century.[26] Among philosophers of education, Dewey is outstanding in his insistence that educational delivery cannot be separated from meta-educational judgments about the role of experience in the way children learn, and that the selection of educational inputs, teaching practices, and curriculum content reflect overall conceptions of human nature, knowledge, and social behavior.[27] This linking of theories of knowing, human nature, and educational philosophy provides answers to the following questions: Why, despite a significant appeal for it, is instruction in critical thinking not a central feature of educational processes? Why have other movements for education reform such as multicultural education and education for raising students' self-esteem received more media attention and official endorsement? Does the critical thinking advocacy lack intrinsic persuasive power?

First, proposals for infusing critical thinking should be expected to meet opposition in an intellectual environment dominated by assumptions that human beings are basically flawed—irrational, emotional, materialistic, genetically predisposed, or culturally determined—for the advocacy of critical thinking draws much from the writings of philosophers who posit the decisive significance of reasoning in human affairs. Second, this emphasis on reasoning competes with other explanations of human action, such as God's will, natural laws, human nature, culture, values, psychological states, social structure, and economic interests. These explanations are manifest in religious doctrines, the biological sciences, and social scientific disciplines such as sociology, economics, anthropology, political science, and psychology. If educational policy makers do not regard reasoning as somehow pivotal to the human experience, the development of reasoning skills will not be prioritized in schools. Third, it is almost exclusively philosophy that promotes the crucial significance of reasoning in human affairs, and philosophy remains "the lost dimension" of educational inputs.[28]

A final reason for the slow institutional progress of critical thinking is that it is incompatible with the education model that prescribes and poses the question: What do teachers teach? In general, answers would refer to disciplines and subject matter. The advocacy of critical thinking poses a different question: *For what* do teachers teach? The answer would be for *educability*. Teaching should be characterized by instruction for the development of critical thinking skills, as a means of promoting educability. The end-product of educational processes cannot be education, or a mere acquisition of knowledge, but respect for knowledge, a commitment to learning, and the possession of specific analytical abilities, reasoning skills, and moral dispositions. If these attributes are to be developed, the organization of schools would have to be grounded in a philosophy of educability that embodies the following propositions:

1. Every human being can learn and realize his or her intellectual and creative potential, if the conditions of learning are conducive to this.
2. Learning is an end and good in itself.
3. Teaching is the most effective way to learn.
4. Schools should serve all intelligences by focusing on the development of students' analytical, reasoning, and empathic skills.
5. The aims of education should be defined by those involved in the practice of educating.

The educability model rests on an assumption that schooling, not the economy, or politics, shapes the quality of social relations; it also embraces a conception of learning as a human obligation, a process so unavoidable that it must be joyfully experienced. Without a commitment to this kind of learning, neither educators nor students will be motivated to transform the educational practices that underlie the state of the economy, politics, and social relations. The critical thinking movement is but a small step in the direction of changing the way human beings construct their being.

The concept of educability underlies critical thinking proposals, although all of its advocates might not agree as to its salience. They would agree, however, that an infusion of critical thinking cannot be realized without a radical departure from the education model. It is this model that disempowers teachers, for it does not enhance the child's passion for knowing/learning. Teachers thereby lose their most important constituency—students who value knowledge and so acknowledge the overarching significance of teaching. It follows that the empowerment of teachers can be achieved by their recognition that, because what takes place in educational institutions is pivotal to the project of human self-realization, the teaching profession should be dedicated to recapturing students' interest in the relationships among learning, reasoning, their personal growth and well-being, and social development. In other words, both teachers' and students' empowerment begins with discussions of the implications of two divergent educational philosophies—education and educability. Educators may seek to change the world, or inspire their students to do so, but only through perfecting the ability to evaluate the quality of thinking about the world. Hence schools must be transformed into "a home for the mind," to use Art Costa's compelling phrase. In such schools, students would be advised: Learn to *learn*, to love learning, for it is the sum and substance of human life. Within this educational philosophy, schools would be organized as places where minds are cultivated as an end in itself, grounded in the ideal of universal human educability, and their curricula guided by a focus on developing criteria-bound and subject-specific reasoning skills. These arguments introduce the concepts around which critical thinking is defined.

Among the advocates and detractors of critical thinking, discussions continue over whether critical thinking is best defined as specific competencies and characterological traits, an educational ideal, an analytic-logical process, a type of verbal behavior, or a field-dependent and content-bound set of analytical procedures.[29] However, this definitional variety generates doubts about the relevance and viability of critical thinking only if their common focus on reasoning is overlooked. Michael Scriven and Richard Paul offer a definition of critical thinking as a process of evaluating structures of thinking (classifications, assumptions, premises, and implications) within standards of clarity, coherence, logical consistency, accuracy, depth, precision, and fair-mindedness.[30] In *Critical Thinking: What Every Person Needs to Survive in a Rapidly Changing World*, Richard Paul offers a variety of tactical and strategic recommendations for infusing critical thinking in educational processes. He argues that the cultivation of critical thinking requires, above all, an understanding of its dimensions—the elements of thinking, intellectual standards, traits of mind or dispositions, and analytical abilities. Teachers cultivate critical thinking when students are challenged to use intellectual standards to assess the elements of thinking—questions at issue, assumptions, premises, purposes, evidence, implications, concepts, and classifications.

Scriven and Paul's definition implicitly rejects relativist and dogmatic theories of knowledge, for they suggest that critical thinking is thinking done within universal intellectual standards. It is a reflective and criteria-bounded process of evaluating the elements of thinking, or reasoned reflection on thinking processes. Critical thinking is not mere questioning, or criticism, for its own sake. Thinking, in the sense of establishing premises and reasoning through conclusions, is critical when the reasoning processes are grounded in standards, self-reflexive, and self-corrective. This means that conclusions, the end-product of reasoning processes, must survive their implications. In this sense, critical thinking is a generic skill, having a high level of transferability across disciplines.

In his "Introduction" to *Curriculum*, Harry Broudy captures the core of Socratic thinking by presenting a series of questions that should be posed in reading a text or engaging in discourse:

What is the argument, the chain or chains of reasoning? What reasons are given for what conclusions, and what reasons are given to support other reasons? . . . What are the author's basic and general beliefs, including some of his significant implicit assumptions? . . . What are the meanings of the author's key terms or concepts? . . . Are the premises credible? . . . Is the reasoning sound? . . . Is the view a comprehensive one that is consistent with cognate views? . . . What is the credibility of the author's argument when compared with other arguments? . . . Is the argument about a significant issue, and does it work for and under the influence of desirable values?[31]

These questions are relevant not only to reading, but to all thinking, knowledge-construction, and argument assessment. One of their implications for educators is that the cardinal objective of teaching should be the cultivation of higher order thinking skills. How else can students aspire to ask Broudy's questions? This focus on reasoning may certainly be challenged, but even the objections raised would have to be justified within intellectual standards. Sound reasoning should be cultivated not because it is reasoning that distinguishes human beings from other species, but because only through the cultivation of such reasoning can disputes over educational issues be resolved.

Within the variety of definitions of critical thinking, there is a consensus among its advocates that rule-governed, disciplined, and consequential reasoning lies at the core of critical thinking. The basic proposition is that reading, writing, speaking, interpreting, and experiencing take place within a network of cognitive processes and elements—questions at issue, premises, purposes, theories, evidence, assumptions, and implications—that are integrated by reasoning. As a cognitive process, critical thinking may be defined as a self-reflective grasping of the structures of thought and subjecting them to (rational, reasonable, logical) standards that facilitate the perception and correction of errors in thinking. When present in discursive activities, critical thinking involves the evaluation of arguments on the basis of agreed-upon intellectual standards, rather than personal or group attributions, custom, authority, and popularity.

The infusion of critical thinking across disciplines involves well-thought-out courses, dialogical and Socratic pedagogical strategies in the classroom, and outcomes assessment with intellectual standards. Through an integrated focus on the elements of reasoning and intellectual standards, reasoning skills and traits such as empathy, integrity, and fair-mindedness can be developed. However, these elements and standards are to be understood, integrated, and applied by the students themselves. Thus teaching for critical thinking skills requires the development of structured, interactive classroom discussions in which students are called upon to evaluate arguments and resolve problems, rather than assimilate and regurgitate information from teachers. Knowledge is not acquired by mere listening, or even through collaborative learning in classrooms. Rather, only when persons engage in standards-based reflection on the information gleaned from listening, observing, or reading do they begin to acquire knowledge. And deep knowledge is reached through critical evaluation, that is, evaluation within specific criteria or standards. These conclusions have a significant implication for teaching practices; they indicate that teachers must abandon the didactic mode of conducting classroom discussions in which teachers talk and students listen. In its place, teachers would Socratically probe students' reasoning, paying attention to the acquisition of specific skills of inferring, analyzing concepts, empathizing with different viewpoints, and evaluating arguments. The presence of these skills is discernible in thinking and problem solving guided by standards of logical consistency, clarity, analytical depth, completeness, and accuracy.

The following guidelines for infusing critical thinking were culled from the literature on critical thinking. Their applicability would vary according to the phase of schooling, but the competencies they nurture are not grade-specific.

1.   Know your subject as thoroughly as possible. However, do not assume that students are to know as much as you do by the end of the course. Rather than seeking to pour all you know into your students' heads, it is advisable to, first, cultivate their desire to know your subject as well as you do. Students learn more and much faster when they value what is being taught, actively participate in the construction of knowledge, and teach others what they are learning.

2.   Introduce students to the lifelong benefits of educability, as part of turning them away from the learn-to-earn dictum. This can be facilitated by discussions of the ideas of learning for earning, learning for life, and *life as learning*. These discussions are critical to the teachers' success, for if students are not committed to Dewey's conception of education as living, not a preparation for future living, the teacher's task is immeasurably more difficult.

3.   Understand the conceptual, strategic, epistemological, and philosophical-educational ramifications of critical thinking. However much these efforts should be supported by administrators, it is primarily up to teachers to grasp the dimensions of critical thinking, through reading as well as participation

in seminars, workshops, and conferences, and introduce them to both colleagues and students.

4.   Provoke discussions that focus on the beliefs (theories) students bring to the classroom, and use the exchanges to introduce the elements of reasoning and intellectual standards. Demonstrate how they can be used to facilitate conclusive intellectual exchanges and resolve disputes.

5.   Move your courses and subjects away from the principles of the education model into a conception of education as perpetual and disciplined cultivation of the mind.

6.   Do not separate coverage of course material from pedagogic practices and tactics. Hence construct lesson plans and courses within a goal of improving coverage through an understanding of basic concepts and the inferential processes underlying problem solving. Indeed, as much as possible, disassemble course material—basic concepts, theories, formulae, and information—into chewable chunks that students can "masticate," modify, and eventually "own."

7.   Abandon the traditional, teacher-lectures students-listen format. While lecturing, pause frequently, and ask if everyone "got it." Ask them to prove it by stating the issue(s) in their own words. Discard the traditional lecture-note-taking style by speaking briefly then asking students to interpret what you said and discuss it among themselves, if need be. Between pauses, ask students to teach their classmates. This ensures that students are in the class "body and soul." Remind them that they will get as much from the class as they put into its organization.

8.   Adopt the maxim that students are to be taught not what to think, but how to reason within a given subject or discipline, which may involve crossing the boundaries among disciplines.

9.   Use the Socratic method for intellectual exchanges in the classroom. This means continually posing questions, without giving the "right" answers, allowing students to "struggle" through their "beliefs" and method of solving problems. Direct their questions to other students. Pose questions as problems, for which you might not have the answer. The objective is to develop *their* inferential skills, and *their* ability to perceive implications and draw valid conclusions.

10.   Regard students as potential or future teachers of your subject. Therefore, give them opportunities to teach you and others in the classroom: We learn best when teaching.

11.   Specify an integrated set of objectives, insert them into classroom practices, and monitor their realization continually.

12.   Pursue a definition of reading/writing and problem solving as reasoning with a pen in hand, and use classroom quizzes to develop the skill of reasoning, whether in literature, mathematics, physics, nursing, sociology, or any other discipline.

13.   As part of involving students in their learning, offer them opportunities to revise your lesson plans and syllabi, as well as standards for evaluating their own work and your teaching. Form groups of rotating members who will read the text in class, solve problems, report on issues, and evaluate one another's

papers. This last feature allows teachers to increase the amount of writing assignments, without "burning out."

14. Emphasize the importance of reading, treating it as a "gateway skill" that is inseparable from reasoning. Indeed, the first class assignment could be a brief paper on "The Benefits of Reading." It should be assessed in the class by groups of students. Group assessment can also be applied to overall assignments. Let students bring first and second drafts of their papers to the classroom for anonymous group evaluations. These discussions and evaluations should be guided by the instructor's interjection with the standards to be used in the assessments.

15. Do not assign a vast amount of reading material, or assign material without making sure that students have grasped basic organizing concepts so that they know how to read productively. Diminish the nonreading of material in two ways. First, ask students to spend the first week browsing through the texts and to return with suggestions on what they think they ought to read. Second, insist on reports from every student on words, phrases, formulae, problems, and arguments in the textbook that they appear incomprehensible. Finally, demonstrate how to use the elements of reasoning for reading by selecting paragraphs from textbooks and exploring the author's purposes, the problems under scrutiny, key assumptions, the various perspectives or paradigms in the texts, the implications of certain arguments, and so on.

16. Assign homework that is integrated with students' extra-curricular activities. For example, ask students to record the expressions of denunciation, rejection, and repudiation in media discussions and everyday conversations.

These recommendations are not exhaustive, and more can be culled from the writings of the critical thinking advocates cited in the "Notes" to this chapter.

As with the definitions of critical thinking, there are significant differences in the strategic and tactical recommendations of its advocates. Some suggest that all educational inputs, beginning in kindergarten, should be imbued with critical thinking pedagogical strategies, curriculum design, and educational goals. Others propose that critical thinking be integrated in the college curriculum as an autonomous course, in social sciences, but not necessarily in natural sciences and the humanities, or even in courses at all, since thinking is subject specific.[32] Still others recommend Socratically taught philosophy in the K-12 curriculum as the best means for developing critical thinking skills. Most of these recommendations, however, are not mutually exclusive. Those that are not share an implicit agreement that mutual criticisms should address reasoning processes not the politics, race, culture, or gender of authors or critics. What should also serve to resolve disputes among advocates of critical thinking is a consensus on expected outcomes—the traits and abilities students are expected to embody as a result of critical thinking instruction.

It is generally agreed that the purpose of critical thinking education reform is the development of sound reasoning within given subjects and disciplines, even to the point of recognizing that different disciplines are largely administrative conveniences. The outcomes of teaching for critical thinking would be attributes that should serve to enhance reasoning within either the natural sciences, social sciences, or the humanities. Students can be expected to be capable of:

1. reflective thinking, or being disposed to use intellectual standards to assess elements of reasoning such as purposes, conceptual structures, assumptions, and classifications, and identify the implications of arguments;

2. recognizing the distinction between belief and knowledge, or justifiable beliefs;

3. being self-motivated learners, that is, committed to principles of educability, rather than "learning to earn";

4. being fair-minded in resolving intellectual disputes by empathizing with viewpoints with which there is disagreement;

5. expressing ethical sensitivity, or being disposed to evaluate the moral consequences of actions for others; and

6. recognizing the common fallacies that plague reasoning.

These "ideals" or expected outcomes by no means exhaust the list of critical thinking dispositions, but they serve to introduce certain divergences between critical thinking and multicultural education /multiculturalism.

Multicultural Education, Multiculturalism, and Critical Thinking: Complementary or Competitive?

Critical thinking may be defined as reasoned reflection on elements of reasoning about given problems, that is, reflection guided by specific intellectual standards. As an ability, it is characterized by a deep evaluation of thinking, beliefs, or actions. Critical thinking dispositions are manifest in certain traits of minds—humility, empathy, integrity, fair-mindedness—and analytical and reasoning processes. These characteristics can be developed through classroom practices that foster analysis of the elements of reasoning, use intellectual standards to assess students' responses and writing, and allow students to take responsibility for their learning. The role of the teacher is to facilitate students' learning not what to think, but how to assess the quality of their own thinking and reasoning in general. Because knowledge is attained only through thinking critically about the reasoning involved in reaching conclusions, students must be continually asked to reflect on their reasoning and the reasoning manifest in all forms of communication and technical processes. To pursue the development of these abilities and dispositions, however, students must value educability, the cultivation of which should be a cardinal mission of schools.

The advocacies of multiculturalism and critical thinking share criticisms of educational practices that disempower teachers, deprive students of opportunities to take charge of learning processes, maintain educational deprivation, neglect different learning styles, restrict instruction to the traditional technique of teacher lectures students take notes and regurgitate for "exams," and ignore the contributions of schooling to overall sociopolitical processes of stability and change. On the other hand, these advocacies diverge considerably with respect to education's rationale and objectives, pedagogical strategies, methods of argument assessment, and conceptions of knowledge. Unlike multiculturalism, the critical thinking advocacy does not go beyond educational processes for its rationale. Critical thinking reforms are aimed at improving the intellectual competencies of all those involved in learning, irrespective of whether this improvement leads to more productive workers, greater social harmony, a strengthening of democracy, socioeconomic equality, or the liberation of the oppressed. Schools cannot be called upon to equalize educational, political, or socioeconomic outcomes, given that the idea of equality still remains one of the most disputable concepts in social sciences.[33] For a similar reason, teachers cannot be advised to teach for the liberation of the oppressed. The following injunction from Peter McLaren should be treated with great caution: "If we want to recruit students to a transformative praxis, students must not only be encouraged to choose a language of analysis that is undergirded by a project of liberation but must affectively invest in it."[34] McLaren's purpose mirrors and legitimizes the Christian Coalition's attempts to establish prayer in schools so that students "affectively invest" in the idea of Christian redemption. By contrast, from a critical thinking perspective, what schools can do is encourage and prepare students to evaluate the philosophical and philosophical anthropological assumptions underlying concepts of equality, Christian redemption, and oppression. Curriculum transformation cannot have as its objective the termination of power imbalances among genders, races, ethnic groups, and classes. What it can aspire to is the development of a consensus on intellectual standards that would lead to mutual agreement and understanding of power, its meaning, relevance, and dispensability.

As indicated above, the promotion of critical thinking is geared to a goal of educability, not education, per se. By contrast, multiculturalism derives from the education model. Most of its advocates recommend increasing the level of information about culture and oppression to foster students' social activism. This recommendation is justified by the claim that schools cannot be separated from politics and power in society, and that teaching/learning must focus on group emancipation and social reconstruction. Thus teachers would be engaged in telling students what to think, politically, rather than teaching them how to process political information and monitor their thinking within standards for its enhancement. Advocates of multiculturalism do consider students as active participants in learning, and insist that teachers respect the cultures and experiences students bring to schools. However, this recommendation is inconsistent with their recognition of ideological distortions in students' beliefs. The gender, racial, ethnic, and class theories through which students interpret events, perceive differences, and acquire identities may be ideological instances that surely require critical scrutiny. An a priori privileging of students' beliefs merely serves to shield these theories from critical evaluation. And indeed, advocates of multiculturalism pay no attention to the literature exposing the fallacies in categorizing human beings according to anatomy, culture, and economic conditions.

Crucial discrepancies appear between critical thinking and multiculturalism with respect to the knowledge embedded in classifications. In both multiculturalism and the standard curriculum, gender, racial, and ethnic categories are explicitly endorsed. These categories are advanced as representations of reality, which by innuendo means things existing independently of forms of signification or perception. The standard curriculum cites "the social reality" of differences to maintain the status quo of race and gender relations, while advocates of multiculturalism promulgate these differences to revolutionize the consciousness of the "oppressed." In both approaches students would be told that racial, cultural, and gender differences are social and political realities. The question that neither poses is: What is *its own contribution* to the formation and consolidation of these differences? What the answer would demonstrate is that the construction of multiculturalism is based on the same methods and categories of that which it seeks to negate.

As indicated, criticisms of gender, racial, and ethnic classifications now represent a sizable literature. The claim that they represent social reality, and therefore should be endorsed, does not indicate analytical depth—one of the intellectual standards recommended for use in critical thinking analyses. In pursuing analytical depth, for example, it could be demonstrated that the concept of racial oppression as well as accusations of racism and sexism represent particular ethical propositions whose assumptions require justification. Offered as explanations of the behavior and decisions of "white males," they present moral-psychological states as the foundation of human decisions. On the other hand, advocates of multiculturalism also note that white males reason about their interests, however badly, and act out the conclusions they reached in their reasoning processes. The downplaying of reasoning, then, cannot be sustained. Indeed, it is through rationally constructed arguments for social justice that the advocates of multiculturalism appeal for an end to various forms of oppression.

Advocates of multicultural education and multiculturalism identify psychological, political, and cultural determinants of patterns of educational underachievement. By contrast, critical thinking advocates point to an instrumentalist educational philosophy that leads to a didactic teaching style and a curriculum geared to transmitting information. Their criticisms of educational practices direct attention to the underlying theories of knowledge, learning, and literacy that constitute an education model. Such a model allows the propagation of "education presidents," "sex education," "drug education," "multicultural education," and "education year," without raising questions about the relationships among schooling, reasoning, and the human experience. Similarly, consistent with their downplaying of the role of reasoning in learning, advocates of multiculturalism make the case that schools should address the cultures that students bring to the classroom. There can be no quarrel with this suggestion. However, it leads to a further question: *How* should teachers address these different cultures? In general, advocates of multicultural education recommend that teachers affirm them. Proponents of critical thinking should demur, for educational experiences are not a continuation of socialization, but a process that subjects all knowledge to critical appraisal. Educational institutions must perform this function, if generations are creatively to enhance or displace given intellectual legacies. Unless education is meant to mirror the content of socialization, teachers need not take students' cultures for granted. Similarly, social studies textbooks need not continue to serve up gender, racial, and ethnic classifications as depictions or reflections of social reality, without addressing the wealth of criticisms of realist claims about knowledge.[35]

Intellectual Diversity through Inclusion of Diverse Social Theories

One issue that necessarily divides the advocacies of multiculturalism and critical thinking is whether schools should be used to foster awareness of racial, ethnic, and gender differences as a means of resistance and social transformation. A variety of scholars, such as bell hooks, Carl Grant, James Banks, Molefi Asante, Henry Giroux, and Peter McLaren regard schools as a site for the mobilization of groups; they therefore recommend the cultivation of differences in order to facilitate group awareness for the struggle against oppression. By contrast, advocates of critical thinking would insist that a focus on differences needs to be justified and that the students' awareness of gender and racial differences can hinder the learning process. What is expressed in the multiculturalist and critical thinking recommendations is divergent conceptions of the aims of education. The multicultural agenda adheres to a principle of constructing educational outcomes to serve institutions and interests beyond the schools: eliminate prejudice about groups, maintain the common culture, celebrate cultural differences, equalize educational opportunities, and liberate oppressed groups. By contrast, advocates of critical thinking suggest that the major purpose of schooling is the development of the capacity for higher order thinking skills among students. Thus students should be initiated into the creative habit of critically thinking about knowledge, not trained to become productive in markets, or motivated and mobilized to change the world, or exhorted to maintain the status quo. Such ends are choices that students must themselves make. What teachers can do is encourage students to be reflective, clear, precise, deep, and logical in their thinking, to subject their assumptions, premises, and purposes to standard-bound evaluations, and to base whatever choices they make on principles of consequential reasoning.

The critical thinker's emphasis on intellectual standards and learning as a process of continual analysis of the concepts embedded in disciplines and theories has significant implications for curriculum development. First, it follows that the curriculum should incorporate the gender, racial, ethnic, and class theories that form much of postcontemporary sociology. These theories advance knowledge in social studies and would enhance intellectual diversity in the curriculum. This inclusion, however, is not equivalent to presenting gender, racial, ethnic, and class experiences as "realities." Rather, these experiences can be assessed as theoretically mediated constructs, and their narratives should be evaluated within intellectual standards. Relatedly, insofar as gender, racial, and ethnic classifications contravene standards of consistency and coherence, educators cannot endorse policies that prefer, or exclude, persons classified as "women," "men," "whites," "heterosexuals," and "people of color." Thus textbooks and faculty must be selected not according to their gender, sexual preferences, skin color, continental origin, or culture, but in relation to clearly specified educational ideals.

The advocacies of multicultural education and multiculturalism concentrate on gender, racial, and ethnic experiences, but fail to analyze the theoretical construction of experiences. This indicates that their objective is to promote not reasoning about experiences and identities, but group images. A critical thinking curriculum would not exclude such experiences. However, educators should note that their formation is influenced by specific premises and assumptions and that the goal of teaching is not to reinforce group experiences and identities, as such, but to enhance students' commitment and ability to reason about them. This commitment may be a prerequisite for an empathic analysis of "white male" prejudices as well as the anguish and anger projected by some of those classified as women, Native Americans, Hispanics, African Americans, Asian Americans, and white ethnics.

A critical thinking social studies curriculum would introduce students to a human perspective on the past, forging considerations of what social relations might have been had human ancestors prioritized a human identity and unearthing the religious, economic, and other intellectual traditions that prevented the emergence of a universal, human self-identification. Such identification may be essential for: (1) a nonjudgmental understanding of variations on (human) culture; (2) appreciation of human achievements in, for example, Inca, Aztec, and Mayan civilizations; and (3) recognition of the interactions among ancient Egyptian, Asian, and Greek civilizations. Indeed, a human self-identification may be crucial to the desire to know about these civilizations, and an imperative if communication is to be based on empathy and reasonableness. All so-called women, men, races, and ethnic groups were, at some time, one another's victims and saviors. What the persistence of these patterns indicates is that human history is largely a story of the ebb and flow of violence and nonviolence, and it may well be the absence of an active human self-identification that is responsible for the easy transformation of human beings into the "others" that are always potentially guilty of something. Do social studies and multicultural education contribute to the consolidation of otherness and the latency of a human identity?

The following outline of social theories introduces analytical components of a human perspective on social relations (Column 6). This perspective remains missing from the history and social studies curriculum. Multicultural education courses also have no space for a rational-humanist paradigm, even though most advocates of multicultural education would agree on the need to cultivate students' reasoning and some form of human self-awareness.

Figure 4.1

Social Theories (GRECH)

	GENDER	RACIAL	ETHNIC	CLASS	HUMAN
Criteria of classification	Anatomical	Anatomical	Cultural	Economic	Species
Explanation	Sexism	Racism	Ethnocentrism	Capitalism	Reasoning
Object of victimization	Women	Non-whites	Non-WASPS	Working class	Human beings
Stratification	Male power	White power	WASP domination	Ruling class	Universal insecurity
Proof structure	Reality	Reality	Reality	Reality	Intellectual standards
Solutions	Legal reforms	Legal reforms	Pluralism	Socialism	Critical thinking

In this scheme, a theory is defined as a logically related set of analytical components: criteria of classification, causation, and methods of demonstration. The above theories may be said to constitute postcontemporary sociological perspectives in that they embody aspects of and yet deviate from mid-twentieth-century functionalist, conflict, and symbolic interactionist sociological theories. As such, they certainly deserve a place in the social studies curriculum.

The viability of a theory stands or falls with the clarity and consistency of its criteria of classification, for classifications are part of and have significant implications for both methods of demonstration and explanations of the object of analysis. As sociologist Richard J. Badham argues: "One of the central features of social classification is the link that it provides between description and explanation. . . . All classifications embody hypothetical explanations or at least limit the kinds of criteria that will be considered as potential explanations."[36] Incoherent classifications necessarily produce incoherent explanations, for the variations in their meanings destabilize the logical connections necessary for a plausible explanation. This state of affairs is discernible in multiculturalists' usages of the concept of culture.

Advocates of multicultural education and multiculturalism present the concept of culture as a category that separates human beings, by their values and practices. This conception of culture allows its fusion with "race," politics, and education. Thus critical multiculturalists conceive teachers as "transformative intellectuals" operating within sites of struggles against oppression. Nevertheless, teaching for political transformation necessarily generates an infinitely regressive politicization of teaching. "Conservative pedagogists" could demand that teachers teach for order and social stability. Moreover, if knowledge and culture are said to belong to races, can criticisms of arguments not be stymied by identifying the interest-bound nature of knowledge and the "race" of a given speaker or teacher? If students and teachers are to be identified as white and black, these questions will be posed: Should "white" teachers teach "black students?" Should not only "black" teachers teach black students? Once persons in educational institutions are racially and culturally classified, and racial-cultural matching is pursued, why not insist on a correspondence for all cultures, all sexual preferences, and all ideologies between students and teachers? Once this principle is set in motion, "students of color" can legitimately "tune out" in classrooms with "white teachers" or on being asked to assimilate "white" knowledge. The teacher's best bet is to teach not for political-cultural transformation, or conservation, but for critical thinking about various conceptions of culture and politics.

Even if it is conceded that U.S. society is culturally diverse, a critical thinking approach would examine: (1) the specific conception of culture involved in the notion that groups have (different) cultures; (2) the educational inputs through which groups come to be perceived as different; and (3) the competitive relationship between reasoning and culture as explanations of behavior. Human behavior is influenced by biological drives, economic interests, values, norms, and interactive social contexts, but, by definition, it is a product of reasoning processes. Culture, understood as practices of symboling that give meaning to things, delimits the range of symbols available to individuals in a given context, for example, in spatially bounded environments. However, it is reasoning that determines the choice of premises, the construction of interests, the decision to adhere to certain values, the adoption of a particular form of self-identification, and the conclusions that are embodied in specific decisions.

The emphasis on the reasoning process underlying behavior introduces a salient difference between critical thinking and multicultural education. Because of its concentration on cultures and ignoring of reasoning processes in behavior, multicultural education does not offer a viable strategy for the behavior modification it advocates. Indeed, its exposition does not specify how behavior is to be transformed through greater awareness of cultural differences. Advocates of multiculturalism seek to remedy this lacuna by introducing the concept of culture as an aspect of domination. Behavioral changes will take place when the oppressed are made aware of the intellectual and cognitive sources of their oppression. But what is to prevent the oppressors from intensifying their oppression on perceiving that the oppressed are becoming more aware of their oppression?

Arguably, information about other cultures and patterns of domination can modify behavior only if it improves the reasoning patterns in the thinking processes that process information. A logically unevaluated presentation of information about Mesoamerican, European, Asian, and African civilizations and cultures would not necessarily alter prejudiced and stereotypical images. The underlying issue is that advocates of multicultural education opt for moral-political denunciations of ideas, rather than assessment of their logical structure. They thereby fail to perceive that so-called Eurocentric and racist ideas are but logically flawed propositions on history and human relations. The recognition and elimination of these ideas would be facilitated by the development of students' ability to think critically, as defined by Barry Beyer: "the process of determining the authenticity, accuracy, and worth of information or knowledge claims."[37] The designation of ideas as racist and Eurocentric is no substitute for an examination of their premises and implications within standards of reasoning. Through the development of their ability to reason and their acquisition of intellectual standards to evaluate knowledge, students can be taught to refute fallacious arguments about races, cultures, and civilizations. Nevertheless, a course on Western civilization need not be taken as indicative of biases against nonwestern civilizations. Its teachers could challenge their students to consider the theses that Western civilization began in the Middle East or in North Africa, that there is no sharp discontinuity between Western and non-Western civilizations, that the European-Asian border is a geographic convenience, if not a fiction, and that the term *civilization* has often been used as a cloak for some very uncivilized practices. A course on Western civilization, then, is not necessarily an exercise in Eurocentrism or an induction into ethnocentrism. What makes the difference is the teacher's commitment to reflecting on various theories and perspectives on events, and the aims of education.

Rather than reinforcing awareness of gender, racial, and cultural differences, the schools' ethos could be grounded in ideas of human educability and intellectual diversity. Thus social science courses would present the structural ramifications of the social theories that ascribe differences to persons and persons to different races, genders, and groups. In keeping with the purpose of educability, educational inputs would raise issues of the relevance, significance, and implications of classifications. One question that would be posed is whether "cultures" can be divided to fit racial attributes and continental configurations. It was by challenging the naturalists' hierarchical racial divisions that Martin Bernal, in *Black Athena*, was able to unearth evidence of complex diffusions and interactions among ancient civilizations and cultures. Western culture, Egyptian civilization, and Greek thought—which allegedly came to the West through Arabic translations—are expressions of human achievements. Indeed, human creativity is never Arabic, Greek, Egyptian, or European, American, male, white, black, or female.

It was Socrates' distinction to notice that all evil comes from human ignorance, and Gandhi's and Martin Luther King Jr.'s genius to recognize that human salvation necessitates a recognition of the humanness of both the oppressed and the oppressors. The colonial and postcolonial policies of Western politicians in the so-called third world cannot be said to be expressive of the Enlightenment or even of instrumental rationality. On the contrary, they were manifestly absurd, as they systematically deprived human beings of educational opportunities and unleashed monumental levels of violence against them. However, "bad" actions do not imply a bad nature. White-male misdeeds, if that is indeed a legitimate description, say nothing about the nature of "white men"—one of many absurd classifications permeating social studies. Neither the infusion of sound moral values among citizens, nor the realization of social justice is compatible with a tolerance of absurdities, which, however, lurk in the best minds.

No inhabitants of any continent have a monopoly on reason. *Some* thinkers have made this untenable claim; they were neither European, male, nor white, for these are equally untenable descriptions. It follows that the West, white people, and men are not embodiments of reason or representatives of the Enlightenment's rational legacies. Indeed, the Enlightenment is not a homogeneous philosophic system, and its legacies are open to evaluation with rational standards. Thus "Eurocentrism," as a negative description of all intellectual creations placed on a certain continent, turns out to be an egregious misnomer. Even so, Kwame Appiah advances a compelling suggestion: "The proper response to Eurocentrism is surely not a reactive Afrocentrism, but a new understanding that humanizes all of us by learning to think beyond race."[38] This thinking beyond hints at the educability of human beings, and it obliges a focus on the faculty of reasoning. This faculty is characteristic of all human beings, but they often reason erroneously. This applies to Aristotle, Voltaire, Hegel, Marx, Wollstonecraft, Einstein, Gandhi, de Beauvoir, Diop, Martin Luther King Jr., Foucault, Habermas, and Bernal. Nevertheless, although arguments may be in opposition, arguers share objectives of clear thinking, understanding, and persuasion. This objective characterizes discourse as a distinctly human project. Its realization requires that those who are deemed oppressors, right-wingers, left-wingers, colonizers, conservatives, liberals, Afrocentrists, and Marxists ought to be regarded as fellow-seekers of sound reasoning, and asked to reflect on the standards with which they evaluate arguments.

NOTES

1.   See Edith Hamilton and Huntington Cairns (eds.), *The Collected Dialogues of Plato* (Princeton, N.J.: Princeton University Press, 1978), *Republic;* Cassirer, *The Philosophy;* Ryland W. Crary and Louis A. Petrone, *Foundations of Modern Education* (New York: Knopf, 1971); U.S. Department of Education, *A Nation of Learners* (Washington, D.C.: U.S. Government Printing Office, 1976).

2.   See Christoffel, Finkelhor, and Gilbarg (eds.), *Up against;* Freire, *Pedagogy;* Carnoy, *Education;* Bowles and Gintis (eds.), *Schooling;* Giroux, *Theory,* Chapter 1.

3.   David T. Kearns, "An Education Recovery Plan for America," in Annual Editions*: Education 89/90* (Guilford, Conn.: Dushkin, 1989), p. 7.

4.   See Robert B. Reich, *Education and the Next Economy* (National Education Association: Washington, D.C. 1987); Lester Thurow, *Head to Head: The Coming Economic Battle among Japan, Europe, and America* (New York: William Morrow, 1992).

5.   James Moffett, "School Reform: Does Business Know Best?" *Phi Delta Kappan* 75, no. 8 (April 1994), pp. 584-590; Daniel Tanner, "A Nation Truly at Risk," *Phi Delta Kappan* 75, no. 4 (December 1993), pp. 288-297.

6.   Paul, *Critical*, p. 13.

7.   Mary Kennedy, "Policy Issues in Teacher Education," *Phi Delta Kappan* 72, no. 9 (May 1991), p. 661.

8.   *Time*, "Adult Literacy in America" (September 20, 1993), p. 75.

9.   See Susan R. Martin, "The 1989 Education Summit as the Defining Moment in the Politics of Education," in Kathryn M. Borman and Nancy P. Greenman (eds.), *Changing American Education: Recapturing the Past or Inventing the Future* (New York: State University of New York Press, 1994), pp. 133-160; Sybil Eakin, "National Education Summit," *Technos* 5, no. 2 (Summer 1996), pp. 16-25.

10.   Goal 5.5 of Goals 2000: Educate America Act is echoed in an open letter (September 18, 1987), drafted by the president of Stanford University, Donald Kennedy, and cosigned by thirty-six other educators: "It simply will not do for our schools to produce a small elite to power our scientific establishment and a larger cadre of workers with basic skills to do routine work. Millions of people around the world now have these same basic skills and are willing to work twice as long for as little as one-tenth of our basic wages. To maintain and enhance our quality of life, we must develop a leading edge economy based on workers who can think for a living. If skills are equal, in the long run wages will be, too. This means we have to educate a vast mass of people capable of thinking critically, creatively, and imaginatively." See Center for Critical Thinking, *Proceedings of the 12th Annual International Conference on Critical Thinking* (Sonoma, Calif.: Center for Critical Thinking, 1992), p. 2. For endorsements of critical thinking in the advocacy of multiculturalism, see Giroux, *Theory*, Chapter 1.

11.   Paul, *Critical*, pp. 4-5. Howard Gardner's remarks are akin to Richard Paul's, and they suggest a coexistence of the education and educability models in colonial America: "By the time of the Revolution, one could discern two broad educational tendencies: a re-creation of the classical education for an elite headed toward higher education and a much broader-based and more practical education slated for the less privileged as well as for those who would make their mark in the commercial world. . . . Common schools might not produce students who were fit for college, but they would ensure that every young person had acquired at least the basic literacies, acquaintance of some texts, and a smattering of scientific knowledge. American patriotism and acceptance of core moral, if not strictly religious, beliefs were a significant part of the agenda of common schools as well." Howard Gardner, *The Unschooled Mind: How Children Think and How Schools Should Teach* (New York: Basic Books, 1991), p. 192.

12.   Lester Thurow writes: "Local governments don't want to pay for first-class schools. . . . As state governments went through their budget-cutting exercise in the 1991 recession, no sector of public spending was cut more than education. . . . In recent years the federal government has come to see education more and more as an individual or local responsibility. Student grants have been converted to student loans, and federal aid to education both at school and on the job is one of the few places where government spending was actually cut under the Reagan administration." Thurow, *Head to Head*, p. 274.

13.   Marx, *Capital*, p. 82.

14.   Gingrich, *To Renew*, p. 143.

15.   For a clear analysis of the philosophical and classical sociological underpinnings of industrial society theory, see Richard J. Badham, *Theories of Industrial Society* (New York: St. Martin's Press, 1986).

16.   Peter W. Cookson Jr. and Caroline Hodges Persell, *Preparing for Power: America's Elite Boarding Schools* (New York: Basic Books, 1985); Kozol, *Savage Inequalities*; Joel Spring, *American Education: An Introduction to Social and Political Aspects*

(New York: Longman, 1990). The proposed voucher system seeks to make this commodity aspect official and explicit. See John E. Chubb and Terry M. Moe, *Politics, Markets and America's Schools* (Washington, D.C.: Brookings Institution, 1990).

17.   See Deborah Verstegen, "Economics and Demographics of National Education Policy," in James G. Ward and Patricia Anthony (eds.), *Who Pays for Student Diversity? Population Changes and Educational Policy* (Newbury Park, Calif.: Sage, 1992), pp. 71-96; Sylvia Hewlett, *When the Bough Breaks: The Cost of Neglecting Our Children* (New York: Basic Books, 1991); Kozol, *Savage Inequalities*; David C. Thompson, "Special Needs Students: A Generation at Risk," in Ward and Anthony (eds.), *Who Pays for Student Diversity?* pp. 97-124.

18.   Gingrich, *To Renew*, p. 141.

19.   Thompson, "Special Needs Students," p. 97. See also Manning Marable and Leith Mullings, "The Divided Mind of Black America: Race, Ideology, and Politics in the Post-Civil Rights Era," *Race and Class* 36, no. 1 (September 1994), pp. 61-72. The authors claim that 95% of the prison population of New York City is African-American. However, 90% of them lack a high school education and more than 50% have less than a sixth grade level of educational ability. Many of these "dropouts" will seek to make do in the underworld and underground economy. Elsewhere it is reported that each year as many as 2.3 million people join the ranks of the functionally illiterate, and 53% of dropouts are unemployed or receiving welfare. The cumulative cost of dropouts to American taxpayers is $75 billion in welfare benefits and lost tax revenues, and 60% of prison inmates are high school dropouts. The annual cost for housing each inmate is $15,000, which is roughly the annual tuition for Harvard, Yale, or Stanford. Among pregnant teenagers, 87% are high school dropouts. It has been suggested that the elimination of dropouts in America would wipe out the entire national debt in about three years.

20.   Gingrich, *To Renew*, p. 151.

21.   Ibid., p. 149.

22.   James Moffett, "On to the Past: Wrong-Headed School Reform," in Annual Editions, *Education 95/96* (Guilford, Conn.: Dushkin, 1995), p. 41.

23.   For an exposé of the levels of officially generated waste and corruption prevailing in both third and first world societies, see Graham Hancock, *The Lords of Poverty* (London: Mandarin, 1994); Martin Gross, *The Government Racket: Washington Waste from A to Z* (New York: Bantam, 1992), and *The Government Tax Racket: Government Extortion from A to Z* (New York: Ballantine, 1994).

24.   As Natalie Isser and Lita Linzer Schwartz write: "The settlement of the colonies was closely associated with religious sects, and therefore the first schools were frequently church-sponsored schools, taught by virtuous ladies or by Protestant divines. Literacy in the service of religion was, indeed, the prime reason for the community-supported schools mandated by the Ould Deluder Act of 1647 in the Massachusetts Bay Colony. The purpose of literacy, then, was to enable each of the colonists to read the Bible for himself (and thus evade the Ould Deluder—Satan). With some modification in other colonies, this philosophy continued to be dominant through the eighteenth century and into the nineteenth century. As a result a tradition existed in which educators considered it their duty not only to train the young to read and write, but also to instill in them proper moral attitudes and wholesome civic feelings. Horace Mann, 'father of the common school,' strongly urged nineteenth century businessmen to support common school education as a means of investing in the future citizens of the young nation—to assure that American youth would be literate, moral, and civic-minded, or patriotic." *The American School and the Melting Pot: Minority Self-Esteem and Public Education* (Bristol, Indiana: Wyndham Hall Press, 1985), p. 79.

25.   Benjamin R. Barber, "America Skips School: Why We Talk So Much and Do So Little," in Annual Editions, *Education, 95/96* (Guilford, Conn.: Dushkin, 1995), p. 11.

26.   See Paul, *Critical*, Chapter 1; Nel Goddings, *Philosophy of Education* (Boulder, Colo.: Westview Press, 1995), Chapter 5.

27.   See *John Dewey on Education*, edited with an introduction by Reginald D. Archambault (Chicago: University of Chicago Press, 1964).

28.   See Lipman et al., *Philosophy in the Classroom*; Proctor, *Education's Great Amnesia*.

29.   See John J. Conley, "Critical Thinking and Educational Assent," *Inquiry: Critical Thinking Across the Disciplines* 11, no. 2 (March 1993), pp. 21-22; Michael Scriven, *Reasoning* (New York: McGraw-Hill, 1976), Gerald Nosich, *Reasons and Arguments* (Belmont, Calif.: Wadsworth, 1981); Arthur Costa (ed.), *Developing Minds: A Resource Book for Teaching Thinking* (Alexandria, Va.: Association for Supervision and Curriculum Development, 1985); Harvey Siegel, *Educating Reason: Rationality, Critical Thinking, and Education* (New York: Routledge, 1988); Ralph Johnson, *Logical Self-Defense* (New York: McGraw-Hill, 1983); Edward Damer, *Attacking Faulty Reasoning* (Belmont, Calif.: Wadsworth, 1987); Matthew Lipman, *Thinking in Education* (Cambridge: Cambridge University Press, 1991); Vincent E. Barry, *The Critical Edge: Critical Thinking for Reading and Writing* (New York: Harcourt Brace Jovanovich, 1992); Connie Missimer, "Where's the Evidence," *Inquiry: Critical Thinking Across the Disciplines* 14, no. 4 (Summer 1995), pp. 1-18; Richard Paul, "Critical Thinking and the State of Education Today," *Inquiry: Critical Thinking Across the Disciplines* 16, no. 3 (Winter 1996), pp. 12-34. For postmodernist criticisms of the first and second "waves" of critical thinking, see Walters (ed.), *Re-thinking*.

30.   Michael Scriven and Richard Paul offer a comprehensive definition: "Critical thinking is the intellectually disciplined process of actively and skillfully conceptualizing, applying, analyzing, synthesizing, and/or evaluating information gathered from, or generated by, observation, experience, reflection, reasoning, or communication, as a guide to belief and action. In its exemplary form, it is based on universal intellectual values that transcend subject matter divisions: clarity, accuracy, precision, consistency, relevance, sound evidence, good reasons, depth, breadth, and fairness. It entails proficiency in the examination of those structures or elements of thought implicit in all reasoning: purpose, problem or question at issue, assumptions, concepts, empirical grounding, reasoning leading to conclusions, implications and consequences, objections from alternative viewpoints, and frame of reference." Michael Scriven and Richard Paul, "Defining Critical Thinking," *1993 Critical Thinking Inservice Handouts* (Sonoma, Calif.: Center for Critical Thinking, 1993), p. 11.

31.   Harry Broudy, "General Introduction," in Martin Levit (ed.), *Curriculum* (Chicago: University of Illinois Press, 1971), pp. 12–15.

32.   See Noddings, *Philosophy*, Chapter 5.

33.   See Frederick Mosteller and Daniel P. Moynihan (eds.), *On Equality of Educational Opportunity* (New York: Vintage, 1972); Terry Eastland and William J. Bennett, *Counting by Race: Equality from the Founding Fathers to Bakke and Weber* (New York: Basic Books, 1979); Pauline Johnson, *Feminism as Radical Humanism* (Boulder, Colo.: Westview Press, 1994), Chapter 4.

34.   McLaren, "White Terror," pp. 68–69.

35.   See Barry Hindess, *Philosophy and Methodology in the Social Sciences* (London: Harvester Press, 1977); Cohen and Hartofsky, *Epistemology*. Richard Badham writes: "It is important to recognize that classifications are not mere reflections of a par-

ticularized 'reality,' but rather are developed for the purpose of understanding or manipulation." Badham, *Theories*, p. 91.

36.   Badham, *Theories*, p. 92.

37.   Barry Beyer, "Critical Thinking: What Is It?" *Social Education* 49, no. 4 (1985), p. 276.

38.   Appiah, "Europe," p. 25.

Bibliography

AACTE Commission on Multicultural Education. "No One Model American." *Journal of Teacher Education* 24, no. 4 (Winter 1973), pp. 264-265.

Agger, Ben. *Gender, Culture and Power*. Westport, Conn.: Praeger, 1993.

Alamdari, Kazem, "The Beijing Conference: A Testimony for Women's Achievements and Reshuffling of Global Alliances." *California Sociologist* 17-18 (1994-1995), pp. 19-39.

Alcoff, Linda, and Elizabeth Potter (eds.). *Feminist Epistemologies*. New York: Routledge, 1993.

————. "Introduction: When Feminisms Intersect Epistemology." In Linda Alcoff and Elizabeth Potter (eds.), *Feminist Epistemologies*, pp. 1-14. New York: Routledge, 1993.

Alexander, Jeffrey. *Fin de Siècle Social Theory: Relativism, Reduction, and the Problem of Reason*. New York: Routledge, 1995.

Allen, Theodore. *The Invention of the White Race*. New York: Verso, 1994.

Allen, Walter R., Edgar G. Epps, and Nesha Z. Haniff (eds.). *College in Black and White: African American Students in Predominantly White and in Historically Black and Public Universities*. New York: State University of New York Press, 1991.

Altbach, Philip G., and Kofi Lomotey (eds.). *The Racial Crisis in American Higher Education*. New York: State University of New York Press, 1991.

Altschuler, Glenn C. *Race, Ethnicity, and Class in American Social Thought 1805-1919*. Arlington Heights, IL: Harlan Davidson, 1982.

Andersen, Margaret, and Patricia Hill Collins (eds.). *Race, Class, and Gender: An Anthology*. Belmont, Calif.: Wadsworth, 1995.

Appiah, Kwame Anthony. "Europe Upside Down: Fallacies of the New Afrocentrism." *Times Literary Supplement* (February 12, 1993), pp. 24-25.

———. *In My Father's House: Africa in the Philosophy of Culture.* New York: Oxford University Press, 1992.

Arendt, Hannah. *The Human Condition.* Chicago: University of Chicago Press, 1958.

Arvizu, S.F. *Demystifying the Concept of Culture: Theoretical and Conceptual Tools.* Sacramento, Calif.: Cross Cultural Resource Center, 1977.

Asante, Molefi. "An Afrocentric Curriculum." *Educational Leadership* 49, no. 4 (December 1991-January 1992), pp. 28-31.

———. *Afrocentricity.* Trenton, N.J.: Africa World Press, 1989.

———. *The Afrocentric Idea.* Philadelphia: Temple University Press, 1987.

———. "The Afrocentric Idea in Education." *Journal of Negro Education* 60, no. 2 (Spring 1991), pp. 170–180.

———. *Afrocentricity: The Theory of Social Change.* New York: Amulefi Publishing Co., 1980.

———. "Afrocentricity and Culture." In Molefi Kete Asante and Kariamu Welsh Asante (eds.), *African Culture: The Rhythms of Unity,* pp. 3-12. Westport, Conn.: Greenwood Press, 1985.

———. *Contemporary Black Social Thought: Alternative Analyses in Social and Behavioral Science.* Beverly Hills, Calif.: Sage Publications, 1980.

———. *Kemet, Afrocentricity and Knowledge.* Trenton, N.J.: Africa World Press, 1990.

———. "Multiculturalism: An Exchange." *The American Scholar* 60, no. 2 (Spring 1991), pp. 267-272.

———. *Rhetoric of Black Revolution.* Boston: Allyn and Bacon, 1969.

———. "Roots of the Truth: Repelling Attacks on Afrocentrism." *Emerge* 7, no. 9 (July-August 1996), pp. 66-70.

———, and Kariamu Welsh Asante (eds.). *African Culture: The Rhythms of Unity.* Westport, Conn.: Greenwood Press, 1985.

Askenasy, Hans. *Are We All Nazis?* Secaucus, N.J.: L. Stuart, 1979.

Association for Supervision and Curriculum Development Multicultural Education Commission. "Encouraging Multicultural Education." In Carl A. Grant (ed.), *Multicultural Education: Commitments, Issues, and Applications,* pp. 1-5. Washington, D.C.: ASCD, 1977.

Bachelard, Gaston. *The New Scientific Spirit.* Boston: Beacon Press, 1984.

Bachrach, Peter, and Morton Baratz. "Decisions and Non-Decisions: An Analytical Framework." *American Political Science Review* 57, no. 2 (1963), pp. 633-642.

Badham, Richard J. *Theories of Industrial Society.* New York: St. Martin's Press, 1986.

Ballantine, Jeanne H. (ed.). *Schools and Society.* Mountain View, Calif.: Mayfield Publishing Co., 1989.

Banks, James A. *Black Self-Concept: Implications for Education and Social Science.* New York: McGraw-Hill, 1972.

———. "The Canon Debate: Knowledge Construction and Multicultural Education." *Educational Researcher* 22, no. 5 (June–July 1993), pp. 4-14.

————. "A Curriculum for Empowerment, Action, and Change." In Christine E. Sleeter (ed.), *Empowerment through Multicultural Education*, pp. 125-141. New York: State University of New York Press, 1991.

————. "Imperatives in Ethnic Minority Education." In Julius Menacker and Ervin Pollack (eds.), *Emerging Educational Issues: Conflicts and Contrasts*, pp. 183-189. Boston: Little, Brown and Co., 1974.

————. "Multicultural Education as an Academic Discipline." In Annual Editions, *Multicultural Education 95/96*, 2nd. ed., pp. 58-62. Guilford, Conn.: Dushkin, 1995.

————. "Multicultural Education: Characteristics and Goals." In James Banks and Cherry A. McGee Banks (eds.), *Multicultural Education: Issues and Perspectives*, pp. 2-26. Boston: Allyn and Bacon, 1989.

————. "Multicultural Education: Development, Dimensions, and Challenges." *Phi Delta Kappan* 75, no. 1 (September 1993), pp. 22-28.

————. "Multicultural Education: For Freedom's Sake." *Educational Leadership* 49, no. 4 (1991), pp. 32–36.

————. "Multicultural Education: Progress and Prospects." *Phi Delta Kappan* 75, no. 1 (September 1993), p. 21.

————. "Multicultural Literacy and Curriculum Reform." *Educational Horizons* 60, no. 3 (Spring 1991), pp. 135-139.

————. "Multiethnic Education and the Quest for Equality," *Phi Delta Kappan* 64, no. 8 (1983), pp. 582–585.

————. *Multiethnic Education: Theory and Practice*. Boston: Allyn and Bacon, 1988.

————. *Teaching the Black Experience: Methods and Materials*. Belmont, Calif.: Siegler/Learon Publishing, 1978.

————. *Teaching Strategies for Ethnic Studies*. Boston: Allyn and Bacon, 1975.

————, and Cherry A. McGee Banks (eds.). *Multicultural Education: Issues and Perspectives*. Boston, Mass.: Allyn and Bacon, 1989.

Banton, Michael. *The Idea of Race*. Boulder, Colo.: Westview Press, 1977.

————. *Race Relations*. New York: Basic Books, 1967.

————. *Racial and Ethnic Competition*. Cambridge: Cambridge University Press, 1983.

————. *Racial Minorities*. London: Fontana, 1972.

————. *Racial Theories*. Cambridge: Cambridge University Press, 1987.

————, and Jonathan Harwood. *The Race Concept*. New York: Praeger, 1975.

Baptise Jr., H. Prentice, and Mira Baptise. "Developing Multicultural Learning Activities." In Carl A. Grant (ed.), *Multicultural Education: Commitments, Issues, and Applications*, pp. 105-112. Washington, D.C.: ASCD, 1977.

Barber, Benjamin R. "America Skips School: Why We Talk So Much and Do So Little." In Annual Editions, *Education, 95/96*, pp. 6-13. Guilford, Conn.: Dushkin, 1995.

Barkan, Elazar. *The Retreat of Scientific Racism: Changing Concepts of Race in Britain and the United States between the World Wars*. Cambridge: Cambridge University Press, 1992.

Barnes, Jonathan. *Early Greek Philosophy*. London: Penguin Books, 1987.

Barrett, Michele. *Woman's Oppression Today: The Marxist-Feminist Encounter.* London: Verso, 1980.

Barry, Vincent E. *The Critical Edge: Critical Thinking for Reading and Writing.* New York: Harcourt Brace Jovanovich, 1992.

Barth, Frederik (ed.). *Ethnic Groups and Boundaries: The Social Organization of Culture Differences.* Boston: Little, Brown and Co., 1969.

———. "Introduction." In Frederik Barth (ed.), *Ethnic Groups and Boundaries: The Social Organization of Culture Differences,* pp. 9-38. Boston: Little Brown and Co., 1969.

Bauer, Peter. *Equality, the Third World and Economic Delusion.* Cambridge, Mass.: Harvard University Press, 1981.

Belkhir, Jean. "Multicultural Education: Race, Gender, and Class: Rethinking the Introductory Textbook in the Academic Disciplines." *Race, Gender and Class: An Interdisciplinary Multicultural Journal* 2, no 2 (Winter 1995), pp. 11-38.

———. "Revised Proposal for a New Section: Gender, Race, and Class." *Race, Gender and Class: An Interdisciplinary Multicultural Journal* 2, no. 2 (Winter 1995), pp. 5-9.

———, Suzanne Griffith, Christine E. Sleeter, and Carl Alsup. "Race, Sex, Class and Multicultural Education: Women's Angle of Vision." *Race, Gender and Class: An Interdisciplinary Multicultural Journal* 1, no. 2 (Spring 1994), pp. 7-34.

Bem, Sandra Lipsitz. *The Lenses of Gender: Transforming the Debate on Sexual Inequality.* New Haven, Conn.: Yale University Press, 1993.

ben-Jochanan, Yosef. *Africa, Mother of Civilization.* Chicago: Black Classic Press, 1971.

Benedict, Ruth. *Race, Science and Politics.* New York: Viking, 1940.

Bennett Jr., Lerone. *Before the Mayflower: A History of Black America.* Chicago: Johnson Publishing Co., 1982.

Bennett, William J. *The Devaluing of America: The Fight for Our Culture and Our Children.* Colorado Springs, Colo.: Focus on the Family Publishing, 1992.

Berger, Peter. *Invitation to Sociology: A Humanistic Perspective.* New York: Anchor Books, 1963.

———, and Thomas Luckmann. *The Social Construction of Reality: A Treatise in the Sociology of Knowledge.* New York: Doubleday, 1967.

Berman, Paul (ed.). *Debating P.C.: The Controversy over Political Correctness on College Campuses.* New York: Laurel Paperbacks, 1992.

———. "The Other and the Almost the Same." *The New Yorker* (February 28, 1994), pp. 61-71.

Bernal, Martin. *Black Athena: The Afroasiatic Roots of Classical Civilization: Vol. I, The Fabrication of Ancient Greece.* New Brunswick, N.J.: Rutgers University Press, 1987.

Bernard, Jessie. *The Female World.* New York: The Free Press, 1981.

Bernstein, Richard. *Dictatorship of Virtue: Multiculturalism and the Battle for America's Future.* New York: Knopf, 1994.

Beyer, Barry. "Critical Thinking: What Is It?" *Social Education* 49, no. 4 (1985), pp. 270-276.

Biddiss, Michael D. (ed.). *Gobineau: Selected Political Writings*. London: Jonathan Cape, 1970.

Blauner, Robert. *Racial Oppression in America*. New York: Harper and Row, 1972.

Bleier, Ruth. *Science and Gender: A Critique of Biology and Its Theories on Women*. New York: Pergamon, 1984.

Bloom, Allan. *The Closing of the American Mind*. New York: Simon and Schuster, 1987.

Boas, Franz. *Race, Language and Culture*. New York: Macmillan, 1948.

———. *Race, Science and Humanity*. New York: D. Van Nostrand, 1963.

———. *The Mind of Primitive Man*. New York: Macmillan, 1966.

Bourdieu, Pierre. *Reproduction in Education, Culture and Society*. London: Sage, 1990.

Bowles, Samuel, and Herbert Gintis (eds.). *Schooling in Capitalist America*. New York: Basic Books, 1976.

Boyer, James. *Multicultural Education: Product or Process?* Kansas City, Mo: Kansas Urban Education Center, 1985.

Bridges, Tom. "Postmodernism and the Primacy of Cultural Difference." *Inquiry: Critical Thinking Across the Disciplines* 9, no. 2 (March 1992), 3-4, 23.

Brier, Peter. *Howard Mumford Jones and the Dynamic of Liberal Humanism*. Kansas City, Mo.: University of Missouri Press, 1994.

Broudy, Harry. "General Introduction." In Martin Levit (ed.), *Curriculum*, pp. 12–15. Chicago: University of Illinois Press, 1971.

Brown, S.C. (ed.). *Philosophical Disputes in the Social Sciences*. Atlantic Highlands, N.J.: Humanities Press, 1979.

Brownmiller, Susan. *Against Our Will: Men, Women, and Rape*. New York: Simon and Schuster, 1975.

Brzezinski, Zbigniew, et al. (eds.). *The Relevance of Liberalism*. Boulder, Colo.: Westview Press, 1977.

Bullivant, Brian M. "Culture: Its Nature and Meaning for Educators." In James Banks and Cherry A. McGee Banks (eds.), *Multicultural Education: Issues and Perspectives*, pp. 27-45. Boston: Allyn and Bacon, 1989.

Butler, Judith. "Contingent Foundations: Feminism and the Question of Postmodernism." *Praxis International* 11, no. 2 (1991), pp. 150-165.

Calabresi, Massimo. "Skin Deep 101." *Time* (February 14, 1994), p. 16.

Callinicos, Alex. *Against Postmodernism: A Marxist Critique*. New York: St. Martin's Press, 1989.

Campbell, Joseph, with Bill Moyers. *The Power of Myth*. New York: Doubleday, 1988.

Carmichael, Stokely, and Charles V. Hamilton. *Black Power: The Politics of Liberation in America*. New York: Jonathan Cape, 1968.

Carnoy, Martin. *Education as Cultural Imperialism*. New York: David McKay, 1974.

Carr, E.H. *What Is History?* Harmondsworth: Penguin Books, 1975.

Cassirer, Ernst. *The Philosophy of the Enlightenment*. Trans. Fritz C.A. Koelln and James P. Pettegrove. Princeton, N.J.: Princeton University Press, 1951.

Cavalli-Sforza, L. Luca, Paolo Menozzi, and Alberto Plazza. *The History and Geography of Human Genes*. Princeton, N.J.: Princeton University Press, 1994.

Center for Critical Thinking. *Proceedings of the 12th Annual International Conference on Critical Thinking*. Sonoma, Calif.: Center for Critical Thinking, 1992.

Center for the New American Community. *Alternatives to Afrocentrism*. New York: The Manhattan Institute, 1994.

Chisholm, Shirley. "Foreword." In D.G. Bromley and C.F. Longino Jr. (eds.), *White Racism and Black Americans*, pp. xv-xxiii. Cambridge, Mass.: Schenkman Publications Co., 1972.

Chubb, John E., and Terry M. Moe. *Politics, Markets and America's Schools*. Washington, D.C.: Brookings Institution, 1990.

Clabaugh, Gary. "The Cutting Edge: The Limits and Possibilities of 'Multiculturalism.'" *Educational Horizons* 71, no. 3 (Spring 1993), pp. 117-119.

Clay, Camille A. "Campus Racial Tensions: Trend or Aberration?" *Thought and Action* 5, no. 2 (Fall 1989), pp. 21-30.

Cohen, Abner. "Introduction: The Lesson of Ethnicity." In Abner Cohen (ed.), *Urban Ethnicity*, pp. 9–24. London: Tavistock, 1974.

Cohen, Jean L. *Class and Civil Society: The Limits of Marxian Critical Theory*. Amherst, Mass.: University of Massachusetts Press, 1982.

Cohen, Robert S., and Mark H. Hartofsky. *Epistemology, Methodology and the Social Sciences*. Boston: Kluwer, 1983.

Collins, Patricia Hill. "Toward a New Vision: Race, Class, and Gender as Categories of Analysis and Connection." *Race, Sex and Class* 1, no. 1 (Fall 1993), pp. 25-46.

———. *Black Feminist Thought: Consciousness and the Politics of Empowerment*. London: Routledge, 1991.

Collins, Randall. *Theoretical Sociology*. New York: Harcourt Brace Jovanovich, 1988.

Conley, John J. "Critical Thinking and Educational Assent." *Inquiry: Critical Thinking Across the Disciplines* 11, no. 2 (March 1993), pp. 21-22.

Conover, Pamela J., and Virginia Gray. *Feminism and the New Right: Conflict over the American Family*. New York: Praeger, 1983.

Conrad, Earl. *The Invention of the Negro*. New York: Paul Eriksson, Inc., 1966.

Cookson Jr., Peter W., and Caroline Hodges Persell. *Preparing for Power: America's Elite Boarding Schools*. New York: Basic Books, 1985.

Cordasco, Francesco. *The Equality of Educational Opportunity*. Totowa, N.J.: Littlefield, Adams and Co., 1973.

Costa, Arthur (ed.). *Developing Minds: A Resource Book for Teaching Thinking*. Alexandria, Va: Association for Supervision and Curriculum Development, 1985.

Craft, Maurice. *Education for Cultural Pluralism*. Philadelphia: Falmer Press, 1984.

Crary, Ryland W., and Louis A. Petrone. *Foundations of Modern Education*. New York: Knopf, 1971.

Crouch, Stanley. *The All-American Skin Game, or, the Decoy of Race: The Long and the Short of It*. New York: Pantheon, 1995.

Cruse, Harold. *The Crisis of the Negro Intellectual: From Its Origins to the Present*. New York: William Morrow, 1967.

Curtin, Philip D. *The Image of Africa: British Ideas and Action, 1789-1850*, vol. 2. Madison, Wisc.: University of Wisconsin Press, 1964.

Dahl, Robert. *Modern Political Analysis*. Englewood Cliffs, N.J.: Prentice-Hall, 1963.

Daly, Mary. *Gyn/Ecology: The Metaethics of Radical Feminism*. Boston: Beacon Press, 1978.

Damer, Edward. *Attacking Faulty Reasoning*. Belmont, Calif.: Wadsworth, 1987.

Davis, F. James. *Who Is Black?: One Nation's Definition*. University Park, PA: Pennsylvania State University Press, 1991.

de Beauvoir, Simone. *The Second Sex*. Trans. H.M. Parshley. New York: Vintage Books, 1974.

de Montellano, Bernard Ortiz. "Multicultural Pseudoscience: Spreading Scientific Illiteracy among Minorities." *Sceptical Inquirer* 16 (Fall 1991), pp. 46-50.

Delmar, Rosalind. "What Is Feminism?" In Juliet Mitchell and Ann Oakley (eds.), *What Is Feminism? A Re-Examination*, pp. 8-33. New York: Pantheon, 1986.

Delphy, Christine. *The Main Enemy*. London: Women's Research and Resources Centre, 1977.

Derber, Charles, *The Wilding of America: How Greed and Violence Are Eroding Our National Character*. New York: St. Martin's Press, 1996.

Dewart, Janet (ed.). *The State of Black America 1990*. New York: National Urban League, 1991.

Dewey, John. *On Education*. Edited with an introduction by Reginald D. Archambault. Chicago: University of Chicago Press, 1964.

Diop, Cheikh Anta. *The African Origin of Civilization*. New York: Lawrence Hill and Co., 1974.

———. *Civilization or Barbarism: An Authentic Anthropology*. New York: Lawrence Hill, 1991.

———. *The Cultural Unity of Black Africa*. Chicago: Third World Press, 1978.

Doty, Roxanne. "The Bounds of 'Race' in International Relations." *Millennium* 22, no. 3 (Winter 1993), pp. 443–461.

D'Souza, Dinesh. *The End of Racism*. New York: Simon and Schuster, 1995.

———. *Illiberal Education: The Politics of Race and Sex on Campus*. New York: The Free Press, 1991.

Dunn, Frederick. "The Educational Philosophies of Washington, Du Bois, and Houston: Laying the Foundations for Afrocentrism and Multiculturalism." *Journal of Negro Education* 62, no. 1 (1993), pp. 24-34.

Durant, Will, and Ariel Durant. *The Age of Voltaire*. New York: Simon and Schuster, 1965.

Dworkin, Andrea. *Letters from a War Zone*. New York: Lawrence Hill, 1993.

———. *Intercourse*. New York: The Free Press, 1987.

———. *Our Blood: Prophecies and Discourses on Sexual Politics*. New York: Harper and Row, 1976.

———. *Pornography: Men Possessing Women*. New York: Perigee Books, 1981.

———. *Right Wing Women*. New York: Perigee Books, 1983.

————. *Woman Hating*. New York: E.P. Dutton, 1974.

Eakin, Sybil. "National Education Summit," *Technos* 5, no. 2 (Summer 1996), pp. 16-25.

Early, Gerald. "The Anatomy of Afrocentrism." In Center for the New American Community, *Alternatives to Afrocentrism*, pp. 12-15. New York: The Manhattan Institute, 1994.

————. "Understanding Afrocentrism: Why Blacks Dream of a World Without Whites," *Civilization* (July/August 1995), pp. 31-39.

Eastland, Terry, and William J. Bennett. *Counting by Race: Equality from the Founding Fathers to Bakke and Weber*. New York: Basic Books, 1979.

Education Commission for the States. *Action for Excellence: a Comprehensive Plan to Improve Our Nation's Schools*. Denver, Colo.: ECS, 1983.

Ehlstain, Jean B. *Public Man, Private Woman*. Princeton, N.J.: Princeton University Press, 1981.

Eisenstein, Zillah. "Some Notes on the Relations of Capitalist Patriarchy." In Zillah Eisenstein (ed.), *Capitalist Patriarchy and the Case for Socialist Feminism*, pp. 41-55. New York: Monthly Review Press, 1979.

Epperson, Terrence. "The Politics of Empiricism and the Construction of Race as an Analytical Category." *Paper Presented at the 116th Annual Spring Meeting of the American Ethnological Society*, Santa Monica, California, April, 14-16, 1994.

Epps, E.G. *Cultural Pluralism*. Berkeley, Calif.: McCathan Press, 1974.

Epstein, Cynthia Fuchs. *Deceptive Distinctions: Sex, Gender, and the Social Order*. London: Yale University Press, 1988.

Faludi, Susan. *Backlash: The Undeclared War against Women*. New York: Crown Books, 1991.

Faris, Robert. *Chicago Sociology, 1920-1932*. Chicago: University of Chicago Press, 1970.

Farrell Jr., Walter C., and Cloyelle K. Jones. "Recent Racial Incidents in Higher Education: A Contemporary Perspective." *ISSR Working Papers in the Social Sciences* 4. Los Angeles, Calif.: UCLA Institute for Social Science Research, 1989.

Farrell, Warren. *The Myth of Male Power*. New York: Simon and Schuster, 1993.

Ferguson, Margaret, and Jennifer Wicke (eds.). *Feminism and Postmodernism*. London: Duke University Press, 1994.

Figes, Eva. *Patriarchial Attitudes*. London: Faber and Faber, 1970.

Firestone, Shulamith. *The Dialectic of Sex: The Case for Feminist Revolution*. New York: Bantam Books, 1970.

Flannery, Danielle D. "Adult Education and the Politics of the Theoretical Text." In Barry Kanpol and Peter McLaren (eds.), *Critical Multiculturalism: Uncommon Voices in a Common Struggle*, pp. 149-163. Westport, Conn.: Bergin and Garvey, 1995.

Flax, Jane. "Postmodernism." In Micheline R. Malson, Jean F. O'Barr, Sarah Westphal-Wihl, and Mary Wyer (eds.), *Feminist Theory in Practice and Process*, pp. 51-73. Chicago: University of Chicago Press, 1989.

Foucault, Michel. *Power/Knowledge: Selected Interviews and Other Writings 1972-1977*. New York: Pantheon, 1980.

Fox, M., and D. Ward. "Multiculturalism, Liberalism, and Science." *Inquiry: Critical Thinking Across the Disciplines* 10, no. 4 (December 1992), pp. 3-6, 11.

Francis, Patricia L. "A Review of the Multicultural Education Literature." *Race, Gender and Class: An Interdisciplinary Multicultural Journal* 2, no. 2 (Winter 1995), pp.49-64.

Franklin, Raymond, and Solomon Resnick, *The Political Economy of Racism*. New York: Holt, Rinehart and Winston, 1973.

Fraser, Nancy, and Sandra Lee Bartky (eds.). *Revaluing French Feminism: Critical Essays in Difference, Agency, and Culture*. Bloomington, Ind.: Indiana University Press, 1992.

Freire, Paulo. "Foreword." In Henry Giroux, *Theory and Resistance in Education: A Pedagogy for the Oppressed*, pp. ix-x. Westport, Conn.: Bergin and Garvey, 1983.

———. *Pedagogy of the Oppressed*. New York: Herder and Herder, 1971.

French, Marilyn. *The War against Women*. New York: Summit Books, 1992.

Friedan, Betty. *The Feminine Mystique*. New York: Norton, 1963.

Fukuyama, Francis. *The End of History and the Last Man*. New York: The Free Press, 1992.

Fuss, Diana J. "'Essentially Speaking': Luce Irigaray's Language of Essences." In Nancy Fraser and Sandra Lee Bartky (eds.), *Revaluing French Feminism: Critical Essays in Difference, Agency, and Culture*, pp. 95-112. Bloomington, Ind.: Indiana University Press, 1992.

Garcia, Jesus, and Sharon L. Pugh. "Multicultural Education in Teacher Preparation Programs: A Political or Educational Concept?" *Phi Delta Kappan* 74, no. 3 (November 1992), pp. 214-219.

Gardner, Howard. *Multiple Intelligences: The Theory in Practice*. New York: Basic Books, 1993.

———. *The Unschooled Mind: How Children Think and How Schools Should Teach*. New York: Basic Books, 1991.

Gates Jr., Henry L. "Critical Remarks." In David Goldberg (ed.), *Anatomy of Racism*, pp. 319-329. Minneapolis, Minn: University of Minnesota Press, 1990.

———. "Good-bye, Columbus? Notes on the Culture of Criticism." In David Theo Goldberg (ed.), *Multiculturalism: A Critical Reader*, pp. 203-217. Oxford: Blackwell, 1994.

———."Introduction: Writing 'Race' and the Difference It Makes." In Henry L. Gates Jr. (ed.), *"Race," Writing and Difference*, pp. 1-20. Chicago: University of Chicago Press, 1986.

———. "Whose Canon Is It, Anyway?" *New York Times Book Review* (February 26,1989), pp. 1, 44-45.

Gay, Geneva. "Building Cultural Bridges: A Bold Proposal for Teacher Education." In Annual Editions, *Multicultural Education, 95/96*, pp. 34-40. Guilford, Conn.: Dushkin, 1995.

———. "Curriculum Design for Multicultural Education." In Carl A. Grant (ed.), *Multicultural Education: Commitments, Issues, and Applications*, pp. 94-104. Washington, D.C.: ASCD, 1977.

——. "Ethnic Minorities and Educational Equality." In James Banks and Cherry A. McGee Banks (eds.), *Multicultural Education: Issues and Perspective,* pp.183-189. Boston: Allyn and Bacon, 1989.

Gay, Peter. *The Enlightenment: An Interpretation, Vol. II, The Science of Freedom.* New York: Alfred A. Knopf, 1969.

Genet, Jean. *The Blacks: A Clown Show.* Trans. Bernard Frechtman. New York: Grove Press, 1960.

Gilder, George. *Men and Marriage.* Gretna, L.A.: Pelican 1986.

Gingrich, Newt. *To Renew America.* New York: Harper/Collins, 1995.

Giroux, Henry A. *Border Crossings: Cultural Workers and the Politics of Education.* New York: Routledge and Kegan Paul, 1992.

——. "Series Foreword." In Barry Kanpol and Peter McLaren (eds.), *Critical Multiculturalism: Uncommon Voices in a Common Struggle,* pp. ix-xi. Westport, Conn.: Bergin and Garvey, 1995.

——. "Insurgent Multiculturalism and the Promise of Pedagogy." In David Theo Goldberg (ed.), *Multiculturalism: A Critical Reader,* pp. 325-343. Oxford: Blackwell, 1994.

——. "The Politics of Insurgent Multiculturalism in the Era of the Los Angeles Uprisings." In Barry Kanpol and Peter McLaren (eds.), *Critical Multiculturalism: Uncommon Voices in a Common Struggle,* pp. 107-124. Westport, Conn.: Bergin and Garvey, 1995.

——. "The Politics of Post-Modernism: Rethinking the Boundaries of Race and Ethnicity." *Journal of Urban and Cultural Studies* 1 (1990), pp. 5-38.

——. "Rethinking Education in the Age of George Bush." In Annual Editions, *Education 91/92,* pp. 10-12. Guilford, Conn.: Dushkin, 1991.

——. *Theory and Resistance in Education: A Pedagogy for the Oppressed.* Westport, Conn.: Bergin and Garvey, 1983.

——, and Stanley Aranowitz. *Postmodernism and Education.* Minneapolis, Minn.: University of Minnesota Press, 1991.

Glazer, Nathan. "A New Word for An Old Problem: Multicultural 'School Wars' Date to the 1840s." In Annual Editions, *Multicultural Education 95/96,* pp. 74–77. Guilford, Conn.: Dushkin, 1995.

Goddings, Nel. *Philosophy of Education.* Boulder, Colo.: Westview Press, 1995.

Goldberg, David Theo. "Introduction: Multicultural Conditions." In David Theo Goldberg (ed.), pp. 1-41. *Multiculturalism: A Critical Reader.* Oxford: Blackwell, 1994.

——. *Racist Culture: Philosophy and the Politics of Meaning.* Cambridge: Blackwell, 1993.

—— (ed.). *Multiculturalism: A Critical Reader.* Oxford: Blackwell, 1994.

Gollnick, Donna M., and Philip C. Chinn. *Multicultural Education in a Pluralistic Society,* 2nd. ed. New York: Merrill, 1990.

Goodlad, John I. "Better Teachers for Our Nation's Schools." *Phi Delta Kappan* 72, no. 3 (November 1990), pp. 185–194.

Gossett, Thomas F. *Race: The History of an Idea in America.* New York: Schocken Books, 1965.

Gould, Stephen Jay. *The Mismeasure of Man*. New York: W.W. Norton, 1981.

Grant, Carl A. "Anthropological Foundations of Education That Is Multicultural." In Carl A. Grant (ed.), *Multicultural Education: Commitments, Issues, and Applications*, pp. 29-39. Washington, D.C.: ASCD, 1977.

————. "So You Want to Infuse Multicultural Education into Your Discipline? Case Study: Art." *The Educational Forum* 57, no. 1 (Fall 1992), pp. 18-28.

————, and Christine E. Sleeter. *Turning on Learning: Five Approaches for Multicultural Teaching Plans for Race, Class, Gender, and Disability*. Columbus, Ohio: Merrill, 1989.

Gray, Paul. "Whose America?" *Time* (July 8, 1991), pp. 13-17.

Greeley, Andrew. *Why Can't They Be Like Us: America's White Ethnic Groups*. New York: E.P. Dutton, 1971.

Gross, Martin. *The Government Racket: Washington Waste from A to Z*. New York: Bantam, 1992.

————. *The Government Tax Racket: Government Extortion from A to Z*. New York: Ballantine, 1994.

Guillaumin, Colette. "The Idea of Race and Its Elevation to Autonomous Scientific and Legal Status." In UNESCO, *Sociological Theories: Race and Colonialism*. Paris: UNESCO, 1980.

Gutierrez, Kris D., and Peter McLaren. "Pedagogies of Dissent and Transformation: A Dialogue about Postmodernity, Social Context, and the Politics of Literacy." In Barry Kanpol and Peter McLaren (eds.), *Critical Multiculturalism: Uncommon Voices in a Common Struggle*, 125-147. Westport, Conn.: Bergin and Garvey, 1995.

Gutmann, Amy (ed.). *Multiculturalism: Examining the Politics of Recognition*. Princeton, N.J.: Princeton University Press, 1994.

Habermas, Jurgen. *The Philosophical Discourse of Modernity: Twelve Lectures*. Trans. Frederick Lawrence. Cambridge Mass.: MIT Press, 1987.

————. *The Theory of Communicative Action: Volume 1, Reason and the Rationalization of Society*. Trans. Thomas McCarthy. Boston: Beacon Press, 1981.

Hall, Raymond L. *Black Separatism in the United States*. Hanover, N.H.: University Press of New England, 1978.

Hamilton, Edith, and Huntington Cairns (eds.). *The Collected Dialogues of Plato*. Princeton, N.J.: Princeton University Press, 1978.

Hancock, Graham. *The Lords of Poverty*. London: Mandarin, 1994.

Harding, Sandra. "Is Science Multicultural? Challenges, Resources, Opportunities, Uncertainties." In David Theo Goldberg (ed.), *Multiculturalism: A Critical Reader*, pp. 344-370. Oxford: Blackwell, 1994.

Hardt, Ulrich H. (ed.). *A Critical Edition of Mary Wollstonecraft's A Vindication of the Rights of Women: With Strictures on Political and Moral Subjects*. New York: Whitson Publishing Co., 1982.

Harvey, David. *The Condition of Postmodernity: An Enquiry into the Origin of Cultural Change*. Cambridge: Blackwell, 1990.

Hawkesworth, Mary. *Beyond Oppression: Feminist Theory and Political Strategy*. New York: Continuum, 1990.

Herrnstein, Richard J., and Charles Murray. *The Bell Curve: Intelligence and Class in American Life*. New York: The Free Press, 1994.

Herskovits, Melville J. *Franz Boas: The Science of Man in the Making*. New York: Charles Scribner's Sons, 1953.

———. *Man and His Works: The Science of Cultural Anthropology*. New York: Knopf, 1965.

———. *The Myth of the Negro Past*. Boston: Beacon Press, 1958.

Hewlett, Sylvia. *A Lesser Life: The Myth of Women's Liberation in America*. New York: William Morrow and Co. 1986.

———. *When the Bough Breaks: The Cost of Neglecting Our Children*. New York: Basic Books, 1991.

Hilliard III, Asa G. "Why We Must Pluralize the Curriculum." *Educational Leadership* 49, no. 4 (December 1991-January 1992), pp. 12-13.

———. Lucretia Payton-Stewart, and Larry O. Williams. *Infusion of African and African-American Content in the School Curriculum*. Morristown, N.J.: Aaron Press, 1990.

Hindess, Barry. *Philosophy and Methodology in the Social Sciences*. London: Harvester Press, 1977.

———, and Paul Q. Hirst. *Pre-capitalist Modes of Production*. London: Routledge and Kegan Paul, 1975.

History-Social Science Curriculum Framework and Criteria Committee. *History-Social Science Curriculum Framework for California Public Schools Kindergarten through Grade Twelve*. Sacramento, Calif.: California State Board of Education, 1988.

Hobbes, Thomas. *Leviathan*. New York: Collier, 1962.

Hollins, Etta R., Joyce E. King, and Warren C. Hayman. *Teaching Diverse Populations: Formulating a Knowledge Base*. New York: State University of New York Press, 1994.

Holmes, Cleo H. "Notes on Pragmatism and Scientific Realism." *Educational Researcher* 21, no. 6 (August-September 1992), pp. 13-17.

hooks, bell. *Killing Rage: Ending Racism*. New York: H. Holt and Co., 1995.

Horsman, Reginald. *Race and Manifest Destiny: The Origins of American Racial Anglo-Saxonism*. Cambridge, Mass.: Harvard University Press, 1981.

House, Ernest R. "Realism in Research." *Educational Researcher* 20, no. 6 (1991), pp. 2-9.

Howard, Gary. "Whites in Multicultural Education: Rethinking Our Role." *Phi Delta Kappan* 75, no. 1 (September 1993), pp. 36-41.

Howe, Irving. "The Value of the Canon." *New Republic* (February 18, 1991), pp. 40-47.

———. "What Should We Be Teaching?" *Dissent* (Fall 1988), pp. 477-479.

Humm, Maggie (ed.). *Modern Feminisms: Political, Literary, Cultural*. New York: Columbia University Press, 1992.

Hunter, William A. *Multicultural Education through Competency-Based Teacher Education*. Washington, D.C.: American Association of Colleges for Teacher Education, 1974.

Isser, Natalie, and Lita Linzer Schwartz. *The American School and the Melting Pot: Minority Self-Esteem and Public Education.* Bristol, Ind.: Wyndham Hall Press, 1985.

Jacobs, Paul, and Saul Landau (eds.). *To Serve the Devil: Natives and Slaves: A Documentary Analysis of America's Racial History and Why It Has Been Kept Hidden,* vols.1 and 2. New York: Random House, 1971.

Jacoby, Russell, and Naomi Glauberman (eds.). *The Bell Curve Debate: History, Documents Opinions.* New York: Random House, 1995.

Jaggar, Allison. *Feminist Politics and Human Nature.* Totowa, N.J.: Rowman and Allanheld, 1983.

James, George G.M. *Stolen Legacy.* San Francisco, Calif.: Julian Richardson Associates, 1976.

Jean, Clinton M. *Behind the Eurocentric Veils: The Search for African Realities.* Amherst, Mass.: University of Massachusetts Press, 1991.

Jensen, Arthur. *Genetics and Education.* New York: Harper and Row, 1972.

Johnson, Pauline. *Feminism as Radical Humanism.* Boulder, Colo.: Westview Press, 1994.

Johnson, Ralph. *Logical Self-Defense.* New York: McGraw-Hill, 1983.

Johnson, Roosevelt (ed.). *Black Scholars on Higher Education in the 70's.* Columbus, Ohio: ECCA Publications, 1974.

Johnstone Jr., Henry. "Philosophy and Argument Ad Hominem." Inquiry: *Critical Thinking Across the Disciplines* 12, nos. 3–4 (November-December 1993), pp. 25-29.

Jones, Mary McAllester. *Gaston Bachelard, Subversive Humanist: Texts and Readings.* Madison, Wisc.: University of Wisconsin Press, 1991.

Kallen, Horace. *Cultural Pluralism and the American Idea.* Philadelphia: University of Pennsylvania Press, 1956.

———. *Culture and Democracy in the United States.* New York: Boni and Liverwright, 1924.

Kandal, Terry R. *The Woman Question in Classical Sociological Theory.* Miami: Florida International University Press, 1988.

Kanpol, Barry, and Peter McLaren. "Introduction: Resistance Multiculturalism and the Politics of Difference." In Barry Kanpol and Peter McLaren (eds.), *Critical Multiculturalism: Uncommon Voices in a Common Struggle,* pp. 1-17. Westport, Conn.: Bergin and Garvey, 1995.

Karenga, Maulana. *Introduction to Black Studies.* Inglewood, Calif.: Kawaida Publications, 1982.

———. *Essays in Struggle.* San Diego, Calif.: Kawaida Publications, 1978.

Kearns, David T. "An Education Recovery Plan for America." In Annual Editions: *Education, 89/90,* pp. 6-10. Guilford, Conn.: Dushkin, 1989.

Kelly, David H. "Egyptians and Ethiopians: Color, Race, and Racism." *The Classical Outlook* (Spring 1991), pp. 77–82.

Kendall, Frances E. *Diversity in the Classroom: A Multicultural Approach to the Education of Young Children.* New York: Teachers College Press, 1983.

Kennedy, Mary. "Policy Issues in Teacher Education." *Phi Delta Kappan* 72, no. 9 (May 1991), pp. 658-665.

Kerber, Augustus, and Barbara Bommarito (eds.). *The Schools and the Urban Crisis*. New York: Holt, Rinehart and Winston, 1963.

Kerner, Otto. *Report of the National Advisory Commission on Civil Disorders*. New York: E.P. Dutton and Co., 1968.

Keyes, Alan. *Masters of the Dream*. New York: William Morrow, 1995.

Keynes, John M. *The General Theory of Employment Interest and Money*. New York: Harcourt, Brace and World, 1935.

King Jr., Martin Luther. "Letter to a Clergyman from Birmingham City Jail" (April 16, 1963).

Klatch, Rebecca. *Women of the New Right*. Philadelphia: Temple University Press, 1987.

Kohn, Alfie. "The Truth about Self-Esteem." *Phi Delta Kappan* 76, no. 4 (December 1994), pp. 272-283.

Kohn, Marek. *The Race Gallery: The Return of Racial Science*. London: Jonathan Cape, 1995.

Kozol, Jonathan. *Illiterate America*. New York: Doubleday, 1985.

―――. *Savage Inequalities: Children in America's Schools*. New York: Crown Publishers, 1991.

Kristeva, Julia. *Strangers to Ourselves*. Trans. Leon S. Roudiez. New York: Columbia University Press, 1991.

Kroeber, Alfred, and Clyde Kluckhohn. *Culture, A Critical Review of Concepts and Definitions*. Cambridge, Mass.: Harvard University Peabody Museum of American Archaeology and Ethnology Papers, 1952.

Ladner, Joyce. *The Death of White Sociology*. New York: Vintage, 1970.

Lasswell, Harold, and Abraham Kaplan. *Power and Society: A Framework for Political Theory*. New Haven, Conn.: Yale University Press, 1965.

Lecourt, Dominique. *Marxism and Epistemology: Bachelard, Canguilhem and Foucault*. Trans. Ben Brewster. London: New Left Books, 1975.

Leech, Kenneth. "'Diverse Reports' and the Meaning of 'Racism.'" *Race and Class* 28, no. 2 (Autumn 1989), pp. 82-88.

Lefkowitz, Mary. *Not Out of Africa: How Afrocentrism Became an Excuse to Teach Myth as History*. New York: Basic Books, 1996.

―――. "The Origins of Greece and the Illusions of Afrocentrists: Not Out of Africa," *New Republic* (February 10, 1992), pp. 29-36.

Leo, John. "A Fringe History of the World." *U.S. News and World Report* (November 12, 1990), pp. 25-26.

Leone, Bruno (ed.). *Racism: Opposing Viewpoints*, rev. ed. San Diego, Calif.: Greenhaven Press, 1986.

Lester, Joan S. "Stages in the Diversity Process." *Black Issues in Higher Education* 10, no. 4 (January 27, 1994), pp. 64-65.

Levesque, George A. "Black Culture, the Black Esthetic, Black Chauvinism: A Mild Dissent." *The Canadian Review of American Studies* 12, no. 3 (Winter 1981), pp. 275–284.

Levin, Michael, "Responses to Race Differences in Crime," *Journal of Social Philosophy* 23, no. 1 (Spring 1992), pp. 5-29.

Levine, Donald N. "On the History and Systematics of the Sociology of the Stranger." In William A. Shack and Elliott P. Skinner (eds.), *Strangers in African Societies*, pp. 21-36. Berkeley, Calif.: University of California Press, 1979.

Levine, George (ed.). *Realism and Representation: Essays on the Problem of Realism in Relation to Science, Liberation and Culture.* Madison, Wisc.: University of Wisconsin Press, 1993.

Levine, Molly M. "The Use and Abuse of Black Athena." *American Historical Review* 97, no. 2 (April 1992), pp. 440-463.

Limbaugh, Rush. *See, I Told You So.* New York: Pocket Books, 1993.

———. *The Way Things Ought To Be.* New York: Pocket Star Books, 1993.

Lipman, Matthew. *Thinking in Education.* Cambridge: Cambridge University Press, 1991.

———, Ann M. Sharp, and Frederick S. Oscanyan. *Philosophy in the Classroom.* Philadelphia: Temple University Press, 1980.

Lorber, Judith. *Paradoxes of Gender.* New Haven, Conn.: Yale University Press, 1994.

Loury, Glenn C. *One By One from the Inside Out: Essays and Reviews on Race and Responsibility in America.* New York: The Free Press, 1995.

Lukes, Steven. *Power: A Radical View.* London: Macmillan, 1974.

Lynch, James. *The Multicultural Curriculum.* London: Batsford Academic and Educational Ltd., 1983.

———. *Multicultural Education.* London: Routledge and Kegan Paul, 1986.

———. *Multicultural Education in a Global Society.* New York: The Falmer Press, 1989.

———. *Multicultural Education: Principles and Practice.* London: Routledge and Kegan Paul, 1986.

Lyotard, Jean-François, *The Postmodern Condition: A Report on Knowledge.* Minneapolis, Minn.: University of Minnesota Press, 1993.

Macionis, John J. *Society: The Basics.* Englewood Cliffs, N.J.: Prentice-Hall, 1992.

Madhubuti, Haki R. *Enemies: The Clash of Races.* Chicago: Third World Press, 1978.

Malik, Kenan. "Universalism and Difference: Race and the Postmodernists," *Race and Class* 37, no. 3 (March 1996), pp. 1-18.

Marable, Manning. "The Beast Is Back: An Analysis of Campus Racism." *The Black Collegian* 19, no. 1 (September–October 1988), pp. 52-54.

———, and Leith Mullings. "The Divided Mind of Black America: Race, Ideology, and Politics in the Post-Civil Rights Era." *Race and Class* 36, no. 1 (September 1994), pp. 61-72.

Martel, Erich. "Multiculturalism, Not Afrocentrism for D.C. Public Schools." *Journal of the Educational Excellence Network* 10, no. 2 (February 1991), pp. 44-48.

Martin, Susan R. "The 1989 Education Summit as the Defining Moment in the Politics of Education." In Kathryn M. Borman and Nancy P. Greenman (eds.), *Changing American Education: Recapturing the Past or Inventing the Future?* pp. 133-160. New York: State University of New York Press, 1994.

Martusewicz, Rebecca A., and William M. Reynolds (eds.). *Inside Out: Contemporary Critical Perspectives in Education*. New York: St. Martin's Press, 1994.

Marx, Karl. *Capital*. New York: International Publishers, 1977.

———. *Economic and Philosophic Manuscripts of 1844*. New York: International Publishers, 1970.

———. *A Contribution to the Critique of Political Economy*. New York: International Publishers, 1970.

———, and Friedrich Engels. *The Communist Manifesto*. New York: Monthly Review Press, 1964.

Matthews, Fred. "Cultural Pluralism in Context: External History, Philosophic Premises and Theories of Ethnicity in Modern America." *Journal of Ethnic Studies* 12, no. 2 (Summer 1984), pp. 63-79.

Mayhew, Leon H. (ed.). *Talcott Parsons on Institutions and Social Evolution: Selected Writings*. Chicago: University of Chicago Press, 1982.

Mazuri, Ali, and Tobi Levine (eds.). *The Africans*. New York: Praeger, 1986.

McCarthy, Cameron, and Michael Apple. "Class, Race, and Gender in American Educational Research: Toward a Nonsynchronous Parallelist Position." In Lois Weis (ed.), *Race, Class, and Gender in American Education*, pp. 9-39. New York: State University of New York Press, 1988.

McCormick, Linda. "Cultural Diversity and Exceptionality." In Norris G. Haring and Linda McCormick (eds.), *Exceptional Children and Youth: An Introduction to Special Education*, 5th ed., pp. 48-75. Columbus, Ohio: Merrill, 1990.

McDiarmid, G. Williamson. "What to Do about Differences?: A Study of Multicultural Education for Teacher Trainees in the Los Angeles Unified School District." *Journal of Teacher Education* 43, no. 2 (March-April 1992), pp. 83–93.

McInerney, Peter K. (ed.). "The Twenty-ninth Oberlin Colloquium in Philosophy," *Philosophical Studies* 61, nos. 1-2 (February 1991).

McKnight, C.C., F.J. Crosswhite, J.A. Dossey, E. Kifer, J.D. Swafford, K.J. Travers, and T.J. Cooney. *The Underachieving Curriculum: Assessing U.S. School Mathematics from an International Perspective*. Champaign, Ill.: Stipes, 1987.

McLaren, Peter. "White Terror and Oppositional Agency: Toward a Critical Multiculturalism." In David Theo Goldberg (ed.), *Multiculturalism: A Critical Reader*, pp. 45–74. Oxford: Blackwell, 1994.

Meier, August, Elliot Rudwick, and Francis L. Broderick (eds.). *Black Protest in the Twentieth Century*. Indianapolis, Ind.: Bobbs-Merrill, 1965.

Menacker, Julius, and Ervin Pollack (eds.). *Emerging Educational Issues: Conflicts and Contrasts*. Boston: Little, Brown and Co., 1974.

Meyers, Diana T. *"The Subversion of Women's Agency in Psychoanalytic Feminism: Chodorow, Flax, Kristeva."* In Nancy Fraser and Sandra Lee Bartky (eds.), *Revaluing French Feminism: Critical Essays in Difference, Agency, and Culture*, pp. 136-161. Bloomington, Indi.: Indiana University Press, 1992.

Millet, Kate. *Sexual Politics*. London: Sphere, 1971.

Mills, C. Wright. *The Power Elite*. New York: Oxford University Press, 1959.

Missimer, Connie. "Where's the Evidence," *Inquiry: Critical Thinking Across the Disciplines* 14, no. 4 (Summer 1995), pp. 1-18.

Mitchell, Juliet. *Psycho-Analysis and Feminism.* New York: Vintage, 1975

———. *Women: The Longest Revolution.* New York: Pantheon Books, 1984.

———, and Ann Oakley (eds.). *What is Feminism? A Re-Examination.* New York: Pantheon, 1986.

Modgil, Sohan, Gajendra K. Verma, Danka Mallick, and Celia Modgil (eds.). *Multicultural Education: The Interminable Debate.* London: Falmer Press, 1986.

Moffett, James. "On to the Past: Wrong-Headed School Reform." In Annual Editions, *Education 95/96.* pp. 40-44. Guilford, Conn.: Dushkin, 1995.

———. "School Reform: Does Business Know Best?" *Phi Delta Kappan* 75, no. 8 (April 1994), pp. 584-590.

Money, John, and Patricia Tucker. *Sexual Signatures: On Being a Man or a Woman.* Boston: Little, Brown and Co., 1975.

Moore, Henrietta L. *A Passion for Difference.* Indianapolis: Ind.: Indiana University Press, 1994.

Moses, Wilson J. "In Fairness to Afrocentrism." In Center for the New American Community, *Alternatives to Afrocentrism*, pp. 16-22. New York: The Manhattan Institute, 1994.

———. *The Golden Age of Black Nationalism, 1850–1925.* New York: Oxford University Press, 1978.

Mosteller, Frederick, and Daniel P. Moynihan (eds.). *On Equality of Educational Opportunity.* New York: Vintage, 1972.

Muir, Donald E. "Race: The Mythic Root of Racism." *Sociological Inquiry* 63, no. 3 (August 1993), pp. 339–350.

Murray, Albert. *The Omni Americans: New Perspectives on Black Experience and American Culture.* New York: Outerbridge and Dienstrfrey, 1970.

Murray, Charles, and Richard J. Herrnstein. "Race, Genes and I.Q.—An Apologia." *New Republic* (October 31, 1994), pp. 27-37.

Natanson, Maurice A. (ed.). *Philosophy of the Social Sciences: A Reader.* New York: Random House, 1963.

National Council for the Social Studies. *Curriculum Guidelines for Multiethnic Education.* New York: Anti–Defamation League of B'nai B'rith, 1983.

National Congress of Black Faculty Newsletter. "New Jersey Multicultural Studies Project" (Spring 1993), p. 2.

National Review. "Special Issue on Multiculturalism." February 21, 1994.

National Urban League. *The State of Black America 1994.* New York: AG Publishing, 1994.

Newsletter on Intellectual Freedom 40, no. 5 (September 1991).

Nieto, Sonia. *Affirming Diversity: The Sociopolitical Context of Multicultural Education.* New York: Longman, 1992.

Norris, Christopher. *What's Wrong with Postmodernism?* Baltimore, Md.: Johns Hopkins University Press, 1993.

Nosich, Gerald. *Reasons and Arguments.* Belmont, Calif.: Wadsworth, 1981.

Olson, James. *The Ethnic Dimension in American History*, vol. 1. New York: St. Martin's Press, 1979.

Omi, Michael, and Howard Winant. *Racial Formation in the United States: From the 1960s to the 1990s*, 2nd. ed. New York: Routledge and Kegan Paul, 1994.

Ortnar, Sherry, and Harriet Whitehead (eds.). *Sexual Meanings: The Cultural Construction of Gender and Sexuality*. Cambridge: Cambridge University Press, 1981.

Outwaithe, William. *New Philosophies of Social Science: Realism, Hermeneutics, and Critical Theory*. New York: St. Martin's Press, 1988.

Paglia, Camille. *Vamps and Tramps: New Essays*. New York: Vintage Books, 1994.

Palter, Robert. "Black Athena, Afro-Centrism, and the History of Science." *History of Science* 31 (1993), pp. 228-287.

Parker, James. *Ethnic Identity*. Washington D.C.: University Press of America, 1983.

Parkin, Frank. *Marxism and Class Theory: A Bourgeois Critique*. London: Tavistock, 1979.

Patchen, M. *Black-White Contact in Schools: Its Social and Academic Effects*. Lafayette, Ind.: Purdue University Press, 1982.

Paul, Richard. *Critical Thinking: What Every Person Needs to Survive in a Rapidly Changing World*. Sonoma, Calif.: Foundation for Critical Thinking and Moral Critique, 1990.

———. "Critical Thinking and the State of Education Today." *Inquiry: Critical Thinking Across the Disciplines* 16, no. 3 (Winter 1996), pp. 12-34.

Perlmutter, Philip, and Walter E. Williams. "Racism Is No Longer Prevalent." In Bruno Leone (ed.), *Racism: Opposing Viewpoints*, pp. 144-151. San Diego, Calif.: Greenhaven Press, 1986.

Pine, Gerald, and Asa Hilliard III. "Rx for Racism: Imperatives for America's Schools." *Phi Delta Kappan* 71, no. 8 (April 1990), pp. 593-600.

Pinkney, Alphonso. *Red, Black, and Green: Black Nationalism in the United States*. London: Cambridge University Press, 1976.

———. *The Myth of Black Progress*. Cambridge: Cambridge University Press, 1986.

Polsby, Nelson. *Community Power and Political Theory*. London: Yale University Press, 1963.

Popper, Karl. *Realism and the Aim of Science*. Totowa, N.J.: Rowman and Littlefield, 1983.

Poulantzas, Nicos. *Classes in Contemporary Capitalism*. London: New Left Books, 1975.

———. *Political Power and Social Classes*. London: New Left Books, 1973.

Proctor, Robert E. *Education's Great Amnesia: Reconsidering the Humanities from Petrarch to Freud with a Curriculum for Today's Students*. Bloomington, Ind.: Indiana University Press, 1988.

Quine, William V. *Word and Object*. Cambridge, Mass.: Technology Press of MIT, 1960.

Ravitch, Diane. "A Culture in Common." *Educational Leadership* 49, no. 4 (December 1991–January 1992), pp. 8-11.

————. "Diversity and Democracy: Multicultural Education in America." *American Educator* 14, no. 1 (Spring 1990), pp. 16-20, 46-48.

————. *The Great School Wars, New York City, 1805–1973: A History of the Public Schools as Battlefields of Social Change.* New York: Basic Books, 1974.

————. "Multiculturalism: An Exchange." *The American Scholar* 60 (Spring 1991), pp. 272-276.

————. "Multiculturalism: E Pluribus Plures." *The American Scholar* 59 (Summer 1990), pp. 337-354.

————. *The Schools We Deserve: Reflections on the Educational Crisis of Our Times.* New York: Basic Books, 1985.

————. *The Troubled Crusade: American Education, 1945-1980.* New York: Basic Books, 1983.

Redman, Ray Ben (ed.). *The Portable Voltaire.* New York: Viking, 1949.

Reich, Robert B. *Education and the Next Economy.* National Education Association: Washington, D.C. 1987.

Reminick, Ronald. *Theory of Ethnicity: An Anthropologist's Perspective.* Lanham, Md: University Press of America, 1983.

Renzetti, Claire M., and Daniel J. Curran. *Women, Men and Society.* Boston: Allyn and Bacon, 1992.

Reynolds, Larry T., and Leonard Lieberman. "The Rise and Fall of 'Race.'" *Race, Sex and Class* 1, no. 1 (Fall 1993), pp. 109-127.

Robinson, Cedric. "Ota Benga's Flight through Geronimo's Eyes: Tales of Science and Multiculturalism." In David Theo Goldberg (ed.), *Multiculturalism: A Critical Reader*, pp. 388-405. Oxford: Blackwell, 1994.

Root, Maria P.P. (ed.). *Racially Mixed People in America.* Newbury Park, Calif.: Sage, 1992.

Rorty, Richard. *Philosophy and the Mirror of Nature.* Princeton, N.J.: Princeton University Press, 1979.

Rothberg, Robert. *The Mixing of Peoples: Problems of Identity and Ethnicity.* New York: Greylock, 1978.

Rothenberg, Paula S. (ed.). *Racism and Sexism: An Integrated Study.* New York: St. Martin's Press, 1988.

Russell, Kathy, Midge Wilson, and Ronald Hall. *The Color Complex: The Politics of Skin Color among Blacks.* New York: Harcourt Brace Jovanovich, 1992.

Ryan, Francis J. "The Perils of Multiculturalism: Schooling for the Group." *Educational Horizons* 71, no.3 (Spring 1993), pp.134-138.

Sargent, Lyman Tower. *Contemporary Political Ideologies: A Comparative Analysis*, 7th ed. Chicago: Dorsey Press, 1987.

Sayers, Janet. *Biological Politics: Feminist and Anti-Feminist Perspectives.* London: Tavistock, 1982.

Sayers, Sean. *Reality and Reason: Dialectic and the Theory of Knowledge.* Oxford: Basil Blackwell, 1985.

Schick Jr., Theodore, and Lewis Vaughan. *How to Think with Weird Things: Critical Thinking for a New Age.* London: Mayfield, 1995.

Schlafly, Phyllis. *The Power of the Positive Woman*. New York: Arlington House, 1977.

Schlesinger Jr., Arthur. *The Disuniting of America*. Knoxville, Tenn.: Whittle Communications, 1991.

Schofield, J. *Black and White in Schools: Trust, Tolerance, or Tokenism?* New York: Praeger, 1982.

Scriven, Michael. *Reasoning*. New York: McGraw-Hill, 1976.

————, and Richard Paul. "Defining Critical Thinking." *1993 Critical Thinking Inservice Handouts*. Sonoma, Calif.: Center for Critical Thinking, 1993.

Shipman, Pat. *The Evolution of Racism: Human Difference and the Use and Abuse of Science*. New York: Simon and Schuster, 1994.

Siegel, Fred. "The Cult of Multiculturalism." *New Republic* (February 18, 1991), pp. 34-40.

Siegel, Harvey. *Educating Reason: Rationality, Critical Thinking, and Education*. New York: Routledge, 1988.

————. "On Some Recent Challenges to the Ideal of Reason." *Inquiry: Critical Thinking Across the Disciplines* 15, no. 4 (Summer 1996), pp. 2-16.

Simmel, Georg. *Conflict and the Web of Group Affiliations*. New York: The Free Press, 1955.

Simonson, Rick, and Scott Walker. "Introduction." In Rick Simonson and Scott Walker (eds.), *The Graywolf Annual Five: Multicultural Literacy*, pp. ix-xv. St. Paul, Minn.: Graywolf Press, 1988.

———— (eds.). *The Graywolf Annual Five: Multicultural Literacy*. St. Paul, Minn.: Graywolf Press, 1988.

Sleeter, Christine E. *Multicultural Education as Social Activism*. New York: State University of New York Press, 1996.

————. "Restructuring Schools for Multicultural Education." *Journal of Teacher Education* 43, no. 2 (March-April 1992), pp. 141-148.

————. "The White Ethnic Experience in America: To Whom Does it Generalize?" *Educational Researcher* 21, no. 1 (January-February 1992), pp. 33-35.

————. "White Racism." In Annual Editions, *Multicultural Education 95/96*, pp. 70-73. Guilford, Conn.: Dushkin, 1995.

———— (ed.). *Empowerment through Multicultural Education*. New York: State University of New York Press, 1991.

———— (ed.), and Carl A. Grant. *Making Choices for Multicultural Education: Five Approaches to Race, Class and Gender*. Columbus, Ohio: Merrill, 1993.

————, and Carl A. Grant. "An Analysis of Multicultural Education in the United States." *Harvard Educational Review* 57, no. 4 (November 1987), pp. 421–444.

————, and Carl A. Grant. "Mapping Terrains of Power: Student Cultural Knowledge versus Classroom Knowledge." In Christine E. Sleeter (ed.), *Empowerment Through Multicultural Education*, pp. 49-67. New York: State University of New York Press, 1991.

Smedley, Audrey. *Race: The Evolution of a Worldview*. Boulder, Colo.: Westview Press, 1993.

Smith, Frank. *Insult to Intelligence: The Bureaucratic Invasion of Our Classrooms*. New York: Anchor House, 1986.

Snowden Jr., Frank M. "Bernal's 'Blacks,' Herodotus, and Other Classical Evidence." *Arethusa Special Issue* (Fall 1989), pp. 83-93.

———. "Whither Afrocentrism?" *Georgetown* (Winter 1992), pp. 7-8.

Sowell, Thomas. *Inside Education: The Decline, the Deception, the Dogmas*. New York: The Free Press, 1993.

Spain, Daphne. *Gendered Spaces: Sex Discrimination Against Women*. Chapel Hill, N.C.: University of North Carolina Press, 1992.

Spencer, Jon M. "Trends of Opposition to Multiculturalism." *The Black Scholar* 23, no. 2 (Winter-Spring 1993), pp. 2-5.

Spickard, Paul R. "The Illogic of American Racial Categories." In Maria P.P. Root (ed.), *Racially Mixed People in America*, pp. 12-23. Newbury Park, Calif.: Sage, 1992.

Spring, Joel. *American Education: An Introduction to Social and Political Aspects*. New York: Longman, 1990.

Stam, Robert, and Ella Shohat. "Contested Histories Eurocentrism, Multiculturalism, and the Media." In David Theo Goldberg (ed.), *Multiculturalism: A Critical Reader*, pp. 296-324. Oxford: Blackwell, 1994.

Standifer, James A. "The Multicultural, Nonsexist Principle: Why We Can't Afford to Ignore It." *Journal of Negro Education* 56, no. 4 (1987), pp. 471-474.

Stassinopoulos, Arianna. *The Female Woman*. New York: Random House, 1973.

Steele, Shelby. *The Content of Our Character: A New Vision of Race in America*. New York: St. Martin's Press, 1990.

Steinem, Gloria. *Moving beyond Words*. New York: Simon and Schuster, 1994.

Stent, M.D., W.R. Hazard, and H.N. Rivlin (eds.). *Cultural Pluralism in Education: A Mandate for Change*. New York: Appleton-Century-Crofts, 1973.

Sternberg, Robert. "Instrumental and Componental Approaches to the Nature and Training of Intelligence." In Susan F. Chipman, Judith W. Segal, and Robert Glaser (eds.), *Thinking and Learning Skills, Vol. 2: Research and Open Questions*, pp. 215-244. Hillsdale, N.J.: Lawrence Erlbaum Associates, 1985.

Stocking Jr., George W. "Introduction: The Basic Assumptions of Boasian Anthropology." In George W. Stocking Jr. (ed.), *The Shaping of American Anthropology, 1883-1911: A Franz Boas Reader*, pp. 1-20. New York: Basic Books, 1974.

——— (ed.). *The Shaping of American Anthropology, 1883-1911: A Franz Boas Reader*. New York: Basic Books, 1974.

Stuckey, Sterling. *Slave Culture: Nationalist Theory and the Foundations of Black America*. New York: Oxford University Press, 1987.

Tanner, Daniel. "A Nation Truly at Risk." *Phi Delta Kappan* 75, no. 4 (December 1993), pp. 288-297.

Tavris, Carol. *The Mismeasure of Woman*. New York: Simon and Schuster, 1992.

Teachers for a Democratic Culture. "The State of Academic Freedom 1995." *Democratic Culture* 4, no. 2 (Fall 1995), pp. 6-35.

Thernstrom, Stephan. *The Other Bostonians: Poverty and Progress in the American Metropolis, 1880-1970*. Cambridge, Mass.: Harvard University Press, 1973.

Thompson, David C. "Special Needs Students: A Generation at Risk." In James G. Ward and Patricia Anthony (eds.), *Who Pays for Student Diversity?: Population Changes and Educational Policy,* pp. 97-124. Newbury Park, Calif.: Sage, 1992.

Thompson, John B. *Studies in the Theory of Ideology.* Cambridge: Polity Press, 1984.

Thurow, Lester. *Head to Head: The Coming Economic Battle among Japan, Europe, and America.* New York: William Morrow, 1992.

Tiedt, Pamela L., and Iris M. Tiedt. *Multicultural Teaching: A Handbook of Activities, Information, and Resources.* Boston: Allyn and Bacon, 1990.

Time. "Adult Literacy in America" (September 20, 1993), p. 75.

Tong, Rosemarie. *Feminist Thought: A Comprehensive Introduction.* Boulder, Colo.: Westview Press, 1989.

Trigg, Roger. *Reality at Risk: A Defence of Realism in Philosophy and the Sciences.* Sussex: Harvester Press, 1980.

Tuchman, Barbara. *The March of Folly.* New York: Ballantine Books, 1984.

Turner, Terence. "Anthropology and Multiculturalism: What Is Anthropology That Multiculturalists Should Be Mindful Of It?" In David Theo Goldberg (ed.), *Multiculturalism: A Critical Reader,* pp. 405-425. Oxford: Blackwell, 1994.

Twentieth Century Fund Task Force on Federal Elementary and Secondary Education Policy. *Making the Grade.* New York: Twentieth Century Fund, 1983.

Tye, Kenneth (ed.). *Global Education: School Based Strategies.* Orange, Calif.: Interdependence Press, 1990.

Tylor, Edward. *Primitive Culture: Research into the Development of Mythology, Philosophy, Religion, Language, Art, and Custom.* New York: Brentano's Publishers, 1924.

Tyson-Bernstein, Harriet. *America's Textbook Fiasco: A Conspiracy of Good Intentions.* New York: The Council for Basic Education, 1988.

United States Commission on Civil Rights. *Civil Rights Issues of Euro-Ethnic Americans in the United States: Opportunities and Challenges.* Washington, D.C.: U.S. Government Printing Office, 1979.

United States Commission on Excellence in Education. *A Nation at Risk: The Imperative for Education Reform.* Washington, D.C.: U.S. Government Printing Office, 1983.

United States Department of Education. *A Nation of Learners.* Washington D.C.: U.S. Government Printing Office, 1976.

Van Sertima, Ivan. *African Presence in Early America.* New Brunswick, N.J.: Transaction Books, 1987.

——— (ed.). *Great African Thinkers: Cheikh Anta Diop.* New Brunswick, N.J.: Transaction Books, 1987.

Verstegen, Deborah. "Economics and Demographics of National Education Policy." In James G. Ward and Patricia Anthony (eds.), *Who Pays for Student Diversity? Population Changes and Educational Policy,* pp. 71-96. Newbury Park, Calif.: Sage, 1992.

Vogel, Lise. *Marxism and the Oppression of Women: Toward a Unitary Theory.* New Brunswick, N.J.: Rutgers University Press, 1983.

Walters, Kerry (ed.). *Re-thinking Reason: New Perspectives in Critical Thinking.* New York: State University of New York Press, 1995.

Watkins, William H. "Black Curriculum Orientations." *Harvard Educational Review* 63, no. 3 (Fall 1993), pp. 321-338.

Weber, Max. *Economy and Society: An Outline of Interpretive Sociology. Vol. Two.* Edited by Guenther Roth and Claus Wittich. Berkeley, Calif: University of California Press, 1978.

———. *The Theory of Social and Economic Organization.* Glencoe, Ill.: The Free Press, 1947.

———. *The Methodology of Social Sciences.* Trans. Edward A. Shils and H.A. Finch. New York: The Free Press, 1949.

Webster, Yehudi O. *The Racialization of America.* New York: St. Martin's Press, 1992.

Weedon, Chris. *Feminist Practice and Poststructuralist Theory.* Oxford: Basil Blackwell, 1987.

Weil, Danny. "Towards a Critical Multicultural Literacy." *Inquiry: Critical Thinking Across the Disciplines* 13, nos. 1–2 (February–March 1994), pp. 14-22.

Weis, Lois, and Michelle Fine (eds.). *Beyond Silenced Voices: Class, Race, and Gender in United States Schools.* Albany, N.Y.: State University of New York Press, 1993.

Welsch, Wolfgang. "Transculturality: The Puzzling Forms of Culture Today." *California Sociologist* 17-18 (1994-1995), pp. 19-39.

Welsing, Frances Cress. *The ISIS Papers: The Keys to the Colors.* Chicago: Third World Press, 1991.

West, Cornel. *Race Matters.* Boston: Beacon Press, 1993.

White, Leslie. *The Science of Culture: A Study of Man and Civilization.* New York: Farrar, Straus and Cudahy, 1949.

Wiegman, Robyn. *American Anatomies.* London: Duke University Press, 1995.

Williams, Chancellor. *The Destruction of Black Civilization: Great Issues of a Race from 4500 B.C. to 2000 A.D.* Chicago: Third World Press, 1974.

Williams Jr. Vernon J. *Rethinking Race: Franz Boas and His Contemporaries.* Lexington, Kentucky: The University Press of Kentucky, 1996

Wilson, John. *Thinking with Concepts.* Cambridge: Cambridge University Press, 1963.

Wilson, William J. *The Declining Significance of Race: Blacks and Changing American Institutions.* Chicago: University of Chicago Press, 1978.

Winch, Peter. *The Idea of a Social Science and Its Relation to Philosophy.* London: Routledge and Kegan Paul, 1971.

Wortham, Anne. *The Other Side of Racism: A Philosophical Study of Black Race Consciousness.* Columbus, Ohio: Ohio State University Press, 1977.

———. "Restoring Traditional Values in Higher Education: More Than 'Afrocentrism.'" *The Heritage Foundation* (February 22, 1991), pp. 1-16.

Wren, Thomas E. (ed.). *The Moral Domain: Essays in the Ongoing Discussion between Philosophy and the Social Sciences.* Cambridge, Mass.: MIT Press, 1990.

Wright, Erik O. "Class Boundaries in Advanced Capitalist Societies." *New Left Review* (July-August 1976), pp. 3–41.

————. "Varieties of Marxist Conceptions of Class Structure." *Politics and Society* 9, no. 3 (1980), pp. 323-370.

Wright, Lawrence. "One Drop of Blood." *The New Yorker* (July 25, 1994), pp. 46-55.

Zack, Naomi. *Race and Mixed Race*. Philadelphia: Temple University Press, 1993.

Index

African-American culture, 39
African-American students, 3, 22, 27, 28, 32, 45, 115
Africans in Diaspora, 30
Afrocentric education reform, 26-32
Afrocentricity, and racial classification, 33-42
and humanization, 59-60
Alamdari, Kazem, 75
Allen, Theodore, 123, 127
antiracist education reform, 4-5, 25, 44, 51, 79-87
antirealism, 7, 113, 122
antisexist education reform, 5, 74-79
and radical feminism, 74
Appiah, Kwame Anthony, 40, 91, 104, 108, 117, 151, 195
Apple, Michael, 26
Arendt, Hannah, 134
Asante, Molefi, 27-28, 31-32, 36, 38, 40-45, 59-60, 69, 85, 112, 115, 131, 151, 157, 190
Asian Americans, 26, 127, 191

Badham, Richard, 192
Balkanization, 19, 25, 43
Banks, James, 21, 42, 54, 60, 69-74, 102, 108-111, 114, 131, 140, 190
Baptise, H. Prentice, 18, 24
Baptise, Mira, 18, 24
Barber, Benjamin, 178
Barkan, Elazar, 81

Bennett, William, 51-52, 58, 60, 148
Berger, Peter, 128
Beyer, Barry, 194
Bloom, Allan, 58, 118, 148, 150-151
Boas, Franz, 13, 15-17, 24, 79, 130
Bridges, Tom, 105
Broudy, Harry, 183

Cassirer, Ernst, 106
census, 25, 129, 135
Chinn, Philip, 13, 14
Chisholm, Shirley, 80
Clay, Camille, 26
Collins, Randall, 78
commodification, 8, 9, 137, 144-147, 159, 172-175, 177-180
Cordasco, Francesco, 20
critical pedagogy, 5, 57, 72, 102, 121, 150
critical thinking, definitions, 9, 182-183, 186-190, 198 fn
compared with multicultural education and multiculturalism, 187-190
dispositions, 187
and educability, 187
and education reform, 159, 186
and intellectual diversity, 190-194
and tactics of infusion, 180-186
critiques of education, 170-172
Cruse, Harold, 20
cultural diversity, 1, 2, 5, 19, 24-25, 42, 44, 49-51, 89, 129, 191

cultural domination, 71, 102, 135, 170
cultural nationalism, 6, 20, 26-27, 89,
    108, 110, 129
cultural pluralism, defined, 24
    as basis of multicultural education,
        2-5, 18, 24
    different interpretations of, 19, 24
        8, 15, 18, 19,
    and equality, 24, 31, 42, 45-46, 51,
        69-71, 73, 101
    and Horace Kallen, 18
    and pluralist multicultural education,
        41-46
culture, definitions of, 6, 120, 129-130,
    133-134, 136, 151
curriculum reform, 1, 6, 22, 44, 58, 71,
    74

D'Souza, Dinesh, 83
denunciation, definition of, 157
Derber, Charles, 52, 178
differences, concept of, 133
    cultural, 1, 5, 10, 13-14, 19-21, 23-
        25, 119-122, 130-136
    essentialization of, 5, 72, 76, 123,
    racial, 40, 57, 72, 74, 90-91, 115,
        122, 126, 131, 134, 190,
    and similarities, 133-137
Diop, Cheikh Anta, 33-35, 38-59,
    151, 195
Du Bois, W.E.B., 33, 41, 91
Dworkin, Andrea, 116

E pluribus Unum, 19
Early, Gerald, 16, 30
education model, 8-9, 57, 172-173,
    175-177, 179-182, 185, 188-189
educational underachievement, 3, 6, 13,
    19, 22, 26, 32, 120, 189
Egyptian civilization, 27, 29-30, 194
Enlightenment, 46, 104-107, 115-116,
    122-123, 158-159, 169, 171, 194-
    195
Epperson, Terrence, 81
Epstein, Cynthia, 77
equality of educational opportunity, 1,
    3, 5, 19, 71
essentialism, 76, 82, 95-96fn, 128

Eurocentric, definition of, 115
Eurocentrism, 1, 5, 28, 44, 56-57, 109,
    112, 120, 157, 194, 195

feminism, 71
    kinds of, 76-78
Flannery, Danielle, 149
Flax, Jane, 117, 132
Foucault, Michel, 7, 104, 113, 141,
    146, 195
Fox, M., 107
Francis, Patricia, 69
Freire, Paulo, 7, 57, 71-72, 138-139

Gates Jr., Henry L., 58-59, 108, 110,
    126, 136
gender theory, 74-76, 122
    naturalist variant of, 75-76
    women's liberationist variant, 75
Gingrich, Newt, 51, 170, 172-175,
    177, 180
Giroux, Henry, 50, 72, 102, 108, 119-
    123, 135, 139, 140, 150, 172, 190
Glazer, Nathan, 15
de Gobineau, Arthur, 33-34, 59, 147
Goldberg, David, 81, 147-148, 158-
    159
Gollnick, Donna, 13, 14
Goodlad, John, 49-50
Grant, Carl, 50, 70-74, 102, 131, 140,
    172, 190
ground rules of discourse, 156-158
Gutierrez, Kris, 122

Habermas, Jurgen, 104, 107, 154-156,
    158, 195
Harvey, David, 115, 145
Herrnstein, Richard, 25, 91-93
Hilliard III, Asa, 21, 31, 59-60, 80
hooks, bell, 117, 190
House, Ernest, 137, 173
Howard, Gary, 84, 94, 126, 152
human identity, 49, 191
human nature, 8, 50, 60, 117, 134, 141,
    147, 171, 177, 180-181
human perspective, 10, 50, 54, 58-59
human species, 30, 76, 127, 130, 143,
    144, 154

intellectual standards, outlined, 9-10
  absence of, 118, 136, 148, 170, 179
  agreement on, 60, 155, 158, 170,
    184, 189
  relevance to discussions, 10, 42,
    153, 158, 179, 194

Jean, Clinton, 6, 37-38, 104, 141, 158
Jensen, Arthur, 6, 19-20, 27, 91

Kallen, Horace, 16-18, 24
Kandal, Terry, 78
Kanpol, Barry, 50, 72, 74, 102, 135
Kearns, David, 170
Kendall, Frances, 80
Kennedy, Mary, 171
Keyes, Alan, 51
Keynes, John Maynard, 87
King Jr., Martin Luther, 134, 194-195
Kluckhohn, Clyde, 130
Kristeva, Julie, 66 fn, 119
Kroeber, Alfred, 130

language games, 7, 104-105, 107, 155,
  158
Lester, Joan, 70
Levesque, George, 39
Lillard, Richard, 169
Limbaugh, Rush, 51, 149
logical reasoning, 8, 34-35, 52, 83, 85-
  86
Lukes, Steven, 142-144
Lynch, James, 48, 49, 50
Lyotard, Jean-François, 7, 104, 107,
  113, 115, 122, 141, 155, 156, 158

Macionis, John, 89
male domination, 76
Malik, Kenan, 123
Marx, Karl, 27, 37, 77-78, 87-89,
  105, 107, 110, 119, 122, 137,
  139-147, 150, 157, 173, 195
McCarthy, Cameron, 26
McCormick, Linda, 23
McLaren, Peter, 50, 72, 74, 102, 121-
  122, 124, 131, 136-137, 147,
  188, 190
Modgil, Sohan, 69
Moffett, James, 176

monoculturalism, 44, 72, 109
Moore, Henrietta, 118
moral values, 44, 52, 169, 175
Moses, Wilson, 125
Muir, Donald, 127
multicultural agenda, and social
  theories, 87-89
multicultural education, definitions of,
  8, 14, 49, 54, 69-70
  aims of, 13-14
  analytical shortcomings of, 57-58
  evolution into multiculturalism, 4-5,
    70-74
  globalist and rational-humanist
    approaches to, 48-51
  intellectual origins of, 15-21
  justifications for, 21-24, 57-58, 71,
  pluralist approach to, 42-48
multiculturalism, definitions of, 5-
  10, 160fn
  analytical foundations of, 101-103
  and capitalist commodity
    production, 143-148
  conservative, 72, 91-94, 121
  critical, 5, 7, 50, 71, 72, 74, 94,
    102, 118, 119, 121, 123, 129,
    131-132, 137-138
  difference, 72, 74, 121, 129, 131-
    132
  and ground rules of discourse, 148-
    159
  insurgent, 72, 94, 102, 119-123
  and oppression, 137-139
  and postmodernist theory of
    knowledge, 103-118
  and power, 139-143
  resistance, 102
Murray, Charles, 25, 91-93

Nieto, Sonia, 70, 72, 102
Nietzsche, Friedrich, 101

Olson, James, 132

Paglia, Camille, 108, 116
Pan-Africanism, 6, 27, 29, 88, 91
Paul, Richard, 171-172, 182
Perlmutter, Philip, 83
political domination, 5, 91, 119

postmodernism, definition of, 104
  and the Enlightenment, 103-104,
    107
  and multiculturalism, 112-116, 122,
    123, 149, 157, 159
power, definitions of, 140-143
  and interests, 142-144

racial classification, illogicalities of,
    122-127
  and IQ, 91-94
  and reality, 90, 136
racial theory, 28, 81, 83-85, 87, 89,
    91, 123, 192
  liberationist variant of, 28, 75, 83,
    89-91, 108
  naturalist variant of, 75, 89
racism, definitions of, 82-83, 124-125,
    127
  alleged pervasiveness of, 80-81
  relationship to racial classification,
    81-82, 124-125
  various usages of, 81-84
Ravitch, Diane, 15, 32, 42-46, 60, 69,
    115, 150, 151, 157
realism, 7, 103, 105, 113, 122, 128,
    137, 177
  and the culture concept, 129-133
reasoning processes, 3, 124, 171, 183,
    186-189, 193
reasoning, soundly, 4, 86, 106, 150,
    186, 195
  within intellectual standards, 9
refutation, definition of, 158
rejection, definition of, 157
repudiation, definition of, 157
Robinson, Cedric, 90, 118
Rorty, Richard, 105, 115
Ryan, Francis, 14

Schlesinger Jr, Arthur, 17, 42-43,
    44, 60, 69
Scriven, Michael, 183
sexism, definitions of, 56-57, 75-76
  as part of women's liberation

feminism, 88, 91
  origins and alleged pervasiveness of,
    75
Shohat, Ella, 102
Siegel, Harvey, 115
Simonson, Rick, 151
single cultures, 3, 6, 16, 17, 25, 57, 79,
    87, 130, 133
Sleeter, Christine, 50, 60, 70-72,
    74, 102, 131, 140, 152, 153
Smedley, Audrey, 110
social constructionism, 77, 81, 111,
    115, 128-129
social theories, gender, racial, ethnic,
    class, 88
  gender, racial, ethnic, class, and
    human, 194
Spencer, Jon, 29, 88, 110
Stam, Robert, 102
Steele, Shelby, 79, 82, 108, 132
Stocking Jr., George, 13, 16

Thernstrom, Stephan, 27
Thompson, David, 175
transcultural, 24-25, 56-57, 59, 177
Turner, Terrence, 129
Tylor, Edward, 25, 110, 130

values education, 51-53
Voltaire, François-Marie Arouet, 106,
    116, 180, 195

Walker, Scott, 151
Ward, D., 107
Weber, Max, 7, 88, 105, 110, 140-142,
    146-147, 173
Weedon, Chris, 77
Weil, Danny, 120, 133
West, Cornel, 39-40
Western civilization, 28, 30, 33-34, 46,
    52, 101, 194
White, Leslie, 25, 131
Williams, Walter, 83
Wortham, Anne, 83, 108, 115

About the Author

YEHUDI O. WEBSTER teaches in the Sociology Department at California State University. He holds degrees from Warwick University, London University, and Warsaw University. Dr. Webster is the author of *The Racialization of America* (1992), which was selected as the Outstanding Book published in 1992 on Human Rights in the United States.